WATCHDOG ON THE POTOMAC:

A Study of the Comptroller General of the United States

Joseph Pois
University of Pittsburgh

University Press of America™

Copyright © 1979 by

University Press of America, Inc.™

4710 Auth Place, S.E., Washington D.C. 20023

Printed in the United States of America

ISBN: 0-8191-0691-7

Library of Congress Catalog Card Number: 78-66276

TABLE OF CONTENTS

PREFACE

The term "U.S. General Accounting Office" conjures up the image of a large governmental agency totally immersed in recording the financial transactions of the Federal establishment. This erroneous impression of an agency that actually plays an astonishingly vital role in the political process is compounded by the fact that the head of the Office carries the title Comptroller General, which some construe as a completely separate entity and which, on occasion, is even confused with the Comptroller of the Currency, a Treasury Department official. Two other factors contribute to the misunderstanding and obscurity that tended to envelop the GAO (the acronym by which the agency is known in the Federal Government): the aloofness that -- at least until recently -- had generally characterized its operations and the unusual mix of legislative and executive functions, the full implications of which are not readily perceived by the uninitiated.

Having some awareness of the ascendant, albeit not widely discerned, position of the GAO in the Government's power structure, this writer was surprised and gratified when Elmer B. Staats, shortly after assuming the Comptroller Generalship in 1966, requested him to undertake a study of the trends in the GAO's "program, operations and relations with other government agencies, the Congress, and the public." Staats accorded the writer complete independence, gave him unrestricted access to GAO personnel and records in both Washington and the field, and actively facilitated contacts with Congressional members and staff, Executive Branch officials, and defense contractors. The writer's membership for nine years on the Comptroller General's Consultant Panel was most helpful in obtaining in-depth insights into GAO policies, plans, operations, and problems.

The initial product of the study was an analysis prepared for the Comptroller General's use. This was followed by a draft manuscript, the revision of which had to be deferred indefinitely because of academic and consulting commitments. In 1976, an analysis of the GAO conducted at the behest of the Commission on the Operation of the Senate afforded the writer an excellent opportunity to update his information. By that time, he had already resigned from the Consultant Panel, thereby averting possible criticism that such relationship was not congruent with objectivity of approach in preparing the definitive draft.

The decade that elapsed since the study's inception witnessed far-reaching changes in the role, priorities,

practices, and influence of the Comptroller General.
These developments need to be perceived in the context
of shifts of power between the Congress and the Executive
Branch and the pressure for greater governmental openness
and accountability, a thrust to which Watergate obviously
gave vast impetus.

A fascinating aspect of the GAO is the amazing extent
to which the reports and pronouncements of the Comptroller
General, as well as his clashes with the Executive Branch
including the President, throw light on numerous facets of
the national scene. Whether it be public policy issues, the
quality of agency management, or the positions taken by
governmental luminaries, GAO activities yield invaluable
information as well as perspectives that are often provocative. But the Comptroller General's increasingly intimate involvement in not only the Government's operations
but also decision-making needs to be more fully understood
by the Congress and others concerned with the structure and
dynamics of the Federal Government. This study, therefore,
seeks to portray the growth, current dimensions, and impacts
of the Comptroller General's power with the hope that it
will facilitate a much-needed reexamination.

Chapter 1

THE GENERAL ACCOUNTING OFFICE - A CITADEL OF POWER

> The principal witness today is the man we have
> been talking about -- the Comptroller General,
> the Honorable Elmer B. Staats. Perhaps he
> will provide some answers to our questions,
> and in particular alleviate some of the fears
> expressed that he has become the head of a
> "fourth branch of government."[1]

The characterization of the General Accounting Office
as a fourth branch of government would puzzle most people
since there is a general unawareness of the scope and impact of the functions performed by the GAO, headed by the
Comptroller General.[2] It is true that there has been a
cascading of events that have pushed the GAO into the public limelight. For example, its report on Cambodia's
seizure of the S.S. Mayaguez was discussed heatedly during
the 1976 Presidential Campaign, but few could have explained
why the GAO had concerned itself with such a delicate international matter. Similarly, public attention is evoked
when the GAO issues reports on such wide-ranging subjects
as: war on organized crime, acquisition of weapons systems,
defective cardiac pacemakers, alcoholism programs for Federal employees and military personnel, and even the world
population explosion. But, whether it be such inquiries or
even the Comptroller General's challenges of Presidential
proposals, the underlying motif of GAO activities has not
elicited the incisive Congressional scrutiny that it merits.

For that matter, Congress, in its thrust to assert itself more vigorously vis-a-vis the Executive Branch, has
been prone to expand the Comptroller General's authority
without relating such actions to a well-conceived frame of
reference. The result has been an aggregate of GAO power,
the implications of which have been perceived by few.
Senator Metcalf's comment quoted at the beginning of this
chapter might be the forerunner of the development of a more
balanced Congressional approach to the mission of the Comptroller General.

THE VARIEGATED NATURE OF GAO

Ever since it was established by the Budget and Accounting Act, 1921, GAO has had a multi-faceted role which
encompasses far more than assistance to the Congress, as
vital as that responsibility may be. The fact that so much
of the GAO activity is expressed in terms of audits reflects
the emphasis which the Comptroller General places upon this

1

responsibility. Coupled with the audit role is an imposing aggregate of responsibilities which places the Comptroller General in a position of power that is distinctly
atypical so far as governmental auditors are concerned.
Hence, the GAO contrasts sharply with the three other
agencies (Congressional Budget Office, Congressional Research Service, and Office of Technology Assessment) that
also serve the Congress in a supportive or informational
capacity but which essentially have this single mission.
While recognizing that one of the GAO's major objectives
is to render maximum assistance to Congress, its committees, and Members, the Comptroller General has recently
stipulated that this is subject to consistency "with our
responsibilities as an independent, non-political, agency."
The Comptroller General identifies GAO's other functions
as: auditing the programs, activities, and financial operations of Federal departments and agencies; helping to
improve Federal agency financial management systems;
settling claims and collecting debts; and providing legal
services.[3]

The mix of GAO's responsibilities

The role and impact of the GAO must be viewed in the
context of the diverse character of the totality of activities performed by the agency. The Comptroller General
has appropriately observed that the GAO "has the biggest
audit, monitoring and oversight job in the world." This
statement, as impressive as it is, does not convey the
complex of tasks performed by the GAO. The agency's
spectrum is brought out by the listing of estimated staff
year requirements for fiscal 1978 as presented in the
House Appropriations Committee hearings for that year:[4]

Special work mandated by statute	120
Direct assistance to committees and Members of Congress	1,459
Reviews of programs, under current statutes, for economy, efficiency, and effectiveness	2,325
Examination of agencies' financial systems, transactions, accounts, and reports	225
Financial management improvement	167
Claims settlement and debt collection activities	103
Legal services and decisions	205
Executive direction and management services	571
Total estimated staff years for fiscal 1978	5,175

2

This enumeration conveys something of the heterogeneity of the GAO activities but not the far-reaching implications of these different elements. For example, "Legal services and decisions" embraces the tasks which the Comptroller General performs in an adjudicative capacity when he rules on questions as to availability of appropriations and when he disposes of protests from unsuccessful bidders.

GAO's direct assistance to the Congress is discussed separately, but such categorization of activities should not obscure the fact that the other functions performed by the GAO reinforce its supportive role for the Congress. For example, the self-initiated reviews of economy, efficiency and program effectiveness, which have centrality in the functioning of the GAO, are indispensable in underpinning GAO's capability to be of service to the Congress.

THE RATIONALE FOR AN INDEPENDENT AUDIT AGENCY

The issues that have been posed as to the GAO have never involved any doubt as to the essentiality of such an independent audit agency. The concept of having such an instrumentality for implementing the accountability of Government agencies is almost unchallengeable. It has been said that "one of the most widespread, significant, and complex control devices employed in bureaucracies consists of separate monitoring organizations for inspecting and reporting on performance."[5] Professor W.J.M. Mackenzie has observed that without audit there is no accountability, and hence an absence of control.[6]

The consensus just described begins to fade as issues arise concerning the objectives, depth, and breadth of the reviews made by the GAO and the manner in which the agency articulates its findings and recommendations. Such challenges are to be expected by any audit agency that seeks to be incisive and forthright in its approach. In fact, it has been contended that "the effectiveness of separate monitoring agencies can be maintained only if a definite tension exists between their members and the members of the operating bureaus they monitor."[7] Moreover, with greater awareness that monitoring activities have dysfunctional aspects, they cease to be regarded as an unmixed blessing and are viewed more realistically. Checking on accountability can be pushed to a point so that it becomes a drag on the dynamism, initiative, and creativity of operating personnel.[8] The hypothesis has been advanced that those subject to audit modify their behavior to conform with criteria which they believe the auditor will apply.[9]

Recent developments have accentuated the issue as to how deeply the GAO should go into the substantive aspects

of agency operations. The polemics have revolved in large
measure around the fact that GAO's authority extends far
beyond the strictly auditing area and permits the agency
not merely to audit transactions after they have been consummated but to directly affect the day-to-day operations
of the Government. The blend of functions performed by
the GAO under the direction of the Comptroller General impelled one writer to state that, in his opinion, "the Comptroller General is a quasi-legislative, quasi-executive,
and a quasi-judicial officer."[10]

GAO'S LEGISLATIVE BACKGROUND AND RELATED DEVELOPMENTS

The GAO as a statutory creation has been the subject
of both legislative proposals and enactments that have
profoundly affected the scope of the Comptroller General's
authority and the constraints upon its implementation.
Hence, the manner in which the GAO presently functions and
what existing trends portend need to be viewed in the context of the legislative history and related developments.

Thrust of GAO legislation since 1921

The GAO legislation affecting GAO since its creation
in 1921 has sought to achieve several different purposes:
relieve the GAO of the need to process innumerable individual transactions that imposed a back-breaking paper
workload on the agency; effect decentralization and thereby
do away with the insularity which kept GAO cloistered in
Washington buildings rather than going out into the agencies;
provide a statutory basis for collaboration between the GAO,
Treasury, and Office of Management; provide a broader frame
of reference for GAO's auditing activities; recognize agency
financial management responsibilities without at the same
time attenuating the authority vested in the GAO; and
strengthen the GAO as a resource for the Legislative Branch.
As to the latter, recent developments reflect a marked departure from the earlier Congressional ambivalence, if not
refusal, to strengthen and fully utilize GAO's supportive
capabilities. The impact of this reversal in attitude has
been somewhat attenuated by the action which Congress has
taken to strengthen the Congressional Research Service and
to establish two new support agencies: the Congressional
Budget Office and the Office of Technology Assessment.

The post-1921 legislation demonstrates that Congress
has been reasonably responsive to recommendations for effecting GAO improvements. However, at least until recently,
Congress has been resolutely averse to any redefinition of
the Comptroller General's authority that would detract from
his basic power. This has made the current questioning
attitude on the part of some Congressional leaders all the
more traumatic for the GAO.

4

Establishment of GAO by Budget and Accounting Act, 1921

Those drafting the Budget and Accounting Act of 1921 sought to deal with two facets of the Government's financial management: the budgetary process and accountability. As to the problem of accountability, there was concern over the fact that checking on the stewardship for public funds had been left to the Executive Branch.[11]

The earlier laws enacted to strengthen the Government's fiscal controls reached their zenith in the Dockery Act of 1894. This Act provided for six auditors in the Treasury Department who were assigned to designated departments and were made responsible for examining the respective accounts and certifying the balances therein. Balances so certified were final and conclusive upon the Executive Branch, subject to the appeal of the Comptroller. This latter official, in addition to having appellate authority with respect to determinations made by the auditors, was given authority to render decisions on the legality of proposed expenditures in advance of actual payments.

The 1921 Act abolished the Comptroller of the Treasury and the six auditors and transferred their powers and duties to the General Accounting Office created by the Act. The balances certified by the Comptroller General were made final and conclusive upon the Executive Branch of the Government (Section 304). These provisions were followed by Section 305 providing that the GAO settle "all claims and demands whatever by the Government of the United States or against it, and all accounts whatever in which the Government of the United States is concerned, either as debtor or creditor. . ." The authority flowing out of these two Sections has placed the GAO in an unusual position of power vis-a-vis the Executive agencies. The fact that the legislation envisaged the Comptroller General as far more than an auditor was reflected in Section 309 making the Comptroller General responsible for prescribing administrative appropriation and fund accounting in the several departments and establishments.

It is only after vesting the GAO and Comptroller General with what might be termed non-audit responsibilities that the Budget and Accounting Act of 1921 delineates his audit role. Interestingly enough, the statute does not use the term "audit" in this connection but states that the Comptroller General "shall investigate, at the seat of government or elsewhere, all matters relating to the receipt, disbursement, and application of public funds. . ." (Section 312). The same section calls upon the Comptroller General in the regular report he is required to submit to the Congress, or in special reports "to make recommendations looking to greater economy or efficiency in public expenditures."

Combination of functions: a cause celebre

This combination of responsibilities and, probably more so, the manner in which this far-reaching aggregate authority was exercised became an irritant very quickly within the Government and was the target for political scientists and public administrators who found it difficult to reconcile such a setup with what they considered to be accepted theory. The initial administration of these responsibilities was characterized by emphasis on: (1) the issuance of Comptroller General's decisions that broadly defined the scope of that official's authority and made little, if any, attempt to recognize the problems and realities of the administrative process, and (2) the highly centralized examination of individual transactions on the basis of what appeared to be an extremely fault-finding approach.

It was no surprise, therefore, that in 1937 the President's Committee on Administrative Management was sharply critical of the array of powers of the Comptroller General:

> This system results in divided authority and responsibility for the proper expenditure of public funds and the accounting therefor: it deprives the President of essential power needed to discharge his major executive responsibility. Equally important, it deprives the Congress of a really independent audit and review of the fiscal affairs of the Government by an official who has no voice in administrative determinations, which audit is necessary to hold the Administration accountable.[12]

The Committee recommended that the Comptroller General be divested of his authority to prescribe accounting systems and that this task be transferred to the Secretary of the Treasury. Similarly, it proposed the reallocation of the responsibility for settling claims and accounts from the Comptroller General to the Treasury Department. Mindful of the stress and strain that had been engendered by the Comptroller General's decision-making, the Committee recommended that the Attorney General be authorized to render binding decisions on questions of the jurisdiction of the Secretary of the Treasury to settle public accounts, but not on the merits of the case. In effect, the Committee conceived of the Comptroller General exclusively as an auditor and recommended that his title be changed to Auditor General and that the General Accounting Office be redesignated as the General Auditing Office.

6

In submitting these proposals, the Committee took cognizance of the fact that, in 1932, President Hoover had recommended to the Congress that the power to prescribe accounting systems be transferred to the Executive Branch. Hoover had argued that "accounting is an essential element of effective administration, and it should be developed with the primary objective of serving this purpose." The Committee also called attention to the fact that a special committee of the United States Chamber of Commerce had, in 1934, recommended "that all accounting activities be removed from the Comptroller General and placed in a General Accounting Office directly responsible to the President."[14]

Although Congress reacted adversely to the Committee's recommendations, the Committee report had a profound effect in molding a distinctly unfavorable image of the Comptroller General and the GAO. The sweeping criticisms leveled at the GAO were followed by the Mansfield book[15] severely castigating the Comptroller General and supporting the indictment with a bill of particulars that had long-lasting effects in terms of detracting from the stature of the Comptroller General, at least insofar as political scientists and public administrators were concerned.

Centralized nature of audits

As has already been intimated, the vulnerability of the Comptroller General to the Mansfield type of criticism did not stem entirely from his having been vested with powers that ordinarily come within the ambit of the Executive Branch. The manner in which he discharged his audit responsibilities could not possibly evoke confidence or respect on the part of those who understood the methodology of the independent auditor. The Comptroller General's audit work was carried out primarily through central desk audits of documents in Washington; it had more of a clerical rather than a truly professional character. Fifteen years elapsed before some progress was made towards auditing in the field.[16] It took such cataclysms as the Depression of the '30's and World War II to overcome the inertia and resistance that the GAO had shown with respect to adopting accepted auditing practices. Measures subsequently enacted by Congress afforded statutory underpinning for the more enlightened audit approach.

The Government Corporation Control Act of 1945

The Government Corporation Control Act of 1945[17] was significant not only from the standpoint of requiring GAO audits of Government corporations but also stating explicitly that such audits should be made "in accordance with the principles and procedures applicable to commercial corporate transactions. . ." This mandate for an audit conforming to accepted auditing practices had vital "spill-over" effects, the impact of which changed the tone of GAO's operations and gave it the professional stature that had been so sorely lacking. The implementation of the statutory requirement necessitated the recruitment of many accountants with true professional credentials; it resulted in the ascendancy of the certified public accountant in not only the newly-established Corporation Audits Division but also throughout the organization.[18] Corporation audits have become a relatively minor aspect of GAO's total work program. However, the professional thrust for which they were a catalyst has in no way been abated by this development.

Legislative Reorganization Act of 1946

In 1946, Congress adopted a provision that gave every appearance of Congressional desire to make the fullest utilization of the GAO in the Legislative oversight of expenditures. Section 206 of the Legislative Reorganization Act of 1946 reads as follows:

> The Comptroller General is authorized and directed to make an expenditure analysis of each agency in the Executive Branch of the Government (including Government corporations), which, in the opinion of the Comptroller General, will enable Congress to determine whether public funds have been economically and efficiently administered and expended.

This could have represented a monumental turning point in establishment of the GAO as a highly effective and meaningful resource for Congress. But this proved to be an abortive step. Congress was not yet ready to make the GAO such an active participant in the discharge of its oversight responsibility.

Joint Financial Management Improvement Program

The initiation of the Joint Financial Management Improvement Program, which was announced by the Comptroller General in 1948, was a momentous step towards establishing a continuing collaborative relationship between the GAO and the two Executive Branch Agencies deeply concerned with the Government's financial management, i.e., the Bureau of the Budget (later redesignated the Office of Management and Budget) and the Department of the Treasury. The essence of this program has been a cooperative working relationship between the three agencies directed to the improvement of accounting throughout the Federal Government.[19] The pro-

8

gram's effectiveness as a cohesive influence was enhanced
by the broader perspective it developed over the years.
This joint endeavor so impressed the First Hoover Commission that it received the Commission's endorsement. In
light of the widespread support which the program evoked,
it was not surprising that the Budget and Accounting Procedures Act of 1950 gave it a statutory basis.[20]

The Joint Financial Management Improvement Program,
which is discussed at some length subsequently, has, whatever its shortcomings, afforded a very useful bridge between the GAO and the key fiscal agencies of the Executive
Branch. The program, in a sense, has been something of a
substitute for the statutory reallocation of certain of the
Comptroller General's responsibilities. It has sought to
make his accounting system authority more compatible with
what many would regard as the optimal allocation of responsibilities between the independent audit agency and
the Executive Branch.

Federal Property and Administrative Services Act of 1949

In 1949, the Congress, for the first time, gave specific statutory recognition to the concept that the non-
corporate audits conducted by the GAO should be decentralized. The Federal Property and Administrative Services
Act of 1949, in directing the GAO to audit property accounts and transactions, stated that: "such audit shall
be conducted as far as practicable at the place or places
where the property or records of the executive agencies
are kept. . ."[21] The Act also provided that the audit
should include but not necessarily be limited to an evaluation of the effectiveness of internal controls and audits.
Finally, a reference to "generally accepted principles of
auditing" added further emphasis to the Congressional expression of intent that these audits conform to accepted
standards.

The Comptroller General recognized that the implementation of this Act would "require the utilization of the
same type of personnel needed for the corporate audits. . ."[22]
He went out of his way to declare that the GAO had turned
over a new leaf and that its stodginess was a thing of the
past. He described it as no longer "hide-bound and wedded
to antiquated methods," but as now being "in a fluid state,
alert and alive to modern procedures."[23]

First Hoover Commission Report - 1949

The First Hoover Commission was very restrained in
its approach to possible reallocation of the Comptroller
General's responsibilities. It hazarded the observation

9

that "accounting is primarily the responsibility of the executive branch."[24] Using this viewpoint as a spring-board, the Commission recommended that an Accountant General be established under the Secretary of the Treasury with authority to prescribe general accounting methods and enforce accounting procedures. But, apparently seeking to avoid a direct confrontation with respect to the Comptroller General, the Commission recommended that such methods and procedures be subject to the approval of the Comptroller General "within the powers now conferred upon him by Congress." To further assuage the protagonists of the GAO, the Commission said: "We believe there is no inherent conflict between the present position of the Comptroller General and our recommendation to create the position of Accountant General."[25]

The Commission was similarly circumspect with respect to the Comptroller General's authority to settle accounts and claims. It has been pointed out earlier in this chapter that GAO critics contend this responsibility is one that properly comes within the purview of the Executive Branch. The Hoover Commission contented itself with recommending that the practice of sending millions of expenditure vouchers to Washington be stopped insofar as possible and that "a spot sampling process at various places where the expenditure vouchers and papers are administratively checked might be substituted for much of the procedure for bringing all these documents to Washington."[26] The conciliatory stance taken by the Commission vis-a-vis the GAO repudiated, for the most part, the recommendations of its Task Force.[27]

Indicative of Congressional sensitivity with respect to the Comptroller General's prerogatives is the fact that the proposal for establishment of an Accountant General within the Treasury Department was the only budget and accounting recommendation of the Commission which was rejected outright in Congressional consideration of the Budget and Accounting Act of 1950. Both the House and Senate Committees opined that the Comptroller General's authority to prescribe accounting requirements was essential to legislative control of appropriations and expenditures in the Executive Branch "and must be held inviolate." The reports stated that this matter was really none of the Hoover Commission's business since the proposal primarily concerned the Legislative Branch over which the Commission "had no jurisdiction in conducting its survey for reorganization in the Federal Government."[28]

Accounting and Auditing Act of 1950

The Accounting and Auditing Act of 1950[29] is one of

10

the most important statutory landmarks in the development of the GAO since the enactment of the Budget and Accounting Act, 1921.[30] The Act's completeness and specificity with respect to the GAO contrast markedly with the general and sometimes cryptic language of those provisions of the 1921 legislation relating to the Comptroller General's accounting and auditing responsibilities.

A significant feature of the Act is the declaration of Congressional policy as to: the purposes of the Government's accounting; the consideration to be given to the needs and responsibilities of both the Legislative and Executive Branches; the responsibility of the Executive Branch for the maintenance of accounting systems and for reporting on the financial operations of Executive agencies; the purpose of the audits conducted by the Comptroller General as an agent of the Congress; and the emphasis to be placed on effecting improvements in the financial process and on the elimination of duplication. The Act also calls for GAO cooperation with Executive agencies in the development of their accounting systems and, at the same time, makes such systems subject to approval by the Comptroller General on the basis of "conformity with the principles, standards, and related requirements prescribed by him."

The 1950 Act requires the heads of Executive agencies to establish and maintain systems of accounting and internal control. It provides that the Comptroller General consider such internal agency facilities in determining his own auditing procedures and the extent of the examination which he makes of accounting documents. The Act also establishes a firm legal basis for the Comptroller General conducting his audits in the places where the accounts and other records of the respective Executive Agencies are maintained. Finally, the Comptroller General is authorized to discontinue the maintenance of various accounting records "when in his opinion the accounting systems and internal control of the Executive, Legislative, and Judicial agencies are sufficient to enable him to perform properly the functions to which such accounts relate."

Second Hoover Commission Report - 1955

The report of the Second Hoover Commission[31] made no recommendations designed to change the responsibilities or authority of the Comptroller General. The Commission's approach to this facet of its inquiry was undoubtedly conditioned by the resentment that Congress had shown when the First Hoover Commission submitted proposals changing the statutory role of the Comptroller General. However, the 1955 report on budget and accounting contained recom-

11

mendations affecting the frame of reference within which
the Comptroller General discharges his responsibilities,
particularly those relating to financial management systems.

The Commission reiterated the 1949 recommendation for
a performance or program budget,[32] a concept that was a
harbinger of the more sophisticated planning-programming-
budgeting (PPB) approach, in the implementation of which
the GAO became deeply involved. The Commission recommended the use of the accrual basis in the Executive budget and Congressional appropriations.[33] It also recommended that accrual accounting be employed by Executive
agencies[34] and a requirement to that effect was enacted by
the Congress.[35] The GAO has been unremitting in its efforts directed to compliance with this statutory mandate.

The importance of adequate internal auditing within
the Federal departments and agencies was emphasized by
the Commission, which pointed out: "It does not take
the place of the external auditing by the Comptroller
General."[36] The Commission recognized the managerial
utility of internal auditing as well as its usefulness
in facilitating the Comptroller General's work. The push
which the Commission gave to internal auditing was unquestionably a potent force in stimulating Congressional
interest in, and active support of, efforts to strengthen
such activities within the Executive Branch.

Legislative Reorganization Act of 1970[37]

Although the Comptroller General has insisted that
the Budget and Accounting Act of 1921 afforded the GAO a
tenable basis for extending its reviews far beyond the
finance sphere, the 1970 Legislative Reorganization Act
unquestionably strengthened his position markedly by man-
dating that he review and evaluate the results of Government programs and activities in response to Congressional
directives or upon his own initiative. These reviews were
to include cost-benefit studies, and the Comptroller General was required to have available in the GAO employees
experts in analyzing and conducting such studies.

The Act was significant not only for legitimizing
program reviews but also for authorizing either House and
any committee of either House or any joint committee to
order the Comptroller General to conduct these reviews,
provided the committee had jurisdiction over the programs
and activities that were involved. This was a sharp departure from the 1921 Act which had restricted the authority to order Comptroller General's "investigations and
reports" to only the two Houses and those committees having
jurisdiction over revenues, appropriations, and expenditures.

Although GAO had brushed this limitation aside and responded to the requests of all committees, the 1970 change
is still important as tangible Congressional recognition
that GAO's role is of such breadth that it can be expected
to be of assistance in the total range of Congressional
concerns. These provisions were included in Title II of
the Act which carried the heading "Fiscal Controls"; another provision directed the Comptroller General to establish under the GAO such a unit as he considered necessary
to carry out the provisions of that Title. The Act also
called upon the Comptroller General to cooperate with the
Secretary of the Treasury and the Director of OMB in:
(a) developing, establishing, and maintaining: a Government-wide information and data processing system for budgeting and fiscal data and (b) standard classifications
of programs activities, receipts, and expenditures of
Federal agencies. Both the content and structure of the
Act were indicative of Congressional recognition of GAO
as an important resource in discharging the budgetary responsibilities of the legislative branch.

The thrust for more effective utilization of GAO by
the Congress is also manifested in the 1970 provisions as
to: (a) the manner in which the Legislative Branch is to
be apprised of, and furnished, GAO reports; (b) assisting Congressional committees, on the basis of such reports,
in their consideration of proposed legislation, including
requests for appropriations; and (c) the requirement that
agencies furnish Congressional committees written statements of the action they have taken concerning recommendations made in GAO reports.

At the same time that the Legislative Reorganization
Act of 1970 broadened GAO's role as a supportive agency
for the Congress, it took what might be regarded as a
countervailing step when it redesignated the Legislative
Reference Service in the Library of Congress as the Congressional Research Service and evidenced the intention
that the Service should have the capability for "rendering
to Congress the most effective and efficient service" and
for "responding most expeditiously, effectively, and efficiently to the special needs of Congress." The Service
was given the duty of assisting committees in "the analysis, appraisal, and evaluation of legislative proposals
. . . or of recommendations submitted to Congress by the
President or any executive agency." Thus, the Act was
double-edged in that it expanded GAO's statutory mandate
but also buttressed another source of assistance to the
Congress.

Technology Assessment Act of 1972[38]

The establishment of the Office of Technology Assessment in 1972 carried forward the trend to broaden the supportive services available to the Congress and, in effect, to make it less dependent upon the GAO. The Act provides: "The basic function of the Office shall be to provide early indications of the probable beneficial and adverse impacts of the applications of technology and to develop other coordinate information which may assist the Congress."

Congressional Budget and Impoundment Control Act of 1974[39]

The Congressional Budget and Impoundment Control Act of 1974 has far-reaching ramifications for the GAO, especially with respect to the manner in which it serves the Congress. Title VIII - Fiscal and Budgetary Information and Controls, expanding upon the Legislative Reorganization Act of 1970, further defines and strengthens the role which the Comptroller General is to play in cooperation with the Secretary of the Treasury, the Director of the Office of Management and Budget, and the Director of the newly-created Congressional Budget Office in developing, establishing, maintaining, and publishing standard terminology, definitions, classifications, and codes for Federal fiscal, budgetary, and program-related data and information. It requires the Comptroller General to conduct a continuing program to identify and specify the needs of the committees and Members of the Congress for fiscal, budgetary and program-related information. The Comptroller General is also given the task of assisting committees in developing their information needs; and he is required to critique the recurring reporting requirements of the Congress and its committees.

The provisions of Title VIII together with the enlarged GAO program evaluation role set forth in Title VII, represent a formidable enhancement of GAO's responsibilities in connection with the budgetary process, particularly as it relates to the Congress. In seeking to achieve more effective participation in budgetary decision-making, Congress is manifestly looking to the GAO as an agency having the expertise that can aid immeasurably in carrying this thrust to a successful conclusion.

Title X of the 1974 Act - Impoundment Control, requires the Comptroller General to review all deferrals and rescissions of budget authority which the President proposes and to advise the Congress as to their legality and impact. The Comptroller General is empowered to bring suit to effect the freeing of budget authority not made available as required by the Act. This deep involvement of the Comptroller General in the implementation of a newly-enacted and highly significant Congressional con-

14

straint on Presidential control of governmental expenditures again bespeaks the fact that Congress attributes
to the GAO a role far more encompassing than that ordinarily associated with an audit agency. It also reflects
a propensity on the part of Congress to look to the
Comptroller General when it needs a surrogate to effectuate its edicts.

The 1974 Act reinforced the Congressional espousal
of program evaluations that had been articulated in the
Legislative Reorganization Act of 1970. The 1970 mandate for such evaluations was supplemented by the requirement that the Comptroller General, "develop and
recommend to the Congress methods for review and evaluation of Government programs and activities carried on
under existing law." It is noteworthy that a separate
title of the Act is devoted almost in its entirety to
program reviews and evaluation, demonstrating that this
technique, that had been nurtured by the Comptroller
General, had attained fruition at least insofar as Congressional acceptance was concerned.

Just as the 1970 Legislative Reorganization Act had
a double-edged impact upon the GAO, so did the 1974 legislation. One of the principal features of the Congressional
Budget and Impoundment Control Act of 1974 was the establishment of the Congressional Budget Office, the primary
responsibility of which is to assist the Committees on the
Budget of both Houses. The broad range of tasks inherent
in the CBO's responsibilities inevitably impinge upon
GAO's involvement in the budget process.

The General Accounting Office Act of 1974[40]

The broad horizons which Comptroller General Staats
envisaged for the GAO made him anxious to divest his agency
of responsibility for the detailed audits of transportation
payments, a relatively prosaic task requiring a large complement of lower grade employees. Hence, he was grateful
that the General Accounting Office Act of 1974 transferred
this function to the General Services Administration.
The audits of government corporations which, as described
elsewhere, had a profound influence in establishing the
professional stature and broad gauge audit approach of
GAO ultimately became a comparatively minor component of
GAO's total program. Responding to the wishes of the Comptroller General, the 1974 Act reduces the required frequency of corporate audits to once in every three years.
The third change effected by the legislation was to extend
the GAO audit authority to certain non-appropriated funds.

In advocating the transfer of the transportation audit

15

function, Comptroller General Staats said: "The basic
reason for proposing the transfer of this operation is
that by its very nature it is primarily an operating
function of the Executive Branch."[41] The Comptroller
General has not displayed similar eagerness to divest
himself of other functions such as approval of accounting
systems which, as is brought out later, the Comptroller
General considers "executive" in nature. This demonstrates
that the Comptroller General is not at all averse to discharging executive functions if they fit into the power
base he espouses for the GAO.

Federal Election Legislation[42]

Congressional proclivity for dumping responsibilities
upon the GAO regardless of their relevance to the fundamental mission of the Government's central monitoring
agency was evidenced in the involvement of GAO in the administration of the legislation relating to the financing
and control of campaign expenditures for Federal elections.
Two acts, one of which became effective in 1972 and the
other in 1973 vested important responsibilities in the
Comptroller General, mainly relating to compliance with
the requirements for the disclosure of campaign expenditures. The Office of Federal Elections was created in
GAO to carry out these functions.

As the 1972 Presidential campaign gained momentum,
the GAO found itself deeply enmeshed in the hurly burly
of the political scene. An outpouring of newspaper, tele-
vision, and radio reports and comments followed the announcement by GAO that it had referred to the Department
of Justice its finding that "apparent and possible violations" of the Election Campaign Act had been committed by
the Finance Committee to Reelect the President. The report assumed an especially dramatic quality because of
its implications in terms of the funds found in the possession of the individuals involved in the Watergate
break-in.

The Comptroller General had to process thousands of
reports required to be filed by political committees and
candidates, prepare necessary listings, conduct audits
and investigations of committee and campaign activities,
and make referrals to the Department of Justice for possible prosecution. The Comptroller General had objected
to having these responsibilities thrust upon him; and
he was undoubtedly relieved when they were transferred to
the Federal Election Commission established in 1974.[43]

GAO INTERACTION WITH OTHER CONGRESSIONAL SUPPORT
AGENCIES

GAO has enjoyed primacy as a supportive agency for the Congress. However, the foregoing legislative history brings out that Congress has strengthened the informational resources available to it through the establishment of the Congressional Budget Office, Congressional Research Service, and the Office of Technology Assessment.[44] Furthermore, there has been a marked expansion in the staffs of Congressional committees and individual members. Finally, the Comptroller General has taken a firmer position with respect to not permitting the direct assistance rendered Congress to divert the GAO from other responsibilities such as self-initiated reviews. Hence, there are at least the beginnings of a recasting of GAO's supportive role in relation to that of the other resources Congress can tap.

GAO relations with CBO, CRS, and OTA

In their review of the 1976 appropriation requirements for the Legislative Branch, both the House and Senate Committees on Appropriations expressed concern that there was insufficient coordination among the activities of the Congressional Research Service, General Accounting Office, and the Office of Technology Assessment. In its report, the Senate Appropriations Committee reiterated concern that GAO involvement in technology might result in overlap with the work of OTA. It went on to state that Congress expected OTA "to take the lead role in assessments of the impact of technology applications."[45] The Committee was also apprehensive that the GAO might be expanding unduly that component of its staff engaged in budget and program analysis and Congressional information and budget support activities. It apparently felt that there might be unnecessary overlap between GAO and the newly-established CBO.

GAO generally feels that there are no significant difficulties in the relations between it and the Congressional Research Service. GAO and CRS perceive their respective approaches to problems as being so different as to almost preclude any overlap. The Acting Director of CRS, observing that the Service made timely responses to the requests from the Congress, was probably thinking of the relatively extended periods of time required for completion of the in-depth type of analysis ordinarily involved in a GAO study.[46] It is also worthy of mention that a CRS Report is ordinarily issued over the name of the particular staff member responsible for it. This contrasts sharply with the fact that a report issued by GAO is an institutional product for which the GAO as such takes responsibility.

The Comptroller General informed a House Appropriation Subcommittee that he felt that the relationship with CBO

had been worked out satisfactorily and that there is no
duplication. The Comptroller General was not so reassuring
in discussing GAO relationships with OTA.[47] This might
strike some as all the more surprising in light of the
fact that the Comptroller General is by statute an ex-
officio member of the Technology Assessment Advisory Council of OTA. The GAO contends that coordination between it
and OTA could be strengthened if OTA checked with GAO before making a definitive decision to go ahead with a project. GAO's overtures on this score have been unsuccessful;
and OTA has continued to defer any coordination with GAO
until after the decision has been reached to proceed with
a project.

The problem is not entirely one of duplication of effort but also selecting the agency which can best be responsive to the needs of the particular committee or individual Member. Much depends upon the perception which Members and their staffs have of the respective competences
of the several agencies and also upon the relationships
which they have developed with them. Moreover, even the
most precise carving out of responsibilities will not in
itself suffice. Congress should expect meaningful continuing collaboration among these agencies; its interest
on this score can do much to stimulate such interaction
and counteract any tendency toward aloofness or insularity.

Although coordination between the four agencies presents no truly serious problems at the present time, there
is some question as to whether integration of these activities should continue indefinitely to be dependent upon
relatively informal arrangements worked out by them, and
which reflect the interaction of the personalities involved. As CBO and OTA, which were established relatively
recently, develop and give further expression to their
roles, effective coordination may become more difficult.
The demands which Congress makes upon the four agencies
may have to be channeled systematically if these supportive services are to be utilized in a manner that enables
them to serve the Congress in a complementary fashion
rather than competing with each other by engaging in
activities that are unnecessarily duplicative.

IMPACT OF INDIVIDUAL COMPTROLLERS GENERAL

The evolution of the GAO has been very much influenced
by the backgrounds, personality attributes, and values of
those who occupied the office of Comptroller General. The
fact that the agency has been so responsive to the thinking
of those serving in the top post is due in part to the extended statutory term of the Comptroller General, i.e.,
fifteen years. Those serving under this official realize

18

that his is not a transitory tenure and that they will be subject to his direction for a relatively prolonged period. Another factor that buttresses the Comptroller General's impact is the leeway which he has in determining the specific activities of the Office, and more particularly how these will be implemented. The statutory enactments discussed in the foregoing have left the Comptroller General with considerable discretion as to how his organization will function; this enables the individual to place his own firm imprint upon the agency. The GAO's operational style at any one point of time can best be understood only if one considers the individual then serving as Comptroller General.

Working relationships with the Congress circumscribe the Comptroller General's freedom of action; but, at the same time, these have been so tenuous that the Comptroller General has frequently been very much on his own. One writer says: "the Comptroller General of the United States sits upon a lonely eminence of authority within his department."[48] As time slips by and practices become more institutionalized, the incumbent may find it more difficult to deviate markedly from what has been established. He may feel reluctant to overturn what has become the accepted way of doing things. On the other hand, changes in the milieu including Congressional attitudes may motivate a new Comptroller General to effect relatively sweeping changes.

Comptroller General McCarl

The first Comptroller General, J.R. McCarl, was appointed by President Harding; he was a lawyer who had served as private secretary to Senator George W. Norris of Nebraska and prior to his appointment was Executive Secretary of the National Republican Congressional Committee. McCarl, as the initial incumbent, was in an unusually strategic position to mold the concept of the GAO. He epitomized the watchdog role with all of its restrictive overtones.[49] McCarl quickly became a stormy petrel in Washington. One of his staff has described him as a "strict constructionist." This quality, together with his unwillingness to delegate authority within the organization and a penchant for injecting himself into important policy matters, made the GAO a disruptive force in the total governmental process. Daenecke gives several cases as illustrative of McCarl's hamstringing the Executive Branch:

He blocked a $25,000,000 Canada-to-the-Gulf tree belt project fostered by President Franklin Roosevelt as a drought curb;

19

he returned to the then Secretary of the
Interior Ickes, also Public Works Administrator, an ambitious $100,000,000 slum
clearance plan; refused to allow Secretary of Agriculture Henry A. Wallace to
purchase surplus lambs with drought funds,
and criticized the War Department while
forcing new bids for the $10,000,000
Army motorization program on the ground
that the first bids were restrictive and
did not allow free competition.[50]

Perhaps even more irritating to Executive Branch agencies than disagreements on major issues such as these was
McCarl's pettifogging approach to small expenditure items.
He apparently found it a challenge to question and disallow
expenditures of relatively trivial size. This proclivity
was undoubtedly strengthened by the fact that such heroics
on the part of the Comptroller General intrigued the press
and were the subject of many newspaper stories picturing
McCarl as the fiscal watchdog staving off attempts to mis-
use or purloin public funds. One news item tells of Mc-
Carl's disallowing an expense account payment of $1.50 for
an official who left Washington at 6:00 P.M. and ate dinner
on the train. McCarl ruled that the employee had ample
time to eat before leaving home and, more important, that
Congress had failed to make an appropriation to pay a man
for a meal on the train when he could and should have
taken it at his own expense.[51]

McCarl retired on June 30, 1936 at the end of his
statutory term; but President Roosevelt, completely dis-
enchanted with the Office of Comptroller General, did not
fill the position until March, 1939 when Fred Herbert Brown,
a former Senator from New Hampshire was appointed. In the
interim, the Assistant Comptroller General, Richard N.
Elliott, served as the Acting Comptroller General. Brown
resigned in 1940 because of illness; and his brief tenure
had little, if any, effect upon the development of the GAO.

Comptroller General Warren

Lindsay C. Warren, who assumed the duties of Comptroller General on November 1, 1940, brought to the office
extended experience and considerable prestige as a member
of the House of Representatives. His position was also
enhanced by the fact that he accepted the appointment only
after repeated overtures by President Roosevelt.

Warren was quick to deemphasize the enforcement role
of the GAO and to portray its mission in broader perspective. He was manifestly mindful of the antagonisms that

had developed between the GAO under the leadership of
McCarl and the Executive Branch. Warren sought to bind
the wounds and arrive at a rapprochement between his
Office and the Executive agencies.

> Its task is great. Its possibilities as
> a helpful force in the Government have not
> yet been fully reached. I would not regard
> its mission as entirely performed if it
> should serve merely as a fiscal policing
> force for the detection of improper use or
> disposition of public funds and as an of-
> fice for the certification and collection
> of balances found to have been improperly
> used.[52]

However, shortly thereafter, Warren emphasized the
GAO's role as an arm of the Congress and tied in the
creation of the GAO with implementation of the constitutional provision that "no money shall be drawn from the
Treasury but in consequence of appropriations made by law."
He termed the principle of legislative control of the
purse as being in the front rank of United States demo-
cratic institutions.[53] This pronouncement was not surprising in light of Warren's Congressional career. In
later reiterating his emphasis on the GAO's participation
in Congressional oversight of expenditures, Warren appeared
to be intimating that his broader approach did not contemplate any relaxation of GAO's efforts to serve as Congress'
instrumentality for enforcing "its control of the purse,
insuring that its appropriations are equally applied in
accordance with its directive and limiting enactments."[54]
In this respect, Warren shared some of McCarl's thinking;
and he, in fact, referred to McCarl's remarks on the background of Congressional financial control.[55]

Warren stated that "the chief functions of the Office
are to determine by audit and other means the lawfulness
and justice of public accounts and claims and, except
wherever other disposition is provided by law, settle them
accordingly, and to investigate and report to the Congress
matters affecting public finances."[56] But, at the same
time, Warren worked zealously to change the image that the
GAO had acquired under the McCarl regime and that had made
for serious estrangement between the Office and the Executive Branch. His launching of the Joint Financial Management Improvement Program previously described is symptomatic of his sustained effort to make the GAO more acceptable
to Executive agencies.

The excellent relations Warren had with the Congress
placed him in a formidable position to influence the fate

of proposed legislation with respect to the GAO. He was
constantly on the alert to resist what he thought might
be legislative attempts to weaken that agency. Conversely,
his stamp of approval upon legislative proposals involving
the GAO could be a potent force in effecting their enactment.

When, because of ill health, Warren resigned in 1954,
he sent a letter to each senator and congressman in which
he told them of his resignation and commented on his performance as Comptroller General. In this valedictory,
Warren directed attention to GAO accomplishments in the
financial management area, and praised the Joint Financial
Management Improvement Program; ever on the alert to rebuff attempts to narrow the scope of GAO's authority, he
warned against efforts to "destroy the effectiveness of
the General Accounting Office." He beseeched Congress to
give the GAO its wholehearted support and "vigilant safe-
guarding of its functions and powers."[57]

Comptroller General Campbell

When Joseph C. Campbell took over as Comptroller General in December 1954, GAO had, for the first time, as its
chief a person coming from the accounting profession. Unlike his predecessors, Campbell was not a lawyer and had
not served in the Congress. His previous Government service was as a member of the Atomic Energy Commission; prior
to this, he had been Vice President and Treasurer of Columbia University. While serving in this latter capacity, he
came to know Dwight Eisenhower, who, at the time was President of Columbia.

As is brought out in the next chapter, the fact that
Campbell's background was so different from that of his predecessors afforded a rationale for subjecting him to hostile
questioning during the Senate hearings on his nomination.
It was to be expected that a person with Campbell's orien-
tation would carry forward the trend towards increased professionalism within the GAO. He initially perceived the
role of the agency from the perspective of the public accountant.[58] Subsequently, Campbell saw GAO's role in broader
dimensions. He described it as including both examining
the manner in which Government agencies discharge their
financial responsibilities with respect to public funds and
making recommendations looking to greater economy and efficiency in public expenditures.[59]

The Campbell regime diverged sharply from that of Warren's, at least insofar as relations with Congress and the
Executive agencies were concerned. According to many
knowledgeable persons, Campbell stressed output of reports,
especially those of a fault-finding character. The follow-

22

ing is representative of such evaluations. "Campbell was
a very peculiar man and few people would say they knew
him. There was something in his ego that was satisfied
by newspaper headlines concerning GAO findings. . . . He
pressured GAO divisions to get out more and more reports
with the result that Congress was not able to digest them."
The Campbell critics contended that the quality of reports
was subordinated to quantity and that staff promotions were
influenced by the volume of deficiency findings made by the
individuals. On the other hand, some who served under
Campbell feel that he was misunderstood; they refer to his
high standards of integrity and his anxiety lest GAO's independence and objectivity be compromised. Perhaps the
mystique and aloofness with which Campbell surrounded himself made for unnecessary friction and disagreement. Speaking of Campbell's tenure, an editorial in a professional
journal observed:

> A problem of increasing concern to many in
> the Federal Government has been the ten-
> dency of the General Accounting Office for
> some years to be in the Government but not
> of the Government. . .[60]

Comptroller General Staats

The appointment of Elmer B. Staats as Comptroller General in 1966 brought to the office an individual whose career had been almost in its entirety within the Executive
Branch of the Government. Continuity of his service in the
Bureau of the Budget and the fact that he had served as
Deputy Director under four Presidents afforded him both
broad perspective as to the Federal Government as well as
an understanding in depth of the many different aspects of
the Federal establishment. His numerous appearances before
Congressional committees and other contacts with members
of Congress afforded him savoir-faire in handling relationships with the Legislative Branch. This quality was reflected in the highly favorable reaction of Congress to his
nomination. Staats' adeptness in testifying before committees has contributed immeasurably to solidifying GAO relations with Congress.

The insights which Staats had acquired into Federal
agencies, their programs, and problems have facilitated
more effective utilization of GAO resources. Similarly,
his familiarity with the operations of the Federal agencies
have been invaluable in making for better relationships between them and the GAO.

In his first Annual Report, Comptroller General Staats
underlined the importance of GAO efforts directed toward

"assisting Congress in maintaining the surveillance so
necessary for effective legislative oversight of a vast
complex of Governmental programs and operations."[61]   At
the same time, Staats -- apparently mindful of the skepticism and even hostility on the part of many agencies
with respect to the GAO, stated:

> An important part of the work of the General
> Accounting Office is providing assistance to
> the agencies of the Government in bringing
> about greater effectiveness, efficiency, and
> economy in the conduct of their programs and
> activities.[62]

Staats has emphasized GAO reviews as a vehicle for
checking on Federal agency management. He stated that one
of GAO's primary missions would continue to be reports to
the Congress reflecting the independent judgment of GAO on
the effectiveness, efficiency, and economy with which governmental programs are carried out.[63]   Greater breadth of
the audit and review activities of the GAO is only one of
several indicia of Staats' determination to make his Office
a more potent and meaningful force in the total Governmental
process. Staats personally plays a pivotal role in the efforts to strengthen relations with the Legislative Branch
and, in that connection, to keep the GAO attuned to Congressional needs. Constrasting sharply with this deference
to the Congress is the strong stand the Comptroller General
has taken vis-a-vis the Executive Branch in asserting his
decision-making authority, as exemplified in the Philadelphia Plan ruling and the steps he took to enforce the decision despite the Attorney General's disagreement with it.[64]

As an advocate of a very broad approach to the role of
the GAO, Staats often finds himself in a dilemma because of
numerous proposals to push the GAO into areas that might
well overtax GAO's capabilities to deal adequately with them.
The Comptroller General is faced with the quandary of how to
keep the GAO responsive to challenges that appropriately
come within its sphere and at the same time steer clear of
responsibilities that do not comport with a tenable concept
of a central monitoring agency.

GAO'S CHANGED MILIEU

The inherent caution and conservatism of an audit
agency has not inhibited GAO responsiveness to the vast
economic, technological, social, and political changes in
its milieu.

Size and complexity of Federal Government

A consolidated Federal budget of $459.4 billion pro-
posed by President Carter for fiscal 1978 compares sharply
with $3.3 billion in 1922, the first year of the GAO's
existence, even after allowing for the reduced purchasing
power of the dollar and a difference in the basis of com-
puting the budgetary totals. The size has been accompanied
by a dispersion of Government facilities throughout the
world and the proliferation of separate programs and organization units. But it is not merely the number and size of
Governmental programs that strain the resources of GAO;
the diversity, complexity, and technical character of Governmental undertakings pose many problems for such an audit
agency.

The monolithic character which the Federal Government
has assumed cuts two ways so far as the GAO is concerned.
It makes both Congress and the public even more convinced
of the need for an independent instrumentality for monitoring this tremendous complex. But the gargantuan nature of
the Government, the number of separate agencies, and the
prodigious volume of transactions mean that the GAO has to
rethink its operations so that it can keep its workload
within manageable proportions. The ever-growing size of
the Federal establishment is conducive to the crystallization and acceptance of the concept of a central monitoring
agency that places greater emphasis upon agency self-ap-
praisals and that focuses its own efforts upon special
problems and situations.

Defense spending

The very size of defense expenditures, $111.9 billion
proposed by President Carter for fiscal 1978, would in itself require GAO to direct much of its effort to the defense establishment. At the same time, the military tradition, the problems stemming from the confidentiality of
essential data, the magnitude and complexity of the operations, the strength of the military industrial complex,
and the ties between the Defense establishment and key
Congressional committees and members, all add up to a climate that until recently had impeded deep GAO penetration
into Defense expenditures.

Increased financial assistance to state and local governments

The 1978 budget prepared by President Ford recommended
$71.6 billion of outlays for grants-in-aid to state and lo-
cal governments, an amount more than thirty times the 1950
grants.[65] The expenditures entailed in this financial assistance, which has become an increasingly large segment of
the Federal Budget (16.3 per cent in 1978 versus 5.3 in 1950)
are not within the audit authority of the GAO in the absence

25

of special statutory provisions. However, "numerous laws enacted in recent years and authorizing Federal grants-in-aid, cost sharing programs, and other financial assistance specifically provide for GAO audit and access to records of recipients."[66] Entirely apart from statutory mandates, the volume of grants-in-aid and the increasing interaction between the programs and operations of the several levels of government afford a rationale for the Comptroller General reaching out beyond the Federal Government and addressing himself to improved financial management at subnational levels of government.

Expanded use of Government contractors

The expansion of the Federal Government has been felt not only in the increased numbers of military and civilian personnel but also in the volume of services and materiel obtained on a contractual basis. Whereas previously one thought of the Government contractor primarily in terms of suppliers of commodities required for Governmental operations or for the construction of public works, contractors are now the source of a wide range of services, some of which are integral aspects of Federal programs. The dependence of Government upon contractors is a development that has basic implications of both an operational and policy character.[67] The dependence is not one-sided; in a significant number of cases, contracts awarded by the Government comprise a high proportion of the total volume of the enterprise. In some cases, the dichotomy between status as a Government agency and that as a private corporation becomes distinctly fuzzy. The Comptroller General has found that an increasing component of his total responsibilities relates to Governmental contractors.

In many instances, an agency may have a choice between performing activities directly through its own personnel and facilities and procuring them on a contractual basis. As discussed in the chapter dealing with the GAO's role in Government procurement, this has given rise to problems in the resolution of which the Comptroller General has had an important part.

The vastness of the spending incurred by the defense establishment on the basis of contractual arrangements has given broader dimensions to Government procurement. This refers to not only the budgetary implications but, equally important, the public policies involved. There are disturbing problems as to waste of funds, exorbitant profits, and incompatibility between the public interest and the pressures brought to bear by Government contractors. Public and Congressional discussions make frequent critical references to the military-industrial complex.

It is not only commercial enterprises that are involved in contractual undertakings with the Federal Government. Contractual relationships between Government and educational and scientific institutions have given rise to what Don Price referred to as "an improvised form of federalism."[68] These contractual arrangements between Government and private organizations add to the tasks that a monitoring agency should be expected to perform in following through on the implementation of public programs.

As the distinction between the private and public sectors becomes less sharp and as the quality of the performance of Governmental functions becomes more dependent upon the skills, diligence, and standards of the Government contractor, the GAO must look increasingly beyond the functioning of the agencies proper. A truncated appraisal is inevitable unless the GAO sees an activity as a totality and as encompassing all facets whether they be carried out by Government personnel or be entrusted primarily or in part to those entering into contractual commitments with the Government.

Impact of advances in management technology

The tremendous strides in managerial technology have constrained GAO to enter into areas that call for skills that had not been part of the regular audit discipline. This has made it essential for GAO to adopt a multidisciplinary approach which will enable it to evaluate operations that involve the application of these new managerial tools and also permit the GAO itself to utilize such techniques in connection with its own operations.

The Comptroller General reported that the "Federal Government spends over $10 billion annually to use computers and related resources for its activities."[69] The extensive use of computers throughout the Government has led Congress to look to the GAO as a means for assuring that automatic data processing installations have a sound basis and do not merely represent the whims of administrators who are bemused by computers. Within the Federal Government, the question of effecting savings in the utilization of ADP equipment should not obscure the importance of making certain that the Government is fully realizing the managerial potentialities of such equipment. The Comptroller General has directed attention to the significant impact which the use of ADP systems has had "on operations in almost every major agency of the Government." This aspect assumes added relevance in view of GAO's effectiveness approach to its audit function.

Congress has shown increasing interest in the use of

the systems approach to the analysis of problems and the
importance of making certain that the Government is in a
position to avail itself of more sophisticated analytical
tools. A Congressional committee report specifically referred to the GAO as being one of the agencies which might
play a role in furthering the use of systems technology to
solve the burgeoning social and community problems.[70] As
the earlier discussion brought out, the Legislative Reorganization Act of 1970 and the Congressional Budget Act of
1974 include provisions directed to making GAO a vehicle
for facilitating Congressional utilization of advanced
analytical techniques as well as strengthening the informational resources available to the Legislative Branch.
The mounting Congressional interest in this facet of its
operations was undoubtedly stimulated by the push for
widespread application of Planning-Programming-Budgeting
(PPB) throughout the Executive Branch, even though this
move was ill-fated. Similarly the current Congressional
interest in the zero base approach will inevitably make
for greater receptivity to more disciplined decision-making.

GAO's public image

Reference has already been made to public awareness
and misconception of the GAO. Yet public pressure can be
a potent force for obtaining consideration of a monitoring
agency's findings and recommendations and bringing about
appropriate action.

The press is the key medium for creating the GAO image.
But public media have a proclivity for seizing upon GAO's
findings of shortcomings and, sometimes, giving a distorted
impression. The result is to irritate the particular agencies that are concerned and place them even more on the defensive with respect to GAO's reviews. A top GAO official
has observed: "We are cast in the role of pouncing upon
the agencies insofar as the press is concerned." He went
on to comment that "unfair criticism not only hurts the
agency covered by the report but also the GAO." The same
official referred to certain news stories as "inflammatory."
It is obvious that the press may push a GAO lead to a point
that the GAO itself is disturbed by the exaggerated or
erroneous impression the public receives. The GAO is not
unmindful that this elicits tension, resentment, and even
hostility on the part of the agencies. Yet Comptrollers
General, in an apparent eagerness to avoid relative anonymity, have been prone to aid and abet sensationalism in
news stories on the GAO.

The newspaper stories that depict the GAO in sleuth-
like terms such as "top capital muckraker"[71] undoubtedly
help to stimulate public interest in the Comptroller General

28

but tend to undermine GAO stature within the Government and may even cause more roadblocks to be thrown up against its inquiries. The public is led to look upon the GAO as a good source for the disclosure of scandal but does not conceive of the agency as an instrumentality for the evaluation of programs and operations and the formulation of findings and recommendations directed to their improvement.

Comptroller General Campbell tended to create a GAO image of being the safeguard against scoundrels and imcompetents who had access to public funds. Although Comptroller General Warren adopted and implemented a more constructive concept of the GAO, what came through in the press conjured up the image of the Comptroller General as something of an Horatius fighting off villainous attempts to raid the public treasury. Thus, one news story was headed: "Scowling is Part of Controller General Warren's Job."[72]

Staats has worked incessantly to effect wider and better coverage of the GAO by the media. He has made himself accessible to the press and has used interviews to explain GAO's role and operations: Staats' emphasis upon public relations together with the newsworthy character of many of the GAO reports have not only afforded GAO activities greater publicity but have also evoked editorial support for the Comptroller General's recommendations.

The press stories that have come out since Comptroller General Staats took office reflect a more sophisticated understanding of the GAO. However, media awareness of the GAO is not as widespread as some might surmise. A radio commentator puzzled as to why the GAO was concerning itself about the Navy's eight-inch gun exclaimed:

> The GAO pops up in the news frequently, but most of us haven't the slightest idea what it is, and the press never tells us anything more than "investigative arm of Congress." How does it manage to have a staff person who knows naval guns, and how did he find out the new one can't hit his targets? Help "Washington Press Corps." Tell us what it's all about.

Although, when taken to task by the GAO the commentator admitted that there was wider press coverage of GAO than he had been aware of, he pointed out that such a story "sinks without a trace. I checked around and found that like me, a number of quite knowledgeable people to this day are ignorant of the activities of the GAO."[73]

Some comments are critical and/or still picture the

GAO in accounting terms. A magazine article alleged that
GAO: (a) has "a tremendous number of time-serving hacks
just sitting around pushing pencils and dreaming of the
day they can retire." (b) "is critically afflicted with
accountants' mentality" and (c) "spends far too much time
in trivial studies and far too easily intimidated by tough
rascals in the Executive Branch and in the bureaucracy."[74]
But, despite this diatribe, the article conceded GAO is
"really a pretty good ol' dog." One article gave a com-
pletedly outmoded picture of GAO's modus operandi when it
related that GAO personnel "pour over the federal government books to ferret out waste, bungling, and outright
thievery."[75] The same article referred to a disquieting
criticism by a Republican official impugning the non-par-
tisanship of the GAO. An earlier news story, "Watchdog
GAO May be Monster," accused GAO of strong pro-Democratic
bias and contended that it "was mostly quiet as far as
national publicity until Johnson was succeeded by Richard
Nixon."[76] The fact that such accusations are rare reflects
the favorable press reaction which GAO more typically elicits. One business publication went all out in its evaluation and not only stated that GAO "has acquired the clout
to cut off Congressional appropriations and check Presidential power" but also prophesized that it "is destined to
grow even more powerful under the Carter Administration."[77]
A newspaper, reacting to the range of important matters
explained by GAO, titled its story, "Watchdog GAO Draws
Blood on Big Issues."[78]

GAO PARADOXES

     It is not only the heterogeneity of GAO functions
that engenders misconception. Understanding the GAO is
made more difficult because of the number of paradoxes
which it reflects.

     The semantics in themselves are confusing. The sta-
tutory use of two separate terms -- Comptroller General
of the United States, and General Accounting Office --
tends to make for the misconception that they are two distinct organizational entities. The terminology obscures
the fact that the Comptroller General is the head of, and
discharges his responsibilities through, the GAO. The
name "General Accounting Office" is in itself misleading
since the GAO no longer does any accounting for the Federal Government. Another semantic difficulty is encountered in connection with the term "audit." Most of the
so-called audits now made by the GAO deal only indirectly,
if at all, with agency financial operations and condition
and do not result in the preparation or verification of
financial statements as in the case of the more typical
audits. For the most part, the audits made by the GAO are

evaluations of programs and operations. Confusion also stems from the fact that the professional accountant still is the keystone of its technical staff -- aside from those employed in the Office of the General Counsel. The important role of the individuals having professional accounting credentials has been open to increasing question as GAO embarked upon projects that call for a multidisciplinary approach.

The accounting facade of the agency obscures the crucial role that the legal staff plays in the discharge of the Comptroller General's responsibilities. Those who rely unduly upon the watchdog metaphor for obtaining an understanding of the GAO may not be aware of the fact that much of the Comptroller General's influence is exercised through the output of the legal staff. The decisions issued by the GAO have profound effects upon Government operations. Additionally, the GAO's legal role encompasses the settlement of claims by and against the Government and the resolution of the protests of unsuccessful bidders.

The very manner in which the Comptroller General is appointed is something of an incongruity. Although clearly a component of the Legislative Branch, the Comptroller General is appointed, as is also the Deputy Comptroller General, by the President. This method of selecting the Comptroller General, based on constitutional considerations, is increasingly difficult to reconcile with the trend to give this official a more vital role in the legislative process. This arrangement, as is observed subsequently, is currently being challenged by some Members of Congress.

The GAO finds itself caught in the contradiction of seeking to be of service to the Government agencies and at the same time functioning as independent critic. This role conflict is intensified by the fact that accounting systems are subject to approval of the Comptroller General, whose efforts in this area have been difficult to reconcile with the interests, priorities, and preferences of Executive Branch agencies.

The much vaunted independence of the GAO presents still another paradox. The realities implicit in the GAO's relations with the Congress circumscribe this independence. The working accords that have developed between GAO and Congressional committees, individual Members, and Congressional staffs, are not all compatible with full freedom of action on the part of the GAO.

GAO finds itself in a Scylla and Charybdis situation posed by the expanding size of the Federal Government. The Office, since the Warren regime, has proudly trumpeted a

policy of restraint as to its budgetary needs. The stance
of relatively modest expenditure requirements is particularly becoming to a monitoring agency, but yet it might impair the capability to discharge adequately the responsibilities entrusted to it.

The outpouring of Comptroller General reports, many
of which evoke little interest even on the part of the
Congress, presents something of a contradiction. GAO is
concerned about stimulating greater awareness and utilization of its reports; and yet their very volume sets up a
formidable obstacle to the achievement of this goal.

It is surprising to find that the GAO, an adjunct of
the Legislative Branch, has become something of an administrative management instrumentality in the Executive Branch.
It is the only agency that deals with the operating levels
of all Government establishments on a continuing basis.
This perhaps indicates that the GAO's role may, on a pragmatic basis, best be conceptualized in a manner that is not
fully compatible with the doctrine of separation of powers.

HOW SHOULD GAO BE EVALUATED?

One can reasonably assume that independence as to content of work program and the manner in which reviews are
conducted and reported upon is inherent in the concept of
a central monitoring agency. When the agency is, as in
the case of the GAO, a creature of statutory enactment,
rather than constitutional provisions and is considered
part of the Legislative Branch, the independence needs to
be viewed in the context of this legal status. But, even
in such a situation, the audit agency should be expected
not to compromise on independence as to the manner in which
it initiates and conducts its examinations and articulates
its findings.

Objectivity of approach is important in the monitoring
concept; a corollary is the disassociation of such an
agency from responsibilities that involve its participation
in activities that come within the ambit of its audits or
other examinations. This raises the question as to when it
is appropriate for the central monitoring agency to express
its views at a stage when they can influence decision-making by the responsible administrators. It accentuates the
problem of the auditor counseling management without becoming so involved as to preclude a completely objective post
review.

Ready access to relevant information is patently a
sine qua non of effective central monitoring. The word
"ready" bears emphasis since data obtained only after pro-

tracted negotiations or even a sharp confrontation may involve delay that militates seriously against the usefulness
of the findings. A closely related point is the comprehensiveness of audit authority in terms of the governmental
agencies subject to examinations by the auditor. The more
delicate facets of such comprehensiveness relates to the
extent to which the legislative and judicial branches come
within the purview of the monitoring agency.

Independence and objectivity as well as broad authority are of little avail unless the audit agency has the
requisite expertise to conduct its reviews in a competent
manner. Its requirements on that score depend upon how
the purposes, breadth, and depth of its examinations are
perceived.

Financial accountability can be assumed to be at best
the point of departure for the audits. Inquiries as to
efficiency, i.e., sound utilization of resources, appear
to be well accepted. Far more difficult to resolve is the
question as to the extent to which the auditor should seek
to ascertain the effectiveness with which operations
achieve the purposes envisaged for them. The limits are
being pushed still further so as to encompass the evaluations of the programs themselves and to pass judgment on
policies. It is not only a matter of having the essential
talents or skills to make such analyses but also the desirability and feasibility of having the central monitoring
agency inject itself into this area. In any event, the
auditor seeking to develop these "frontier" aspects should
be expected to maintain a balanced program that does not
relegate its less glamorous efforts to a low priority.
Another constraint which the monitoring agency should recognize in broadening the scope of its reviews is the importance of not being catapulted into the political mael-
strom to an extent that brings into play pressures that
threaten the independence of the agency.

Finally, the audit agency should conduct its reviews
in a manner that minimizes tensions in the agencies under
review and that evokes confidence in the validity of its
findings and the soundness of its recommendations.

FOOTNOTES - Chapter 1

1. Senate, Hearings Before the Subcommittee on Reports, Accounting, and Management of the Committee on Government Operations. GAO Legislation, 94th Cong., 1st Session, 1975, p. 3.

2. See Peter Gruenstein, "The GAO: A General Account-ing." The Nation, June 4, 1973.

3. Comptroller General of the United States, 1975 Annual Report, p. 1.

4. Statement of Comptroller General Staats Before Legisla-tive Subcommittee, House Appropriations Committee, February 3, 1977.

5. Anthony Downs, Inside Bureaucracy (Boston: Little, Brown & Company, 1967), p. 148.

6. W.J.M. Mackenzie, "Foreword" in E.L. Normanton, The Accountability and Audit Of Governments (New York: Frederick A. Praeger, 1966), p. vii.

7. Anthony Downs, op. cit., p. 149.

8. Fritz Morstein Marx, The Administrative State (Chi-cago: University of Chicago Press, 1957), p. 13.

9. Neil C. Churchill and Louis N. Teitelbaum, "Auditing and Managerial Control - A Hypothesis," in Organi-zational Decision Making, ed. by Marcus Alexis and Charles Z. Wilson (Englewood Cliffs, N.J.: Pren-tice-Hall, Inc., 1967), p. 423.

10. Eric Daenecke, A Study of the United States General Accounting Office with Emphasis on the Period Since 1938 (unpublished Ph.D. Dissertation, The American University, 1960), p. 222.

11. See Senate, Committee on Government Operations, Financial Management in the Federal Government, S. Doc. 11, 87th Congress, 1st Session, 1961, p. 3. Some interesting insights into the background of the Act are found in Margaret L. MacFarlane and Judith Hatter, "Personalities Contributing to the Enactment of the Budget and Accounting Act, 1921." GAO Review, Fall 1971, pp. 57-71.

12. President's Committee on Administrative Management, Report of the Committee With Special Studies (Washington, D.C.: Government Printing Office, 1937), p. 22.

13. Ibid., p. 25.

14. Ibid., p. 24.

15. Harvey C. Mansfield, The Comptroller General (New Haven: Yale University Press, 1939).

16. General Accounting Office, Policy and Procedures Manual for Guidance of Federal Agencies, Title I, Section 5.2.

17. 59 Stat. 597.

18. Comptroller General of the United States, 1945 and 1949 Annual Reports (Washington, D.C.: Government Printing Office), p. 3 and p. 31, respectively.

19. Comptroller General of the United States, 1949 Annual Report, p. 11.

20. Budget and Accounting Procedures Act of 1950, Section 111 (f).

21. 63 Stat. 377, Section 206 (c).

22. Comptroller General of the United States, 1949 Annual Report, p. 31.

23. Ibid.

24. Commission on Organization of the Executive Branch of the Government, Report on Budgeting and Accounting in the Executive Branch, H. Doc. 84, 81st Congress, 1st Session, 1949, p. 39.

25. Ibid., p. 41.

26. Ibid., p. 43.

27. Commission on Organization of the Executive Branch of the Government, Task Force Report on Fiscal, Budgeting and Accounting Activities (January 1949).

28. Senate, Committee on Expenditures, S. Rep. No. 2031, 81st Congress, 2nd Session, 1950, p. 4, and House, Committee on Expenditures, H. Rep. 2556, 81st Congress, 2nd Session, 1950, p. 5, on Budgeting and Accounting Procedures Act of 1950.

29. 64 Stat. 832. The Budget and Accounting Procedures Act of 1950 provided that Part II of Title I of that Act may be cited as the Accounting and Auditing Act of 1950.

30. See Ellsworth H. Morse, Jr., "The Accounting and Auditing Act of 1950 - Its Current Significance to GAO." The GAO Review, Summer 1975, p. 23.

31. Commission on Organization of the Executive Branch of the Government, Budget and Accounting, 84th Congress, 1st Session, 1955.

32. Ibid., p. 11.

33. Ibid., pp. 22-25.

34. Ibid., pp. 36-38.

35. 70 Stat. 782.

36. 1955 Commission Report, op. cit., p. 50.

37. Public Law 91-510.

38. Public Law 92-484.

39. Public Law 93-344.

40. Public Law 93-604.

41. Statement of Elmer B. Staats Before the House Subcommittee on Legislation and Military Operations, June 5, 1974.

42. Public Law 92-178 and Public Law 92-225.

43. Public Law 93-443.

44. The four agencies are dealt with in Congressional Support Agencies - A Compilation of Papers Prepared for the Commission on the Operation of the Senate, 94th Congress, 2nd Session, 1976. The author prepared the paper "The General Accounting Office as a Congressional Resource." Section VII of the Final Report of the Commission (December, 1976) also deals with the support agencies.

45. Senate Report 94-262, p. 35.

46. Transcript of Commission on Operations of the Senate Inquiry on CRS, p. 64.

47. House Hearings on Legislative Branch Appropriations
    for 1977, pp. 376 and 379.

48. Normanton, op. cit., p. 297.

49. See Comptroller General of the United States, 1926
    Annual Report, pp. 1-2 for McCarl's concept of the GAO.

50. Daenecke, op. cit., p. 64.

51. Baltimore Sun, December 15, 1929.

52. Comptroller General of the United States, 1942
    Annual Report, p. 1.

53. Comptroller General of the United States, 1944
    Annual Report, p. 1.

54. Comptroller General of the United States, 1945
    Annual Report, p. 1.

55. Ibid.

56. Comptroller General of the United States, 1949
    Annual Report, p. 1.

57. Letter from Comptroller Lindsay Warren, to All Members
    of Congress, March 31, 1954.

58. Comptroller General of the United States, 1956
    Annual Report, p. 1.

59. Comptroller General of the United States, 1958
    Annual Report, p. 1.

60. Federal Accountant, Volume 14, No. 4 (Summer 1965), p. 9.

61. Comptroller General of the United States, 1966
    Annual Report, p. 7.

62. Ibid., p. 31.

63. Elmer B. Staats, "The General Accounting Office - How
    Its Activities Support Federal Management of Federal
    Programs," in The GAO Review, Spring 1967, p. 3.

64. See Chapter 7.

65. Budget of the United States Fiscal Year 1978 Special
    Analyses, p. 273.

66. <u>Legislation Relating to the General Accounting Office</u> - Office of the General Counsel, January 1975, p. D-i.

67. Victor K. Heyman, "Government by Contract: Boon or Boner?" <u>Public Administration Review</u>, Spring 1961.

68. Don K. Price, <u>Government and Science</u> (New York: Oxford University Press, 1962), p. 66.

69. Comptroller General of the United States, <u>1971 Annual Report</u>, p. 49.

70. Senate, Committee on Labor and Public Welfare, Hearings Before Subcommittee, Employment, Manpower, and Poverty, <u>Systems Technology Applied to Social and Community Problems</u>, 91st Congress, 1st Session, June 1969.

71. <u>Houston Chronicle</u>, January 30, 1974.

72. <u>Washington Star</u>, April 30, 1950.

73. William Wood, <u>CBS Radio News</u>, November 11, 1976 and January 4, 1977.

74. <u>Playboy Magazine</u>, November 1974.

75. <u>Chicago Tribune</u>, September 14, 1976.

76. <u>Columbus Evening Dispatch</u>, July 15, 1973.

77. <u>Dun's Review</u>, February 1977.

78. <u>The Pittsburgh Press</u>, December 5, 1976.

Chapter 2

THE COMPTROLLER GENERAL'S CONGRESSIONAL CONSTITUENCY

The basic intent in creating the General Accounting Office and the position of Comptroller General was to strengthen congressional authority over and involvement in fiscal matters, both by assuring independence in the performance of functions previously vested in Treasury officials and by furthering Congress' ability to obtain candid information.[1]

GAO'S CONGRESSIONAL CLIMATE

In making the above pronouncement, the Comptroller General was mindful of the fact that the GAO is a statutory creature and that Congress not only is the key factor in determining the agency's responsibilities and authority but also allocates the resources available to it. The frame of reference of the Comptroller General's activities is determined in large measure both by the explicit requests and directives that emanate from the Congress and also the manner in which the Comptroller General anticipates and seeks to respond to what he deems to be Congressional expectations.

The increased Congressional sentitivity as to the dominance of the President in the total Governmental process has colored the role, approach, and activities of the Comptroller General. As Congress began to assert its prerogatives more aggressively and reached out for more meaningful participation in Governmental decision-making, it assayed the relevant resources available to it. In short, Congressional frustrations stemming from a feeling of impotence or even futility in dealing with the Executive Branch spurred Congress to make more effective use of the GAO. At the same time, there is a more questioning Congressional attitude as to the mix of legislative and executive functions vested in the GAO, the manner in which the Comptroller General is appointed, and the independence of the Comptroller General vis-a-vis Congress.

Until relatively recently, those concerned over Congress' weakness in relation to the Executive Branch would decry the Legislative Branch's paucity of informational and analytical resources. But there has been a marked expansion of, if not explosion in, such resources, and Congress now has the problem of marshalling its supportive services so as to make effective use of them. A writer, who headed his article "The Bloated Branch," emphasized

39

the large numbers of both personal and committee staff employees of the Congress and warned that, unless the "phenomenal growth in legislative personnel and facilities is curbed, Congress' quest for authority will yield only conflict and further public mistrust."[2]   It is not only a matter of numbers of personnel and the expenditures they entail but, even more significantly, the power which Congressional staff exercise in legislative analyses and decision-making.[3]   Hence, as is brought out elsewhere, the staff is a major factor in determining the manner in which Congress utilizes the GAO. The informational and analytical resources -- other than the GAO -- presently available to Congress are all the more impressive when one considers not only the personal and committee staffs, but also the Congressional Budget Office, Congressional Research Service, and the Office of Technology Assessment.

CONGRESSIONAL PERCEPTION OF THE GAO

It would be simplistic to present a stereotyped image of the GAO which purportedly is shared by all Congressional committees, their staffs, and individual Members. However, certain reactions which were elicited in the course of this study merit mention, either because of the relative frequency with which they were experienced or because of their insightful or provocative character.

GAO has generally stood firmly in the good graces of the Congress, particularly so far as public expressions of Congressional members are concerned. Whatever reservations or criticisms committees or Members may have with respect to the GAO, they have ordinarily not been articulated on the floor of either the House or the Senate. Some criticisms are found in Committee reports; but, typically, they are of a relatively restrained character.

Former Senator Paul Douglas was effusive in his praise of the GAO.[4] He stated that his impression was not only distinctly favorable but of the highest, and that GAO was "one of the few ways to keep the bureaucracy on its toes." Bewildered by the complexities of the Executive Branch and frequently hard-pressed to contend with the expertise of those deeply involved in the formulation and management of programs, Congress has ordinarily been receptive to the assistance it can obtain from the GAO. Looking upon the Comptroller General as an ally in its dealings with departments and other agencies, Congress has not been prone to be either incisive or perceptive in its relations with the GAO. Perhaps, too, there may be some feeling that Congressional criticisms of the GAO tend to reflect upon the Congress itself. Moreover, as has already been mentioned, Members of Congress in many instances have relatively few direct contacts with the Comptroller General or his representatives and, therefore, see GAO through the eyes of their own staff assistants or the staffs of the committees on which they serve.

Laudatory comments on the GAO are not infrequently voiced on the floor of the Senate and House. Some are undoubtedly motivated by respect for, and confidence in, the output of GAO. Others are induced, at least in part, by the Member's reliance upon GAO findings to support proposals or points of view of which the Member is a protagonist. Still others appear to be something of a gambit to steer the GAO into particular areas of inquiry. The staff director of a key subcommittee remarked: "Some people in Congress have excessive confidence in the GAO and may become servants of the GAO."

GAO's experience in connection with the Holifield hearings, discussed in Chapter 8, was atypical in that the Office was subjected to penetrating inquiry into some of its basic operations and certain alleged shortcomings were discussed in the public limelight. A committee staff member remarked: "GAO should not be bawled out in public as in the case of the Holifield hearings." The considerable freedom that GAO enjoyed from critical scrutiny made it all the more unprepared to cope adequately with the far-reaching criticisms leveled at it during the Holifield hearings. This undoubtedly accounted, in some measure, for the abject manner in which the GAO responded to its critics. Similarly, the questions raised recently by Senator Metcalf and Representative Brooks apparently were unusually disconcerting to the Comptroller General, unaccustomed as he has been to such challenges. Even Congressmen who view the mission of the GAO rather narrowly still deem it to be indispensable. A Member, who was critical of the GAO, nevertheless considered it essential: "We must have some way to assure the American people that the stewardship for their funds is being adequately watched."

Just as Congress has markedly varying degrees of knowledgeability as to the GAO and its potentialities, similarly there are differences in the frequency with which they will tap resources that GAO can make available to them. Some Members are unfamiliar with the GAO; a Comptroller General's representative recalled one Senator saying: "I don't know a damn thing about GAO." On the other hand, a Senator, lauding the GAO for the service it had rendered the Committee of which he was chairman, said in his letter to the Comptroller General: "My only concern is that when other Committees of the Congress learn of these important capabilities of GAO that you will [sic] inundated with more work than you can handle."[5]

THE GAO'S SUPPORTIVE SERVICES FOR CONGRESS

Although GAO's direct assistance to the Congress is
discussed separately, this categorization of activities
should not obscure the fact that the other functions performed by the GAO reinforce its supportive role for the
Congress. Particularly germane are the self-initiated reviews of economy, efficiency, and program effectiveness which
have centrality in the functioning of the GAO. The Comptroller General stated that such work "is as reflective of
congressional interest as we can make it." He asserted that
zero-base budgeting and "sunset" proposals would greatly
depend on effective program evaluation for which GAO has,
by Congressional mandate, important responsibilities.[6]
Staats' observations do not bring out the surprising extent
to which the GAO is injecting itself into the policy area,
a development that is dealt with in chapters that follow.

Direct GAO assistance to the Congress

The Comptroller General directed Congressional attention to the fact that, when he came to the GAO in 1966,
the work which GAO did at the specific request of committees
and Members of the Congress represented about eight per cent
of the effort of a professional staff of about twenty-four
hundred people and that currently this workload represents
thirty-four per cent of a professional staff of about thirty-
eight hundred people.[7] In the category "Direct Assistance
to the Congress," the Comptroller General includes responses
to committee and Member requests; testifying before Congressional committees; providing briefings on Federal
agency programs and activities for committees, Members, and
staffs; assigning GAO staff members for varying periods to
work for committees; developing questions for use during
Congressional hearings; and providing legal opinions and
comments on pending legislation. The Congressionally-
initiated work stems from special provisions written into
the law such as mandates for specific studies, requests
from committee chairmen, and requests from individual Members.[8]

As to the requests which the GAO receives from individual Members of Congress, the Comptroller General estimated that they constituted only about one-third of the
direct assistance and that most staff requirements for
direct assistance come from committee requests. Apparently
in order to forestall the implication that the work entailed
in responding to such committee and Member requests is of
limited utility for Congressional purposes, the Comptroller
General maintained that GAO's experience is that much of
this work "deals with significant matters needed in both
legislative and oversight roles" of the Congress.[9] The

42

Comptroller General was evidently anxious to allay concern
that responses to such requests, particularly those from
individual Members, divert the GAO from more fruitful use
of its facilities. The GAO states that its responding to
requests from individual Members of the Congress "is in
keeping with GAO's nonpolitical, bipartisan character,
since it avoids the implication that GAO limits its assistance to a particular party in the Congress by responding only to requests made by committee chairmen."[10] Despite the importance which GAO attributes to this aspect
of its activities, the Comptroller General announced that
GAO had found it necessary to keep the work categorized
as direct assistance at the same level in 1977 as in the
fiscal year 1976 except for requests under the newly-enacted
energy policy legislation.

Seeking to solidify its position with the Congress,
the GAO had, over the years, made itself responsive to
not only the requests of committees but also individual
Members. Long before the Legislative Reorganization Act
of 1970 provided for the GAO making program and activity
reviews when requested by any Congressional committee
"having jurisdiction over such programs and activities,"
the GAO had committed itself to far-ranging assistance
to committees and Members. The 1921 Act made no reference to assisting individual Members and confined direct
assistance to that "ordered by either House of Congress or
by any committees of either House having jurisdiction over
revenues, appropriations, or expenditures." But, even
prior to the advent of Staats as Comptroller General, a
GAO spokesman had already stated that "we do not limit assistance to the designated committees but respond to the
requests of all committees and, to the extent that staff
is available, to the requests of individual Members."[11]
Later, Staats went out of his way to reaffirm the general
availability of GAO.

> Responding to requests of individual Members
> of the Congress is an important part of the
> work of the General Accounting Office. GAO
> believes that if a Member is concerned about
> a Government operation or action, the Office
> has an obligation to try to assist him if
> possible.[12]

The requests to which Staats alluded range from items
that are of a trivial -- and occasionally even absurd nature -- to matters of considerable moment. This is dealt
with more specifically in Chapter 5. However, it might be
noted at this point that within the GAO there are mixed
reactions with respect to the special reports prepared
for committees and individual Members. Assignments of

43

considerable substance probably impress many of the staff
as affording the GAO the opportunity to serve the Congress
in a direct fashion and to turn out a product that may well
get more than normal attention. These more positive aspects
may not fully allay the irritation or disappointment caused
by the fact that the high priority given these assignments
can mean that other projects have to be delayed or set
aside. Congressional requests that are not particularly
challenging and may even be picayunish in nature can hardly
be expected to generate much staff enthusiasm although they
may, in some instances, have the merit of being capable of
completion in a relatively short period of time. The outspoken reaction of one GAO staff member affords an interesting insight into the thinking which some of the staff
have on this score.

> I am not interested in running errands for every
> nut on the Hill. Some people are very consider-
> ate and able; but some are almost irrational . . .
> You cannot walk away from a job involving a
> Congressional request.

Ultimately the Comptroller General became fearful
lest there develop an imbalance within GAO's work program that would derogate from its ability to discharge
its other responsibilities adequately. On the other hand,
the Comptroller General was undoubtedly mindful of the
fact that the so-called "direct assistance" makes for a
close working relationship with the Congress and is a most
useful vehicle for selling the Congress on the utility of
the GAO. But Staats was also aware that, in addition to
a possible imbalance in GAO workload, the requests flowing
from committees and Members could have a disruptive effect
on the organization.

When a request is obtained from a Member not having
had previous contact with the GAO, a representative of
the Comptroller General will confer with him to see if
the department or other establishment that is involved
can look into the matter. If a prestigious Congressman
such as Senator Proxmire is involved, GAO will "bend over
backwards to serve him." The GAO is not geared to serving
all committees and individual Congressmen; and, in order
to avoid an impossible workload, a great deal of time --
according to one staff member -- must be spent "getting
the Office out of work."

The lack of systematic means within Congress for
screening requests upon the GAO inevitably gets that
agency involved in power plays between committees, subcommittees, and individual Members. Relationships with
a particular committee remained tenuous for some time

because the committee chairman found that "unbeknown to him" GAO, at the request of a committee member, was making a study which came within the purview of the committee. The chairman was vexed and tried unsuccessfully to get the GAO to agree that no study requested by a committee member would be made unless the chairman agreed.

The volume and diversity of the tasks GAO performs for the Congress can be perceived more readily from the fact that during the 15 months ended September 30, 1976, (a) GAO representatives testified before Congressional committees on 172 occasions, (b) 357 reports were completed for committees (these included some addressed to officers of Congress), (c) 295 reports were prepared for Members of Congress, (d) 426 reports on pending legislation were submitted to committees, and (e) 939 responses were made to Members on requests relating to claims by or against the Government.[13]

The advisory role of GAO in connection with legislation merits explication. The familiarity which the GAO has acquired over the years with respect to the Government's programs and operations has placed it in a position to comment on a broad spectrum of pending legislation, including items in which it might have only a tangential interest. In addition, as the Comptroller General has pointed out, the Office may be able to alert committees as to legal or financial implications of legislative proposals that might otherwise be overlooked or the ramifications of which might not have been fully comprehended. In addition to counseling Congressional committees on pending legislation by means of formal reports, the GAO representatives testify at hearings of Congressional committees.

Having GAO representatives testify at committee hearings not only affords the agency the opportunity to make an input into the deliberations but also to solidify relationships with the respective committees. Since personal GAO contacts with the Congress are more typically with staff members than with Representatives or Senators, participation in committee hearings affords GAO representatives a welcome opportunity to meet Members of the Congress face to face. The GAO might well place still further emphasis on consultations with committees and Members, participation in committee hearings, and the furnishing of memoranda to committees and Members, thereby lessening dependence upon formal reports as a means for assisting the Congress.

During the 15-month period ended September 30, 1976, 55 GAO staff members were assigned to the staffs of 18 different committees or subcommittees. Under the provisions of the Legislative Reorganization Act of 1970, these

assignments cannot exceed one year. Relatively few of the
assignments were made to Senate committees, and it is
conjectural whether this is in any way attributable to
the fact that, unlike the House rules, the Senate rules
require that the GAO be reimbursed for the costs of such
services.

In order to facilitate Congressional consideration
of recommendations, which GAO has made to it, an annual
report is submitted to Congress summarizing recommendations
that have not been acted on at the beginning of each session. Copies are sent to cognizant committee chairmen and
ranking minority Members, to assist them "in assessing
Federal programs and agencies."[14]

It bears reiteration that what GAO classifies as
direct assistance is only one aspect of the important services which the GAO renders to Congress. Although an individual category such as this may be singled out for
analysis, one must constantly keep in mind that the several
functions assigned by law to the GAO are so interrelated
that it is their impact as a totality that should be considered in seeking to determine how well GAO serves as a
resource for the Congress.

Congressional oversight

Both the Legislative Reorganization Acts of 1946 and
1970 explicitly made it incumbent upon the standing committees of the two Houses to exercise oversight of the
implementation of those laws the subject matter of which
comes within the jurisdiction of the respective committees.
The 1970 Act uses wording "application, administration and
execution of those laws or parts of laws. . . ."[15] The
Congressional Budget Act of 1974 amended the earlier provisions by adding the following wording:

> Such committees may carry out the required
> analysis, appraisal, and evaluation them-
> selves, or by contract, or may require a
> Government agency to do so and furnish a
> report thereon to the Congress. Such com-
> mittees may rely on such techniques as pilot
> testing, analysis of costs in comparison
> with benefits, or provision for evaluation
> after a defined period of time.[16]

This section is then followed by provisions for review and evaluation by the Comptroller General, all of
which is presented as separate title within the Act,
which title is headed "Program Review and Evaluation."
Manifestly, the legislation reflects the assumption that

review and evaluation would be the keystone of the oversight process. Chapter 5 analyzes the experience and
problems to date in the program evaluation area.

It is interesting that Senators, responding to a
questionnaire of the Commission on Operation of the Senate, indicated that of nine problem areas listed in the
questionnaire, the second most frequently mentioned was:
"Improving access to and the usability of information
available to the Senate in its oversight of the Executive
Branch."[17] This is not surprising in light of the fact
that, with Congressional reassertion of its authority vis-
a-vis the Executive Branch, there is increasing emphasis
on Congress' oversight role as well as the importance of
strengthening its capabilities to discharge this responsibility.[18]

There are varying concepts of what is meant by oversight, although monitoring appears to be implicit in what
is envisaged. The GAO booklet on "Evaluating Federal
Programs" states: "Congressional oversight involves continuous monitoring to insure that the laws enacted by the
Congress are: appropriate, competently administered, and
helping to achieve intended purposes."[19] It is interesting that the GAO then goes on to state that oversight
supports specific Congressional activities including:
authorizing appropriations, making appropriations, re-
newing or amending enabling legislation, and formulating
and enacting new legislation, if necessary. This recognition of the interaction between oversight and the legislative activities of the Congress is appropriate since
semantic niceties may tend to obscure the fact that what
flows out of the implementation of oversight, as, for
example, the evaluation of programs may constitute invaluable information for the legislative process per se.

Professor Morris Ogul maintains that the resurgence
of Congressional interest in oversight stemming from the
Nixon Administration "should be reviewed more as a transitory phenomenon than as the first step toward an en-
during pattern of vigorous legislative oversight." At
the same time, he feels that "the" GAO can be an increasingly useful tool for those very few Congressmen who
have lacked the staff support necessary to oversee effectively."[20]

GAO involvement in the Congressional budget process

The GAO's increasing involvement in the Congressional
budget process is analyzed in Chapter 9 dealing with the
Comptroller General's role in the Government's financial
management. It is not surprising that Congressional desire to deal with the Federal budget in a more incisive

and knowledgeable manner is reflected in greater expectations as to GAO efforts in this area. It is too early to determine the extent to which the newly-established Congressional Budget Office will impinge upon budgetary tasks that GAO would otherwise be discharging for Congress.

STRENGTHS OF THE GAO AS A CONGRESSIONAL RESOURCE

In responding to a query from the Commission on Operation of the Senate as to what it regarded as its "special strengths," the GAO said that these lie "in its independence and nonpartisan status; its hard earned reputation for objectivity, accuracy, and high professional standards; and its broad statutory authority for access to records of the executive branch."

The specific factors contributing to GAO's effectiveness in supporting Congressional legislative and oversight activities can be expressed in even more specific terms: GAO has a staff continually engaged in agency studies not only throughout the United States but also overseas. It reported having auditors physically stationed in over forty different locations in Washington, D.C., as well as in twenty-three different offices and sub-offices throughout the continental United States and in four overseas locations. Apropos of operations outside of the United States, GAO surveys and reviews involved seventy-eight other countries during the fiscal year of 1975. The agency possesses a fund of knowledge and insights into the Governmental structure, processes, and programs garnered through its audits, the dimensions of which, as described elsewhere in this analysis, have expanded over the years. The mass of information which GAO has accumulated over more than fifty years together with the constant up-dating implicit in its studies, enable it to serve as a potent countervailing force to the advantage which the Executive Branch has over Congress with respect to program and operational data.

But this audit work, as invaluable as it is, is not the only reason that the GAO can lay claim to being intimately conversant with the activities, practices, and problems of Government agencies. The authority which it possesses with respect to the approval of agency accounting systems, the settlement of the accounts of responsible officers, the promulgation of decisions as to the spending of appropriations, as well as the important part it plays in the program for the improvement of financial management in the Federal establishment add immeasurably to GAO's expertise in the identification of problems and the formulation of solutions.

GAO is in the advantageous position of having developed over the years a facility for keeping attuned to relevant

developments in the Congress. Through its Congressional
Relations Office, GAO maintains close contact with both
Members and staffs with reference to Congressional requests which are made upon it. In this manner, the GAO
is able to negotiate on demands emanating from the Congress rather than routinely accepting assignments that
might be ill-advised, unduly onerous, or duplicative of
other analyses which the GAO has already made or is conducting at the time.

Despite the fact that it is a statutory creation, the
GAO can reasonably feel that its existence is not dependent upon the vagaries of Congressional reactions and feelings. GAO accomplishments, including the effecting of
substantial financial savings each year in Government
operations,[21] together with its reputation, buttress the
security and independence which a monitoring agency should
have. Furthermore, the increased concern about more effective checks on governmental accountability is a source
of strength for the GAO.

PROBLEMS IN EFFECTIVE CONGRESSIONAL UTILIZATION OF GAO

It is obvious that the GAO has achieved impressive
stature in the Government and has been utilized increasingly by the Congress. Yet one cannot be oblivious of
the fact that there are factors which inhibit the effectiveness with which GAO serves the Congress. Some of
these elements arise from the Congressional "climate"
which conditions relations between the GAO and the Congress; others stem from situations within the Congress;
and still others reflect the manner in which the GAO determines its priorities and processes requests it receives from the Congress.

Impact of Congressional pressures upon independence

The Comptroller General is perennially faced with the
quandary of how to reconcile his independence and the totality of his responsibilities with the pressures emanating from the Congress. This dilemma, explored further at
a later point in this chapter, is accentuated by the fact
that the Comptroller General feels it urgent to have additional authority vested in him so that he may discharge
his responsibilities in a more meaningful manner. For
example, the Comptroller General has, from time to time,
requested Congress to empower him to institute civil actions in the Federal courts in connection with the proposed obligation or expenditure of public funds in a manner which he deems to be illegal. Similarly, the Comptroller General has importuned Congress to authorize him
to bring suit against Federal agencies to compel them to

furnish the requested records. He has also called upon the Congress to vest him with subpoena authority similar to that which has been granted to him in special cases such as in connection with the Energy Policy and Conservation Act.

The fact that the Comptroller General has enunciated a firm stance as to that portion of GAO effort that will be expended upon direct assistance to the Congress represents an encouraging expression of the independence vital to the proper functioning of the GAO. The Congress, in its dealings with the GAO, may not perceive that, unlike CBO, CRS, and OTA, the GAO, when serving as a resource for the Legislative Branch, is discharging only one of the several facets of its role. But it is not merely restraint on the part of Congress that is called for. In considering the assignment of additional tasks to the GAO, whether on a temporary or permanent basis, Congress needs to take into account not only the receptivity of the Comptroller General to such proposals but also the compatibility of these added responsibilities with the GAO's total mission.

Influence of Congressional staff

Many of the contacts which the GAO personnel have with Congress are not so much with Representatives or Senators as with staff members. Hence, the reactions of these individuals have a profound effect upon Congressional-GAO relationships. Because of the pivotal role which Congressional staff have in the legislative process, the GAO must maintain effective relations with staff members and yet, at the same time, must avoid becoming unduly insulated from Senators or Representatives. The GAO is sometimes in the position of not knowing whether it is responding to the interests of Members themselves or needs as identified by the staff. The GAO is prone to defer to influential staff members, and it is not averse to giving obeisance when this appears to be indicated.

One can hardly criticize the Comptroller General and his associates for doing their utmost to sell themselves to the Congress and for forestalling any impression of standoffishness or unreceptivity to the ideas of others, especially those emanating from within the Congress. Yet, in its eagerness to solidify relationships with the committees and Members of Congress, the GAO must not derogate from the independence and objectivity that should be expected of such a monitoring agency. The Comptroller General may, on occasion, find himself under strong pressure to subordinate his position on an issue to the stance taken by a particular committee or influential individual Member.

It is difficult to differentiate between what is appropriate consultation with the committees and their staffs and what might be considered to be an abdication of GAO's position as an independent analyst. Aloofness on the part of the GAO could almost negate efforts to have the Congress effectively utilize the resources which the Comptroller General can make available to it. On the other hand, it would be ill-advised for the Comptroller General to make himself subservient to Congressional committees and Members in order to bring about more intensive Congressional use of the GAO.

Ill-conceived and transient Congressional interests

As is brought out in the discussion of program evaluation, Congress is on occasion prone to make a fetish of such terms as "program evaluation" and "benefit cost analysis" and to show ostensibly a strong interest in having such concepts implemented with the active participation of the GAO. Such interest may prove to be transitory or conceived in such unrealistic terms, especially from the standpoint of the contribution which GAO can make, that GAO finds it difficult to carry out what appears to be the intent of the Congress. The ephemeral character which Congressional concerns may sometimes assume was reflected in a statement which the Comptroller General recently made in testifying before the Senate Committee on Government Operations:

> As you know, Mr. Chairman, Section 202 of the Intergovernmental Cooperation Act of 1968 requires that upon request of any committee having jurisdiction over a grant-in-aid program, GAO will undertake a study to determine among other things the extent to which such program conflicts with or duplicates other grant-in-aid programs. Quite frankly, we are a bit surprised that this provision has attracted little interest.[22]

Volume and availability of GAO reports

In the 15 months ended September 30, 1976, the GAO completed 1380 reports on audits or special studies, of which, as previously noted, 939 were submitted directly to the Congress or to its committees and Members.[23] There is a question as to whether the manner in which the Congress processes the mass of GAO reports submitted to it is conducive to their most effective use for legislative purposes. The reports prepared in response to specific requests by committees and individual Members stand a far better chance of at least perusal than those emanating

51

from studies initiated by the Comptroller General. Congress has sought to make the GAO reports more meaningful; and the Legislative Reorganization Act of 1970 provided for Congressional follow-up on agency implementation of GAO recommendations.[24]

One can understand why the number of agencies and programs coming within the purview of GAO's audit activities may result in a formidable number of reports. This aspect of GAO reports and the signs of delays in their issuance are explored in Chapter 6. As is brought out in the discussion of the GAO's direct assistance to Congress, GAO has deemphasized its dependence upon formal reports as a means for communicating findings and recommendations to the Congress and its committees. Perhaps the Comptroller General is becoming more aware that the mass of documents which it funnels into Congress may overtax the capability of that body to utilize such material effectively, particularly when the other supportive agencies are taken into account. Furthermore, he has undoubtedly recognized that the utility of GAO analyses can be seriously impaired by delays in the availability of their findings.

Need for more viable GAO-Congressional relationship

The Commission on Operation of the Senate recommended "Effective congressional supervision, to improve administrative coherence, insure cooperation, and enhance initiative[25] of the support agencies in providing service to Congress." Although, as already mentioned, the GAO stands apart from Congress' other support agencies, the Commission's recommendation nevertheless is applicable to it. The Government Operations Committees* of the Senate and the House, which are the committees most intimately concerned with the GAO, do not afford the type of relationship that would best assure the most effective utilization of GAO as a supportive service for the Congress. The bewildering array of Congressional assignments is bound to result in a diffusion of effort that tends to undermine GAO's assistance to the Congress. The seriousness of the weakness is aggravated by the vast expansion in the other resources available to Congress, a phenomenon described earlier in this study.

But even more significant is the lack of ongoing in-depth Congressional evaluation of GAO's performance. A House Member, while supporting legislation to improve GAO's audit authority, was nonetheless impelled to remark:

*The Senate Government Operations Committee is presently titled Governmental Affairs Committee.

And who determines the economy, efficiency,
and effectiveness of the General Accounting
Office, to say nothing about the wisdom of
the decision with respect to the priorities
it sets for utilization of its time, manpower, and funds? Who makes these decisions?
The General Accounting Office itself. In
short, the auditor presently audits itself.[26]

Issue Presented by Restricted Distribution of Reports for Committee and Members

Until shortly before the completion of this manuscript, the Comptroller General had indulged in a highly
questionable practice with respect to reports submitted
in response to requests of committees and individual Members. Such reports enjoyed a restricted distribution
which had significant implications in terms of public
policy as well as the relations between GAO and the Congress. Unless the committee or individual Member acqui-
esced, the report was not available for further distribution. Hence, regardless of the nature of the findings
submitted by the Comptroller General, the report could
be kept from not only the public but even the other committees and Members of the Congress until such time as
it was released by the committee or Member that had requested it. This practice continued in spite of the fact
that Sections 232 to 234 of the Legislative Reorganization
Act of 1970 provide for making GAO reports generally available to committees and Members and, in fact, require the
Comptroller General to prepare and transmit to the Congress monthly and yearly listings of the reports issued by
the GAO during the respective periods. However, reports
submitted to committees and Members were not shown in the
monthly listings but were included in the yearly enumeration.

In explaining the special treatment which it accorded
reports prepared for committee and Members notwithstanding
the provisions of the 1974 Act, the GAO referred to the
cautionary note sounded by the House Rules Committee in
its report on the 1970 Act when it was under consideration:

The Comptroller General must exercise some
discretion in deciding what constitutes a
"report." There are times when the Comptroller General and a Member or committee
of Congress have a confidential relationship such as might exist between an attorney or an accountant and his client. Committees frequently ask the Comptroller General for information to be used during
committee hearings in the examination of

witnesses. It would clearly be unwise to
require the Comptroller General to make
the contents of these reports available
on request in advance of their intended use.[27]

Moreover, the Comptroller General advanced the rationale that, in preparing such special reports, the GAO functions as an "extension of the staff of the initiating committee or Member."

However, the Committee's comments can reasonably be
construed as contemplating unusual cases rather than encompassing every report submitted to a committee or Member. The further observation which the Committee on Rules
made concerning the matter appeared to advocate restraint
in the exercise of this "privilege":

> As a general rule, however, it is the intent
> of this legislation that reports prepared by
> the Comptroller General in the normal course
> of carrying out the functions of the General
> Accounting Office should be noted in the
> monthly summary of reports. It is further-
> more expected that Members and committees
> whose views are not in harmony with the sub-
> stance of the reports will not attempt to
> restrict the circulation of these documents.

It could be argued that the independence which is expected of an audit or monitoring agency such as the GAO
was undermined when a disclosure of its findings was in
certain cases entirely out of its hands and completely
within the discretion of a committee or individual Member.
The untenable position in which the Comptroller General
could find himself as a result of this dubious practice
was demonstrated by the controversy that resulted as a result of the manner in which the Comptroller General's reports on the seizure of the U.S. merchant vessel Mayaguez
by Cambodian naval forces in May 1975 was released during
the 1976 Presidential Campaign.[28]

The Comptroller General was requested by Congressman
Dante B. Fascell, Chairman of the House Subcommittee on
International Political and Military Affairs, to review
all aspects of the seizure and the subsequent diplomatic
and military efforts to secure its release. Three reports
were prepared and carried the dates February 11, May 11,
and September 3, 1976. The May 11 report, "The Seizure
of the Mayaguez - A Case Study of Crisis Management," was
by far the most sensitive of the three since it was in
effect a critique of the actions taken by the Executive
Branch. This report was originally submitted in classified

form at the insistence of the President's Adviser for
National Security Affairs, who eventually agreed that
substantial portions of the report could be declassified and released.

Chairman Fascell released the report the day before
the October 6 foreign policy debate between President
Ford and Jimmy Carter. Since the report was critical of
the Administration's handling of the Mayaguez seizure,
the question arose as to whether the timing of the release was not a political strategem by the Democratic-
controlled International Relations Committee of the House
to embarrass the President on the eve of the debate.
The Washington Post concluded: "Of course it was, in
effect, if not by design."[29] Realizing that it appeared
it had engaged in a partisan ploy, the GAO explained that
it "had no control over the release of the report and was
advised only after the release had been made."[30] This
must have struck many as a lame excuse. The Comptroller
General had been placed in a demeaning posture that paved
the way for a long overdue abandonment of the policy that
had compromised GAO independence in the articulation of
its findings.

SENATOR PROXMIRE - GAO'S CONGRESSIONAL TASKMASTER AND ADVOCATE

An individual Member of Congress can be an important
factor in determining GAO priorities and even receptivity
to new responsibilities. During Comptroller General
Staats' tenure, Senator William Proxmire had had a profound impact upon the functioning of the GAO. The agency's
activities have been very responsive to interests of Proxmire, whose demands upon the Office have been legion and
unremitting.

One of the underlying forces that have molded GAO in
recent years has been the influence (this is not meant
pejoratively) which Senator Proxmire has brought to bear
upon the Comptroller General. Other Members of Congress
have had significant interaction with the Comptroller
General, but the Proxmire imprint stands apart and merits
special analysis.

When the Comptroller General has dared to demur to
the Senator's requests or suggestions, he has, as the
recital that follows indicates, felt Proxmire's ire and
has even been sharply rebuked. When the GAO has acceded
to his wishes, the Senator has been lavish in the bestowal
of accolades. Proxmire has had an invaluable ally in
Admiral Hyman Rickover, and the Comptroller General is
understandably reluctant to enter into a confrontation

with these two knowledgeable figures who are so articulate, persevering, and effective in the advocacy of
their views.

Senator Proxmire-Staats' disagreement on Defense Profits study

In November 1968, Comptroller General Staats, while
testifying before the Senate Subcommittee on Economy in
Government, expressed the opinion that it was important
that information on profits realized on different types
of contracts be available for study and use in evaluating
the effectiveness of the types of contracts used. He went
on to state that the GAO knew of no brief and comprehensive
study that had been made on profits actually realized by
defense contractors. In making this observation, Staats
could hardly have been aware of the floodgates that it
would open in terms of difficulties with the Subcommittee.
Senator Proxmire seized upon it immediately and characterized the comment as "the most significant sentence that
we are likely to have in all these hearings."[31] Subsequently, Senator Proxmire inquired of Staats as to what
he would think of "having the GAO, you, the Comptroller
General, conduct a study of this?"[32] Staats replied that
this might be better done by an agency outside of Government. Senator Proxmire was not satisfied with this answer
and stated that he thought the GAO could do it more ex-
pertly and economically than any other group. Defending
the position that he had taken, the Comptroller General
said:

> We, of course, want to assure all of the con-
> tractors that any time that our efforts are
> directed primarily to contract administration
> and to, more particularly, even to the way in
> which procuring agencies exercise their re-
> sponsibilities, this does not reflect on our
> side any concern one way or the other as to
> whether profits are too high or too low.[33]

Staats wrote the Senator shortly thereafter expressing
the belief that the GAO would be severely handicapped in
conducting a study of profits on Defense procurement "because, without additional broad legislative authority, we
could not expect to obtain access to necessary industry
records."[34] He mentioned various alternatives and stated
that the GAO favored an organization that was neither Government nor industry-oriented such as a university foundation. Manifestly seeking to disassociate himself from any
such study, the Comptroller General closed his letter with
a reference to the advantages of having the study made by
such a "non-aligned organization": industry would probably

be more candid in providing the essential information and the results would be more widely accepted as accurate and unbiased by industry and the public.

Staats rebuked by Proxmire

When Comptroller General Staats appeared before Proxmire's Subcommittee on June 13, he addressed his formal statment primarily to the recommendations contained in the Subcommittee's report, "The Economics of Military Procurement." Staats stated that considerable additional resources would be required to implement those recommendations that were directed to the GAO.[35] He had previously mentioned the numerous demands made on the GAO in connection with its multifarious activities.

Whatever the merits of the Comptroller General's observations on the Subcommittee proposals as to the GAO role in defense procurement, they had a very abrasive effect on Senator Proxmire who was in an irascible mood, having just been rebuffed by five defense contractors who had refused to appear before the Subcommittee. The Senator's irritability was probably aggravated by the fact that the Congressional watchdog was recommending that the Defense Department, which the Subcommittee had denigrated, perform certain of the tasks that had been suggested for the GAO. Moreover, Staats' comments did not have the enthusiastic overtones that Proxmire might have expected with regard to his Subcommittee's handiwork. The Senator might have felt that Staats' more conservative approach detracted from the persuasiveness and effectiveness of the Subcommittee's efforts. In any event, Chairman Proxmire's response to Staats' statement had a biting quality:

> Chairman Proxmire. I am very deeply disappointed with this statement, and I think you expected this committee to be disappointed in this statement . . .

> And when a committee of Congress such as this issues a unanimous report making recommendations to the GAO for improving the supply and quality of information as to our defense programs through [sic] Congress, the GAO, while conceding that it would be a good idea to have the new information, makes an excuse on recommendation after recommendation as to why the GAO should not be the one to provide it.[36]

Later in the hearings, Senator Proxmire pointed out that the disclosures to the C-5A overrun had been made by A.E. Fitzgerald of the Defense Department when he appeared

before the Committee, and not by the GAO. He raised the
question whether the GAO should not have discovered that
overrun.[37]   Some questions which Senator Proxmire subsequently sent to the GAO, the answers to which are included
in the hearing record, reflected Proxmire's disenchantment
at that time with the GAO. For example, in one of his
questions, the Senator stated that his overall impression
of the GAO report on the C-5A initiated by Proxmire was
"that there is very little new information."[38]

     It was obvious that tension had been building up over
a period of time so that Proxmire was ready to pounce on
the GAO when an appropriate opportunity presented itself.
These denunciations by an incisive, articulate, and persistent critic such as Senator Proxmire had a chastening
effect upon the Comptroller General. Not many months
elapsed before Staats expressed a willingness to have the
GAO undertake a study of defense contractors' profits.
As to the C-5A, a knowledgeable staff member of GAO observed: "The boss got caught with his pants down on the
C-5A." The discomfiture that Staats experienced in connection with the C-5A controversy must have made him far
more receptive to intensifying GAO's scrutiny of weapons
system acquisitions and to the development of a more systematic means for apprising Congress as to the status of
these programs.

Proxmire attitude toward the GAO

     Proxmire, it can reasonably be assumed, did not con-
template any definitive repudiation of the GAO or the
severance of relations with it. His tactics were apparently directed to establishing a type of relationship more
acceptable to him in the sense that the GAO would be more
mindful of, and even deferential to, the priorities and
approaches he favored.[39]   Proxmire's castigation of the
Comptroller General could have been intended to "ricochet"
and underline in the minds of Defense Department officials
and defense contractors the lack of confidence which Proxmire had in the manner in which military procurement was
being administered. In this and other incidents, the Senator has demonstrated how a Member of Congress can use his
contacts with the GAO not only as a source of information
but also as a springboard for his pronouncements.

     Proxmire has been very astute in identifying and ex-
ploiting the publicity potentialities of findings that can
be attributed to the GAO. Thus, shortly after the June 13
confrontation with Staats, Senator Proxmire, on the basis
of information that had been brought to his attention by
two employees of the B.F. Goodrich Company, requested the
GAO to review certain aspects of the qualification tests

of brakes for A-7D aircraft. The GAO analysis did not, at
least at first blush, give the impression of derelictions
as grave as those subsequently depicted by Senator Proxmire.[40]
Evidently not satisfied with the report, Proxmire obtained,
on July 11, 1969, a letter from the Acting Comptroller General that pinpointed the Goodrich Company's shortcomings in
a manner that was apparently more useful for the Senator's
purposes.[41]   Armed with this report and supplementary letter,
the Senator then presented to the Senate on August 4, 1969,
a lengthy statement on this matter and had the two documents
entered in the <u>Congressional Record</u>.[42]   The Senator, undoubtedly mindful of the public attention such alleged shortcomings could elicit, released a statement on the evening
(Sunday night) preceding the day on which he discussed the
matter on the floor of the Senate. Thus, it gave him a
news story carrying the caption "Goodrich Accused on Air
Force Job," with the subcaption "G.A.O. Charges it Falsi-
fied Tests on Plane Brakes - Charges are Denied."[43]   The
Senator placed both the issue and himself very much in the
limelight and the GAO was a very useful vehicle for that
purpose. Later, the Proxmire Subcommittee held a hearing
on this matter; not only did a GAO representative testify
at the hearing, but the GAO report and supplementary letter
were included in the record.

As a result of the rapport that has been established
between Staats and Proxmire, the latter's comments on the
Comptroller General are now more typically accolades. In
a discussion of the Cost Accounting Standards Board, which
functions under the aegis of the Comptroller General, Proxmire told the Senate that Staats "is an extraordinarily
able man, a man of absolute integrity, a man of nonparti-
sanship, a man who was appointed by President Eisenhower,
and who has served without any partisan reference or without any critical attitude toward defense or any other agency
or certainly toward the private sector."[44]   (Proxmire was
apparently unaware that Staats had been appointed by President Johnson.) One can only speculate as to how resistant
the Comptroller General can be to such blandishments. The
prodding and challenges by a knowledgeable and influential
Member of Congress may, regardless of motivations, constrain the Comptroller General to reexamine the GAO program and make adjustments that appear to be indicated.
Or a Comptroller General hesitant about undertaking certain tasks may do so because of strong expressions of support emanating from Congress. On the other hand, an influential and persevering Senator or Representative may
badger the Comptroller General into an imprudent course
of action. Such pressure may impel the Comptroller General to acquiesce in legislative proposals with respect
to GAO studies or reviews, even though they strike him
to be of doubtful merit.

The Proxmire-Rickover team vis-a-vis the GAO

The influence which an astute member of Congress can bring to bear on the Comptroller General is compounded when he teams up with a member of either the civil or military establishment held in unusually high esteem by both the Congress and the public.

The increased breadth and depth of the Comptroller General's activities in the procurement area reflect not only the imprint of Senator Proxmire but also Admiral Rickover's views as to how the GAO may best serve the Congress in its oversight of Federal procurement -- especially that conducted by the military services. Individually, the Senator and Admiral can be effective advocates of the policies and approaches they favor and can be formidable critics of agencies or officials who incur their disapprobation. Teamed together in their efforts, Proxmire and Rickover can wage an unusually effective battle in winning acceptance of their proposals. They have been able to exert marked influence on the programs and priorities of the GAO.

The reversal of the Comptroller General's stance on GAO making a study of defense contractors' profits reflects the pressure flowing from such joint efforts. When Staats first balked at the GAO undertaking this study, Proxmire readily got Admiral Rickover, who was testifying before the Subcommittee on Economy in Government, to agree that GAO should have been responsive to the Subcommittee's recommendations for such a study. In fact, this afforded Rickover the opportunity to voice his criticism of the GAO's attitude with respect to its role in procurement.[45]

At the same hearing, Admiral Rickover discussed the need for uniform cost accounting standards.[46] Proxmire was so pleased with Rickover's extended testimony, for which one day was set aside, that he characterized it "as one of the most comprehensive critiques of defense procurement ever presented to the Congress."[47]

The very articulate and demanding Admiral was quick to pounce upon the GAO for what he considered to be shortcomings in either the conception or implementation of its program. The credence which Congress is prone to accord the Admiral's observations made his strictures with respect to the GAO of added significance. Testifying before a House Appropriations Subcommittee, Rickover said apropos of the cost accounting standards study that was still under way:

Mr. Chairman, the General Accounting Office
works for Congress. You set them up. You
are their boss. Congress has the responsibility to see to it that the General Accounting Office does a good job on this
study. I think the General Accounting Office needs a nudge from Congress occasionally - as do other Government agencies -
to make sure it does its job.[48]

Illustrative of the Admiral's perseverance in taking
the GAO to task for its failure to perform in the manner
he favors is his criticism, at the same hearing, of GAO's
initial position with respect to the defense profits study.
He challenged Staats' statement that the GAO would need
additional legislative authority in order to conduct such
a study:

The General Accounting Office has all the
legislative authority it needs. This would
be a static world if everyone constantly
studies his charter - like Buddha contemplating his navel - to find reason why he
should not do his job.[49]

Citing some of the studies made by the GAO, Admiral Rickover said that the agency appeared to spend much effort on
minor matters. He told the Subcommittee that he had urged
the Comptroller General to look at broad policy issues
having Government-wide application.

I do not believe the General Accounting
Office should look upon itself as the
Audubon Society looks upon a bird sanc-
tuary - as a secure, inviolate enclave.[50]

In censuring the GAO, Rickover directed the Committee's
attention to the fact that it was Congress, not the GAO,
that recognized the need for uniform cost accounting standards and that pointed out the need for a comprehensive review of defense profits. Similarly, the Admiral credited
the Congress with taking the initiative in investigating
the reasons for cost overruns in major defense programs.
He characterized the GAO posture as being largely negative.
Throwing down the gauntlet, Admiral Rickover, in his concluding remarks on the GAO, said:

If a negative attitude becomes pervasive
in the General Accounting Office, it may
be necessary to establish a new organization which will assume the work that is
not now being done. Part of the genius

of President Franklin Roosevelt was his recognition that you cannot overhaul an entrenched
bureaucracy.[51]

These trenchant remarks by such an esteemed observer
of the governmental scene must have done much to dissipate
GAO's opposition to undertaking a defense profits study
and to even impel it to reverse its position.

One can only conjecture as to what effect Admiral
Rickover's strong views on uniform cost accounting standards had upon that study and the conclusions that were
reached. It bears mention that the New York Times news
story on the GAO study referred to the "Rickover campaign"
on behalf of uniform cost accounting standards and said
that the report "represents in some ways a personal victory for Admiral Rickover over the Defense Department and
the defense industry.[52]

The Proxmire-Rickover pressure upon GAO was not in-
herently dysfunctional. On the contrary, informed and
perceptive critics can be potent countervailing forces
against the bureaucratic inertia and parochialism that
can readily develop in a central monitoring agency. The
danger is that such articulate, persistent, and influential
spokesmen may evoke undue deference on the part of the GAO.
While being completely receptive to ideas that will strengthen the GAO and make it more responsive to the Government's
needs, the Comptroller General can ill afford to permit
considerations of expediency in dealing with these and
other influential personalities to constrain him to compromise the values and priorities that reflect the GAO's sea-
soned, professional judgment.

IMPACT OF CONGRESSIONAL-AGENCY RELATIONS
UPON THE GAO

The relationships which Congress has with the Executive Branch must, for purposes of this analysis, be considered in both overall and specific agency terms. Although it is important to grasp the general tenor of dealings between the Legislative and Executive Branches and
their impact on the functioning of the Comptroller General,
it is equally pressing that one comprehend how Congressional
relations with specific agencies affect the GAO.

GAO-Agency strain engendered by Congressional attitudes

The response of an agency to GAO's activities is conditioned to a significant degree by the nature of the contacts between it and the Congress. Whether it be the Appropriations Committee, Government Operations Committee, or

the committee dealing with the agency's substantive area, the department or other establishment is inevitably mindful of the effect that GAO reports may have upon such relations. The fact that agency officials frequently have to devote an inordinate amount of time to hearings before Congressional committees intensifies their sensitivities about GAO actions that may in any way make such appearances even more difficult or frequent than they otherwise would be. In fact, reports or other materials flowing from the Comptroller General to the Congress may be a catalyst for committees requesting officials to appear before them. As an informational resource for such committees, the GAO may play an important part in determining the lines of committee inquiry and may -- however inadvertently -- trigger a confrontation between the committee and agency officials.

Whether a committee is generally favorable and sympathetic to the agency or whether it leaves the officials with the feeling of having been badgered can have a profound impact upon agency reactions to GAO's efforts in areas of interest to such committees. For example, the House Government Operations Committee's strenuous follow-through on agency accounting systems, subsequently discussed in this study, cut two ways. The Committee's unremitting pressure and sharp criticisms undoubtedly bestirred the agencies to greater effort to develop accounting systems acceptable to the Comptroller General. The other side of the coin is that the Committee's bluster soured agencies so far as this particular facet of the Comptroller General's activities was concerned.

The fact that, as the staff director of a key Congressional committee described it, "Congress still suffers from fault-finding emphasis" inevitably conditions the approach taken by the GAO. The probability of GAO-produced materials setting off or reinforcing a reaction unfavorable to an agency is relatively high because of three factors: inquiries which committees or Members of Congress address to the Comptroller General are usually directed at agency or program shortcomings; GAO staff consciously or otherwise will tend to respond in some measure to Congressional emphasis on the disclosure of deficiencies; and reports submitted by the Comptroller General can often be used to support Congressional criticisms that have already jelled. Furthermore, as one agency official has pointed out, a Congressional inquiry directed to the Comptroller General can be so pinpointed that it precludes disclosure of the full story. This raises a question as to whether it is not incumbent upon the Comptroller General to seek to expand the scope of the study so as to permit more complete presentation of the pertinent facts. Ad-

verting to the use that Members of Congress may make of
GAO materials to harass agencies, a high GAO official
admitted that he did not know "how to get around the
conceded chance that a Congressman might take such information and embarrass an agency on the floor of Congress." Committee attitudes towards agencies vary. One
committee staff member remarked: "GAO schizophrenia probably results from the different committee approaches.
Different committees want different kinds of responses
from the GAO."

Mention is made elsewhere of the ploy to which a
committee or Member of Congress may resort in order to
get information from an agency. Either because of having
been refused or not wishing to incur the risk of confrontation with an agency, the committee or Member may
employ the strategem of calling upon the Comptroller General to ferret out the information. This intermediary
role does not add to the stature of the GAO.

Comptroller General's position on Congressional misuse of GAO materials

The Comptroller General very properly expects Governmental agencies to understand and respond to what he requires of them so that he may discharge his responsibilities. But there is a reciprocal aspect to this relationship which calls for more than lip service by the Comptroller General. The agencies are entitled to expect of
the GAO that it will take affirmative steps to prevent
ill-advised or unfair use of its information gathering
and reporting, on the part of committees or individual
Members of the Congress. It would be naive to think that
the Comptroller General could forestall all improper legislative use of GAO resources. However, he can be more assertive and articulate his concern and even disagreement
with respect to Congressional utilization of GAO output
in a questionable manner. With such a posture, the Comptroller General would be in a more tenable position to
insist upon full agency cooperation in the reviews and
audits conducted by the GAO.

OMBUDSMAN ASPECTS OF THE
GAO

The special reports which the Comptroller General
prepares for the Congress -- more particularly, those in
response to requests from individual Members -- impinge
on the ombudsman implications of the GAO. A significant
number of the inquiries which Members of the Congress
address to the Comptroller General have their origin in
complaints or allegations received from constituents and
others.

The political value which Members of the Congress attribute to the handling of complaints or inquiries from their constituents is undoubtedly a factor in Congressional reluctance to implement the ombudsman concept. Congressional hesitance has been buttressed by the fact that scholars in the field of government and public law have been divided as to the feasibility of applying the ombudsman concept of the Federal Government.[53]

It has been pointed out that the legislative auditor "is the closest parallel to the ombudsman in that he is an independent officer appointed to investigate and report to the Legislature on administrative action."[54] The State Comptroller of Israel has been cited as an outstanding example of how the legislative auditor may function as an ombudsman.[55]

Comptroller General's reluctance to assume ombudsman role

Unlike his Israeli counterpart, the Comptroller General has been averse to developing the ombudsman potentialities of his office. Illustrative of his reluctance was the position which the GAO took at the time that Congressman Betts introduced a bill to give the Comptroller General explicit responsibility for investigating complaints submitted to him and which concerned waste or inefficiency in the use of Government funds and property. The results of any special investigation that was made were, if the Comptroller General deemed them significant, to be reported to the Congress and to the agency involved, setting forth the Comptroller General's findings and recommendations.

In commenting on this bill, the Comptroller General stated that the GAO would have no objection to its enactment since the measure gave the Comptroller General discretion as to the investigation of any complaints: the bill indicated that he was to make an investigation only when the information received by him merited immediate and special consideration.[56] Staats summed up his evaluation by stating that while the GAO did not object to the enactment of the bill, "neither do we offer a recommendation that it be favorably considered." One might surmise that the stance which the Comptroller General took was attributable not only to the general conservatism of the agency but also apprehension that formalizing, and correlatively publicizing, the complaint investigation role of the GAO might impair relations with Members of Congress.

Although the Comptroller General may eschew the ombudsman role as such and although the Congress may be loath to have the GAO designated formally as an instrumentality for the receipt, investigation, and reporting of grievances with respect to the actions of individual officials and agencies, the very nature and functioning of the GAO makes it impinge upon the ombudsman role. In fact, Staats himself told an Appropriations subcommittee: "I suppose we are the nearest counterpart to what the Norwegians call the ombudsman that we have."[57]

A miscellany of public and employee grievances

A wide range of subjects are brought to the attention of the GAO through complaints or inquiries by private citizens, Government employees, and military personnel, most of which are referred to the Comptroller General by Members of Congress.

A letter received by a Senator reported certain facts that had allegedly been given the writer by a Government inspector working in a motor equipment plant. According to the writer, the inspector reported that engines coming off the production line were no good but that the Government continued to buy them. The GAO inquiry disclosed that the commanding officer of the Materiel Command was apparently aware of the problem associated with the particular engine and had initiated a special study of this matter. The GAO deferred further work until completion of this study. Subsequently, it informed the Senator that the report of the consultants had "confirmed some of the allegations made by your constituents." As a result, the Army Chief of Staff directed the Army Audit Agency to review the program for these engines. Although the Army might have arrived at this result even though the GAO had not been drawn into the picture, nevertheless it is reasonable to assume that the GAO inquiry underlined the urgency of this matter in the eyes of responsible officers.

Companies and persons finding themselves enmeshed in the intricacies of Government procedures for procurement or the disposal of surplus property will seek a means to cut through what they consider to be bureaucratic red tape, inertia, or inexcusable delay. A company interested in bidding on a surplus Defense Department item was stalemated in obtaining necessary information. The matter was referred by a Senator to the GAO. Subsequently, the Assistant Comptroller General wrote the Senator saying that he understood that the material in question had been sent to the disgruntled constituent, who later proved to be the successful bidder for the item in question.

A complaint from one of Senator Proxmire's constituents serving in Vietnam was referred to the GAO, which had to delay its review "because of enemy operations within the area." The Army had previously looked into and reported to the Senator on the allegations, which had a certain Gilbert and Sullivan quality. The GAO apprised Proxmire that it was unable to prove or disprove the assertions that: (a) the artillery group commander, in building a handball court, had put a steeple on the top of it so that it would resemble a chapel and (b) the battalion commander had his own personal latrine built with a porch on it and subdued lighting and armrest inside! The report dealt with other complaints such as the manner in which items had been purchased for the officers' club and living conditions in the barracks and personnel bunkers. Whether or not the allegations in this case had merit, the fact that they were investigated independently of any probe within the military was significant.

An inmate at a Federal penitentiary wrote a Congressman, who in turn contacted the Comptroller General, with respect to the prison factory's use of bristles from Russia, Poland, Yugoslavia and Red China, and the use of nylon fiber from France. The prisoner asked the Congressman: "Would you please check with GAO to see whether they have approved the purchases of Communist and French goods and whether such purchases are lawful." Making the most of his correspondence, the inmate also requested that, when the Congressman checked with the GAO, he ask for a copy of the report they filed in June 1964 "about the $100,000 plus home built for the warden here and the book juggling that went on to cover the true cost?" He told the Congressman that he would have written the GAO himself but that this agency was not on the approved list of correspondents for the prisoners' mailbox! In relaying to the Congressman the information it had gathered on this matter, the GAO stated that it was planning to begin a review of selected activities at the particular penitentiary. The charges made by the prisoner were patently not devoid of substance; and the resultant inquiries undoubtedly had a salutary effect.

Inquiries which Senators and Representatives have addressed recently to the GAO on behalf of their constituents have dealt with such matters as to Government costs incurred for Secretary Kissinger's children accompanying him on official trips overseas; alleged minority discrimination by the FAA with respect to advancement and promotion; the cost to the Government of former President Nixon's trip to China; possible criminal conduct of officials involved in the activities discussed in a GAO report; allegations as to an Indian Health Service Hospital; and the cost of maintaining former President Nixon's residence at Key Biscayne.

Should Comptroller General's ombudsman activities be formalized?

The part played by a Senator or Representative in the processing of such complaints or queries is ordinarily nominal; nevertheless, it helps to strengthen the Member's visibility so far as his constituents are concerned. As previously intimated, the political usefulness of receiving and processing constituents' complaints, so far as United States Congress is concerned, is a factor that markedly affects the "climate" for a national ombudsman. A key Congressional staff member, commenting on the ombudsman implications of GAO, expressed the opinion that the Comptroller General could not develop these functions too broadly because they are "so intimately tied up with the Congress itself." He further contended that in the United States the ombudsman role is of such a multiple character that it should not be trusted in its entirety to any one person. It is interesting that the Act setting up the British Parliamentary Commissioner restricted the Commissioner's investigations to written complaints "duly made to a member of the House of Commons by a member of the public," and which are referred to the Commissioner "with the consent of the person who made it, by a member of that House with a request to conduct an investigation thereon."[58]

Even though the existing GAO practice falls short of the full array of tasks contemplated for an ombudsman, it does afford any dissatisfied citizen or employee a medium for articulating his complaints and having them assayed by an agency with resources for making appropriate inquiries. There is, however, lacking any great public awareness of the availability of this investigative facility. So far as the general citizenry is concerned, there is almost exclusive reliance upon bringing complaints to the attention of Members of Congress; hence, those disinclined to do so either because of timidity, political differences, or the feeling that they will receive a "brush-off," are, in effect, bereft of an independent means to have their complaints looked into. There are undoubtedly ways in which the Comptroller General's investigation of complaints could be formalized and be more widely known without making the change appear as any serious threat to the relationships between Members of Congress and their constituents.

If the Comptroller General were to assume a more affirmative stance with respect to the ombudsman facets of his Office, this would be a strong factor in making for much greater public awareness of the GAO and in bridging the large chasm that presently exists between that agency and the public. The vast amount of information which the

GAO accumulates with respect to Federal programs and agencies, the continuing presence of its staff in Government agencies, and the investigative techniques which it has developed make it appropriate for the GAO to function as the formally designated instrumentality for following through on complaints which citizens and Governmental employees may have with respect to the Federal establishment. It has been demonstrated that such complaints can help the Comptroller General in identifying situations that merit his scrutiny. This is an area which deserves further consideration by both the Congress and the Comptroller General. Any exploration of this matter should weigh the ombudsman potentialities of the thrust for inspectors general within the Federal agencies.

THE CRUCIAL ISSUE OF THE COMPTROLLER GENERAL'S INDEPENDENCE

There is general acceptance of independence as a _sine qua non_ of the governmental audit function.[59] Comptroller General Staats is presently concerned over moves within the Congress that impinge upon his independence. So much so that he recently felt impelled to tell the Congress:

> The legislative history of the 1921 Act consistently stressed that the Comptroller General should exercise objective and independent judgment, unfettered by political influence from congressional as well as executive branch sources. This remains as important today as it was perceived to be in 1921, if not more so.[60]

Problems arising from the mix of Comptroller General's functions

In a 1964 opinion[61] of the U.S. District Court which dealt with the unusual blend of responsibilities vested in the Comptroller General, Judge Alexander Holtzoff held that the Comptroller General was acting as an officer of the Legislative Branch of the Government when he scrutinized and reported to Congress on the receipt, disbursement and application of public funds or when he pursued investigations ordered by Congress relating to revenues, appropriations or expenditures. But, according to Judge Holtzoff, the Comptroller General was acting as a member of the Executive Branch of the Government when he discharged his second principal function, i.e., "that of approval or disapproval of payments made by Government departments and other agencies, as well as of settling and adjusting accounts in which the Government is concerned." The opinion went on to say that this dual status was not anomalous since many regulatory commissions fulfill both

legislative and executive functions. However, Judge Holtzoff did not tackle the question of how the Executive Branch
responsibilities could be considered congruent with the GAO
mission of auditing that branch on behalf of the legislative body.

The analysis of GAO's legislative background brought
out that this dualism was not only countenanced but also
tenaciously defended by Congress. Recently, the unusual
mix of functions entrusted to the Comptroller General has
been scrutinized more critically by certain Members of
Congress who were actuated by statements Staats had made
in the suit he brought against the Director of OMB pursuant to the provisions of the Impoundment Control Act of
1974.[62] The Comptroller General maintained that, in conducting this litigation, he was not acting as an agent of
Congress but rather as an independent officer. This
raised the question as to whether the Comptroller General
was asserting independence from the Congress.

In explaining his position to Senator Metcalf,[63]
Staats relied upon the dichotomy which Judge Holtzoff had
enunciated as to the GAO functions. As to those functions
categorized as executive in nature including the authority
vested in him by the Congressional Budget and Impoundment
Control Act, the Comptroller General contends that he can
independently take action but that "it does not mean that
the Comptroller General and the General Accounting Office
are not a part of the legislative branch, but it does
mean that the actions taken are not by direction or with
express approval of Congress or its committees." Staats
then went on to state that it had been a firm policy commitment on his part to make the GAO more relevant to the
needs of Congress. In this connection, he referred to the
direct assistance provided by GAO and expressed the belief
that GAO's "self-initiated work is far more relevant to
the needs of Congress than at any prior time in GAO's
history." For some reason, the Comptroller General did not
explicitly mention the urgency of independence for the
self-initiated reviews that are the basic vehicle for
carrying out GAO's audit or monitoring role. The Comptroller General reminded the Senator of the importance of
the GAO having the attributes of independence and non-
partisanship. "They are not inconsistent with the need
for an agency which can support and be responsive to the
needs of the Congress for assistance and to carry out
delegated authority in a fair, objective and judicial manner." Staats' observations clearly reflect the serious
dilemma which confronts the GAO as it seeks to maintain a
proper balance between the different components of its
multi-faceted role.

Commenting on bills relating to the Comptroller General and GAO, Senator Metcalf referred to the "split personality" of the GAO. The Senator, undoubtedly much to
Staats' consternation, even suggested the possibility of
"splitting the GAO."[64] Congressman Jack Brooks, Chairman
of the House Committee on Government Operations, commented
at a hearing: "There is also legitimate concern about the
status of the General Accounting Office in the general
scheme of the Federal establishment and what effect the
Comptroller's view of that status may have on his relations
with the Congress."[65]

The Congressional questions that have surfaced concerning the existing blend of statutory responsibilities
vested in the Comptroller General were reflected in a
recommendation by the House Government Operations Committee that GAO's function of claims settlement and bid protest reviews be transferred to the Executive Branch. The
Committee argued that this would free GAO to "concentrate
more fully on its primary responsibilities."[66]

It is obvious that the issue of independence of the
Comptroller General is inextricably intertwined with the
atypical array of functions that carry him far beyond the
strictly auditing area. Congress may find itself constrained to grapple with the underlying issue as to the
compatibility of the diversity of GAO activities with the
independence essential to GAO serving effectively as the
central instrumentality for assuring accountability of
Federal agencies and their personnel.

Appointment of the Comptroller General

Congressional reexamination of the manner in which the
Comptroller General and his deputy are appointed has also
involved the issue of independence. As the Comptroller
General became an increasingly important factor in the
functioning of the Congress, it appeared all the more
anomalous that his appointment as well as that of the
Deputy Comptroller General come from the President subject,
of course, to Senatorial confirmation. The method of ap-
pointing the Comptroller General was the subject of a memorandum prepared by the staff of the Senate Committee on
Government Operations at the time that Joseph Campbell was
nominated for the office in 1954. This memorandum explains
the background of the present statutory provision:

> Much thought was given to the inclusion of
> a provision by which the proposed heads -
> the Comptroller General and the Assistant
> Comptroller General - would be appointed by
> the Congress as its agents without any

71

Presidential influence or control. Two major
objections were raised to this latter procedure: (1) That it might involve a constitutional question as to the authority of the
Congress to make appointments of Federal officers or take action which might affect the
power of the President over the appointment
of such officers, and (2) whether or not the
terms of these officers might be terminated
by succeeding Congresses on a possible partisan political basis.[67]

The original version of the Budget and Accounting Act provided that the Comptroller General and the Assistant Comptroller General (now the Deputy Comptroller General) would
serve during good behavior subject to removal by concurrent resolution of the Congress or impeachment. Specific
grounds for removal through concurrent resolution were
set forth in the bill. This bill was vetoed by President
Wilson on the grounds that, if Congress were given the
right to remove by concurrent resolution, this would be
in violation of the constitutional authority vested in the
Chief Executive to remove appointed officers. The bill
subsequently enacted and approved by President Harding provides fixed terms of 15 years for the two officials and
calls for a joint resolution rather than a concurrent resolution to effect removal by Congress, which also has
recourse to impeachment. A joint resolution, unlike a
concurrent resolution, requires Presidential approval in
order to become effective.

Members of the Senate were exercised over the failure
of President Eisenhower to consult them prior to the nomination of Campbell. The Senate hearings on the nomination
clearly reflected the feeling on the part of some Senators
that the selection of the Comptroller General was very much
a concern of the Legislative Branch and was not a decision
that came entirely within the purview of the Chief Executive.

Senator Smith: Mr. Chairman, my interest comes
from the fact that the Comptroller General is
accountable to Congress. He is an agent of
Congress and not an agent of the President, which
would mean to me that the choice should come from
Congress rather than from the President, and, as
I understand it, Mr. Chairman, no one in Congress
was consulted concerning the appointment of Mr.
Campbell.[68]

Senator Gore, appearing as a witness before the Committee,
said:

72

Moreover, there has been a sort of gentle-
men's understanding, so to speak, that the
Comptroller General would be appointed upon
recommendation from the Congress. Advice
and consent with respect to the Comptroller
General, Mr. Chairman, has never been treated
as a mere matter of confirmation. It must
not be so treated now.[69]

The underlying question did not evoke incisive or
continuing interest, and it was only recently that proposals have been advanced for transferring the appointment
power from the President to the Congress. In fact, what
has been presented has represented such a sharp departure
from the existing setup as to appointment and tenure that
the Comptroller General has understandably construed such
proposals as a threat to his independence. He voiced
strong opposition to S.2206 (94th Congress, 1st Session),
which provided for appointment of the Comptroller General
and Deputy Comptroller General by the Speaker of the
House and the President pro tempore of the Senate, fixed
the terms of the Comptroller General and the Deputy at 7
years, and provided for their removal by either the Senate
or House by simple resolution. The Comptroller General expressed concern that such changes would quickly result in
the loss of those qualities that have inspired confidence
and credibility in the actions of the Comptroller General.
Staats made this noteworthy observation:

> By providing the Comptroller General a 15-year,
> nonrenewable term and approximately the same
> retirement arrangements and similar method of
> removal as judges, the Congress wisely, in my
> opinion, made it clear to all concerned that
> the Comptroller General was expected to carry
> out his duties in the same spirit as individuals
> who hold positions on the Federal bench.[70]

Transcendent nature of the independence issue

Implicit in any meaningful Congressional rethinking of
the independence accorded the Comptroller General is the
long overdue reevaluation of the aggregate of functions now
entrusted to that official. Up to this juncture Congress
has allocated responsibilities -- sometimes precipitately --
to the GAO without having a frame of reference for determining the soundness of such actions. The interaction between
the independence of the GAO and the totality of power that
is exercised by the Comptroller General underlines the urgency of incisive Congressional analysis of this Office and,
if need be, the redefinition of its mission and authority.

73

1. Comptroller General of the United States, 1976 Annual Report, p. 1.

2. Milton S. Gwirtzman, New York Times, November 10, 1974. The following are illustrative of the earlier concerns about the paucity of Congressional supportive services. James A. Robinson, Congress and Foreign Policy-Making (Homewood, Ill.: The Dorsey Press, Inc., 1962), p. 7. Richard Bolling, Power in the House (New York: Dutton, 1968), p. 263.

3. "The Hidden Power Elite," Newsweek, January 1, 1977.

4. Interview with Paul Douglas, Washington, D.C., January 23, 1968.

5. Letter of February 28, 1974 from Senator Herman E. Talmadge to Comptroller General Staats.

6. Statement of Comptroller General Staats before Legislative Subcommittee, House Appropriations Committee, February 3, 1977.

7. Hearings Before Subcommittee of the House Committee on Appropriations, Legislative Branch Appropriations for 1977, 94th Congress, 2nd Session, 1976, p. 327.

8. Ibid., p. 40.

9. Ibid., p. 313.

10. General Accounting Office, Answers to Frequently Asked Questions, p. 10.

11. Statement of Acting Comptroller General Weitzel, Hearings Before the Joint Committee on the Organization of the Congress, 89th Congress, 1st Session, 1965, Part 9, p. 1364.

12. Comptroller General of the United States, 1970 Annual Report, p. 14.

13. Comptroller General of the United States, 1976 Annual Report, p. 2-4.

14. Comptroller General of the United States, Summary of Open GAO Recommendations for Legislative Action as of December 31, 1976, February 16, 1977.

15. Public Law 91-510, Section 118.

16. Public Law 93-344, Section 701.

17. Interim Report of the Commission on the Operation of the Senate, March 31, 1976, p. 8.

18. The Conference Report on the 1974 Act made this observation: "The managers consider oversight of executive performance to be among the principal functions of congressional committees and they recognize that the usefulness of program evaluation can be enhanced by the clear expression of legislative objectives and the employment of modern analytic methods." (Senate Report No. 93-924, p. 72.) More recently, the House Committee on Government Operations observed: "The GAO plays an important role in helping Congress carry out its oversight responsibilities -- no examination of the oversight capabilities and accomplishments of Congress would be complete if it omitted the GAO's contributions.Oversight Plans of the Committees of the United States House of Representatives (House Report No. 95-43, p. 3).

19. Ibid., p. 3.

20. Morris S. Ogul, Congress Oversees the Bureaucracy (Pittsburgh: University of Pittsburgh Press, 1976), p. 199.

21. The GAO reported measurable savings of $503 million in fiscal year 1975 directly attributable to its activities. It further stated that $147 million of such savings will continue to be saved annually in future years. For the 15-month period ended September 30, 1976, the GAO listed $532 million of savings attributable directly to its efforts and $1.6 billion attributable to the "combined efforts of GAO and other parties such as the Congress and Federal agencies." See Chapter 3 in the 1975 and 1976 Annual Reports.

22. March 19, 1976 Statement of the Comptroller General Before the Subcommittee on Intergovernmental Relations, Senate Committee on Government Operations, p. 6.

23. 1976 Annual Report, p. 2.

24. Section 236 reads: "Whenever the General Accounting Office has made a report which contains recommendations to the head of any Federal agency, such agency shall -

(1) not later than sixty days after the date of
    such report, submit a written statement to
    the Committees on Government Operations of
    the House of Representatives and the Senate
    of the action taken by such agency with re-
    spect to such recommendations;   and

(2) in connection with the first request for
    appropriations for that agency submitted
    to the Congress more than sixty days after
    the date of such report, submit a written
    statement to the Committees on Appropria-
    tions of the House of Representatives and
    the Senate of the action taken by such
    agency with respect to such recommendations.

25. Toward a Modern Senate - Final Report of the Commission
    on Operation of the Senate, 94th Congress, 2nd Ses-
    sion, December 1976, p. 60.

26. Remarks of Representative Brown in Congressional Re-
    cord, October 20, 1975.

27. House Report No. 91-1215, p. 13.

28. The relevant materials are presented in Seizure of the
    Mayaguez Part IV, Reports of the Comptroller General
    Submitted to the Subcommittee on International Poli-
    tical and Military Affairs, Committee on International
    Relations, 94th Congress, 2nd Session, October 4, 1976.

29. Washington Post, October 10, 1976.

30. New York Times, October 7, 1976.

31. Congress, Joint Economic Committee, Hearings Before
    Subcommittee on Economy in Government, The Economics
    of Military Procurement, 90th Congress, 2nd Session,
    1968, Part 1, p. 15.

32. Ibid., p. 40.

33. Ibid., p. 41.

34. Ibid., p. 43.

35. Congress, Joint Economic Committee, Hearings, The Mili-
    tary Budget and National Economic Priorities, 91st
    Congress, 1st Session, 1969, Part 2, p. 714, et seq.

36. Ibid., p. 721.

37. Ibid., p. 737.

38. Ibid., p. 745.

39. See William Proxmire, Report from Wasteland (New York: Praeger Publications, 1970), p. 95. Also William Proxmire, "The Pentagon vs. Free Enterprise," in Saturday Review, January 31, 1970, p. 14.

40. Comptroller General Report, Review of the Qualification Testing of Brakes for the A-7D Aircraft, B-167023, July 3, 1969.

41. Letter from Acting Comptroller General Lawrence J. Powers to Senator Proxmire, July 11, 1969.

42. Congressional Record, August 4, 1969, S.9066, et seq.

43. New York Times, August 4, 1969.

44. Congressional Record, August 1, 1975.

45. Congress, Joint Economic Committee Hearings on Economics of Military Procurement, 90th Congress, 2nd Session, 1968, p. 83.

46. Ibid., p. 16, et seq.

47. Ibid., p. v.

48. House, Committee on Appropriations, Subcommittee on the Department of Defense Appropriations, Hearings on Department of Defense Appropriations for 1970, 91st Congress, 1st Session, 1969. Part 6, p. 842.

49. Ibid.

50. Ibid., p. 844.

51. Ibid.

52. New York Times, January 19, 1970.

53. Samuel Krislov, "A Restrained View," in Donald C. Rowat, The Ombudsman (London: George Allen and Unwin, Ltd., 1965), p. 246. See also Henry J. Abraham, "The Need for Ombudsman in the United States," in Rowat, op. cit., p. 237; Geoffrey C. Hazard, Jr., "The Ombudsman: Quasi-Legal and Legal Representation in Public Assistance Administration," in Research Contributions of the American Bar Foundation (1959), No. 3; Walter Gellhorn, When Americans Complain (Cambridge: Harvard University Press, 1966), p. 6; and William B. Gwyn, "Transferring the Ombudsman,"

in *Ombudsman for American Government?*, ed. by
Stanley V. Anderson (Englewood Cliffs, N.J.: Pren-
tice-Hall, Inc., 1968), pp. 37-69.

54. Donald C. Rowat, op. cit., p. 32.

55. *The State Comptroller of Israel and His Office at
Work* (Jerusalem: State Comptroller's Office,
1963), p. 28.

56. H.R. 16754, 90th Congress, 2nd Session, 1968.

57. *1968 Hearings, House Subcommittee on Legislative
Branch Appropriations*, op. cit., p. 708.

58. Parliamentary Commission Act 1967, Section 5.

59. See E.L. Normanton, *The Accountability And Audit Of
Governments* (New York: Frederic A. Praeger, 1966),
p. 298.

60. Comptroller General of the United States, *1976 Annual Report*, p. 1.

61. *U.S. ex. rel. Brookfield Construction Company vs.
Stewart*, 234 F.Supp. 94 (DDC 1964).

62. *Staats vs. Lynn*, Civil Action 75-0551 (D.C. for District of Columbia 1975).

63. Letter of October 24, 1975 from Comptroller General
Staats to Senator Lee Metcalf.

64. Senate: Hearing Before the Subcommittee on Reports,
Accounting, and Management of the Committee on
Government Operations. *GAO Legislation* October 2,
1975, Part 1, p. 2.

65. House: Hearing Before a Subcommittee of the Committee
on Government Operations, *Review of the Powers,
Procedures, and Policies of the General Accounting
Office*, December 10, 1975, p. 2.

66. Report of House Committee on Government Operations
to the House Budget Committee in Connection with
1977 Budget Resolutions.

67. Senate, Government Operations Committee, Staff Memorandum No. 83-2-33, November 24, 1954, included in
Financial Management in the Federal Government,
Document No. 11, 87th Congress, 1st Session, 1961,
p. 298.

68. Senate, Committee on Government Operations Hearings, <u>Nomination of Joseph Campbell</u>, 84th Congress, 1st Session, 1955, p. 14.

69. <u>Ibid.</u>, p. 26.

70. <u>GAO Legislation</u>, <u>op</u>. <u>cit</u>., p. 20.

Chapter 3

THE COMPTROLLER GENERAL'S INCREASING
INVOLVEMENT IN THE EXECUTIVE BRANCH

Elmer B. Staats, Comptroller General of the
United States, Plaintiff vs. Gerald R. Ford,
individually and in his official capacity as
President of the United States, et al.,
Defendants.

The very title of this complaint filed with the U.S.
District Court for the District of Columbia on April 15,
1975,[1] epitomizes the steadily increasing involvement of
the Comptroller General in the operations of the Executive
Branch. The lawsuit, which revolved around Presidential
deferral of the use of contract authority for a housing
program, was instituted under the provisions of the Impoundment Control Act of 1974, which is discussed in Chapter 9, dealing with the Government's financial management.
It is true that the Comptroller General was, in effect,
acting as a surrogate for the Congress and, in fact, the
Department of Justice contended that the suit "might just
as conveniently have been captioned 'The Congress of the
United States vs. the President of the United States.'"
Be that as it may, the country had the spectacle of the
Comptroller General as a legal adversary of the President.
The awkwardness of the situation was mitigated when the
President was eliminated as a defendant and the action
was focused on the Director of OMB and the Secretary of
Housing and Urban Development. What could have been a
bitter clash was averted by the Secretary's reactivation
of the program.

As is brought out in the discussion that follows, the
authority which the Comptroller General has over the Executive Branch has made for stress and strain even when
relations were handled adroitly. Ordinarily it was the
agencies to which the Comptroller General's criticisms
and challenges were directed, and the President typically
was involved only tangentially. Now, the broadened ambit
of GAO reviews and studies has carried the Comptroller General into areas that impinge increasingly on Presidential
decision-making with respect to not only programs but --
more significantly -- policies and their implementation
through the Chief Executive's actions.

Several factors have propelled Comptroller General
Staats into functioning as a critic of the President:
Congressional receptivity to counselling by the Comptroller
General as to policy issues; strained Congressional and
Presidential relationships; the development of a multi-

disciplinary staff having policy analysis capabilities
and expertise in specialized areas such as energy; the
competition of the Congressional Budget Office, Congressional Research Service, and the Office of Technology Assessment; and the apparent eagerness of Staats to cap the
final years of his tenure with GAO's attainment of a key
role in the formulation and analysis of policies.

The Comptroller General's reports on the seizure of
the Mayaguez vividly demonstrated the Comptroller General's willingness to evaluate Presidential decisions of
a highly sensitive nature. Staats could maintain that
this was done in response to a Congressional request; but
the subcommittee chairman making the request undoubtedly
sensed the Comptroller General's amenability to conducting
such a study. Another type of GAO critique of Presidential
action occurred when, at the request of Senators Jackson
and Metcalf, GAO evaluated the analysis which was the basis
for President Ford's veto of the proposed Surface Mining
Control and Reclamation Act of 1975. Entirely apart from
such Congressional requests, the studies which the Comptroller General himself initiates increasingly encompass
issues that reach into the White House. Thus a news story
carried the heading "G.A.O. Criticizes Carter Energy Plan
for Failure to Meet its Own Goals." The widening scope of
GAO's inquiries, discussed in Chapter 5, inevitably means
greater possibility of tension between the Chief Executive
and the Comptroller General, a phenomenon that is bound to
impact upon the relations between Executive departments
and establishments and the GAO.

KEY FACTORS IN GAO-EXECUTIVE AGENCY RELATIONS

Basic nature of relations

To analogize Comptroller General-agency relations with
those which the independent public accountant has with his
corporate clients results in fallacies that becloud the
issue. Unlike the public accountant making an audit of a
corporation, the Comptroller General functions on the
basis of a legal mandate which is backed up by statutory
authority, albeit deemed inadequate by the Comptroller General, for access to the necessary records. The Comptroller
need have no qualms about the possibility of being dismissed
as a client. Neither need he worry about whether the disclosure of certain information would violate the privileged
relationship of auditor and client. Furthermore, the Comptroller General is completely independent of agencies in
establishing the scope of his examination as well as conducting the examination itself. Finally, the many self-
initiated views often carry the GAO into areas to which
regular auditing skills have limited applicability.

The overriding difference, however, is the authority
of the Comptroller General as to settlement of accounts
and claims and the approval of agency accounting systems.
Furthermore, the role of the GAO as a support agency for
the Congress still further accentuates the dissimilarity
between the Comptroller General's relations with Executive
agencies and those of the auditor in the private sector.

It is unrealistic to assume that there is a standard
pattern to which all agencies conform insofar as their
dealings with the GAO are concerned. What appeared like
an almost idyllic rapport with the Atomic Energy Commission
contrasted sharply with the strain that characterized relations with NASA at one time and which led a GAO executive
to complain that "we have had nothing but problems in connection with that agency." The interaction of personalities,
the attitudes of Congressional committees toward the department or other establishment, and the strength which the
agency derives from statutory provisions and its prestige
are some of the variables. Agency responses to the GAO can
be arranged in a continuum ranging from what one Congressional staff member described as defiance to submissiveness
or undue deference to the GAO. There are not only differences between agencies on this score but also as between
different echelons in the administrative hierarchy.

Operating agencies may feel that the tactics of maintaining satisfactory relations with Congress require them
to deal at arm's length with the Comptroller General or at
least to be wary as to inquiries or reviews emanating from
the GAO. An Assistant Secretary observed: "We do not like
the idea of being close in bed with the GAO." More con-
cretely, those within the Executive Branch may tend to view
GAO as a conduit for feeding information to the Congress
that can embarrass them or undermine their positions in
dealing with Congressional committees or Members. They may
feel that their public image can be threatened by what the
Comptroller General has to say on the basis of the evaluations made by his agency. On the other hand, GAO may be
used by an agency to strengthen its position within the
Executive Branch or in its dealings with the Congress.
Apropos of the latter, an official occupying a highly responsible position in the procurement area said: "We may
hide behind the Comptroller General to protect ourselves
against Congressional pressures."

Impact of individual Comptroller General upon GAO-Agency relations

The stance taken by the Comptroller General is patently
a key factor in the agency reactions evoked by the GAO. The
tight grip, authoritarianism, and hypercritical attitude

that -- as depicted in Chapter 1 -- were hallmarks of
the McCarl regime engendered resentment and defensiveness
on the part of the agencies and even evoked Presidential
hostility. This alienation manifestly precluded any
collaboration, and GAO-agency relations were almost of
an adversary nature. The Warren era effected a rapprochement that was especially welcome because it was such a
marked change from the stress, strain, and mutual antipathy
that had preceded it. The Joint Financial Management Improvement program, although hardly a panacea for the difficulties involved in dealings between the GAO and agencies, at least symbolized a cooperative effort between
the Executive Branch and the Comptroller General. It was
indicative of a relaxation of rigid jurisdictional lines.

The tenure of Comptroller General Campbell carried forward the thrust for professionalism begun under Warren,
which had added to the stature of the GAO and was conducive
to the respect which a central monitoring agency such as
the GAO must command if its efforts are to be fully effective. At the same time, the efforts to penetrate more
deeply into the substantive aspects of agency programs and
operations, coupled with what the agencies considered to
be a proclivity for faultfinding on the part of Campbell,
made for a partial reversion to a feeling of estrangement
and defensiveness on the part of agencies.

With the changeover to Staats as Comptroller General,
agencies expected and have experienced improvement in relations with the GAO. Without detracting from the progress
Staats had made, one can still be skeptical as to the remarks he made in answering a Member's question as to the
receptivity of the agencies to GAO investigations and
audits: " . . . most of the agency heads welcome the fact
that the GAO is in there, because they appreciate having
someone from the outside come and take a look. If there
are problems, they want to know about them."[2]

As eager as Staats had been to solidify relations
with agencies, he is manifestly mindful of the fact that
the GAO functions under Congressional aegis and that the
attainment of smooth working relations with the agencies
must be subordinated to carrying out the mandates which
the Comptroller General receives from the Congress.
However, the Comptroller General is not constrained to
leave GAO-agency relations entirely to the mercy of the
Congressional climate and its vagaries. He can be a positive and creative force in effecting a reasonable reconciliation between the needs and demands of Congress and
the sensibilities of the Executive Branch.

AGENCY PERCEPTIONS OF THE
GAO

Varying agency images of the GAO

The image which agencies have of the GAO has several
distinct aspects. It can be one with respect to the totality of the GAO or in relation to a particular aspect
of the Comptroller General's operations such as agency
audits, financial systems, contract audits, contract appeals, and Comptroller General decisions. Even when the
GAO is viewed in its entirety, much of the image depends
upon the agency's experience with these individual facets
and also the impressions it has generally as to the attitudes, modus operandi, and expertise of the GAO personnel.
The appearance of rigidity on the one hand or dynamism on
the other is a significant factor. Thus, if agencies look
upon the GAO auditors as, in the words of an agency official, being "embalmed" in a certain approach, the implications in terms of GAO-agency relationships are obvious.

Agencies are prone to be critical of the GAO, but they
are quick to accept the concept of an independent monitoring agency such as the GAO and agree with its essentiality.
An agency would be loath to challenge the need for such an
audit facility lest it reflect on the integrity of its own
operations. A Federal official is almost constrained to
show that he has no qualms as to scrutiny by an independent auditor.

It would be erroneous to assume that relations between
GAO and agencies are invariably strained. The deputy administrator of a large Government agency remarked: "We
look at the GAO as another management tool that the administrator has that gives him kind of an objective look."
A departmental official deeply involved in agency financial
management said that he looked upon the GAO as "the high
priest of good accounting practices." The following observation by Assistant Secretary of Defense Shillito demonstrated that an agency, while wincing at some of the results of GAO's endeavors, may not challenge the contribution which these monitoring activities make to the total
governmental process:

> Their reports are published for everyone to
> read and their critical investigations make
> news. Their reports are picked up by some
> Members of Congress who apparently believe
> in the theory that the only way to improve
> the Defense Department's management of the
> $70-$80 billion a year is to keep hitting
> them in the head with a two-by-four. The

theory is that a GAO report, coupled with an
indignant Member of Congress, can get attention. The adverse publicity, frequently an
overkill -- as harsh as it may seem -- will
make the managers of the Defense Department
more careful and make them do a better job
of controlling the programs. There is something to be said for that theory of management. There have been many instances which
warrant the Defense Department's being hit
on the head.[3]

Attributes imputed by agencies to GAO

The agency image of the GAO is inevitably colored by
the sleuth-like nature of certain of GAO's investigative
work, an aspect that cannot be avoided in its entirety if
matters are to be explored incisively. Such investigations
are, in fact, not acceptable to all GAO personnel, who may
feel that they are demeaning and incompatible with professional dignity. A GAO executive referred to the investigative attitude within the GAO that is nurtured in
part by the investigative posture of Congress. "Agencies
feel that GAO is out to get something on them and they,
therefore, may not be responsive to GAO overtures."

The snooping which agencies attribute to the GAO is
an irritant of which the Comptroller General is unquestionably mindful; he needs to make certain that the investigative facets of GAO's operations are handled in a judicious
manner and do not involve the use of tactics that place the
GAO in an untenable position. In connection with GAO's
financial system work in the Department of Defense,
one official of that Department expressed concern that, because of such work, the Department had "GAO looking under
its skirts" on its systems generally. Bemoaning the working arrangements that had been developed, this official
said: "Someone gave away the family jewels so far as I am
concerned." Even allowing for the fact that this official
was prone to look awry at the GAO, one must recognize that
there is a certain burden of proof upon a monitoring agency
to demonstrate that its underlying motif is not of an un-
dercover character.

Closely tied in with the investigative image of the
GAO is the feeling on the part of many agency officials
that the GAO has a propensity for finding shortcomings.
It is not surprising that an operating agency should be
irked by the auditor's identification of deficiencies and
feel that the auditor has a passionate desire to uncover
and report inadequacies. It does not suffice to say that
agencies expressing such feelings are laboring under a

serious misconception. One can still inquire as to how persevering and skillful the GAO is in dispelling such feelings.

GAO staff are very much aware of adverse agency reactions. One mentioned that a common problem is "hostility or indifference by the agency." A top audit supervisor was frank enough to say: "I really can't complain about cooperation. I am enough of a skeptic that I know the damn guy is lying when he says he is happy to see us."

Another criticism voiced frequently during the study was that GAO tended to get into "piddling matters" and reflects an inability to discriminate between trivia and what is significant. Commenting on this alleged shortcoming of the GAO, an agency official said: "They are like beginning clerks. They take more time auditing than it takes to record the transactions on the books." It is significant that the individual making these observations was one who felt that his agency's relations with the GAO were "actually fine." Hence, it can be assumed that his reactions do not stem from dudgeon. Whether or not the feeling that GAO concerns itself unduly with detail is factually correct, the fact that it was found rather widely reflected on the rapport that GAO should seek to develop with agencies.

There appeared to be a pronounced tendency, at least until recently, to look upon the GAO as basically static and deeply rooted in established practices, regardless of statements that may emanate from top-level of the organization. The manner in which the GAO operates was prone to be regarded by agencies as ponderous and unimaginative. A Federal executive formerly with the GAO said: "I don't think that I have seen any professional or philosophical guidance from the GAO in the last half-dozen years." One official felt that rigidity might stem from lack of expertise of individuals in the GAO. This, he said, may necessitate "bucking" the matter up to higher echelons. A related reaction was that GAO approached matters in a way that makes uniformity an end unto itself.

There was a strong feeling on the part of the agencies as to the intransigence of the hard core personnel of the GAO. The agency officials felt that the attitudes and values of the GAO were, therefore, very resistant to change, even when a new Comptroller General assumed office. One official commented: "Staats' heart is in the right place; but can he persuade his staff to go along?" A basic challenge directed to GAO was that their personnel do not have an understanding of agency problems and that they lack a broad-gauge approach. "There is a flaw in the review approach of the GAO. The people who review are in no position to understand the operating implications of what they are reviewing."

87

Effects of expanding scope of GAO reviews upon agency relations

The comprehensive audit philosophy which carried GAO into the evaluations of programs and activities of a specialized, technical, and professional character gave rise to criticism that the Comptroller General was overstepping his bounds and going beyond the Office's competence. GAO findings and recommendations were often criticized to the author on the ground that GAO had not observed appropriate limits as to its capacity to deal with the particular subject matter.

The General Counsel of one of the military services said: "There are areas where we feel it is none of GAO's business." He volunteered the observation that the Service felt GAO was out of its field when it got into questions as to the selection of weapon systems. This comment assumed additional significance in light of the subsequent GAO thrust to become more deeply involved in weapon systems procurement. Similarly, a former Assistant Attorney General stated that the reaction of the Department of Justice was that GAO had the right to look at the financial records but not to inquire as to whether Justice had litigated its cases well. A NASA official expressed himself very strongly on the issue of what came within the proper purview of the GAO. He referred to the "accountant approach" and its emphasis on "detailed documentation." It was his feeling that one runs into trouble when he seeks to evaluate management decisions on the basis of a study of documentation made through the audit approach, "Such as hell, the GAO's staff are not engineers or scientists . . . I do not object to them one damned bit as auditors."

It has already been observed that the expansion in scope of GAO reviews and studies has shown an almost startling crescendo. Hence, Executive agencies have additional reason for speculating on the boundaries of the Comptroller General's inquiries.

Agency reactions vary with different GAO functions

It has already been intimated that agency reactions vary as between the different segments of GAO operations. The rationale for GAO's audits is not challenged; in fact, as already stated, their essentiality and usefulness are widely accepted. However, the manner in which the audits are perceived, carried out, and reported upon were often questioned and even subjected to bitter denunciation.

Unlike the audit work, the financial management system activities were, over the years, challenged from the

standpoint of the propriety of their being performed by
a legislative agency. Despite the fact that this issue
is one of ancient vintage and had been firmly resolved
by Congressional refusal to budge on this score, there
still remained an underlying rancor. GAO tended to be
looked upon somewhat as an interloper in this area. This
attitude intensified the irritation that agencies felt as
a result of the impasses they experienced in seeking GAO
approval of their systems. Staats' simplification of the
procedure for GAO review of agency accounting systems was
bound to improve the situation.

The Department of Defense with its vast weapon acquisition program is particularly concerned with GAO's procurement role. The Holifield hearings presented something
of a nadir in relations between GAO on the one hand, and
Defense procurement officials and contractors on the other.
It was not a question of viewing GAO as an intruder when
it checked on procurement transactions and practices but
rather raising issues as to the fairness and balance of
its findings. The increasing involvement of GAO in oversight of weapons system procurement might make relations
between GAO and the Department of Defense even more delicate than they had been previously. Deputy Secretary of
Defense Packard, while admitting that in defense procurement, "we have a real mess on our hands," went on to say:
"Nor will it help to put the General Accounting Office in
the process of making management decisions. The GAO deserves the highest marks for auditing, but the talents of
a good auditor are not identical with those of a good man-
ager."[4] A separate facet of GAO's activities in the procurement area is that which consists of passing upon bidder appeals. This involvement of the Comptroller General
in decision-making as to the award of contracts has, for
reasons explained later, been relatively acceptable to
agencies.

The Comptroller General's rendering of decisions has
pretty much worked itself into the fabric of the Governmental processes. But agencies may wonder as to how far
the Comptroller General should go in handing down rulings
that are of an important policy nature. This issue, which
was brought into dramatic focus by the Philadelphia Plan
confrontation, is explored more fully in connection with
the discussion of the judicial role of the Comptroller
General.

The Comptroller General cannot afford to be unaware
of how the various aspects of his activities interact from
the standpoint of agency responsiveness to, and evaluation
of, the GAO efforts. His freedom to change the program
"mix" or even the manner in which particular GAO respon-

sibilities are implemented is, to be sure, limited by
statutory requirements, professional standards, and
Congressional directives. But, as was observed earlier
in this chapter, the Comptroller General still has a large
area within which he can maneuver to accommodate the several components of the GAO program into a totality of reasonable acceptability to the agencies.

Intra-agency differences as to GAO-agency relations

GAO relationships with Executive Branch agencies have
to be perceived in terms of the different echelons within
the agencies. Similarly, the various hierarchical layers
within the GAO will have different impacts upon agencies
with which they deal. A subcommittee counsel suggested
the desirability of direct contacts between the Comptroller
General and the respective agency head, who would, in his
opinion, "ordinarily be very ill-informed as to what is
going on in his agency;" he thought that this would be a
means for alerting top departmental executives as to situations which require their attention. Within a particular
government agency, especially one of considerable magnitude,
the interplay between constituent units may result in something of an "interstitial" role for the GAO. In other
words, GAO may serve as a helpful ally of one unit in its
dealings with other components of the organization.

The relations between the GAO and agencies are compli-
cated by the fact that agency personnel who cooperate fully
with the GAO may find that this is looked upon with disfavor
by their superiors. There is an instance in which a cooperative relationship between a Navy flag officer and the GAO
resulted in what GAO considered to be a very useful report.
However, the officer who had been so cooperative, as a result, fell into disfavor. This was brought to the attention
of the Secretary of the Navy by the Comptroller General.

Impact of GAO attitudes on relations with agencies

The perceptiveness and understanding with which GAO
views its "clientele" is a key factor in relations with
agencies. Variations may exist on this score between different levels within the GAO itself. It was observed by
one regional GAO executive that the staff in the field are
more inclined to seek to work out problems with agency
representatives while Washington staff may lean to a more
adversary approach. However, one of the more outstanding
GAO field executives said he supported the practice of
having continued contacts with agencies "so that they know
we are ready to swoop down on them and pluck out a few of
their tail feathers." Regardless of the facade which is
presented to those outside the organization, internally
there can be marked differences as to attitudes towards
the agencies.

The traditional aloofness of the auditor has carried
with it an impersonal attitude that may rapidly be becoming
obsolete as GAO reviews assume an increasingly operational
character and as an interpersonal approach becomes far more
relevant. Apropos of this latter comment, the very modus
operandi of a monitoring agency such as the GAO makes for
a frame of mind which equates objectivity and breadth of
analysis with an arm's length relation. This is coupled
with a strong presumption that shortcomings not only can
be found but should be brought to the attention of persons
outside the agency.

The kind of relationship which GAO should seek to develop in its dealings with agencies cannot be delineated
precisely because of the varying facets of the role that
GAO seeks to discharge. From the perspective of auditing
for the purpose of holding the agency to financial accountability, it may be entirely defensible, if not essential,
for the GAO to maintain an attitude of aloofness. In this
frame of reference, one can understand Comptroller General
Campbell's fears about GAO staff fraternizing with agency
personnel. However, when the GAO seeks to function somewhat in the role of a management advisor or consultant to
the agencies, it manifestly needs a type of rapport that
is not fully consonant with the relationship engendered
by the more critical stance it takes in its audits or critiques of agency operations and programs, especially when
these lead to reports presented to the Congress.

The adverse reactions to GAO's efforts in the financial management area cannot be attributed entirely to inadequacies on the part of the GAO or inertia or negativism
on the part of agencies. The authoritarian position the
Comptroller General took with respect to the approval of
such systems and his serving as a vehicle for "policing"
the program on behalf of Congressional committees, made
for an abrasive effect upon the agencies. Additionally,
it was sometimes difficult for an agency to disassociate
accounting systems activities of the GAO staff from the
regular audit work, a difficulty which undoubtedly had
been compounded by the fact that the same personnel had
at one time handled both tasks.

Agency apprehension of the GAO

GAO agency relations are strongly colored by an under-
tone of apprehension. The status of the GAO as a Congressional instrumentality, its channels of communication to
the Congress, and its access to the press would in themselves make an agency take pause before crossing swords
with the GAO. But the even more direct sanctions which
the GAO possesses in terms of the Comptroller General's

91

decisions and the disallowances of expenditures add immeasurably to its position of power and the concomitant
pressures it can bring to bear upon agencies. An agency
can understandably be disturbed as to the effect which
GAO disclosures may have upon its public image.

Even the more bellicose agency critics of the GAO
have second thoughts about entering into direct confrontations with the Comptroller General. This is evidenced
by the remarks of an agency legal advisor, who was prone
to be vitriolic in his observations on the GAO. This person stated he would proceed on the basis of "to hell with
the GAO" if he had a sound rationale for so advising his
clients. But then he appended the qualification: "Unless the matter is of such consequence that the results
of a mistake would be tremendous." There is unquestionably a definite hesitance on the part of agencies to incur the displeasure of the GAO. An Assistant Secretary
of Defense mentioned the "tendency of people to collapse
when they encounter a GAO report." An agency that views
the GAO as akin to a grand inquisitor may be prone to indulge in what this official described as "weasel justification of the things that are wrong."

Validity of agency reactions

The recital of agency criticisms directed to the GAO
must be evaluated in light of the irritability and defensiveness implicit in the relationship between an audit
agency and those subject to its scrutiny -- especially if
the findings of such reviews are submitted to an outside
body to which the audited organization is accountable.
Officials and other personnel, when responding to inquiries concerning the GAO, are inclined to articulate alleged
shortcomings and not to bestow accolades. Yet, as has been
intimated, the litany of grievances -- however exaggerated
or one-sided the strictures may be -- afford an insight
into factors that becloud relations between the GAO and
Government departments and other establishments.

The proclivity for hurling brickbats at the GAO can
better be understood if account is taken of the fact that
the irascibility of agencies is heightened by the aggregate of authority vested in the Comptroller General. Agencies find themselves dealing with an auditor who cannot
only identify and publicize deficiencies but who can also
inject himself into agency decision-making. Rankled by
the image of power which the Comptroller General presents,
some Federal executives are predisposed to view the GAO
with at least latent hostility. At the same time, there
is within the Federal bureaucracy significant recognition --
some of it grudging -- of the accomplishments of GAO.

GAO's vulnerability to the barbs directed at it by agencies has been lessened by the marked expansion of multidisciplinary talent within its staff. The accolades bestowed upon it by the accounting profession as well as the leadership role it presently has in the governmental auditing field have also weakened the position of agency critics. The unalloyed Congressional support which the Comptroller General could marshal until recently was still another factor that strengthened GAO's position vis-a-vis the agencies. However, the evidence of a more inquiring attitude within the Congress as to the GAO, particularly as it reaches out for additional power, may buttress the position of the agencies.

AGENCY INTERNAL REVIEWS -- THEIR GAO IMPLICATIONS

The interaction between internal evaluations and the GAO

The agency audits and reviews have striking potentialities for complementing GAO efforts in a manner that will either obviate the need for the Comptroller General making certain examinations or that will make it feasible for the GAO and agencies to collaborate in particular analyses. Such sharing of audit tasks would mitigate the tensions too frequently associated with the Comptroller General's review of Executive Branch programs and activities. Effective collaboration also offers a means for strengthening the total audit effort within the Government. A more pragmatic consideration, so far as the Comptroller General is concerned, is that the shedding of certain less alluring tasks enables him to focus more on issues and policies that patently have challenged him. By stressing agency responsibility for constantly checking on its operations, GAO apparently escapes embarrassment when a committee finds that "fraud and program abuse are causing enormous losses" in HEW.[5] Even in an area such as program evaluation, which has captured the Comptroller General's interest, he has found it necessary to stress the role of the agencies lest GAO be overwhelmed by Congressional expectations as to such analyses.

Congressional and GAO push for internal audit

The Accounting and Auditing Act of 1950, in defining the duties of agency heads for the establishment and maintenance of accounting and internal controls systems, requires such systems -- among other aspects -- to provide: "effective control over and accountability for all funds, property, and other assets for which the agency is responsible, including appropriate internal audit."[6] The Act further provides that, in determining the auditing procedures to be followed and the extent of his examination

of vouchers and other documents, the Comptroller General
shall "give due regard to generally accepted principles
of auditing, including consideration of the effectiveness
of accounting organizations and systems, internal audit
and control, and related administrative practices of the
respective agencies."[7] An earlier chapter alluded to the
fact that the Second Hoover Commission had stimulated the
thrust for internal auditing in the Executive Branch.[8]

The GAO has defined the overall objective of internal
auditing to be that of assisting agency management in at-
taining its goals by furnishing information analyses, appraisals, and recommendations pertinent to management's
duties and objectives.[9] It identifies internal auditing
as "a staff and advisory function, not a line operating
function." The GAO envisages internal auditing as encompassing the review of all agency activities and related
management controls and as not being restricted to accounting and financial matters although, of course, including the audit of accounts and financial transactions.[10]

The GAO's position in the internal auditing area was
strengthened immeasurably by the interest and support of
the House Government Operations Committee. In its 1963
statement on this subject, the Committee cited the magnitude of the Federal Government, the number of separate
departments and agencies, and the myriad of Governmental
activities. Using this as a point of departure, the Committee stated that those in charge of departments and
agencies must have the means within their own organizations for discovering and ferreting out inefficiencies
and waste if the monolithic setup the Committee described
was to be operated efficiently and economically. The absence of such means for identifying trouble spots, the
Committee felt, would compound the problem confronting
the President in the formulation of the annual budget and
also those problems confronting the Congress in connection
with both the budget process and its oversight responsibilities.[11]

But, despite this thrust, agency implementation of
the internal audit concept has not proceeded with the verve
that might have been expected. The very nomenclature that
is used gives the impression of a strictly accounting activity having less relevance to management of public activities than it does in the private sector. The GAO reported that "one of the obstacles to improved internal
audit has been the lack of recognition by the higher levels
of management of the benefits to be derived from effective
internal audit."[12]

As recently as 1976, the Comptroller General was still
finding shortcomings in agency establishment of internal

audit capability: some agencies had no internal audit units; some had internal audit staffs too small to provide adequate coverage; and there was a "tendency of some audit groups to emphasize so-called external audits of Federal assistance programs, thereby reducing the amount of internal auditing being performed."[13] While making these observations, the Comptroller General did note that as of June 30, 1975 there were more than 11,600 internal auditors throughout the civilian and defense agencies and that more than $263 million was spent to operate these audit organizations in fiscal year 1975.[14]

Issue as to organizational location of internal audit

The "fundamentals" articulated in 1963 by the House Government Operations Committee with respect to internal audit operations included a statement that all reports and recommendations of the internal audit staff must be submitted in full directly to the agency or department head. Following through on this principle, the GAO has contended that "the internal auditor should be responsible to the highest practical organizational level, preferably to the agency head or to a principal official reporting directly to the agency head."[15] In support of its position, GAO can point to the fact that another fundamental expressed by the Committee was that the central audit agency should be "organized independent of department or agency operations." One can, of course, understand GAO's motivation in seeking to provide organizational safeguards within the respective agencies so that the internal auditors will be insulated from extraneous pressures and not have their findings and recommendations screened or prevented from being presented to top administrative levels. However, an unyielding posture can make something of a fetish of such a concept; and tenacious adherence to it manifestly inhibits willingness to explore the realities of particular situations.

An Assistant Secretary for Administration addressing himself to this problem said:

> I have been through this battle for years, and one of the things that is most frustrating in some of the GAO approach, and I say this with a generally favorable relationship with GAO, is the dabbling in audit organization . . .

The Comptroller General did not recede from his position even when the Bureau of the Budget expressed concern as to the stand taken by the GAO. While agreeing that "it would be undesirable for GAO and the Bureau to hold dif-

95

ferent views on the matter," Staats was unwilling to concede that the GAO's concept required modification.[18]

One can argue that the Comptroller General has inflated the particular issue far beyond what realities justify. This commitment to a theoretical concept can be carried to an extreme which unduly strains relations with agencies and places GAO in the position of appearing to force all agencies into a Procrustean bed. However, one must also recognize that, if the GAO is to place increasing dependence upon the internal audit efforts within the respective agencies, it becomes more understandable why the GAO is so firm in its demands that independence of the internal audit agencies be protected. Furthermore, the inspector general concept, which has strong Congressional advocates, goes -- as is noted in the next section -- beyond the concept enunciated by the Comptroller General.

Fortunately for the GAO, the agencies that were subjected to such vigorous criticism with respect to their internal audit facilities were apparently unaware of the Office's vulnerability as to its own practice in this area. It was not until the middle of 1971 that an internal review unit was established within the GAO. Then, flying in the face of his pronouncements to Executive agencies, the Comptroller General did not make this unit directly responsible to either himself or his deputy.

The move for inspectors general

The concept of an internal monitoring unit directly responsible to the head of the agency has been pushed still further by the current drive for inspectors general, a development that has some features to which the Comptroller General has taken exception. Although the inspector general was a long established functionary in the military, the use of this title in the civil agencies is a relatively recent development. Following the Billie Sol Estes scandal, the Department of Agriculture established an Inspector General. Walter Gellhorn was so impressed with the breadth of the responsibilities entrusted to Agriculture's Inspector General that he concluded that this official "functions to some extent as a sort of departmental ombudsman." In fact, Gellhorn felt that the internal audit as illustrated by this official "offers large hope for continuing advances in the art and science of government."[17] But the Agriculture Department abolished its Inspector General in 1974.

Flowing out of hearings on fraud and program abuse in HEW, the Office of Inspector General was established

96

by statute in that Department in 1976.[18] The House Government Operations Subcommittee on Intergovernmental Relations and Human Resources, which was the driving force in the enactment of this legislation, began hearings in the Spring of 1977 on a bill establishing inspectors general in six additional departments and several other major agencies.[19]

The Committee report recommending enactment of the bill cited deficiencies in the organizational structure, procedures, and resources of agency auditing and investigations.[20] Following the pattern established for HEW, the bill provided that each inspector general shall, together with his deputy, be appointed by the President subject to Senate confirmation and shall: (a) have overall responsibility for the auditing and investigative activities relating to programs and operations of his agency, (b) be under the general supervision of the head of the agency or the officer next in rank below such head, (c) have authority to select personnel independent of his agency head and to protest to Congress reductions made in his budget requests before their submission to Congress; (d) have broad access authority including the issuance of subpoenas enforceable by order of any appropriate U.S. District Court; (e) submit reports not only to the agency head but also appropriate committees and subcommittees of the Congress without further clearance or approval and (f) provide such additional information or documents as may be requested by either House of Congress or, with respect to matters under their jurisdiction by any committee or subcommittee thereof. Recognizing the possibility of overlap with the activities of the Comptroller General, the bill directs each inspector general to give "particular regard" to such activities with a view to avoiding duplications and insuring effective coordination and cooperation.

The Comptroller General expressed his strong support of "the upgrading of the organizational status of the investigative and audit functions and the emphasis on their importance which the bill provides."[21] But he demurred to those provisions that tended to weaken top management's control over the internal audit. It is surprising to find the Comptroller General, who has been criticized for the plethora of reports he submits to Congress, admonishing Representative Brooks that "Congress may get too many reports" because of the bill's provision for quarterly and specialized reports. The Comptroller General's backing of the underlying thrust for inspectors general ties in neatly with his redirection of GAO activities previously alluded to, in the financial accountability area so as "to emphasize audits of systems rather than indi-

vidual transactions."[22] But Executive agencies understandably took a contrary position, so that one newspaper story
carried the heading "Carter Growls at Plans for Fiscal
Watchdogs."[23] The basic agency objection, undoubtedly reflecting the reaction of the new administration, was expressed by an Assistant Secretary Designate at a subcommittee hearing when he observed: "We believe that under
the proposed bill, the office of inspector general would
be viewed more as a congressional investigative arm than
as an organization whose job is to work with management
to improve and preserve the effectiveness, efficiency,
and integrity of the department's operations."[24] But HEW
Secretary Joseph Califano told the Subcommittee of the "already evident accomplishments of his Department's Inspector
General" and referred to the concept of the office as "one
of the most important ideas in years for strengthening the
management of complex Government programs."[25]

GAO advocacy of program evaluations by agencies

Program evaluations present the type of challenge
that comports with Staats' broad concept of the GAO's role.
However, after such evaluations won Congressional acceptance, the Comptroller General recognized the inescapable
disparity between GAO resources and the potential demand
for these evaluations. Having vigorously espoused the
cause of program evaluation, the GAO had to step gingerly
lest it find itself encumbered -- as a result of the 1970
Legislative Reorganization Act -- with a sweeping program
evaluation responsibility of such dimensions as to make
it completely unmanageable. The stance which the Comptroller General enunciated concerning the respective program evaluation responsibilities of the operating agencies and the GAO was attuned to the realities of a vast
and complex governmental setup.

On August 11, 1972 the Comptroller General wrote
committee chairmen urging "that the Congress give careful consideration in authorizing new programs, or in re-
authorizing existing programs, to including in the authorizing legislation specific statutory requirements for a
systematic evaluation by the department or agency involved
of the results of programs in operation." The Comptroller
General might have been anxious to forestall the assumption on the part of Congress that the GAO would have the
primary responsibility for program evaluation throughout
the Federal establishment. In his communication, the
Comptroller General expressed the view that such evaluation is a fundamental part of effective program administration and that responsibility should, therefore, rest initially upon the respective agency. The letter stated that
GAO experience had demonstrated the difficulty of making

program evaluations where the legislation setting up programs fails to set forth program goals or objectives.
Having stated that program evaluation was basically an
agency responsibility, the Comptroller General apprised
the committee chairmen that he had requested GAO staff,
in its conduct of audits, "to give particular attention
to this problem and to include in our advice to the Congress our appraisal as to how well the agencies are performing their evaluation functions."

GAO's increasing dependence upon internal agency reviews

The massiveness of the Federal Government gives the
Comptroller General little alternative to stimulating development of internal and evaluative agencies and encouraging their maintenance of a high level of professional
performance and also to depending in large measure upon
their output. Such agency facilities have far-reaching
potentialities for making GAO-Executive Branch relationships less authoritarian and more collaborative. The progress that can be made in this direction is dependent upon
more than agency willingness and capacity to nurture internal evaluation staffs having unquestionable competence,
broad scope of inquiry, and complete freedom to formulate
and present findings and recommendations. The achievement
of a more viable allocation of audit responsibilities as
between the GAO and agencies also requires that the Comptroller General demonstrate that -- given internal reviews
of high quality -- the GAO will treat them as truly complementary to its own efforts.

The Office of Management and Budget can be a potent
force in buttressing the internal review function. In
its recent report on Federal internal audit, the GAO identified steps it felt should be taken by OMB to strengthen
internal audit capability.[26] If the Office of Management
and Budget and the GAO are persevering in their support of
internal audit and other evaluative activities and, if
they coalesce on a concept as to how these fit into the
total audit program of the Government, the result may well
be a marked transformation of the interface between GAO
and the Executive Branch.

PIVOTAL ROLE OF OFFICE OF MANAGEMENT AND BUDGET (OMB) IN EXECUTIVE BRANCH-GAO RELATIONS

The Bureau of the Budget and its successor, the Office
of Management and Budget, have been very much the bell-
wether in the relations between the Executive Branch and
the Comptroller General. The enunciation of the executive
budget concept and its implementation through the establishment of the Bureau of the Budget by the Budget and

Accounting Act of 1921 were potent factors in strengthening the leadership and control exercised by the Chief Executive. The key role which these accorded the President
in the formulation and presentation of the budget greatly
facilitated the ascendancy of the Chief Executive in the
total governmental process. The establishment of the Comptroller General and the GAO by the same legislation can in
some respects be regarded as a countervailing measure designed to place the Legislative Branch in a more strategic
position to check the Executive. Congress carried this
"defensive" approach still further when it provided for
the Congressional Budget Office in the Congressional Budget and Impoundment Control Act of 1974.

OMB's impressive influence within the Executive Branch
means that it can readily facilitate the efforts of the GAO
or, contrariwise, place formidable obstacles in its way.
Even if the Comptroller General's responsibilities were
restricted to those of a post-audit character, the output
of his Office would still be relevant to OMB's activities.
However, the Comptroller General's authority with respect
to accounting systems and the control which he has over
Government operations because of his settlement and decision
rendering authority make the functioning of the GAO of very
direct concern to OMB. Additionally, the thrust within
Congress to draw upon the GAO for continuing assistance in
connection with policy analysis, oversight, and the budget
process has significant implications in terms of OMB.

GAO'S ILL-FATED EFFORT TO AUDIT THE BUREAU
OF THE BUDGET

Towards the end of the Eisenhower regime, there was
an almost epoch-making confrontation between the Bureau
of the Budget and the GAO. It can be considered a forerunner of the bitter controversy concerning the Nixon
papers. The underlying issue was the privileged status
of records and papers utilized in Presidential decision-
making. The immediate question related to GAO's audit
authority with respect to the Chief Executive and his immediate staff facilities such as the Bureau of the Budget.
The upshot was reaffirmation of the Bureau's immunity from
any truly meaningful scrutiny by the GAO. The stultifying
outcome detracted from the stature of the Comptroller General and weakened his position vis-a-vis the Budget Bureau.

Inception of Project

This study describes other instances of vicarious Congressional searches for information refused it by the Executive Branch, but the debacle of the Comptroller General's
effort to penetrate deeply into the Budget Bureau is unique.

The saga begins with the House Government Operations Committee prodding the Comptroller General into action with
respect to the Executive Office of the President; it
presents a classic case of a Congressional committee attempting to use the GAO as a vehicle for obtaining information that it does not choose to seek on its own.

Early in 1959, Chairman Dawson of the House Government Operations Committee wrote Comptroller General Campbell:

> The White House activities are clearly within
> the purview of your duty and authority under
> the laws enacted by congress. Moreover, the
> inclusion of many and diverse functions in
> the Executive Office of the President makes
> possible an asylum from accountability under
> the protective aegis of the White House.[27]

The letter closed with a specific request that the Comptroller General include in his current audits a "comprehensive audit of the Executive Office of the President." Although reluctant to undertake such a project, the Comptroller General apparently felt that there was no alternative to acceding to Chairman Dawson's request. Hence,
Campbell stated that, as GAO staff resources were expanded,
the Office would undertake to make "appropriate reviews
of these agencies. We hope to undertake this work during
the first part of the fiscal year 1960."[28]

Comptroller General rebuffed by Budget Bureau and White House

Five months later, the Comptroller General wrote
Maurice Stans, the Budget Director, stating that the GAO
had "recently initiated a review of the Executive Office
of the President, including the activities of the Bureau
of the Budget." Apparently anticipating some challenge
by the Bureau, Campbell reminded the Director of the Bureau of the Budget that this work was being done in accordance with the provisions of the Budget and Accounting
Act, 1921, and the Accounting and Auditing Act of 1950.[29]
Campbell informed Stans that the GAO review had been
"materially impeded by refusals or unnecessary delays in
furnishing us with pertinent information." The Bureau
had reacted to the GAO's request for internal staff documents with this comment:

> . . . we are not at liberty to divulge the
> nature of the advice and recommendations
> made to the President or members of his
> staff prior to Presidential action . . .

Expressing disagreement with the Bureau's intention to examine the pertinent files and screen out items which it did not consider appropriate for submittal to the GAO, the Comptroller General stated:

> . . . we alone must determine whether audit requirements have been satisfied. To accomplish the independent audit contemplated in the legislation to be carried out by the General Accounting Office, it is absolutely essential that we be completely free of any restrictions in determining the scope of a review.

A memorandum written by the GAO's General Counsel refers to a "further meeting" on December 17, 1959 to discuss the proposed comprehensive audit, apparently with particular reference to the White House proper. In explaining the decision to restrict the GAO to "strictly fiscal records" of the White House, the memorandum presents an interesting interpretation and application of the separation of powers doctrine:

> The decision by the White House representatives was taken upon the ground that, under our form of government and our Constitution, the President, the popularly elected head of the Executive Branch of the government, is responsible for the conduct of his office to the electorate -- not to either of the other two branches of the Government. (Similarly, the other two branches owe no such responsibility to the President.) Further, because the records and files maintained in the President's immediate office are his personal papers, such papers cannot, under the Separation of Powers doctrine, be compelled by another branch of the Government -- any more than those of another branch can be compelled by the President. Nor, therefore, should such papers be yielded to another branch or agency thereof if the basic design of our form of government and our Constitution is to be observed.

Both Chairman Dawson and the Committee's General Counsel thought that the GAO should proceed with the Budget Bureau audit, notwithstanding the limitations imposed on access to records.

Budget Bureau's conciliatory gesture

Subsequently, the Budget Director wrote the Comptroller General stating that the Bureau was anxious to cooperate with the GAO in the performance of its statutory duties.[30]   Director Stans said he believed the Bureau had made available all of the materials and information which the Comptroller General's auditors had requested "with the exception of various items which contain advice, opinions, suggestions, or recommendations by persons in the Executive Branch to each other or to their supervisors."

Then, setting forth the underlying rationale for the course of action which the Bureau had taken, Stans went on to say:

> . . . But, whether prepared by members of our staff or by others in the Executive Branch, and whether for the use of the Bureau of the Budget or of the White House, communications and documents in our files which contain advice and recommendations are subject to the same considerations as the evaluation reports discussed in the President's quoted letter.[31] I have discussed this matter with the President, and he has confirmed my understanding that I am bound by the views which he expressed in his letter to you.

Replying to Stans' letter, the Comptroller General commented that, in view of the statutory authority of the GAO, that agency could not agree that the considerations advanced by Stans justified withholding information needed by the GAO in "fulfilling our statutory responsibilities."[32] However, Campbell stated that GAO was willing on a trial basis to follow a middle course and attempt to perform its audit even though it did not have complete access to the Bureau's records.

The Bureau prevails vis-a-vis the GAO

The ultimate result of these proposals and counterproposals was that the GAO decided to discontinue its audit of the Bureau's "principal function;" and Chairman Dawson was informed on September 12, 1960 that GAO had "suspended indefinitely" its review of those Bureau functions dealing with the formulation, review, and execution of the Federal Budget. However, the GAO continued its work relating to some of the Bureau's other activities. Shortly after President Kennedy was inaugurated in 1961, Congressman Dawson wrote Campbell:

> It occurs to me that . . . it would be advisable for your office to call to the

103

attention of the new Administration officials
the difficulties you have encountered. It may
be that you will find the new Administration
ready to cooperate in the audit.[33]

Goaded on by Congressman Dawson and showing something
of a Don Quixote persistence and resilience, Comptroller
General Campbell informed the new Director of the Bureau
of the Budget, David Bell, "The Bureau of the Budget is
hereby formally designated for comprehensive audit by
this Office."[34]

In June 1961, the Comptroller General reported to Congress on Bureau activities under the management improvement
program and those activities for promoting charges for services and commodities furnished by the Government.[35] "We
found it necessary to suspend our review of a third, and
the Bureau's most important function -- the formulation,
review, and execution of the Federal budget -- because of
denials of access to pertinent records and documents." Even
within the circumscribed sphere, GAO was critical of the
Bureau's leadership and assistance to Executive agencies;
and Stans, who was no longer Budget Director, characterized
the report as "inaccurate and misleading in many respects."[36]

The Bureau's stance unaffected by change in administration

The following month, the new Director of the Budget,
David Bell, sent a lengthy letter to Chairman Dawson in
reply to the Congressman's request for his views on the GAO
report.[37] The most significant aspect of the Bell letter
was the manner in which he dealt with the issue of GAO access to Budget Bureau records. Bell said he recognized
that there could be situations where it would be inappropriate to disclose communications between the President and
the Bureau of the Budget Director or the staff analyses
and recommendations upon which such communications are
based, without Presidential concurrence.

Congressman Dawson's reaction to the Bell letter was
to request the Comptroller General to resume his audit of
the Budget Bureau,[38] and he so notified Bell on the same
day. There was an interchange of correspondence between
Bell and Campbell concerning the Dawson request. The Comptroller General was not to be put off by Bell's interpretation[39] as to what he regarded as a resolution of the
matter. He replied with a recapitulation of the trials
and tribulations that had been encountered by the GAO in
its attempts to make a comprehensive audit of the Bureau.[40]

Bell might have felt that letting the matter drag
over an extended period of time would be the best approach

to the very obvious impasse between the Bureau and the GAO. When his departure from the Bureau was imminent, Bell wrote the Comptroller General stating that Kermit Gordon, his successor, would be glad to discuss the matter further with Campbell if he should so desire. In something of a valedictory, Bell expressed his views concerning the matter at issue.

> The particular documents in question are the working materials which underlie the Director's advice to the President. Nevertheless, they constitute only a small part of the Bureau's records. For these reasons, it would be my hope that mutual agreement could be reached on the exclusion of such documents from the scope of the audit. If it were possible to do this, I am sure that the comprehensive audit could be resumed and completed to your satisfaction.

With Kermit Gordon's assumption of the directorship of the Budget Bureau, this matter went into limbo.

One can only conjecture as to the extent to which the Director of the Bureau of the Budget and the Comptroller General were speaking as protagonists of the prerogatives of the Chief Executive and the Congress respectively, and the extent to which expressions of concern on this score were more of a facade for bureaucratic sensitivity as to their own authority. Whatever their motivations, however, the locking of horns placed the loser -- the Comptroller General -- in an awkward position so far as future relations with the other agency were concerned. Certainly GAO's stature suffered from its abject submissiveness to what could be regarded as untenable requests from a committee chairman.

THE CHALLENGE OF EFFECTING COOPERATION BETWEEN GAO AND OMB

Lack of close working relations between GAO and Budget Bureau

The relations between the Bureau of the Budget and GAO were described by a Bureau official as in a "state of sporadic hostilities interspersed with episodes of close cooperation," at least up to the assumption of the Comptrollership General by Staats. This official attributed the lack of rapport to what he felt was the ingrained philosophy of GAO, i.e., that it is solely the servant of the Congress. "GAO," he said, "has jealously guarded its isolation from the Executive Branch, its independence, its objectivity, its notion that it is the guardian of

public morality." However one may feel as to the validity
of this characterization of the attitude of the GAO, the
fact that it was viewed in these terms by a top Budget
Bureau official was indicative of a sharp split between the
two agencies. This functionary did not attribute the arm's
length relationship entirely to the GAO. He pointed out
that the Budget Bureau was "equally polarized to the view
that it is the personal staff of the President; that it is
part of his mind; that it is here to protect the flanks
of the President against unreasonable criticisms." Such
an adversary relationship militated heavily against meaningful collaboration between the Bureau and GAO in the improvement of public management. In light of this setting, one
could hardly expect very much to come from the provision
of the Budget and Accounting Act that the Comptroller General "shall furnish such information relating to expenditures
and accounting to the Bureau of the Budget as it may request
from time to time."

A fundamental weakness in relationships between the
two agencies was the lack of firm underpinning. A Bureau
official, speaking of GAO's relations with other overall
agencies of the Government, said: "This is a terrible
mixed-up bag highly influenced by personal relationships
that intentionally have been kept non-institutional." Another official observed that relationships between the GAO
and the Bureau had been influenced considerably by the
successive incumbents of the Office of the Comptroller
General. A former Bureau Director similarly referred to
the impact of the personalities of the Director and the
Comptroller upon the interaction between the two agencies.
He was of the opinion: "Given reasonably competent men,
there is no reason why you cannot get along;" in this
connection, he referred specifically to the good relationships between Budget Director Webb and Comptroller General
Warren. On the other hand, as has already been observed,
the incumbents of the two offices were often at loggerheads
during the Eisenhower era.

Strain imposed by comprehensive audit concept

The comprehensive audit concept, which is discussed
at some length in Chapter 5, aggravated tensions between
the Bureau and the GAO. The Comptroller General's desire
to make unlimited examinations of management throughout
the Executive Branch put the Budget Bureau on guard. This
reaction was brought about at least in part by the fact
that, implicit in the comprehensive audit as conceived by
the GAO, is the demand for broad access to information.
The skirmish which GAO had with the Bureau when it attempted to make a comprehensive audit of the Bureau and
which has just been depicted, probably added to whatever

misgivings the Bureau might have had initially with respect to this broad-scale type of audit.

A Bureau official who criticized the GAO's comprehensive audits was irked apparently not by the basic concept
but the manner in which it was implemented by the GAO. He,
in fact, took issue with those of his colleagues who felt
that the GAO had neither the responsibility nor competence
for evaluating management. This official went along with
the idea that Congress is entitled to have comprehensive
audits made by an instrumentality controlled by it and that
this is not precluded by the doctrine of separation of
powers. He regretted that an accommodation had not been
worked out between the GAO and the Bureau with respect to
these audits.

It was an opportunity for GAO and the Bureau
of the Budget to make common cause but it
failed because it was badly engineered,
poorly staffed, and undertaken unilaterally.

In evaluating these criticisms, one needs to be mindful of the fact that, as is brought out in the next section, the Bureau of the Budget had over the years phased
itself out of much of its management activities and thereby
by its own default created a void which the GAO attempted
to fill at least in part.

Budget Bureau's withdrawal from the management field

As the Budget Bureau placed increasing emphasis upon
the program planning, evaluation, and review facets of its
tasks and as the skills, interest, and priorities of econ-
omists became more dominant in the functioning of the Bureau, there was a marked diminution in the Bureau's concern
and leadership with respect to the strictly managerial aspects of the Government. There had been widespread awareness of this development by those within the Bureau, on
the part of the agencies, and even -- within the Congress --
although to a somewhat lesser degree. A top Budget Bureau
official was impelled to comment:

We have been submerged in program decisions
in later years. It has been a long time
since we have had a rooting, tooting public administration man as a director.

The administrative management facet of the Bureau's responsibilities, which was initiated with considerable vigor during the directorship of Harold Smith and very carefully nurtured by him, was almost totally eclipsed by the Bureau's
deep involvement in agency programs. The planning-programming-
budgeting system, which the Bureau strove to implement through-

out the Government made this trend all the more pronounced. The paths of the Bureau and GAO had sharply diverged with respect to the management area. A Bureau staff member, commenting on the Bureau as having "backed away" from management improvement, put it this way:

> Kermit Gordon was strictly relaxed with respect to GAO audits of a management character. This attitude has been carried forward by subsequent directors.

Even before the announcement of the reorganization[42] plan establishing the Office of Management and Budget, President Nixon had evinced an interest in revitalizing the Budget Bureau's managerial efforts. The Presidential message accompanying the Plan said that the new Office represented "more than a mere change of name for the Bureau of the Budget. It represents a basic change in concept and emphasis, reflecting the broader management needs of the Office of the President. . . Improvement of Government organization, information and management systems will be a major function of the Office of Management and Budget. It will maintain a continuous review of the organizational structures and management processes of the Executive Branch, and recommend needed changes." However, the revitalization of OMB's management function tends to be inhibited by the dominance of the budgeting process within the Office. One writer dealing with this phenomenon comments: "With the departments, as within the Congress, the management component [of OMB] suffers from its association with the budgeting component, and from the universal antipathy toward the activities of the examiners."[43]

Countervailing developments in OMB-GAO relationships

The fact that Staats spent most of his professional career in the Bureau of the Budget and played such an important part in its leadership could cut two ways. On the one hand, this background afforded him contacts, insights, and understanding that could facilitate a much better accommodation between the GAO and OMB than had existed in the past with its predecessor. However, his background could impel persons in OMB -- either because of hypersensitivity or because of Congressional criticisms directed at it -- to feel that Staats has been reaching out for some of the tasks that he performed as Deputy Director of the Budget. OMB cannot be unmindful of the fact that Staats' intimate knowledge of its predecessor as well as his demonstrated ability to mobilize Congressional support make him a formidable competitor.

Furthermore, as is described in Chapter 9, both the Legislative Reorganization Act of 1970 and the Congressional

Budget and Impoundment Control Act of 1974 gave the GAO
responsibilities in connection with the budget process
which OMB might have felt intruded into its domain.   In
fact, the Budget Bureau reacted negatively in commenting
on a provision, that was later incorporated in the 1970
Act, for the Comptroller General to participate in the
development, establishment, and maintenance of a standard
data processing and information system for budgetary and
fiscal data for use of the Federal Government.   The Bureau
felt that there had been full cooperation with the Comptroller General in the past on such matters and that such
a statutory provision was not necessary.   Its more significant criticism of the provision was:

> . . . we have considerable doubt as to the
> wisdom of a provision which might inject the
> Comptroller General - an official of the
> legislative branch - directly into the bud-
> getary processes of the executive branch.[44]

In his comments on the bill, Staats sought to make
it clear that his interpretation of the provisions was
that they did not contemplate any overlap between the responsibilities that would be vested in the GAO and those
of the Bureau.   He construed the GAO's role as seeing that
the particular needs of Congress were met.[45]   However reassuring the Comptroller General may be, the realities
are that the GAO has become increasingly involved in Congressional evaluation of the budget proposals emanating
from the Executive Branch.   The Director of OMB and the
Secretary of the Treasury are now required by statute to
report to Congress annually on their plans for addressing
what the Comptroller General has identified and specified
as to the needs of committees and Members of Congress for
fiscal, budgetary, and program-related information contemplated by the Congressional Budget Act of 1974.[46]   It is
noteworthy that, in reporting on the progress toward the
implementation of the Congressional mandate, the Comptroller
General commented: ". . . we and the committees will have
to increase individual dealings with executive agencies."
After making appropriate reference to the "cooperative
spirit" of OMB and Treasury, the Comptroller General low-
ered the boom:

> However, we wish to specifically note that
> cooperative spirit between the two branches
> will not be sufficient, by itself, for the
> satisfactory achievement of the objective
> of improved information for the Congress.
> In our judgment, it will require large in-
> creases in the resources allocated to the
> tasks by central executive branch agencies,
> particularly OMB.[47]

The possibility of OMB being irked by such GAO criticisms may be increased by the fact that the Congressional Budget Office established by the 1974 Act could also make for defensiveness by OMB as to its prerogatives under the Executive budget concept.

THE CHANGING PATTERN OF GAO - EXECUTIVE BRANCH RELATIONS

The changes in GAO-Executive Branch relations need to be perceived in the context of the profound recasting which GAO's role has been undergoing. The more sharply defined image of GAO as a Congressional surrogate concerned with far more than audits as ordinarily understood inevitably impacts upon agency and even Presidential attitudes toward the Comptroller General. For that matter, the Comptroller General's increasing coverage of national issues has significant implications in terms of relation with not only the Executive departments and establishments but also the Chief Executive. These developments, in turn, must be viewed against the backdrop of the burgeoning resources which the Congress now has at its disposal to assist it in the analysis and evaluation of Executive Branch operations and proposals. The cumulative impact of the inquiries which these diverse and sometimes competing legislative agencies address to the Executive Branch can engender strain that will be particularly felt by the GAO as one of the more demanding agencies. The Commission on the Operation of the Senate identified the need for improved coherence and cooperation among the four Congressional support agencies;[48] progress in that direction would contribute to smoother GAO relations with the Executive Branch.

FOOTNOTES - Chapter 3

1. Civil Action No. 75-0551 U.S. District Court, District of Columbia, 1975.

2. House, Committee on Appropriations, Hearing Before a Subcommittee, Legislative Branch Appropriations for 1974, 93rd Congress, 1st Session, 1973, p. 475.

3. House, Committee on Appropriations, Hearings Before a Subcommittee, Department of Defense Appropriations for 1970, 91st Congress, 1st Session, 1969, Part 6, p. 389.

4. Address at Armed Forces Management Association Dinner, 1971.

5. House, Committee on Government Operations, Department of Health, Education and Welfare (Prevention and Detection of Fraud and Program Abuse, House Report 786, 94th Congress, 2nd Session, 1976, p. 5.

6. Section 113 (a).

7. Section 117 (a).

8. Commission on Organization of the Executive Branch of the Government, Report on Budget and Accounting (Washington, D.C.: United States Government Printing Office, 1955), pp. 59-60.

9. General Accounting Office, Internal Auditing in Federal Agencies, 1974, p. 1.

10. Ibid., pp. 4 and 5.

11. House, Committee on Government Operations, Survey of Selected Activities, Eighth Report, Part 1, Efficiency and Economy in Government, Department of Commerce, House of Representatives 456, 88th Congress, 2nd Session, 1964, p. 9.

12. General Accounting Office, GAO Views on Internal Auditing in the Federal Agencies (Washington, D.C.: U.S. Government Printing Office, 1970), p. 24.

13. Comptroller General Report, An Overview of Federal Internal Audit F6MSD-76-50, November 29, 1976.

14. Ibid., p. 5.

15. General Accounting Office, Policy and Procedures Manual for Guidance of Federal Agencies, Title 3, p. 100.

16. Letter from Comptroller General Elmer B. Staats to Dwight A. Ink, Assistant Director, Bureau of the Budget, February 9, 1970.

17. Walter Gellhorn, When Americans Complain (Cambridge: Harvard University Press, 1966), p. 120-121.

18. Public Law 94-505.

19. H.R. 8588, 95th Congress, 1st Session.

20. House Committee on Government Operations, Establishment of Inspector General in Certain Executive Departments and Agencies, House Report 95-584, 95th Congress, 1st Session, 1977.

21. Letter from Comptroller General Elmer B. Staats to Chairman Jack Brooks, House Committee on Government Operations, May 23, 1977.

22. House Committee on Appropriations, Hearing Before a Subcommittee, Legislative Branch Appropriations for 1977.

23. Pittsburgh Press, May 25, 1977.

24. Statement of William A. Medina, Assistant Secretary-Designate for Administration, Department of Housing and Urban Development Before the House Committee on Government Operations, Subcommittee on Intergovernmental Relations and Human Resources. May 24, 1977. See also Subcommittee Hearings, Establishment of Offices of Inspector General, 95th Congress, 1st Session, 1977.

25. Subcommittee Hearings, op. cit., p. 463.

26. An Overview of Federal Internal Audit, op. cit., pp. 18-19.

27. Letter from Chairman William L. Dawson, House Government Operations Committee to Comptroller General Joseph Campbell, February 9, 1959.

28. Letter from Comptroller General Joseph Campbell to Congressman William L. Dawson, June 30, 1959.

29. Letter from Comptroller General Joseph Campbell to
    Maurice Stans, Director, Bureau of the Budget,
    November 30, 1959.

30. Letter from Maurice Stans, Director, Bureau of the
    Budget, to Comptroller General Joseph Campbell,
    January 4, 1960.

31. "The Presidents," quoted letter "refers to President
    Eisenhower's letter of September 15, 1959, written
    in connection with his refusal to furnish the GAO
    certain International Cooperation Administration
    information. This is discussed in the next chapter.

32. Letter from Comptroller General Joseph Campbell to
    Maurice Stans, Director, Bureau of the Budget,
    January 18, 1960.

33. Letter from Chairman William L. Dawson, House Govern-
    ment Operations Committee, to Comptroller General
    Joseph Campbell, January 24, 1961.

34. Letter from Comptroller General Joseph Campbell to
    David Bell, Director, Bureau of the Budget, Feb-
    ruary 21, 1961.

35. Comptroller General Report, Review of Selected Acti-
    vities of the Bureau of the Budget, B-133209,
    June 1961.

36. Letter from Maurice Stans to Comptroller General
    Joseph Campbell, August 12, 1961.

37. Letter from David Bell, Director, Bureau of the Bud-
    get, to Chairman William L. Dawson, House Government
    Operations Committee, September 14, 1961.

38. Letter from Chairman William L. Dawson, House Govern-
    ment Operations Committee, to Comptroller General
    Joseph Campbell, August 18, 1961.

39. Letter from David Bell, Director, Bureau of the Bud-
    get, to Comptroller General Joseph Campbell, May
    8, 1962.

40. Letter from Comptroller General Joseph Campbell to
    David Bell, Director, Bureau of the Budget, July
    12, 1962.

41. Letter from David Bell, Director, Bureau of the Bud-
    get, to Comptroller General Joseph Campbell,
    December 12, 1962.

42. <u>Reorganization Plan No. 2 of 1970</u>.

43. Gary Bombardier, "The Managerial Function of OMB:
Intergovernmental Relations as a Test Case."
<u>Public Policy</u>, Vol. 23, No. 3 (Summer 1975), p. 317.

44. Letter from Wilfred H. Rommel, Assistant Director
for Legislative Reference, Bureau of the Budget,
to Chairman William L. Dawson, House Government
Operations Committee, April 2, 1969.

45. Letter from Comptroller General Elmer B. Staats to
Chairman William L. Dawson, House Government Operations Committee, February 20, 1969.

46. Public Law 93-344, Section 801.

47. Comptroller General Report, <u>Program on Improving
Fiscal, Budgetary, and Program-Related Information for the Congress</u>, PAD-76-64, August 30, 1976,
pp. 22-23.

48. <u>Toward a Modern Senate. Final Report of the Commission on the Operation of the Senate</u>, 94th Congress, 2nd Session, 1976, p. 60.

Chapter 4

COMPTROLLER GENERAL'S ACCESS TO INFORMATION[1]

The matter of access to information and records
is absolutely basic and fundamental to all state
audit; if executive departments are ever allowed to withhold or delay it on a plea of policy or interest, then the auditors might as well
assume that arbitrariness has become the rule
for the conduct of government, and accordingly
shut up their shop.[2]

THE BROAD IMPLICATIONS OF THE ACCESS ISSUE

The vital character of GAO access to information

Pivotal to the discharge of the Comptroller General's
audit responsibilities is access to information in agency
and contractors' files and records. Since access is the
sharp cutting edge of the audits, the keystone of GAO's
role, it is not surprising that the Comptroller General
is more and more prone to take up the cudgels whenever
such access is challenged. Section 313 of the Budget and
Accounting Act requires all departments and establishments
to furnish the Comptroller General such information as he
may require of them "regarding the powers, duties, activities, organization, financial transactions, and methods
of business of their respective offices." The Comptroller
General and his duly authorized personnel are given "access to and the right to examine any books, documents,
papers, or records of any such department or establishment"
for the purpose of securing such information. There are
numerous special statutory provisions applying to particular programs that provide for the Comptroller General's
access to documents and records.

The access which the independent audit agency has to
information needs to be viewed in both de jure and de facto
terms. However sweeping the statutory mandate,[3] its real
impact may be undermined significantly by negative agency
reactions coupled with the lack of effective means to implement such statutory requirements. While Congressional
support of GAO's demands can significantly reinforce the
Comptroller General's requests for information, they do
not necessarily assure agency compliance.

Extent of GAO access problems

Access cannot be considered entirely from the standpoint of whether GAO can ultimately obtain the desired information; the crucial factor is the relative ease and

promptness with which the data are furnished. Time-con-
suming negotiations involve a process of attrition that
may seriously impede GAO's efforts and make for excessive
demands upon staff time. Moreover, delays of this type
can detract from the timeliness of the report that is issued. A top GAO official pointed out that the access issue has assumed greater importance as GAO audits have become more far-reaching in nature.

Staats initially had been prone to minimize the access
problem and to at least present the facade of being sanguine
as to the satisfactory resolution of difficulties that did
arise. However, in his 1969 statement to the Senate Subcommittee on Executive Reorganization, the Comptroller General included a recital of Executive agency roadblocks to
GAO's obtaining information.[4] In his 1971 Annual Report,
he referred to GAO experiencing "increased difficulties
in obtaining access to agency information and documents
needed to carry out its responsibilities."[5] The Comptroller
General stated that these difficulties occurred principally
in relation to international matters and identified the
Departments of Defense and State as culprits. But he also
alluded to the refusal of the Federal Deposit Insurance
Corporation to permit GAO unrestricted access with the result that it was unable to "fully discharge its responsibilities for auditing" the corporation.[6] Shortly after the
annual report containing this complaint was presented to
the Congress, Staats found himself locking horns with the
Treasury Department, a long-time adversary, on an access
issue involving the Lockheed loan guarantee.

When he prepared his 1975 Report, the Comptroller General, apparently deeming it politic to minimize his access
difficulties, stated: "Most Federal agencies cooperate
satisfactorily with us."[7] Yet, only a few months after
the conclusion of the period covered by that report, the
Comptroller General submitted to a Senate Subcommittee "a
summary of some examples of the numerous and long outstanding problems GAO has had in obtaining records of Federal
agencies."[8] The fact that he was testifying in support of
legislation to strengthen his access authority impelled the
Comptroller General to depict the situation in much stronger
terms and to set aside the ambivalence he had been demonstrating.

GAO concept of its authority

GAO seems to have viewed its access authority in all-
embracing terms. It has gone so far as to say that the
policy enunciated in the statutes "does not admit the propriety of any restrictions on our legal authority other
than those specifically contained in law." This statement
is followed by the assertion that the right of unrestricted

116

access to needed records is based not only on laws enacted
by Congress but is inherent in the nature of the duties
and responsibilities of the GAO.[9] In reaffirming this
position, the Comptroller General contended that full access as he conceives it, is essential to the effective
discharge of the GAO role "as an oversight arm of the Congress."[10] It is important to be cognizant of the fact that
the unrestricted access to which GAO lays claim embraces
not only what might be considered the regular records of
agencies but also: (a) "the opinions, conclusions, and
recommendations of persons directly engaged in programs
that are an essential and integral part of operations,"
and (b) "agency internal audits and other evaluative studies."
This broad ambit together with GAO demands for documents of
a sensitive nature have inevitably evoked resistance, at
least on the part of more powerful and prestigious agencies.

GAO strategy in dealing with access problems

The manner in which GAO deals with specific confrontations on the access issue reflects a pragmatic approach.
The Comptroller General must, when a particular situation
arises, determine how far the matter should be pressed in
light of the stress and strain that will be engendered and
the significance of the rejection to the full exercise of
the Comptroller General's audit authority. The initial
GAO reaction is undoubtedly that of doing battle when confronted with a refusal of access to information that appears to be essential to the performance of the GAO's
functions. The Office can ill afford to be cut off from
data that are the lifeblood of meaningful analyses; but
it cannot be completely obdurate. One Department of Defense official said: "GAO negotiates like hell when they
are turned down on requests for information." The GAO
might, on occasion, find that it has overreached itself
and requested information that is not indispensable to the
discharge of its responsibilities.

In thinking of how firmly it should insist upon compliance with a particular request, GAO undoubtedly considers several factors: the relevance and importance of
the information being sought; the bargaining position of
the specific agency vis-a-vis GAO; Congressional and public interest in the subject which GAO is exploring; and
the support that GAO can expect from Congressional committees and/or individual Members. A factor which appears
to be looming larger in the Comptroller General's approach
to access problems is the cumulative effect which agency
refusals or delays have upon the general attitude of the
Executive Branch. This, together with increasing Congressional interest, as well as the post-Watergate thrust

for openness in government, are perhaps the major elements
in the more outspoken and firmer manner with which the
Comptroller General is currently dealing with the access
issue.

The judgment and restraint shown by GAO personnel
in demanding access to records have a profound effect on
the degree of antagonism or resistance that may be engendered. Indiscriminate or arbitrary demands for records
that do not appear relevant to the scope of the GAO's inquiry leave the impression that the auditors are engaged
in a fishing expedition or are overreaching themselves.
Illustrative of this reaction are the comments made by
one official:

> We have a minor problem with the GAO on one
> fund which is a non-appropriated fund and has
> special legislation. In fact, the legisla-
> tion provides that no other office of the
> Government, except the Secretary of the
> Treasury and the President may review the
> operations of this fund. The GAO has made
> a number of direct requests for information
> on it; they have been turned down by the
> Secretary. Yet continually the auditor as-
> signed there will try to make other inquir-
> ies back into the data they want on this
> particular fund. You can give them "E"
> for effort. . . they do that to us all the
> time.

A top GAO official observed: "Speaking frankly, I think
some of our auditors go too far." Yet attempting to define precise limits may circumscribe the audit efforts
and detract from their effectiveness.

Congressional implications of GAO access to information

Hovering in the background of the access problem is
the part that Congress plays in facilitating or impeding
GAO's obtaining information that it requests from agencies.
Refusing GAO access is not merely a challenge to that
agency but something of a rebuff to the Legislative Branch,
of which the GAO is a component.

Since Congress itself has experienced difficulties
in obtaining information from the Executive Branch, it
may, at least on occasion, not feel that it can do much
to help the GAO. However, where the GAO is handling a
specific assignment made by a Congressional committee and
where the committee has firmly expressed the determination
that the GAO be furnished the necessary information, the

agency would ordinarily be more receptive to requests. But, as is brought out in cases cited subsequently, even strong Congressional support of a GAO inquiry may not remove all roadblocks to the acquisition of the information which the GAO deems necessary.

An agency may be reluctant to accord GAO access to information because of the possibility that such material will ultimately wind up in the hands of the Congress as a whole or some of its committees or individual Members. Hence, even though an official may feel confident that the information would be handled discreetly and fairly by the GAO, he may fear that the Office -- willingly or not -- will serve as a vehicle for the transmittal of the information to Congress, where it may be used to embarrass or hamstring the agency. A Senator or Representative knowing that the GAO has certain information in its files may request that this information be made available to him. Or a Member may use the GAO as an intermediary for obtaining the information, feeling that there is a better chance of procuring it if the request comes from the GAO. Senator Margaret Chase Smith's use of the GAO to obtain a summary of "the Sam Phillips report" (relating to the Apollo disaster) prepared within NASA is an example of such a situation. The fact that GAO, as in this case, becomes a conduit for placing agency documents at the disposal of Congress complicates the access issue. The Comptroller General has pointed out that it would be difficult for the GAO to refuse a Congressional request for information that is physically in the hands of his agency. Yet, for the GAO to be placed in a "messenger" role does not comport with the stature that should characterize the Government's independent audit agency.

REASONS ADVANCED FOR DENIAL OF ACCESS

Executive privilege implications of GAO access

The doctrine of executive privilege (the Chief Executive's right to withhold information from the Congress and the courts), which Raoul Berger labeled as a "myth" in his monumental study[11] and which was so crucial in the Watergate saga, can be viewed as the fountainhead for agency refusals to furnish information to the GAO.

In discussing the 1960 Foreign Aid dispute, a former Legal Advisor to the Department of State said the issue as to the right of the President to withhold papers and records from the Congress had "been disputed since the failure of the St. Clair expedition in the very first years of the Republic, without ever developing a 'case' that was decided by, or even submitted to a court." Professor

Paul Freund commented: "The issue of executive privilege is one aspect of a reexamination by Congress of the larger subject of relations between Congress and the President."[12] This latter observation is particularly apposite to any study of the GAO in view of the fact that the Office is essentially an instrumentality of the Congress. The Nixon confrontations brought the issue into the judicial limelight.[13] The Supreme Court held in U.S. vs. Nixon that, while there is a presumptive privilege for Presidential communications, it is the judiciary and not the President that must, in each case, determine the applicability of executive privilege. This holding needs to be viewed in the context of the Court's concern with protecting the integrity of criminal justice by promoting full disclosure of all the facts within the framework of the rules of evidence. One writer comments that "it will be contained and regarded as an exceptional case in which the Court intervened because of the complicity of the executive in the issue and the likelihood of disability on his part to disinterestedly exercise executive privilege."[14]

The GAO attitude with respect to executive privilege was expressed some years ago by its General Counsel (now the Deputy Comptroller General) before a Congressional committee inquiring into the production of documents by NASA.

> Mr. Keller: . . . in the absence of a judicial ruling going to Section 313, and how it fits in with the doctrine of executive privilege, I feel that the General Accounting Office has a right under the law, under Section 313, to have access to any documents that the Comptroller General considers necessary in the performance of his duties.[15]

Prior to Watergate, there had been Presidential pronouncements that reflected a feeling on the part of the Chief Executives that the invoking of executive privilege is a serious step to be taken only on the basis of clearcut justification and subject to Presidential approval. Responding to an inquiry from Congressman John E. Moss, President Kennedy, on March 7, 1962, said: "Executive privilege can be invoked only by the President and will not be used without specific Presidential approval."[16] In his letter, President Kennedy assured the Congressman that his administration would cooperate to the fullest in obtaining the widest public accessibility to Governmental information. This was followed by President Johnson's statement "that the claim of 'executive privilege' would continue to be made only by the President."[17] Upon Nixon's assumption of the Presidency, Congressman Moss wrote him, pointing out the position taken by both Presi-

dents Kennedy and Johnson and expressing the hope that
President Nixon would "favorably consider the reaffirmation of the policy which provides, in essence, that the
claim of 'executive privilege' would be invoked only by
the President." In his reply of April 7, 1969,[18] President Nixon expressed the belief that the scope of executive privilege must be very narrowly construed and stated
that "under this Administration this privilege will not
be asserted without specific Presidential approval." The
President enclosed a copy of the memorandum he had issued
to the heads of Executive departments and agencies establishing a procedure that governed compliance with Congressional demands for information. In the memorandum,
he stated that executive privilege would not be used without specific Presidential approval and set up a procedure
governing the invocation of the privilege.

At first blush, these Presidential pronouncements
might appear to have limited resort to executive privilege
to very few cases and, in effect, assured Congress and,
in turn, the GAO of relatively ready access to any information desired by them. But it is not the relative frequency
with which the Chief Executive invokes executive privilege
that sets the stage for agency responsiveness to Congressional or GAO requests for more sensitive types of information. The crucial factor determining the climate for
such interplay between the Legislative and Executive
Branches -- at least insofar as the latter is concerned --
is the probability that the President will uphold agency
rejection of access when a truly critical situation arises.
The 1971 Foreign Aid controversy discussed later in this
chapter was a dramatic demonstration that, notwithstanding
Presidential expressions of amenability, the Chief Executive can be unyielding in refusing information. It is not
difficult for a Chief Executive to find a rationale for
denying requested data. In this instance, President Nixon
expressed concern that "unless privacy of preliminary exchange of views between personnel of the Executive Branch
can be maintained, the full frank and healthy expression
of opinion which is essential for the successful administration of government would be muted."[19]

Senator Ervin, in addressing the Senate on legislation
designed to strengthen GAO access, pointed out that Comptroller General Staats had differentiated between executive
privilege and agency privilege, whereby executive officials
refused to furnish particular records or documents which
they do not consider "appropriate for GAO review." The
Senator felt that he himself had experienced agency privilege when the Department of the Army refused his request
for certain documents regarding military surveillance of
airlines saying they would be of no use to the subcommittee
of which he was chairman.[20]

121

Denials of access to budgetary information

The Office of Management and Budget Circular A-10,
(Revised 11/12/76), states:

> The confidential nature of agency submissions,
> requests, recommendations, supporting materials
> and similar communications should be maintained,
> since these documents are an integral part of
> the decision-making process by which the Presi-
> dent resolves budget issues and develops recom-
> mendations to the Congress. Presidential bud-
> get decisions are not final until the budget it-
> self is transmitted to the Congress. Amendments
> to the budget and supplemental budget requests
> may also follow the transmittal of the budget.
> Budgetary material should not be disclosed in
> any form prior to transmittal by the President
> of the material to which it pertains. The head
> of each agency is responsible for preventing
> premature disclosures of this budgetary infor-
> mation.

Comptroller General Staats has pointed out that this
Circular has given rise to difficulties in connection with
requests for projections on future costs of programs. It
is his opinion that the agencies have misunderstood or
misinterpreted the intent of the Circular.[21] Whatever
the merits of the Comptroller General's criticisms, it
is evident that the OMB directive affords the agencies an
effective excuse for rejecting GAO informational requests that can be regarded as in any way impinging upon
the budgetary area. It can at least be surmised that
Executive Branch agencies take a cue from the Office of
Management and Budget as to how readily they should furnish information to the GAO. As was brought out in the
previous chapter, relations between the central budget
agency and the GAO have not been such as to establish a
climate most conducive to disclosure by Executive agencies. Symptomatic of the underlying OMB attitude are the
remarks of one of its former top officials:

> The difficulty was that persons would demand
> information from agencies without having the
> competence and maturity to analyze what they
> saw. . . After a few bitter experiences,
> the Executive Branch began to freeze up, to
> fend off approaches from the GAO, to exhibit
> all the usual signs of diminished confidence
> in the GAO.

The Comptroller General may assert that the agency compliance with the OMB directive violates the duty which Section 313 of the Budget and Accounting Act imposes upon all departments and establishments to furnish information to him. The agency or OMB can advance the counter-argument that to give the Comptroller General the information he requests would negate the concept of the Executive budget that is articulated in the Budget and Accounting Act, 1921, and which can reasonably be contended to be a basic feature of that legislation. The implications of the clash of viewpoints with respect to this particular facet of the access to information issue were brought out in the discussion of GAO relationships with OMB. The problem may become more acute as Congress seeks to make greater use not only of GAO but also the Congressional Budget Office as staff resources for assisting the Legislative Branch in connection with the budget process. Such utilization would underline the question as to how much of the budgetary materials compiled within the Executive Branch should be made available to the Congress and its supporting agencies.

The GAO was rebuffed when it requested copies of the agency responses to a letter of the Director of OMB concerning contracting-out of in-house functions. The letter was written pursuant to a directive from President Ford. OMB informed the Comptroller General that it had not yet presented the agency submissions to the President and that until the completion of the Chief Executive's review, "the dissemination of the agency proposals outside the Executive Branch would clearly be inappropriate." The Acting Director of OMB went on to say that "to his knowledge Section 313 has never been construed to authorize the Comptroller General access to agency recommendations and advice prior to Presidential action thereon."[22]

Internal agency documents

Closely tied in with the issue of executive privilege is the reluctance or resistance that agencies manifest with respect to providing the GAO with documents which they consider to be of a strictly internal character. This question was invoked in the Foreign Aid confrontation mentioned above; it was also raised in the Lockheed controversy discussed subsequently. Prior to these incidents, the Comptroller General told the Senate Subcommittee on Executive Reorganization that it is questionable whether withholding this type of information can be labeled as executive privilege: "In our opinion there is no way in which a specific line can be drawn as to information which should be regarded as 'internal' as against information which should be available to the Legislative Branch."[23]

Explaining their reluctance to make available to the GAO information which they considered to be strictly of an internal character, agencies mention the inhibiting effect that such availability may have upon the frank and full interchange of viewpoints within the organization. It is contended that the possibility of scrutiny by the GAO may well deter an employee or consultant from a candid expression of opinion. Agency sensitivity as to giving the GAO access to internal memoranda is intensified when such documents reflect conflicting viewpoints which might cause the outsider to raise questions concerning the ultimate decision or action that was taken. Still another factor is a consideration already alluded to, namely, the possibility of such internal documentation subsequently being turned over by the GAO to the Congress.

One agency official stated that his problem was not with the GAO seeing such internal memoranda but their publishing such materials in the GAO reports "particularly when they pick and choose among the divergent views." It was his contention that GAO picks out those internal memoranda supporting the conclusion reached by the GAO and ignores or makes no mention of contrary views set forth in other memoranda.

An agency executive said that he was not so much concerned with the GAO report itself as he was with what happened the next time that a scientist, an engineer, or another technician was asked to make a review for his agency. He felt that such an individual would be prone to ask: "Gee, how much privacy do I have to really express myself?" Another agency official said: "We are concerned about how responsibly the data obtained will be treated in total context of the agency operations. We have instances where specific pieces of paper -- individual pieces of paper -- they can be a trip report or a memorandum, are made the major basis for a particularly critical point in the report." An agency that had been most cooperative in making this type of information available to the GAO had an understanding with the GAO that any reference to other than the official departmental position should be cleared with the agency before being used.

Agency officials seem to agree that much depends upon the calibre of GAO personnel examining these internal documents and the judgment that they reflect in the utilization of such materials: "But it really gets down to GAO's ability to have the type of personnel on board that can measure up to the type of job they have to do. And, if they get a bookkeeping mentality for this, we're all in trouble if we go to complete disclosure." One official told of emphasizing to the GAO that his organization did

124

not expect to have internal documents with different
staff views played against each other in the GAO report.
"And we have emphasized that if they went to that we
would crack down real hard."

Agency clearance of reports, discussed separately
in this study, affords an opportunity for the agency to
protest to the GAO against what it deems to be the improper use or misinterpretation of the internal documents
made available to the GAO. If such reports are not submitted for clearance, as is frequently the case with respect to those prepared pursuant to Congressional requests, then the agency, of course, is deprived of the
chance to take exception before the report is issued.

Need for analysis of specific instances of agency refusal of·access

The issues that have arisen in connection with access
involve a number of variables: type of agency; nature of
the subject matter embraced by the GAO inquiry; personalities, whether it be the Comptroller General, Members
of Congress, or the career or political officials of the
Executive Branch; and the prevailing climate as to disclosure of public business. The impact of these variables
can be discerned only by an analysis -- such as follows --
of a cross section of access denials, as well as capitula-
tions, compromises, or acquiescences experienced by the GAO.
It has been previously noted that Comptroller General Staats
has resorted to a recital of access rebuffs in his advocacy
of legislation to buttress GAO capability to obtain information.

ACCESS CONFRONTATIONS WITH THE DEPARTMENT OF DEFENSE

The perennial negativism of DOD

The defense establishment has posed an especially sensitive area with respect to access to information. Yet the
magnitude of defense expenditures, together with the multiplicity, complexity, and importance of issues involved in
the management of these vast resources, make it all the
more urgent that the Comptroller General be in a position
to subject the military services to meaningful scrutiny.

The recurring disagreements between GAO and the Department of Defense and the individual military services
with respect to availability of information for examination
by the GAO have defied satisfactory resolution. Military
tradition is one factor, as for example, in the refusal to
permit the GAO to see Inspector General reports in their
entirety. Another aspect of DOD's stance is the sensitivity
of the military with respect to subjecting its decision-
making to outside scrutiny.

125

It might have been expected that the top civilians, especially those in the overall Department of Defense, would be more receptive to furnishing information to the GAO and that they would have some inhibiting effect on the negativistic attitude of the military. However, civilian officials within the Defense establishment seem prone to become allies of the professional military personnel in staving off the informational requests of GAO. The more critical and inquiring attitude that Congress is increasingly manifesting towards the defense establishment has engendered a climate that is significantly more conducive than what has existed heretofore to GAO's obtaining the information it requests.

Refusal of access to inspector general report -- a cause celebre

The issue with respect to GAO's access to DOD records reached a boiling point when in 1958 the Comptroller General was refused access to a survey which the Air Force Inspector General had made of the management of the Air Force Ballistics Missile Program. Comptroller General Campbell brought this rebuff to the attention of the House Committee on Government Operations; and, as a result, the Special Subcommittee on Government Information held hearings.[24]

Prior to these hearings, Secretary of the Air Force James H. Douglas, in replying on July 30, 1958 to the Comptroller General's request, said:

I firmly believe that the goal of objective self-criticism can be attained only if the Inspector General's organization has the assurance that its reports will, without exception, be kept within this Department. . . . The release of such reports to persons outside the Department would have a serious adverse effect on the effective administration of the Department.[25]

The Secretary, accordingly, rejected the Comptroller General's request but stated that he has asked that a summary of the findings of fact contained in the Inspector General's report be prepared and forwarded to the GAO. In a letter to the Chairman of the Special Subcommittee, Campbell contended that GAO could not discharge its statutory responsibilities without having access to reports resulting from such internal reviews.[26] In support of his contention, the Comptroller General said that the subjects covered in the report denied to the GAO presented internal management evaluations which were clearly a part of "internal

126

audit and control" that the Accounting and Auditing Act of 1950 specifically requires the Comptroller General to consider in the conduct of his audits. But Secretary Douglas was unbending. When testifying before the Sub-committee, Douglas expressed the opinion that the Department of Defense regulation which says that such reports will not be released except with the Secretary's approval "rests solely for its validity on executive privilege."[27]

Eisenhower's involvement in the issue of GAO access to inspector general reports

At a press conference on November 5, 1958, President Eisenhower was questioned with respect to the Department of Defense and Air Force refusal to make reports available to the GAO. Eisenhower, apparently unaware of all the implications of the question, observed that his interrogator was "obviously talking about some special thing that I would have to study before I could make -- give an answer." Then, although he had first expressed an appropriate cautionary note, the President went on to say: "I have stated this time and time again: I believe that every investigating committee of the Congress, every auditing office, like the GAO, should always have an opportunity to see official records if the security of our country is not involved."[28] The reporter directed Eisenhower's attention to the fact that the refusal of access had been made under executive privilege, but the President refused to comment further.

Congressman Clare E. Hoffman of Michigan, who espoused the Department of Defense cause, was understandably upset by the implications of President Eisenhower's remarks and wrote him to inquire whether the President meant to imply "that the complete text of Inspector General reports, including recommendations, be made available to Congress and the General Accounting Office."[29]

The President replied immediately, manifestly now anxious to show complete acquiescence in the stand taken by the Air Force. Having reconsidered the position that he had taken only the week before, the President expressed an entirely different approach to the problem:

> And in my judgment the public interest is not necessarily served by divulging the advice, suggestions or recommendations which sub-ordinate employees periodically make to their superiors. In this connection, recommendations of inspectors general have been a most useful advisory tool in administering the military departments; and historically,

recommendations and other advisory matter
in such reports have not been released. I
think this practice is the correct one[30] and
is in the best interest of the Nation.

The Presidential letter threw the Subcommittee hearing
into something of a tailspin, and it adjourned almost immediately after Hoffman read the correspondence between
himself and President Eisenhower. The Committee on Government Operations, in its report dealing with this matter, sharply criticized the position taken by the Air Force.[31]

Congressional protestations on inspector general issue of no avail

Obviously, rejection of a GAO request tends to be a
challenge to the prerogatives of Congress, which can readily
be drawn by such a refusal into a confrontation with the
Executive Branch. The Air Force incident has been cited
by Professor Berger as illustrating "the lengths to which
the claim of privilege has been pushed and the frivolous
grounds on which disobedience of a statute has been based,
if indeed one ground more than another can be deemed to
extenuate the disobedience."[32] Yet, however unyielding the
position of the defense establishment and however loud
the Congressional outcries, the resolution of the issue
as to GAO access to Inspector General reports has remained
on dead center.

At about the same time as the embroilment between the
Air Force and the GAO, the Navy refused to make available
to the GAO an "uncensored" version of a procurement review
report evaluating the work of the Military Sea Transportation Service.[33] Although the report was not one prepared
by the Inspector General, the Navy claimed that it came
within the purview of the Defense Department restriction
because it was an "Inspector General type of report."[34]
In support of the Navy's refusal, the General Counsel of
the Navy said:

In any event, I think there should be no doubt
about our legal authority for not disclosing
this advisory material on occasion. This
authority is the well-known executive privilege, which is founded upon the Constitution
and its doctrine of separation of powers.[35]

The House Government Operations Committee inveighed
against what it termed "administrative arrogance" in claiming a power "above the duly enacted laws, which can be
used to cover up waste, inefficiency -- or worse."[36] But
such bombastic statements have apparently made little impact.

Staats' abortive efforts to obtain greater access to DOD information

Shortly after assuming office, Comptroller General
Staats sought to overcome the DOD resistance that had bedeviled his predecessor. Writing to Deputy Secretary of
Defense Cyrus Vance, Staats identified two types of access
problems that GAO had in the Defense Department:

1. Ready access to reports prepared on examinations made by the Inspectors General or by
   other staff organizations who render what
   are referred to as "Inspector General-type"
   reports.

2. Ready access to uncensored files of the
   Department.[37]

The Comptroller General, in requesting reconsideration of
DOD's stance, pointed out that Inspector General reports
had broadened tremendously in scope so that they might
even include management surveys. It was Staats' contention that the line of demarcation between the reports of
an Inspector General and those of internal auditors was
not very clear and that "the problem reduces itself to
a decision to withhold reports depending upon what organizational unit performed the study rather than upon the
nature of the subject matter." He was referring to the
fact that the Comptroller General has been given access
to internal audit reports. As to access to uncensored
departmental files, the Comptroller General stated that
the withholding of opinions, conclusions, and recommendations had been extended by operating personnel to include
correspondence in the official files so that the GAO was
not permitted to use such sources as a procurement file
until it had been screened and there had been removed
from it what was considered to contain opinions, conclusions, or recommendations.

Staats subsequently received a letter from Paul Nitze,
who had succeeded Vance. Nitze stated that the Department
of Defense policy which had last been restated in 1958 em-
bodied "many years of experience in seeking to reach a
mutual accommodation with the General Accounting Office
. . . one that strikes a balance between the auditor's
needs for the facts to enable him to discharge his responsibilities and our own needs for orderly and effective
management."[38] The Undersecretary drew a distinction between
audit and inspection reports on the basis of the auditor
existing entirely apart from the commander whereas the inspector "is an extension of the commander's authority and
stands in a subordinate-superior relationship."

As to the Comptroller General's request for "ready access to uncensored files of the Department," Nitze stated that this posed very difficult problems; and he pointed out the very sensitive character of materials in the files of the Defense Department. Then, apparently seeking to show some effort to effect a reconciliation of viewpoints between the two agencies, Nitze said: "In short, while I would consider improper a request for a 'fishing expedition' through raw files, I do not believe that we should insist on exact document identification; rather, a rule of reason is called for, between these extremes."

GAO's access difficulties in connection with F-111 review

Undersecretary Nitze, in his letter to Staats, referred to such special situations as the F-111 review and stated that in such cases "the door is always open for arrangements to fit the needs of a particular case." This statement would imply that DOD and GAO had been able to work out an accommodation that afforded the Comptroller General's representatives the access to information they deemed necessary for the purpose of their studies. Yet GAO experienced many trials and tribulations in seeking the necessary data. The GAO's analyses in connection with the F-111 (TFX) are discussed in Chapter 8 dealing with the GAO's role in procurement.

Following a request in 1963 by Senator McClellan, the GAO attempted to obtain "the cost estimates and related cost data actually used by the Secretary in reaching his decision to award the TFX contract to General Dynamics." Reporting that these efforts were completely fruitless, Comptroller General Campbell said "both Secretary McNamara and Secretary Zuckert stated to our representatives that the conclusions reached by them were on the basis of their judgment rather than on independent cost studies."[39] A GAO representative testified that some of the records which had been prepared at the time the initial Air Force estimate was assembled, were destroyed "in accordance with their normal procedures."[40] In its subsequent investigative work, the GAO ran into other access problems.

On August 15, 1966, Senator McClellan requested the GAO to assist his Subcommittee in securing full and accurate information on seven specific items concerning the F-111 as well as obtaining "any and all other information pertinent to the inquiry being pursued by the Subcommittee and which will be of assistance to it in resolving and reporting to the Congress on issues involved." Apparently mindful of some of the experiences that GAO had in dealing with the Department of Defense, Senator McClellan said in his letter: "Should any difficulty be experienced in developing or obtaining this information from the Department of Defense or its contractors, we would appreciate your reporting this promptly to the Subcommittee."[41] He attached a copy of the letter he had addressed to the Secretary of Defense the same day requesting his "personal and official cooperation" in the GAO study and specifically asking him to direct the Secretaries of the Air Force and the Navy and their subordinates to furnish the information deemed necessary by the Comptroller General.

According to the GAO representative, the DOD directives, ostensibly designed to implement GAO access, created an atmosphere of fear and caution on the part of the Defense personnel involved in the F-111 work. He stated that every piece of paper desired by the GAO required a formal request and the submission of the document through channels. The McClellan Subcommittee was apprised of these developments, and the Senator wrote Secretary McNamara concerning the difficulties that were being encountered. Senator McClellan, citing the experience of the Subcommittee's own staff, said: "As many as three officials were assigned as observers for all interviews. Freedom of discussion disappeared, and the persons interviewed were obviously inhibited and guarded in their responses."[42] According to the GAO investigator, Senator McClellan's intervention "did no good at all. Matters got worse and are still that way; I ran into these same conditions just yesterday."

GAO's continuing access difficulties in the defense area

Whether it be DOD or the Department of State, Staats' efforts to obtain what might be considered sensitive information concerning defense matters continue, from time to time, to be repeated. In 1971, the State Department refused GAO requests for records relating to U.S. occupation costs in Berlin.[43] Permission to visit Vietnam to observe distribution of U.S. military equipment to Thai and Korean troops was denied; furthermore, the Departments of State and Defense sent messages stating that GAO representatives should be discouraged from consulting host country officials or agencies.[44]

In seeking to respond to a request by Senator Proxmire -- in his capacity as Chairman of the Senate Subcommittee on Priorities and Economy in Government -- for a comprehensive review of military airlift requirements, the GAO requested access to the Joint Strategic Capabilities Plan. GAO had been apprised by Air Force officials that review of this plan was essential to its work. Although representatives of the Joint Chiefs of Staff agreed that access to the Plan was essential to the analysis the

131

Senator had requested, the representatives "reiterated their policy not to grant access to the plan outside the military." Whereupon, GAO terminated its work on the request, in which Senator McClellan was also interested.[45]

The GAO inquiry into the seizure of the Mayaguez in 1975 and the subsequent diplomatic and military efforts to secure its release patently involved highly delicate subject matter. The GAO reported that it "had been restricted by the executive branch from analyzing the decision-making process involved in the management of this crisis and, consequently, our review was basically limited to an analysis of the implementation of the decisions which were made."[46]

The Comptroller General has become more critical and articulate concerning refusals to furnish defense-related information requested by the GAO. The inquiring and critical attitudes of Congress and the public with respect to the Nation's defense policies and programs and their implementation make it opportune for the GAO to flex its muscles in the pursuit of information it considers essential to its reviews in the defense area.

GAO EXCLUSION FROM THE INTELLIGENCE COMMUNITY

Comptroller General Staats, explaining GAO reluctance to initiate reviews of intelligence operations, cited limited legal authority;[47] this factor includes instances where monies are accounted for solely on certification by the head of an agency. Staats stated that there are also "serious practical considerations which further inhibit our ability to perform meaningful reviews" such as the problem of obtaining special security clearances; the difficulty of developing acceptable arrangements for reporting GAO findings and conclusions on such sensitive subject matter; and "the restrictive policy established to maintain security by the intelligence agencies." However, the disclosures of questionable practices on the part of the intelligence community and a much firmer and inquiring attitude on the part of Congress have undoubtedly strengthened GAO's position vis-a-vis intelligence agencies.[48]

GAO's capitulation to the CIA access denial

The Central Intelligence Agency presents a particularly interesting study of the dilemma that confronts the GAO when it impinges on the intelligence function. CIA immunity from meaningful audit is based on the type of special statutory provision mentioned by Staats:

132

The sums made available to the Agency may be
expended without regard to the provisions of
law and regulations pertaining to the expenditure of Government funds; and for objects
of a confidential, extraordinary, or emergency nature, such expenditures to be accounted
for solely on the certificate of the Director
and every certificate shall be deemed a sufficient voucher for the amount therein certified.[49]

An official of CIA estimated that this clause removed
from GAO's purview 45 to 50 per cent of the total agency
expenditures, with the agency itself determining which
expenditures justified special treatment areas.

At first, GAO accommodated itself to this dichotomy,
but then found itself in a quandary when it adopted the
comprehensive audit approach, which was hardly compatible
with the relatively truncated audit that it had been making
of the CIA. This dilemma impelled Comptroller General
Campbell to decide in 1959 that it would be desirable to
expand its CIA audit work.[50] Some months later, Allen W.
Dulles, Director of the CIA, wrote the Comptroller General
expressing the belief that the GAO could expand its audit
activities "in a considerable portion of the Agency" but
stating that "we should reach agreement on certain fundamental aspects." Having given some evidence of a desire
to cooperate with the GAO, Dulles proceeded to delimit the
scope of GAO's review so as to make it acceptable to CIA.
Directing the Comptroller General's attention to Section 8
quoted above, Dulles said:

A comprehensive audit of the sort now conducted
by the General Accounting Office in other agencies, if applied to our so-called vouchered expenditures, would necessarily reach into the
confidential operations which they support and
which are protected by my special authority under Section 8 of the Act. In these instances,
therefore, the comprehensive audit would have
to be limited so as to remain outside the area
of sensitive security operations.[51]

Replying to Dulles' letter, Campbell stated that it
seemed possible for the GAO to expand its CIA audit into
a considerable part of the agency's activities, even
though its reviews would be outside the area of sensitive
security operations. However, the Comptroller General
went on to say that "in the event it appears after a
trial period that our reviews are limited to such an extent that we cannot effectively and constructively accom-

plish any worthwhile objectives, we will have to consider whether the audit should be continued."[52]

In 1961, Campbell concluded that the restrictions imposed upon GAO's audit precluded access sufficient "to make comprehensive reviews on a continuing basis that would produce evaluations helpful to the Congress." Hence, the GAO planned to discontinue its audit of CIA activities.[53] Importuned by both Dulles[54] and Chairman Carl Vinson of the House Committee on Armed Services,[55] Campbell continued the GAO's "limited program"[56] in CIA. But, in 1962, shortly after John McCone, Dulles' successor, called off a conference with the Comptroller General, Campbell informed Congressman Vinson that GAO still felt that "under existing security restrictions on our audit of CIA activities we do not have sufficient access to effectively accomplish any worthwhile audit objectives at CIA on a continuing basis."[57] By this time, Congressman Vinson was apparently reconciled to the cessation of GAO efforts in connection with the CIA. In responding to Campbell's letter, Vinson expressed the belief that the restrictions the GAO met in its audits of CIA were necessary for the proper performance of CIA's intelligence activities and should be maintained. Vinson said that he would accept the Comptroller General's conclusion that he should withdraw from further audit activities in CIA.[58]

The Comptroller General obviously could not evoke strong support from Congress in this confrontation with CIA. The agency, sensing this Congressional attitude, became all the more adamant in its refusal to permit the GAO to expand the scope of its audits.

Justice Department rebuff to GAO in its study of FBI domestic intelligence operations

Attorney General Edward H. Levi proved to be intransigent in his rejection of the procedures proposed by GAO for verifying the accuracy of information which the FBI provided it in connection with the review of the Bureau's domestic intelligence operations.[59] Levi's apparent underlying rationale was that "investigative material in the possession of the government has traditionally occupied a special status in our legal system and has been accorded careful protection against unnecessary dissemination." The Attorney General further stated: "In short, it is my view of the law that powers implicit in GAO's charter do not include the examination of investigative files by non-law enforcement personnel."[60] The request of Chairman Rodino of the House Judiciary Committee that Levi reconsider his rejection of GAO's verification proposal was of no avail, and the Comptroller

General, in submitting his report, therefore, stated that
"we cannot adequately assure the Committee and the Congress
that our findings are complete."

An important postscript to this incident is the fact
that the Justice Department ultimately receded from this
negativistic stance on GAO access to FBI files after "more
than seven months of secret negotiations involving Kelley
[FBI Director], Comptroller General Staats, head of the GAO[61]
Attorney General Edward H. Levi and congressional leaders."
The mounting attacks upon the secretiveness that had en-
veloped the FBI could not be resisted for long, and the Attorney General capitulated albeit that -- as reported by the
Washington Post -- the Comptroller General had to agree to
various compromises "that saw the GAO give up its demand
for unrestricted access to FBI records and the bureau concede the principle of outside review." In light of earlier references to Congressional use of the GAO as a vehicle to "extract information" from the Executive Branch,
it is very significant that the GAO was reported as pro-
mising not to "serve as a conduit for congressional committees
or members seeking to obtain FBI files or documents."[62]

FOREIGN AID CONTROVERSIES OF 1960
AND 1971 - PANDORA'S BOXES

The Foreign Aid program sparked two bitter controversies -- one involving President Eisenhower and the other
President Nixon -- in connection with Legislative Branch access to executive agency information. Both cases were essentially confrontations between the Congress and the Executive Branch, into which the Comptroller General was drawn.

Inception of the 1960 dispute

Toward the end of the Eisenhower regime, the GAO found
itself enmeshed in a dispute resulting from a Congressional
subcommittee seeking to use GAO as a medium for effecting
compliance with Congressional requests for documents. Before the battle was over, both the President and Attorney
General were drawn in; the result was something of a debacle
for the GAO.

On October 31, 1960, Congressman Porter Hardy, Jr., as
Chairman of the Foreign Operations and Monetary Affairs Subcommittee of the House Committee on Government Operations
had sent a letter to Secretary of State Christian A. Herter,
requesting that he furnish the Subcommittee copies of documents relating to the U.S. Aid program in countries included
in an attached list, which was designated as secret. Shortly
thereafter, Congressman Hardy wrote the Comptroller General,
enclosing a copy of a letter to the Secretary of State and

relating that he had asked the Deputy Secretary for
Congressional Relations, to make the documents available
no later than November 14.[63] The requested documents included investigative files on three individuals and Inspector General reports on seven South American countries.
Hardy further told Campbell that the Subcommittee had met
the previous day to receive the documents from the Inspector General's office but the materials had not been
produced. He then went on to refer to a statutory provision that materials relating

> "to the operation or activities of the Office
> of Inspector General and Comptroller shall be
> furnished to the General Accounting Office and
> to any committee of the Congress, or any duly
> authorized subcommittee thereof, charged with
> considering legislation or appropriation for,
> or expenditures of, such Office upon request
> of the General Accounting Office or such com-
> mittee or subcommittee as the case may be."

The same day, moving with marked alacrity or perhaps
having been forewarned by Congressman Hardy, the Comptroller
General wrote the Secretary of State calling his attention
to the statutory requirements and winding up his letter
with something of an ultimatum as to possible cutting off
of funds available for the Office of the Inspector General
and Comptroller.[64]

Comptroller General invokes sanctions on basis of State Department refusal

Secretary of State Herter, in his reply to Campbell,
stated that the Office of Inspector General and Comptroller
had prepared only one evaluation report and that the facts
set forth in this report had been furnished to the Subcommittee on November 14. However, the Subcommittee had
been informed that, pursuant to Presidential policy previously expressed, the recommendations contained in the
report could not be furnished.[65] As to the investigative
material, Secretary Herter said:

> It is the position of this Department, in keep-
> ing with basic Executive Branch policy, that in-
> vestigative files and reports are confidential
> documents of the Executive Branch of the Govern-
> ment and that Congressional or public access to
> them is not in the public interest. . . . As the
> Subcommittee was informed on November 14, the
> specific request discussed above was being taken
> up with the President. The President subse-
> quently approved this Department's withholding
> the investigative materials in question.

In the closing paragraph of his letter, Secretary Herter informed the Comptroller General that the State Department was of the view that the statutory provision cited by Campbell did not provide for cut-off funds for expenses of the Office of the Inspector General and Comptroller upon failure to furnish the Subcommittee the information requested. He enclosed a memorandum setting forth the reasons for this position.

The Comptroller General counterblasted with a lengthy letter setting forth the legal reasoning in support of the contention that the statutes did provide for the cut-off of funds and presenting the Secretary with the warning that "unless the documents are furnished by December 9, 1960, program funds will no longer be available for expenses of the Office of the Inspector General and Comptroller, and any such use of program funds after that date will be disallowed by this Office."[66] Probably with one eye directed at the Congress, Campbell dismissed the constitutional issues raised by the Secretary of State with the comment:

> . . . we would not be justified in failing to carry out a statute enacted by the Congress in order to avoid the raising of a constitutional issue. The question of the constitutionality of a statute is for decision by the courts rather than by this Office.

Campbell sent copies of his letter to the President, Budget Director, Secretary of the Treasury, and the chairmen of various Congressional committees.

The following day, Gerald D. Morgan, Deputy Assistant to the President, requested the Attorney General for his opinion as the Comptroller General's action.[67] The President, in the meantime, had issued a certificate forbidding the furnishing of the documents that had been requested. Eisenhower stated that such certification was made pursuant to a statutory provision which the Comptroller General had contended did not apply to requests for information relating to the operation of the Office of the Inspector General and Comptroller. On December 13, the Comptroller General informed the Secretary of State that he understood that the documents requested had not been furnished and that he was, therefore, advising him "that mutual security program funds are not available to liquidate obligations incurred after December 9, 1960, with respect to operations of the Office of the Inspector General and Comptroller and any such payments made will be disallowed by this Office."

The President intervenes with Attorney General's support

137

In an opinion dated December 19, 1960, Attorney General Rogers ruled that the Comptroller General's interpretation of the statutory provision in question was erroneous insofar as he deemed that it operated to cut off the funds in question.[68] Rogers based his ruling upon (a) the Presidential authority to determine when it is not in the public interest to disclose to Congress information of the Executive Branch and (b) the constitutional doctrine of the separation of powers. The Attorney General felt that the Constitution precluded "any indirect encroachment by Congress upon this authority of the President through resort to conditions attached to appropriations" such as the Comptroller General was relying upon. This ruling is particularly interesting in light of the current sharpening differences between the two branches of government.

Armed with the opinion from the Attorney General, President Eisenhower issued instructions to the Secretaries of State and Treasury which directed that, until the end of President Eisenhower's term of office on January 20, 1961, vouchers might be certified and paid covering the expenses of the Office of Inspector General and Comptroller out of mutual security program funds as theretofore.[69]

Battle ended with change in administration

An internal GAO memorandum reports that Congressman Hardy received a telegram from President-elect Kennedy which was followed by a phone call from Dean Rusk concerning this matter. Kennedy and Rusk, according to the memorandum, requested that the new Administration be allowed a short period of time after January 20, 1961 to go into the problem and try to work out a satisfactory solution with the Subcommittee. GAO apparently advised the counsel for the Subcommittee that compliance with this request would not complicate the GAO's position. Chairman Hardy wrote Rusk who, of course, had not yet assumed the Office of Secretary of State, stating that request for the documents would be withdrawn temporarily, but that this action was taken "without prejudice to the rights of either the Executive or Legislative Branch."[70] The Comptroller General then informed the Secretary of State that, in light of the withdrawal of the Subcommittee's request, the GAO would have no objection to the use of mutual security funds to liquidate obligations for the Office of the Inspector General and Comptroller incurred on and after January 20, 1961. He reserved judgment on transactions prior to January 20.[71]

The Comptroller General had been placed in the unenviable position of having to serve as an intermediary in a very critical clash between the Executive and Legisla-

tive Branches. The Presidency came off best in this controversy; and Campbell had to stage a retreat that did
not add to the stature of his Office. Several months
later, the Comptroller General, apparently seeking to
salvage whatever he could from this disconcerting incident, wrote the Secretary of State expressing disagreement with the opinion of the Attorney General and voicing
the view that it is the responsibility of the GAO to carry
out Congressional mandate unless a court of competent juris-[72]
diction has determined that mandate to be unconstitutional.
At the same time the Comptroller General said:

> . . . we do not regard the opinion of the for-
> mer President, whether based on an advisory
> opinion of the former Attorney General or
> otherwise, as affecting the action which the
> General Accounting Office is authorized to
> take in settling the accounts of the depart-
> ments, which action is by law final and con-
> clusive on the Executive establishment.

Then, in order to dispose of the loose ends that had
been left as a result of his pronouncements, the Comptroller
General announced that on the basis of the "workable arrangement" entered into between the Department of State and
the Subcommittee on Foreign Operations and Monetary Affairs,
his Office would take no further action with respect to the
period prior to January 20, 1961, during which mutual security program funds were utilized "in contravention of our
prior instructions."

A writer, commenting on President Kennedy's handling
of the matter said:

> In the end, and after intricate maneuvering,
> he did not join issue on the same ground as
> President Eisenhower. His situation, as well
> as his attitude toward Congress, was differ-
> ent. An arrangement was worked out whereby
> the Subcommittee Chairman, but not its mem-
> bers, could see the disputed papers under
> limited and controlled conditions. Soon
> afterward, Congressman Hardy went to another[73]
> subcommittee, and the battle went unrenewed.

The 1971 controversy's origin - DOD refusal of Senate Committee requests for information

The foreign aid access dispute which came to a head
in 1971 apparently began in 1969 when Senator Fulbright,
as Chairman of the Senate Committee on Foreign Relations,
wrote Secretary of Defense Laird concerning the Defense

Department's refusal to give GAO personnel "access to certain planning information and other documents concerning the training" of foreign military personnel under the military assistance program.[74] The item which proved to be critical was the Five Year Plan for the program, which Laird categorized as "a staff study, an entirely tentative planning document at the staff level." The Secretary stated that he seriously doubted that the release of the entire plan would be in the public interest.[75]

The request of the Foreign Relations Committee was renewed in 1971, and Fulbright took the opportunity to request that either the Committee be furnished with several documents, including the Five Year Plan, "or that the President formally invoke executive privilege as authority to withhold them." The Senator cited other examples of GAO inability to obtain necessary information from the Defense Department and observed that the refusal of departments and agencies to give the GAO access is the same as denying that information to the Congress.

Senate invokes sanction with backing of GAO

When Laird failed to respond, the Foreign Relations Committee voted on July 28, 1971 to suspend all funds for the foreign military assistance program thirty-five days from that date unless the Secretary complied with its request.[76] The sanction invoked by the Committee was a proviso in the Foreign Assistance Act of 1971 stipulating that funds made available under that Act should not be used for any country, project, or activity if within 35 days an agency had not supplied to the GAO or any appropriate Congressional committee a document requested with respect to the administration of such assistance. The statute made an exception if the President certified that he had forbidden the furnishing of the requested material and gave his reason for so doing.

Laird retorted with the statement that the Defense Department had no document or documents which constituted a Five Year Plan for the program. Fulbright then called upon the Comptroller General for his views as to the Committee's invocation of the provision for the suspension of funds. Staats ruled that the 35-day period commenced on July 28 and that all funds for the Military Assistance Program would cease to be available at the expiration of that period unless the material in question was furnished or the President made the appropriate certification.[77] Whereupon, the Chief Executive directed the Secretaries of State and Defense not to make available to the Congress the planning data that the Foreign Relations Committee had been seeking.

While this confrontation was reaching its zenith, the
Senate Appropriations Subcommittee on Foreign Operations,
chaired by Senator Proxmire, had also expressed concern
over the rebuffs which the GAO had experienced in requesting information from the Defense and State Departments.
Citing a "bill of particulars" set forth in a statement
by the Director of GAO's International Division, Proxmire
said it portrayed "an almost unbelievable series of incidents in which these two giant departments engaged in a
game of cat and mouse with General Accounting Office in-
vestigators."[78]

The heated exchange with the Defense Department afforded Fulbright a springboard for releasing a lengthy,
detailed memorandum which the GAO had prepared in response
to his request that it compile a list of recent, significant instances in which the Office had been denied access
to Executive Branch records or materials.[79]

The Congressional hostility engendered by the stance
taken by the Defense and State Departments manifestly
posed a threat to the pending appropriation for foreign
aid. Secretary Rogers undertook to placate the Senatorial
critics by assuring Senators Proxmire and McGee "that it
would be 'reasonable' for the Administration to supply
Congress with rough projections on economic and military
aid in the next five years."[80]

INTERNAL REVENUE SERVICE REFUSAL OF
ACCESS - GAO THE FINAL VICTOR

An access to information controversy which had rankled
the Comptroller General for many years revolved around the
refusal of the Internal Revenue Service to give the GAO[81]
access to Federal tax returns and related IRS records.
The issue was brought into focus by a GAO request in 1966
for information relative to state income tax refunds.
The GAO was apparently seeking to review the Service's
controls and procedures in connection with taxpayer reporting of such refunds on Federal tax returns. In furnishing
this information, the Commissioner said: "We are pleased
to furnish the following information requested in your
memorandum which does not fall within the categories of
information precluded from disclosure." This was not the
type of response for which the GAO had hoped; and it set
off a clash of viewpoints which was not finally resolved
until late in 1977. The GAO-IRS dispute ultimately involved not only the tax returns and IRS records but also
the Bureau of Alcohol, Tobacco, and Firearms. As to the
latter, the GAO stated that "in accordance with the precedent set up by the Internal Revenue Service the Bureau
. . . does not permit GAO access to records relating to

141

the administration of laws contained in the Internal
Revenue Code on distilled spirits, tobacco products,
and certain firearms."[82]

Ostensible agreement quickly disappeared and the issue remained

On November 16, 1967, Comptroller General Staats
wrote Commissioner Sheldon Cohen to confirm an understanding that the two officials had reached concerning GAO's
access to IRS records and information.[83] Commissioner
Cohen, replying to Staats' letter, said that he felt that
Staats had "captured well the substance and the spirit of
our discussion."[84] However, this apparent resolution of
the access problem quickly vanished into thin air when
Cohen directed Staats' attention to the opinion of the
Bureau's Chief Counsel holding that administration of the
Internal Revenue Code by the Commissioner "is not subject
to review by the Comptroller General either specifically
or in general."[85]

When the General Counsel of GAO expressed disagreement with the position taken by IRS,[86] the Chief Counsel
of the Service prepared a lengthy opinion in which he conceded that not all matters concerning the administration
of the Internal Revenue Service are outside the scope of
GAO activity. This opinion observed that the Service had
furnished or would furnish information to the GAO on such
matters as payment of personnel, purchase of supplies,
rental and use of office space, the accounting for money
received and "general housekeeping details which concern
every Federal department or agency." The Chief Counsel
pointed out that there was an obvious distinction between
consideration of such matters and the analysis of the
income reporting practices of the taxpayers which the
GAO had proposed to conduct.[87] Armed with this opinion,
Commissioner Cohen wrote Staats: "Thus, federal tax returns and related records can be made available to you
only where the matter officially before GAO does not involve administration of those laws."[88]

Treasury continued to be adamant in resisting what
it considered to be GAO encroachments upon its prerogatives. In turn, Staats reacted with tenacity to this and
other Treasury refusals of access such as that in connection with the Lockheed loan guarantee discussed in the
next section. Late in 1976, GAO issued a report entitled
"How the Internal Revenue Service Selects Individual Income Tax Returns for Audit,"[89] that perhaps reflected some
softening in Treasury's position.

Staats' perseverance finally paid off. A modest

first step taken in the form of an amendment to the Tax
Reform Act of 1976 was followed by the 1977 enactment of
clarifying legislation authorizing the Comptroller General
to conduct audits of the IRS and the Bureau of Alcohol,
Tobacco and Firearms.[90]   The GAO is given access to tax
returns and information in connection with these audits --
as provided in the 1976 Act -- but the Joint Committee on
Taxation may, by a two-thirds vote, disapprove such an
audit within 30 days after receiving notice that an audit
is to be undertaken. The Comptroller General expressed
the belief that this measure would "finally resolve the
long-standing conflict between our Office and the IRS
and ATF as to our authority and access to records."[91]

LOCKHEED LOAN GUARANTEE IMPASSE - AN-
OTHER TREASURY REBUFF TO GAO

GAO's trials and tribulations in obtaining information
from the Executive Branch came into the public limelight in
1972 following Secretary of the Treasury Connally's firm
refusal to give GAO access to those internal records of
the Emergency Loan Guarantee Board[92] relating to its decision-making process. The financial crisis of the Lockheed Aircraft Corporation had led to the creation of the
Board which consisted of the Secretary of the Treasury, as
Chairman, the Chairman of the Federal Reserve Board, and
the Chairman of the Securities and Exchange Commission and
which was, in Senator Proxmire's words, "to bail out the
Lockheed Corporation from its financial difficulties with
a $250 million loan guarantee."[93]   It can reasonably be
assumed that the Treasury Secretary was the Board's moving force; in fact Samuel R. Pierce, Jr., the General
Counsel of the Treasury served as the Board's Executive
Director. Connally contended that "it was not the intent
of Congress that the decisions of the Board be reviewed by
the General Accounting Office."[94]   He brushed aside Staats'
assertions that the Comptroller General's statutory authority entitled the GAO to the access it was seeking. Staats
had argued "that there would have been no reason for the
Congress to repeat this authority in connection with the
Emergency Loan Guarantee Act."[95]

Senator Proxmire came to the aid of GAO;[96] but Connally refused to testify before the Senate Banking, Housing
and Urban Affairs Committee on the administration of the
loan guarantee to Lockheed. Proxmire charged that the
Secretary of the Treasury had deliberately insulted Congress by his refusal.[97]   The New York Times editorialized:
"The mystery is why the Treasury is putting up such heavy
resistance to the GAO."[98]   The editorial went on say that
the GAO had "both the right and the duty, as Mr. Staats
insists, to look into the emergency board's handling of

143

the Lockheed loan guarantee." The <u>Times</u> then became the
vehicle for an unusual exchange of letters between Government officials concerning the Lockheed issue. The letters
afford a helpful crystallization of the conflicting theses
that underlie the access issue; they also reflect the
sharp class of viewpoints evoked by the access issue.
Pierce wrote:

> It is only those internal records of the board
> relating to its decision-making process to which
> access by the GAO has been denied, and this de-
> nial was in accordance with law.[99]

Paul G. Dembling, the GAO's General Counsel, wrote
to make the <u>Times</u>' readers "aware of the shallow basis
upon which Mr. Pierce defends his position."[100] He referred to GAO's role in assisting the Congress in making
informed judgments concerning the efficiency and effectiveness with which agency programs are being administered.
Proxmire entered the "battle of letters" pointing out that
the information which the GAO was seeking included "several
credit analyses of Lockheed prepared at taxpayer expense
by the New York Federal Reserve Bank."[101] He argued that,
unless the GAO had access to the requested data, it would
have no way of knowing whether the Board complied with
the law in approving the loan guarantee.

Pierce refused to let the matter rest and stated there
was no inconsistency between the Board's willingness to
supply information to the Congress and its position that
the "Budget and Accounting Act of 1921 does not authorize
unlimited GAO access to its internal memorandums."[102]
An earlier section of this chapter pointed out that agencies have been particularly sensitive about revealing to
the GAO documents which they felt to be of an internal
nature. A very significant aspect of the Pierce retort
was his point that the Board's position was not novel and
that "over the years, many executive agencies . . . have
disputed GAO claims to unlimited access to executive records." Pierce neatly referred to the fact that the Deputy Comptroller General only a few weeks previously had,
in Pierce's words, told a Congressional subcommittee "that
several executive agencies are currently denying GAO unlimited access to their records." Here Pierce identified
what was undoubtedly a sore point for the Comptroller
General, i.e., the growing number of instances of access
refusal made Executive agencies less reluctant to cross
swords with the GAO on this issue.

DISPUTES WITH NASA - ILLUSTRATIVE
OF THE INTERNAL DOCUMENT ISSUE

NASA had been particularly sensitive with respect to
GAO's requests for documents that the agency considers to
be of a strictly internal character. The "Phillips Report" incident, which has already been mentioned in a prior
portion of this discussion, contributed greatly to this
sensitivity.

Report of Review Group at Goddard Space Flight Center

Another case that highlighted the issue was the GAO
request for a copy of "Report of Orbiting Astronomical
Observatory Failure Review Group for OAO-1 Flight." Dr.
John F. Clark, Director of the Goddard Space Flight Center,
said he had "deliberately put together a team composed
wholly of technical specialists from outside the OAO project, many of whom had disagreements with project personnel
concerning the design or implementation of various systems
of hardware of OAO . . ."[103] According to Dr. Clark, the
Review Group, in the introduction to the report, stated
that it had worked "from a deliberately skeptical viewpoint
and have produced, in this report, a severe critique of
OAO problems."

James Webb, NASA Administrator, sent a copy of this
letter to Staats and made this salient observation:

> Dr. Clark's letter illustrates the diffi-
> culty of having people from the GAO who are
> not fully familiar with the process that can
> produce success in such complicated equipment
> as the Orbiting Astronomical Observatory use
> quotations from reports as a measure of the
> system rather than recognizing that they are
> only a part of the process that leads to
> success.[104]

Webb said that he was prepared to release the report at
the Comptroller General's request under the conditions
that Dr. Clark had stated in his letter, i.e., delete
the signature page and schedule so that the identity of
the Review Group would be protected and prohibit the
taking of notes from or the copying of the report. A
few months later, GAO and NASA agreed on procedures with
respect to GAO access to sensitive NASA materials.

NASA's refusal to furnish reports of source selection boards

Some years before the Goddard Space Flight Center
incident, there had been a far more serious disagreement
with respect to the underlying issue, i.e., whether it is
incumbent upon an Executive agency to give the GAO or a

145

Congressional committee access to findings and/or recommendations intended for internal agency use and which are not binding upon those responsible for making the definitive decisions. This question led to a donnybrook between Comptroller General Campbell and Dr. T. Keith Glennan, who was NASA Administrator at that time.

The controversy had its inception in the refusal of NASA to furnish information to the House Committee on Science and Astronautics. The specific information which Glennan refused to submit to the Committee was the reports of two boards which had advised him in connection with the selection of two contractors. In explaining his unwillingness to make these reports available, Dr. Glennan had written the Committee:

> Since this document discloses the personal judgments of subordinates made in the course of preparing recommendations to me, I am sure you will agree with me that it would not serve the interests of efficient and effective administration of this agency for such a document to be reviewed by anyone outside of NASA.[105]

Shortly after these refusals by the NASA administrator, the Committee Chairman wrote the Comptroller General requesting him to make an evaluation of the bids, the proposals, and negotiations leading up to the two contracts, and the NASA procurement procedures.[106] As in the case of the controversy in connection with the State Department's Inspector General and Comptroller -- discussed earlier in this chapter -- this was an instance of a Congressional committee which, having been refused information by an Executive agency, turned to the Comptroller General to have him pull the proverbial chestnuts out of the fire.

When the Comptroller General complained to Dr. Glennan that GAO had been denied permission to examine the report of the Source Selection Board that had dealt with the North American Aviation contract, the Administrator pointed out that a similar request received from the Committee Chairman had been denied and that the reasons for not making the documents available to the Committee were equally applicable to the GAO.[107] The Comptroller General, having referred to Section 313(a) of the Budget and Accounting Act dealing with the right of access, Glennan retorted with the statement: "As you know, the privilege of the Executive to withhold documents in cases such as this has a constitutional rather than a statutory basis and, accordingly, is unaffected by the statute cited in your letter of August 19." There was a similar exchange

146

of letters in connection with the McDonnell Aircraft Corporation contract.

At the hearings which the Committee held on Glennan's refusal to produce the requested documents, Glennan was unyielding with respect to the position he had taken and cited statements that President Eisenhower had made as being directly applicable to the particular case. When he was specifically asked as to whether the President had advised him to exercise executive privilege in this matter, Dr. Glennan said, "I discussed this matter with the President personally and with his staff. The position I take has his approval."[108]

Although this incident did not have the same headline aspect as the State Department disputes, the denouement was just about the same. In the end, the Comptroller General suffered a sharp rebuff, and the Committee terminated its efforts once it realized it was confronted with a formidable adversary adamant in his resistance.

GAO PROBLEMS WITH THE BANK REGULATORY AGENCIES

The Federal Reserve System, Comptroller of the Currency (Treasury Department), and the Federal Deposit Insurance Corporation have momentous regulatory authority in the banking field. Neither the Federal Reserve nor the Comptroller of the Currency is subject to GAO audit. The arguments advanced against extending the Comptroller General's audit authority to these two agencies relate to not only the issue of autonomy but also the delicate nature of the material entailed in any thoroughgoing examination. The FDIC, although coming within GAO's purview, had consistently denied the GAO unrestricted access to examination reports, files, and other records with respect to banks which the Corporation insured.[109] This refusal impelled the Comptroller General to state that the GAO cannot "fully discharge our audit responsibilities with the Federal Deposit Insurance Act" and to qualify his audit reports accordingly.[110] The obdurate stance of FDIC was undoubtedly encouraged by the resistance which the Federal Reserve and the Comptroller of the Currency had shown to the Comptroller General's derogating from "the long-established tradition that reports of examinations of commercial banks should be kept confidential."[111]

Despite the perennial and strenuous efforts of Chairman Wright Patman of the House Committee on Banking and Currency, the Federal Reserve was able to fend off statutory authorization of GAO audits; Chairman Arthur Burns said that such action "would unwisely inject a third

147

party into the sensitive area of monetary policy."[112]
Comptroller General Staats, testifying the next day before the same Senate committee as Chairman Burns, challenged
the supposition that a GAO audit would interfere with the
independence of the Federal Reserve System and its monetary
policy-making machinery. Staats had previously observed
that many of the Government operations audited by GAO "are
equally, if not more sensitive than the Federal Reserve
System operations."[113]

But, in 1976, these three pivotal bank regulatory
agencies found themselves under considerable adverse pressure because of recent large bank failures and, in the
words of GAO, "public disclosure that supervisory agencies'
lists of 'problem banks' had lengthened." Hence, the "tri-
umvirate" agreed to having the GAO make an "unprecedented
study of the effectiveness of State and national bank supervision" by the three agencies. The latter had been urged
by the House Committee on Banking, Currency, and Housing
to accept this voluntary audit; a key factor in such acquiescence was "the agencies' fears that if they do not consent
to audits, concern over problem banks will boil over into
even more severe encroachments on their independence."[114]
The Comptroller General attributed the agencies' capitulation more immediately to "the heavy congressional interest
in the area."

What made the consent to this study even more porten-
tous was the agencies' agreement that the GAO would have
"unlimited access to their bank examination reports and
other related records, provided we would not disclose any
information about specific banks, bank officers, or bank
customers."[115] The accord which the Comptroller General
was able to elicit from such formidable antagonists had --
despite its limitation to the one study -- important implications for more ready acceptance of GAO access. A voluminous report on the study was issued in January 1977.

The thrust for subjecting the three Federal bank regulatory agencies to GAO audit intensified; and, in June
1977, the House Government Operations Committee recommended
the Federal Banking Agency Act (H.R. 2176) which would
authorize the GAO to conduct independent audits of these
agencies. In its report, the Committee referred to "the
widespread concern about the adequacy and effectiveness
of Federal Banking agency operations."[116] This measure
was still pending at the time that this manuscript was
completed.

THE COMPTROLLER GENERAL'S BID FOR
STATUTORY BUTTRESSSING OF GAO
ACCESS

The progress which GAO has made in resolving its access difficulties has not been rapid or far-reaching enough to convince Comptroller General Staats that such problems are no longer a major concern of GAO. Furthermore, increased Congressional emphasis on its oversight of the Executive Branch, as well as the underlying thrust for fuller governmental disclosure, are propitious to moves to strengthen GAO capability to obtain information it requests pursuant to Section 313 of the Budget and Accounting Act, 1921, or other authority. Similarly, the Comptroller General's access difficulties with the private sector, especially Government contractors, have made him anxious to obtain the means to enforce his requests from "nonfederal persons and organizations." This latter facet of the access issue is dealt with in Chapter 8.

Staats proposes that the Comptroller General be vested with authority to back up his requests for information from Federal departments and establishments by bringing U.S. District Court action to compel the respective agency heads to furnish such material.[117] The Comptroller General would be represented by his own counsel, while the Attorney General would be authorized to represent the defendant officials. As to contractors and others in the private sector who are subject to GAO access, the Comptroller General seeks the authority to issue subpoenas. In case of disobedience to such a subpoena, the Comptroller General, under the provision proposed by Staats, would be able to invoke District Court aid in requiring the production of the records involved.

Staats has argued that Title III (he inadvertently omitted reference to Title II) of S.2268, on which he was testifying, "does not expand our statutory authority relating to access to records of Federal agencies, contractors, and recipients of Federal assistance. It merely establishes a strengthened procedure for obtaining the records to which we are entitled by law."[118] However tenable this line of reasoning, it should not becloud the fact that the legal remedies sought by the Comptroller General would greatly enhance the impressive aggregate of power already vested in him.

Even if Congress accedes to the Comptroller General's proposals, it would be imprudent of the GAO to invoke such authority except under very compelling circumstances. Precipitate resort to the legal remedies sought by the Comptroller General could result in Pyrrhic victories. For that matter, the courts might -- at least on occasion -- adopt a highly questioning attitude as to the tenability of the informational requests which GAO seeks to enforce through judicial intervention. On the other hand, the enactment of the proposed legislation would symbolize strong

Congressional support of GAO access and thereby inhibit
agencies from entering into confrontations with the Comptroller General. This impact, together with the existence of an ultimate legal sanction, might make it a rar-
ity for a situation to arise in which the Comptroller General would consider recourse to judicial assistance in effecting compliance with his requests for information.
Congressional adoption of the GAO-initiated measures will
not obviate the need for the Comptroller General's discreet handling of specific cases of access as they arise
so as to maintain a proper balance between the needs of
the GAO and the legitimate concerns of the agencies involved.

Footnotes - Chapter 4

1. Those aspects of this problem that concern Governmental contracts are for the most part dealt with in Chapter 8, Comptroller General's Role in Government Procurement.

2. E.L. Normanton, The Accountability And Audit Of Governments (New York: Frederick A. Praeger, 1966), p. 302.

3. One legal writer maintains that "Section 313 is arguably less broad than it first appears." Thomas D. Morgan, "The General Accounting Office: One Hope For Congress To Regain Parity Of Power With The President." 51 North Carolina Law Review 1279, (1973), 1352.

4. Senate, Committee on Government Operations, Hearings Before Subcommittee, Capability of GAO to Analyze and Audit Defense Expenditures, 91st Congress, 1st Session, 1969, p. 35.

5. Comptroller General of the United States, 1971 Annual Report, pp. 6 and 13.

6. Ibid., p. 79.

7. Comptroller General of the United States, 1975 Annual Report, p. 7.

8. Statement of Elmer B. Staats, Comptroller General of the United States, Before the Subcommittee on Reports, Accounting, and Management of the Committee on Government Operations. U.S. Senate, On S.2268, 94th Congress, October 2, 1975.

9. General Accounting Office Comprehensive Audit Manual, Chapter 14, p. 1.

10. October 2, 1975 Statement, op. cit.

11. Raoul Berger, Executive Privilege: A Constitutional Myth (Cambridge: Harvard University Press, 1974).

12. Abram Chayes, "A Common Lawyer Looks at International Law." 78 Harvard Law Review 1396, (1965), p. 1400, and Paul A. Freund, "The Supreme Court, 1973 Term, Foreword: On Presidential Privilege." 88 Harvard Law Review 13, (1974), p. 36.

13. 418 U.S. 683 (1974). Professor K.C. Davis observes: "The Court clearly gave the doctrine of executive privilege a constitutional base when it said: 'Nowhere in the Constitution . . . is there any explicit reference to a doctrine of confidentiality, yet to the extent this interest relates to the effective discharge of a President's powers, it is constitutionally based.'" Kenneth Culp Davis, Administrative Law Cases-Text-Problems (St. Paul, Minn.: West Publishing Co., 1977), p. 576.

14. Edwin S. Rhodes, "From Burr to Nixon," 35 Federal Bar Journal 218, 227 (1976).

15. Congress, House, Committee on Science and Astronautics, The Production of Documents by the National Aeronautics and Space Administration for the Committee on Science and Astronautics, Hearings, 86th Congress, 2nd Session, 1960, p. 16.

16. Letter from President Kennedy, March 7, 1962 in The GAO Comprehensive Audit Manual. The letter was written to Congressman Moss as Chairman of the Special Government Information Subcommittee of the Committee on Government Operation.

17. Letter of April 2, 1965 to Congressman John E. Moss, cited in Congressional Record, April 15, 1969. H.2634.

18. Ibid., 2634-35.

19. New York Times, September 1, 1971.

20. Congressional Record, June 21, 1973.

21. Capability of GAO to Analyze and Audit Defense Expenditures, op. cit., p. 35.

22. Letter from Acting OMB Director, Paul H. O'Neill to Comptroller General Elmer B. Staats, October 26, 1976.

23. Capability of GAO to Analyze and Audit Defense Expenditures, op. cit., p. 35.

24. House, Committee on Government Operations, Hearings Before Subcommittee, Availability of Information from Federal Departments and Agencies, Part 16, Department of Defense, 7th Section, (Air Force-GAO), 85th Congress, 2nd Session, 1958.

25. Ibid., p. 3572.

26. Ibid., p. 3571.

27. Ibid., p. 3691.

28. Ibid., p. 3706.

29. Ibid.

30. Ibid., pp. 3706-3707.

31. House, Committee on Government Operations, Availability
     of Information from Federal Departments and Agencies
     (Air Force Refusal to the General Accounting Office),
     House of Representatives 234, 86th Congress, 1st
     Session, 1959, p. 83.

32. Raoul Berger, "Executive Privilege vs. Congressional
     Inquiry," UCLA Law Review, Vol. 12, No. 5, August
     1965, p. 1114. Professor Berger, together with Dean
     Frank C. Neuman and Professor Kenneth Culp Davis
     had been retained in 1959 to advise the Comptroller
     General as to his right to insist on delivery of
     the Inspector General's report in question.

33. Statement by Secretary of the Navy before Government
     Operations Committee, Subcommittee on Government
     Information, April 23, 1959.

34. House, Committee on Government Operations, Availability
     of Information From Federal Departments and Agencies,
     (Navy Refusal to the General Accounting Office),
     H. Rept. 1224, 86th Congress, 2nd Session, 1960, p. 43.

35. Ibid., p. 45.

36. Ibid., p. 4.

37. Letter from Comptroller General Elmer B. Staats to
     Cyrus R. Vance, Deputy Secretary of Defense, June
     5, 1967.

38. Letter from Paul Nitze, Undersecretary of Defense, to
     Comptroller General Elmer B. Staats, November 26, 1967.

39. Senate, Committee on Government Operations, Hearings
     Before Subcommittee, TFX Contract, 88th Congress,
     1st Session, 1963, p. 876.

40. Ibid., p. 886.

41. Letter from John L. McClellan, Chairman, Permanent Sub-
     committee on Investigations, to Comptroller General,
     August 15, 1966.

42. Letter from John L. McClellan, Chairman, Permanent Subcommittee on Investigations, to Secretary of Defense Robert S. McNamara, March 31, 1967.

43. October 2, 1975 Statement of Comptroller General Staats, op. cit.

44. Ibid.

45. Letter from Comptroller General Elmer B. Staats to Senator William Proxmire, March 2, 1976.

46. Reports of the Comptroller General of the United States. Submitted to the House Subcommittee on International Political and Military Affairs. Seizure of the Mayaguez. Part IV, 94th Congress, 2nd Session, 1976, p. 59.

47. Statement of Elmer B. Staats before the Select Committee on Intelligence. House of Representatives, July 31, 1975.

48. Symptomatic of this change is the position taken by the Deputy Executive Director of the Commission on the Organization of Government for the Conduct of Foreign Policy:

> Congress should put CIA and other intelligence agencies under the fiscal and managerial audit of the General Accounting Office comparable to all other executive agencies. . . . The GAO is fully capable of dealing with the sensitive aspects of intelligence programs with complete security and dependability. To say otherwise is to use secrecy as an excuse to escape oversight. Washington Post, May 4, 1976.

> A similar view was expressed by Professor Paul Kircher of UCLA in a newspaper article headed, "Why Not Sic the GAO on the CIA." Los Angeles Times, March 5, 1976.

49. Section 8(b) Central Intelligence Agency Act of 1949 as amended 63 Stat. 208, 50 USC 403(a).

50. Letter from Comptroller General Joseph Campbell to Honorable Paul J. Kilday, Chairman, Special Subcommittee, Central Intelligence Agency, House Committee on Armed Services, May 29, 1959.

51. Letter from Allen W. Dulles, Director, CIA, to Comptroller General Joseph Campbell, October 16, 1959.

52. Letter from Comptroller General Joseph Campbell to Allen W. Dulles, Director, CIA, October 21, 1959.

53. Letter from Comptroller General Joseph Campbell to Congressman Paul Kilday, May 16, 1961.

54. Letter from Allen W. Dulles, Director, CIA, to Comptroller General Joseph Campbell, May 17, 1961.

55. Letter from Carl Vinson, Chairman, House Armed Services Committee, to Comptroller General Joseph Campbell, May 18, 1961 and Letter from Comptroller General Campbell to Congressman Carl Vinson, May 23, 1961.

56. Internal GAO memorandum of June 11, 1962.

57. Letter from Comptroller General Joseph Campbell to Congressman Carl Vinson, June 21, 1962.

58. Letter from Congressman Carl Vinson to Comptroller General Joseph Campbell, July 18, 1962.

59. Report by the Comptroller General to the House Committee on the Judiciary, FBI Domestic Intelligence Operations -- Their Purpose and Scope: Issues That Need to be Resolved GGD-76-50, February 24, 1976.

60. Ibid., p. 180.

61. Washington Post, June 2, 1976.

62. Ibid.

63. Letter from Chairman Porter Hardy, Jr., House Foreign Operations and Monetary Affairs Subcommittee to Comptroller General Joseph Campbell, November 15, 1960.

64. Letter from Comptroller General Joseph Campbell to Secretary of State Christian A. Herter, November 17, 1960.

65. Letter from Secretary of State Christian A. Herter to Comptroller General Joseph Campbell, November 22, 1960.

66. Letter from Comptroller General Joseph Campbell to Secretary of State Christian A. Herter, December 8, 1960.

67. A White House release of December 23, 1960 contained: (a) Mr. Morgan's letter, (b) the Presidential certificate referred to subsequently in this discussion,

and (c) the letter of December 22, 1960 from Attorney General Rogers to the President summarizing
the opinion he had given the President with respect to this matter.

68.   41 Opinions of Attorney General 507 (1960).

69.   Letter from President Dwight D. Eisenhower to Sec-
      retary of State Christian A. Herter, December 23, 1960.

70.   Letter from Chairman Porter Hardy, Jr. to Dean Rusk,
      January 3, 1961.

71.   Letter from Comptroller General Joseph Campbell to
      Dean Rusk, January 18, 1961.

72.   Letter from Comptroller General Joseph Campbell to
      Secretary of State Dean Rusk, May 16, 1961.

73.   Abram Chayes, "A Common Lawyer Looks at International
      Law," op. cit., p. 1402.

74.   Letter from Senator J.W. Fulbright to Secretary of
      Defense Melvin Laird, May 21, 1969.

75.   Letter from Secretary of Defense Melvin Laird to Sen-
      ator J.W. Fulbright, June 26, 1969.

76.   New York Times, July 30, 1971.

77.   New York Times, August 19, 1971.

78.   Congressional Record, July 12, 1971.

79.   Letter from Acting Comptroller General R.F. Keller
      to Senator J.W. Fulbright, September 10, 1971 re-
      fers to the Senator's request.

80.   New York Times, September 9, 1971.

81.   1969 Hearings Before the Senate Subcommittee on Exec-
      utive Reorganization, op. cit., p. 20 and p. 36.

82.   Senate Hearing Before the Subcommittee on Reports,
      Accounting and Management of the Committee on Gov-
      ernment Operations, GAO Legislation, 94th Congress,
      1st Session, 1975, p. 59.

83.   Letter from Comptroller General Elmer B. Staats to
      Sheldon Cohen, Commissioner, Internal Revenue
      Service, November 16, 1967.

84. Letter from Commissioner Sheldon Cohen to Comptroller General Elmer B. Staats, November 24, 1967.

85. Letter from Commissioner Sheldon Cohen to Comptroller General Elmer B. Staats, November 29, 1967.

86. General Accounting Office Internal Memorandum on the Audit of the Internal Revenue Service, undated.

87. Memorandum from Lester R. Uretz, Chief Counsel, IRS to Sheldon Cohen, Commissioner, May 20, 1968.

88. Letter from Commissioner Sheldon Cohen to Comptroller General Elmer B. Staats, June 6, 1968.

89. GGD-76-55. November 5, 1976.

90. Public Law 95-125 signed by President Carter on October 11, 1977.

91. House Report 95-480, 95th Congress, 1st Session, July 1, 1977, Appendix B.

92. Emergency Loan Guarantee Act - Public Law 92-70.

93. Congressional Record, April 25, 1972.

94. Letter from Secretary of the Treasury John M. Connally to Comptroller General Elmer B. Staats, March 30, 1972.

95. Letter from Comptroller General Elmer B. Staats to Secretary of the Treasury John B. [sic] Connally, February 10, 1972.

96. Congressional Record, op. cit.

97. New York Times, May 4, 1972.

98. New York Times, May 7, 1972.

99. Letter from Samuel R. Pierce, Jr., General Counsel of the Treasury to Editor, New York Times, May 21, 1972.

100. Letter from Paul G. Dembling, General Counsel, U.S. General Accounting Office to Editor, New York Times, June 4, 1972.

101. Letter from Senator William Proxmire to Editor, New York Times, June 9, 1972.

102. Letter from Samuel R. Pierce, Jr., General Counsel of the Treasury to Editor, New York Times, June 21, 1972.

103. Letter from John F. Clark, Director, Goddard Space Flight Center to James E. Webb, Administrator, NASA, October 4, 1967.

104. Letter from James E. Webb, Administrator, NASA, to Comptroller General Elmer B. Staats, October 11, 1967.

105. House, Hearings Before the Committee on Science and Astronautics; The Production of Documents by the National Aeronautics and Space Administration for the Committee on Science and Astronautics, 86th Congress, 2nd Session, 1960, No. 1, p. 34.

106. Ibid., pp. 84 and 112.

107. Ibid., p. 85.

108. Ibid., p. 62.

109. Letter from Chairman Joseph W. Barr of FDIC to Comptroller General Joseph Campbell, Ibid., February 2, 1965, and Letter from Chairman Kenneth Randall of FDIC to Comptroller General Elmer B. Staats, March 26, 1968.

110. Letter from R.F. Keller, Acting Comptroller General to Chairman Robert E. Barnett, FDIC, September 2, 1976 is a recent expression of the GAO position.

111. Statement of J.L. Robertson, Vice-Chairman, Board of Governors of the Federal Reserve System, before the Subcommittee on Banking and Currency, House of Representatives, on H. Rept. 12754, September 14, 1967.

112. Statement by Arthur F. Burns, Chairman, Board of Governors of the Federal Reserve System before the Senate Committee on Banking, Housing, and Urban Affairs, October 20, 1975.

113. Senate Subcommittee Hearing on GAO Legislation, op. cit., p. 70.

114. "Banks Watchdogs Agree to an Audit," Business Week, May 17, 1976.

115. Federal Supervision of State and National Banks. A Study by the Comptroller of the U.S. OCG-77-1, January 31, 1977, p. 1.

116. House Committee on Government Operations, Federal Banking Agency Audit Act, 95th Congress, 1st Session, House Report 95-492, p. 3. See also

hearings of House Commerce, Consumer, and Monetary Affairs Subcommittee on H.R. 2176, March 2 and 3, 1977.

117. See Titles II and III of S.2268, 94th Congress, 1st Session, August 1, 1975.

118. Senate Subcommittee Hearing on GAO Legislation, op. cit., p. 38.

Chapter 5

THE COMPTROLLER GENERAL'S WIDE-RANGING
REVIEWS AND STUDIES

> We audit the programs, activities, and financial
> operations of Federal departments and agencies,
> and their contractors and grantees to:
>> Evaluate the efficiency, economy,
>> legality, and effectiveness with
>> which they carry out their finan-
>> cial, management, and program
>> responsibilities.
>> Provide the Congress and agency
>> officials with objective infor-
>> mation, conclusions, and recom-
>> mendations.[1]

Reviews and studies which ultimately find expression
in what are categorized as audit reports are the basic
means for the Comptroller General discharging his monitoring responsibility. These activities are the pivotal element of the Comptroller General's role in holding agencies
to accountability. The breadth and depth of the GAO's
audit program are obscured by semantic confusion. The
wide spectrum of subject matter coming within the ambit
of GAO audits is almost staggering.

Confusion as to the nature of GAO audit activities
does not stem entirely from the fact that what the GAO
labels an audit may vary from a brief reply to a simple
inquiry to an analysis requiring many man-years of effort.
The word "audit" conjures up in the minds of many people
the examination made by independent public accountants to
enable them "to express an opinion as to the fairness of
the [financial] statements, their compliance with generally accepted accounting principles and the consistency
of the application of these principles with that of the
preceding period."[2] But, in fact, relatively little of
GAO's auditing effort is directed to tasks that call for
the application of the auditing skill of one trained in
accounting. It is true that, insofar as Government corporations are concerned, the audits conform to the concept of audit as ordinarily understood. However, this
type of audit work does not loom very large in the total
auditing effort of GAO.

The reviews, for which the GAO uses the rubric "auditing" are increasingly concerned with the manner in
which agencies discharge their responsibilities and the
evaluation of programs. As the Comptroller General points
out, GAO auditing "includes not only examining accounting

161

records and financial transactions and reports, but also
checking for compliance with applicable laws and regulations; examining the efficiency and economy of operations;
reviewing the results of operations to evaluate whether
the desired results, including legislatively prescribed
objectives, have been effectively achieved."[3] Although
some audit assignments may not cover all of the aspects
to which the Comptroller General has referred, it is
highly significant, especially from the standpoint of
Congressional oversight, that the GAO audit can be so all-
embracing.

The effort entailed in the activities the Comptroller
General categorizes as audits is reflected in the fact that,
during the 15-month period ended September 30, 1976, GAO
made 909 surveys and 1716 reviews of government programs
and activities in the United States, 3 U.S. territories,
and 67 other countries.[4] A survey, as distinguished from
a review, consists of obtaining working information and
analyzing it to identify matters deserving detailed information.

THE EVER-EXPANDING SCOPE OF GAO AUDITS
AND THE PRODIGIOUS VARIETY OF SUBJECTS
THEY COVER

Initiation of audits

The outpouring of GAO audit reports impels one to
speculate on how the GAO determines what reviews and special studies are to be made and the relative priorities
to be assigned to them. A significant number of reports
are made in response to requests from committees or individual Members of the Congress.[5] Such requests receive
a high priority and ordinarily are handled much more expeditiously than audits initiated within the GAO. The
fact that a report is labeled as having been requested
by a committee or individual Member should not obscure
the fact, as is brought out in Chapter 2, that GAO may,
on occasion, stimulate the request and, in fact, even
phrase the letter that the committee or Member sends to
the GAO. The response to a request may require less than
one staff day or many hundreds of staff days. This range
is indicative of the diversity of such requests, an aspect discussed subsequently. Suffice it to say, at
this point, that there is a fortuitous element in whether
the report is one initiated by the Comptroller General or
one requested by a Congressional committee. Thus, a report on AID projects in Colombia[6] was of the first type;
while a secret report on economic assistance to the Dominican Republic was prepared at the request of, and submitted to, the House Subcommittee on Inter-American Affairs.[7]

The hard core of the Comptroller General's audit program consists of reviews initiated within the GAO. The
Comptroller General stresses the fact that, in planning
such work, the GAO looks first to the needs and interests
of Congress and, in that connection, maintains contacts
with committees. Other considerations which enter into
the GAO's planning of self-initiated work are:

(a)   The importance of programs and activities
       judged by such means as public impact,
       amount of expenditures, investment in
       assets, and amount of revenues.

(b)   The newness of programs and activities.

(c)   Public criticism indicating the need
       for corrective action.

(d)   The extent and recency of prior work
       by GAO or by agency internal review
       and evaluation groups.[8]

In order to facilitate the systematic channeling of
its audit activities, the GAO has identified twenty-nine
major Federal program or issue areas which are to receive
priority attention in deciding which self-initiated reviews to undertake. These areas include such spheres of
inquiry as automatic data processing, health, energy,
military preparedness, law enforcement and crime prevention, tax policy, and water.[9] The fields of inquiry are
used not only for planning purposes but also in keeping
the GAO's top management apprised as to the status of its
current operations. Of equal, and perhaps even greater,
import is the perspective reflected in the Comptroller
General's statement as to the underlying thrust of this
approach to the programming of GAO's operations: "We
have an opportunity second to none in Government -- to
look beyond individual agencies and programs to the broader problems and issues facing the Nation."[10] Such a broad
frame of reference is the antithesis of the parochialism
which some might attribute to an audit agency.

It is apparent that, while seeking to have its audits
responsive to Congressional needs, the GAO also takes into
account which programs, activities or operations should
be audited by the GAO in its monitoring capacity even though
such audits may not at the time appear to be germane to matters currently of interest to the Congress. For that matter, the GAO may undertake a review knowing that it will not
be of immediate interest to the Congress but feeling that,
in terms of a longer range perspective, such a study may
well prove to be of utility to the Legislative Branch. One

163

cannot brush aside the consideration that such a GAO audit
may yield results that will serve as a catalyst in ultimately stimulating Congressional interest in the particular
subject matter.

In some cases, Congress might, as exemplified by the
GAO study of the Economic Opportunity Program, enact a
statutory directive calling upon GAO to conduct a specific
review. Illustrative of how a Congressional committee may
prod the GAO into including particular projects in that
part of the work program which is internally generated is
the impact a report of the House Government Operations Committee which was very critical of GAO's audit effort in
Vietnam and expressed the opinion "that the GAO has been
deficient in carrying out its statutory responsibility for
auditing and reviewing the foreign operations activities
of responsible audit and inspection agencies."[11] The Comptroller General subsequently wrote the Committee Chairman
and, referring to the Committee's report, described what
the GAO had done in Vietnam from July 1, 1966 to June 30,
1968.[12] Staats stated:

> We believe that we are complying with this
> recommendation of the Committee, i.e., that
> GAO should establish a continuous presence
> in Southeast Asia.[13]

Dilemmas in the allocation of audit activity

The criticisms leveled at the GAO as a result of the
disclosures of the C-5A overruns reflect something of the
dilemma that confronts the agency in determining the allocation of its audit resources. The huge defense expenditures understandably made it appear untenable, at least
insofar as the casual observer was concerned, for the
GAO to be looking into matters that did not appear to be
of great moment. Just about the time that Congressional
criticisms were reaching a zenith with respect to defense
contracts, the GAO -- in addition to reports on subjects
of readily recognizable importance -- was issuing reports
on "Improvements in the Management of Government Parking
Facilities;"[14] "Activities of the Office of the Government Comptroller of the Virgin Islands;"[15] and "Opportunities for Better Service and Economies Through Standardization of Pharmacy Items and Consolidation of Bulk
Compounding Facilities - Veterans Administration."[16]
Some might well have reacted to such studies with the
feeling that GAO audit efforts required for these more
limited reviews could have been expended far more fruit-
fully in vital areas that offered greater possibilities
for the identification of major shortcomings. Similarly,
little enthusiasm might have been evoked by the report on

"Savings in Shipments of Printed Matter from Japan to Points in the Pacific,"[17] even though this did involve the Department of Defense. Yet the Comptroller General would be ill-advised to completely brush less glamorous reviews aside in favor of those that are palpably of much more moment or general concern.

It is fairly obvious that the preferences and interests of the audit personnel and the familiarity they already have with particular subject matter might exert a strong influence in the selection of projects. Furthermore, there could be a tendency to establish ties with particular subjects or problems with resultant reluctance to move into other areas. The recently prescribed issue areas afford at least a frame of reference for methodical programming of GAO's vast audit activities. The other supportive facilities now available to Congress have added another dimension to the determination of reviews that are to be initiated by the Comptroller General. There are steadily increasing possibilities of unnecessary overlapping and duplication of effort between the GAO and the other research and analytical resources utilized by the Congress.

The amazing spectrum of GAO audit reports

The output of GAO reports reflects a heterogeneous mix that ranges from the more orthodox reports on financial accountability[18] that even include an audit of the House Beauty Shop, to those dealing with vital national and international issues involving the United States.

Some of the studies initiated by the Comptroller General deal with problems or issues which Congress is considering or which it can reasonably be assumed will be on the legislative agenda in the near future. Thus, the Comptroller General, reacting to both Presidential and Congressional interest in deregulation, gave Congress "an overview of the current debate on Government regulation."[19] The energy problem is very high in GAO priorities, so much so that a separate division was established to deal with this area. The Energy and Minerals Division has been prolific in the production of materials; during the 15-month period ended September 30, 1976, GAO completed 102 energy-related reports, 73 of which were Congressional and 29 were addressed to agency officials.[20] Indicative of the depth of GAO's penetration into energy problems is its report seeking "to identify those energy issues that are most in need of attention."[21] This was followed by a report in response to the request of a subcommittee chairman, summarizing GAO views on the significant issues facing five major energy agencies during the 95th Congress and discussing GAO past efforts on energy questions during the 94th Congress.[22] The Comptroller General's probing into the international arena led to a report evaluating the adequacy and effectiveness of U.S. and internal controls over peaceful nuclear programs.[23]

Other self-initiated reviews, more modest in scope, can also be perceived as responsive to Congressional needs in connection with its legislature or oversight responsibilities. This panoply of reports encompasses such diverse subjects as alcohol abuse among military personnel,[24] Federal effort to combat organized crime,[25] space shuttle facility,[26] New York City's fiscal outlook,[27] management of agricultural exports,[28] aircraft mid-air collisions,[29] immigration policy,[30] and audits of Government corporations.[31] Reports relating to procurement, particularly the acquisition of weapons systems, are not only concerned with the processes but also substantive questions as to the items for which the Government is contracting. These reports are discussed in Chapter 8 dealing with procurement.

A third category of reports stemming from reviews initiated by the Comptroller General deals with subjects that seem to stretch to the utmost the GAO audit mandate even when construed in the broadest terms. Thus, one can readily be taken aback when he finds Comptroller General reports carrying such titles as "An Evaluation of the U.S. Early Warning System in the Sinai,"[32] "Learning Disabilities: The Link to Delinquency Should be Determined, but Schools Should do More Now,"[33] "Audit of the Procurement System of the State of Oregon: A Case Study,"[34] "State and County Probation: Systems in Crisis,"[35] and "The Clemency Program of 1974"[36] (for the return of Vietnam era draft evaders and military deserters).

The numerous reports prepared in response to requests of committees and individual Members sometimes are catalysts for involving the GAO in issues of critical importance. Thus, what the Comptroller General described as an "unprecedented study," "Federal Supervision of State and National Banks," was made at the request of several Congressional committees.[37] A request by the Chairman, Senate Committee on Governmental Affairs, led to a report on the employment of Americans in international organizations.[38] Another request from the same Committee afforded a springboard for the expression of GAO views on the World Food Program.[39] Following an inquiry by Senator Kennedy, the Comptroller General reported on "Implementation of Economic Sanctions Against Rhodesia."[40] In answer to a request from Senator Gaylord Nelson, three reports were prepared on food additives, the last of which dealt with the volatile subject of saccharin.[41] The reports on the seizure of the Mayaguez,

166

discussed earlier, were unusually dramatic instances of
how a committee request can afford the Comptroller General
a rationale for concerning himself with a matter that
ordinarily would not be deemed to come within the audit
purview. Apropos of sensitive subjects, Senator Humphrey
apprised the Senate of highlights of the GAO reports he had[42]
requested on the readiness of U.S. combat forces in Europe.
Some requests even go so far as to call upon the GAO not
merely to report but to monitor operations of an agency such
as the Federal Energy Administration.[43] Some years before,
the Joint Committee on Atomic Energy had requested the GAO
to maintain a continuing review of the Senate Antiballistic
Missile System:

> The purpose of having the General Accounting
> Office review the Sentinel Program is to pro-
> vide the means for continuing surveillance of
> the economy, efficiency, and effectiveness of
> the program within the reasonable availability
> of manpower of the General Accounting Office
> coincident with the high security nature of
> the program.

The Comptroller General subsequently reported that
approximately 30 GAO staff members were assigned to this
work on a continuing basis and that the review covered
operations of both the Atomic Energy Commission and the
Department of Defense. Staats further stated that this
was an unusual type of review for the GAO in that it contemplated that the GAO would have its personnel located
at the sites in the contractors' offices so that they
could report currently any problems that developed on
the way.[45]

But the potpourri of committee and Members' requests
often involves matters of more limited significance and
occasionally some of dubious merit. Responding to a request from Congressman Jack Brooks, the GAO made a visual
inspection of gifts received by former President Nixon
and even furnished photos of the items.[46] A letter from
Senator Gaylord Nelson led the GAO to investigate "whether
Monterey cheese imported from New Zealand under the quota
category of 'other cheese' is being used in place of
cheddar cheese in the manufacture of American-type processed cheese or cheese foods."[47] A request from Congressman Gross required analysis of the refurbishing of the
offices of the Secretary of the Interior; one conclusion
reached by the GAO was that the procurement of the furni-
ture and furnishings was not made in accordance with the
applicable Federal regulations, and the Comptroller General
informed the Congressman that the GAO intended to take exception in the accounts of the responsible fiscal officers.[48]

167

The total amount involved in the GAO review was $39,400, which might impel one to question whether this represents the best utilization of the Office's resources.

Senator William Proxmire is a perennial "client" of the GAO; in addition to matters of great consequence, he has called upon the Comptroller General to report on such subjects as: gifts given by U.S. Presidents since 1970 and an unsolicited mailing of certain materials by the Treasury Department to members of the American Economic Association.[49] One request from Senator Proxmire's office smacked of snooping that hardly adds to the lustre of GAO; it called upon the Comptroller General "to discreetly determine the specific U.S. Government program under which a recent visitor came to the United States."[50]

A third category of Congressional requests calls for the Comptroller General looking into matters that, while perhaps not of the greatest moment, are nevertheless patently germane to Congressional legislative or oversight responsibilities. For example, the Chairman of the House International Political and Military Affairs Subcommittee requested information on the number of Americans working on military or military-related projects in Saudi Arabia, including the number of these employees readily ascertainable as Jewish or female.[51] An analysis initiated by Senator Proxmire revealed not only shortcomings in the system for distributing petroleum and related supplies under the control of the Navy Fuel Supply Office in Bangkok, Thailand, but also confirmed allegations as to theft.[52] A request from Senator Margaret Chase Smith resulted in GAO's preparation of a report summarizing NASA's management review of North American Aviation, Inc. activities.[53] This was the so-called "Sam Phillips Report," about which NASA was very sensitive because of the Apollo program tragedy that took the lives of three astronauts. Some other subjects in this third category which the Comptroller General has explored at the instigation of committees or Members have been: hazing and the amount of combat training at the service academies;[54] the Japanese acquaculture program;[55] the opium problem;[56] the effect of the sale of wheat to Egypt on U.S. wholesale and retail prices;[57] mismanagement in the U.S. Postal Service;[58] and the collapse of part of a Federal building in Miami, Florida.[59]

THE EVOLUTION FROM ROUTINE AUDITS TO PROGRAM EVALUATIONS

The stature, recognition, and influence which the GAO presently enjoys contrast sharply with the pedestrian approach and limited credibility that characterize the earlier years of its existence. The primary factor in this metamorphosis was the marked change in the manner in which

168

the Comptroller General conceptualized the scope of the audits and their implementation.

Change in the GAO audit concept

It has already been pointed out that for many years GAO's audits consisted primarily of a centralized review in Washington of documents transmitted by the respective Government agencies. At one time, this centralized examination not only included the review of transactions after they had been consummated but also a pre-audit in which, prior to payment, the GAO examined vouchers after they had been administratively approved.

Comptroller General McCarl contended that the pre-audit appeared necessary for the protection of the Government's interests pending the enactment of legislation to effect separation of disbursing officials from the spending agencies.[60] He had previously recommended to Congress that such a separation be made on the grounds that the subordinate position of the disbursing officer subjected him to administrative influence and control. McCarl also cited what he considered to be the more positive advantages of the pre-audit: retention of Federal funds in the Treasury until determination was made that they were properly payable for the purposes proposed; protection afforded disbursing officers against liability for erroneous or illegal payments which could not be recovered from others; avoiding hardships to payees who might otherwise be called upon to make refunds to the Government; and saving the time that otherwise would have to be expended on the paper work in connection with the settlement of differences. The pre-audit was phased out over a ten-year period, 1942-52. This step received its impetus from Comptroller General Warren's efforts during World War II to enable the GAO "to keep abreast of the rapid acceleration in war-time activities and expenditures."[61]

It has been pointed out earlier that the pressures of World War II also made for some relaxation in GAO's tenacious adherence to the performance of its auditing work on a highly centralized basis. The enactment of the Corporation Control Act (1945) and the Budget and Accounting Procedures Act of 1950 were major forces in moving the GAO from centralized, desk audit review of financial transactions to audits that were conducted at the sites of operations and that were in conformity with the accepted auditing practices of the public accounting profession. However, it was some time before the full impact of this change was felt insofar as Washington processing of individual items was concerned.

Until the latter part of 1975, the GAO was responsible

169

for determining the correctness of charges the Government
paid for freight and passenger transportation services.
This entailed the centralized audit of millions of bills
of lading and transportation requests -- 4.2 million and
2.6 million respectively in fiscal year 1975. The GAO
would effect recovery of overcharges directly from the
carriers. The size and routine character of this activity
created a dilemma for Comptroller General Staats, who was
seeking to focus the agency's operations on far more challenging tasks such as the evaluation of programs and operations. As indicated previously, Staats was finally able
to obtain legislation that enabled the transferring of the
transportation audit function to the General Services Administration in October 1975.[62] It is interesting that
the Comptroller General stated that the GAO had "strongly
supported this change on the basis that the initial audits
of such expenditures are an Executive Branch function."[63]
But, since the Comptroller General still holds on firmly
to other functions to which the Executive Branch can lay
tenable claims, it seems that the motivating factor in the
transfer was the relatively prosaic nature of the transportation audit.

<u>Settlement of accountable officers' accounts - completely
recasted</u>

In the past, a significant volume of GAO's auditing
work was done in connection with the settlement of accounts
of those who had either received and disbursed Government
funds or who certified amounts for payment. These settlement audits review transactions for which the certifying,
disbursing, and collecting officers are accountable and
determine amounts for which they are liable because of
transactions deemed to be illegal or improper. As has
previously been pointed out, Section 304 of the Budget and
Accounting Act transferred to the Comptroller General the
responsibility for effecting settlements and further provided that the balances certified by the Comptroller General should be final and conclusive upon the Executive
Branch of the Government. The legal implications of the
Comptroller General's settlement function and the power
he has derived from this responsibility are discussed in
Chapter 7 -- the Judicial and Legal Counselor Roles of
the Comptroller General. At this juncture, we are concerned with the audit ramifications of the settlement
function.

The detailed and tedious nature of the work involved
in settlement of accounts on the basis of the examination
of individual transactions was not compatible with the increasing professionalism and multidisciplinary approach
of the auditing staff. One GAO official observed that

"except in the military, the settlement function is at
the bottom of the totem pole." At the same time, some
within the GAO felt that the settlement function generally
serves a useful purpose, particularly from the standpoint
of the psychological effect that it has upon those responsible for the certification or actual disbursement of expenditures.[64] For reasons explained subsequently, the
Comptroller General was reluctant to relinquish the settlement function, especially from the standpoint of any
statutory change. But he was anxious to relieve the GAO
of the need to expend considerable time and effort on this
phase of its activities.

The Comptroller General decided upon a sweeping revision of the manner in which the GAO conceives and imple-
ments its settlement responsibilities. In a memorandum
addressed to heads of Federal departments and agencies,
Staats apprised them of the revised approach that would
be applicable thereafter.[65] Rather than indicating something of a retreat from the position previously taken by
the GAO, the statement stressed the responsibilities that
the Accounting and Auditing Act of 1950 imposes upon the
heads of Executive agencies. The Comptroller General reminded agency officials that Section 113 of the Act requires the head of each Executive agency to establish
and maintain systems of accounting and internal controls,
including appropriate internal audit, designed to provide,
among other features: "effective control over and accountability for all funds, property, and other assets
for which the agency is responsible." Pressing this point
further, the Comptroller General said that this includes
"providing assurance of the legality, propriety and correctness of disbursements and collections of public funds."
At the same time, Staats took the opportunity to remind
the addressees that the agency accounting systems are required by the Accounting and Auditing Act to conform to
the principles, standards, and related requirements which
the Comptroller General prescribes under the mandate of
that Act. Having indicated that the primary responsibility
with respect to accountable officers was that of the agencies, the Comptroller General announced that GAO audit of
such officers would henceforth place its major emphasis
on the adequacy and effectiveness of the accounting and
internal controls, including internal audit. Under the
new approach, the GAO audit would include selective examinations of individual transactions, which would be the
basis for issuing notices of exceptions and for otherwise
advising the agencies of irregularities that are found.
Staats has reaffirmed GAO determination "to emphasize
audits of systems rather than individual transactions."[66]

The far-reaching overhaul of the settlement function

reflected the underlying change in the GAO approach to
its audit responsibilities. It bespeaks not only a willingness, but a positive desire, to shed the task of reviewing
a multiplicity of individual transactions. The internal
memorandum issued for the implementation of the new policy
stated that it should be carried out to the extent permissible "in accord with our basic audit policy of directing
our resources and talents to the areas in which they can
be most effectively used to fulfill the greatest apparent
need and benefit to the government."[67] Moreover, as has
already been intimated, the change in policy was affirmative recognition that this type of work was not conducive
to the professional stature of the agency and that it detracted from GAO's attractiveness as a career. It re-
directed emphasis from the scrutiny of masses of items
and determining disallowances to reviewing effectiveness
of the underlying systems. To that extent, it made the
GAO settlement role less vulnerable to criticisms such as
those voiced by the President's Committee on Administrative Management, discussed earlier in this study.

Inception of comprehensive audit concept

The term "comprehensive audit" played an unusually
important part in the recasting of GAO's operations; its
enunciation set in motion a process that culminated in the
1970 legitimization of broad-gauged reviews. The evolution presents an interesting case study of how an agency
can seize upon a concept, however vague, and then through
trial and error utilize it as a means for expanding the
scope of its operations. The very ambiguity and elusive-
ness of the concept can be elements of strength in organizational strategy. Once having served its purpose, the
concept can be replaced by one that appears to be more
suitable. An analysis of this development is useful for
more than an understanding of GAO background. It can
facilitate identification of some of the problems that
GAO may be expected to encounter in its implementation
of the broad-based review concept which has assumed such
a pivotal position in the Office's audit program.

The activities of the Corporation Audits Division
(established to discharge GAO's responsibilities under
the Government Corporation control Act of 1945) gave rise
to the concept of the comprehensive audit. Comptroller
General Warren indulged in understatement in his 1950 Annual Report when he said that the term "comprehensive
audit" was "not entirely self-explanatory."[68] He followed
this with a definition, the key sentence of which reads
as follows: "The comprehensive audit includes an audit
of receipts, expenditures, and application of public funds;
and embraces the verification of the assets, liabilities,

proprietary accounts, and operating results of Government
departments and agencies in accordance to the extent deemed
practicable and adequate, with generally accepted auditing
principles and procedures applicable to commercial enterprises." The use of the terms "application of public funds"
and "operating results" might be construed to refer to the
broader nature of the audits contemplated by the Comptroller
General. It is significant, however, that the agencies initially selected for comprehensive audit were, to use the
Comptroller General's words "of a predominantly business or
industrial type, and therefore lend themselves readily to
the comprehensive audit approach." This confirms the impression that what Warren had in mind was more of a commercial type of audit. This view was strengthened still further by the fact that the comprehensive audit program was
assigned to the Corporation Audits Division.

It became GAO's goal to extend the comprehensive site
audit programs to all agencies where practical. According
to Comptroller General Warren, the techniques of auditing
Government corporations differed "but little from those
employed in the comprehensive audit program. The chief
difference is that, in the normal course of events, professional opinion is given as to the fairness of the
financial statements of the corporations."[69] The purported
similarity afforded a rationale for discontinuing the corporation audit unit as a separate entity within the GAO;
and, early in 1952, the Corporation Audits Division was
abolished and its functions transferred to the newly-created
Division of Audits. These "and subsequent audits over the
next several years were carried out by or under the supervision of men who had been associated with the Corporation
Audits Division."[70]

The Budget and Accounting Procedures Act of 1950 makes
no reference to the term "comprehensive audit" but does reflect Congressional intent that the Comptroller General's
auditing be conducted in conformity with "generally accepted principles of auditing." Moreover, the Act manifestly contemplates that audits be conducted in the respective agencies rather than having the tremendous flow
of documents into Washington. But the auditing envisaged
by the 1950 legislation appears to be more of a financial
type rather than the all-encompassing kind of examination
which the GAO has stressed. This explains why -- prior
to the Legislative Reorganization Act of 1970 -- GAO officials, in identifying what they considered to be the
statutory mandate for the comprehensive audit, were prone
to refer to the Budget and Accounting Act of 1921, rather
than to the 1950 Act. The crucial wording is found in
Section 312(a) which, in defining the Comptroller General's
investigative responsibility, concludes with this clause:

"and concerning such other matters relating to the receipt,
disbursement and application of public funds as he may
think advisable." The word "application" in this clause
had been -- until the 1970 Act -- the keystone of GAO's
claim for authority to examine into the management of Government agencies. Statutory wording was stretched so that
the GAO might free itself of the constraints imposed by
the assumption that the Comptroller General's audit was
primarily, if not exclusively, concerned with the strictly
financial aspects of an agency and that probing into the
operational facets was justified only when necessary to
cast light upon the financial operations.

The espousal of the comprehensive audit served as the
GAO's vehicle for the assertion and implementation of an
auditing role that concerned itself increasingly with the
managerial and program areas. So much so, that in many
instances the strictly financial analyses were eclipsed.
The culmination of this thrust is reflected in the Comprehensive Audit Manual of the GAO which states that one primary purpose of the audits is: "To evaluate the efficiency,
economy, legality, and effectiveness with which Federal
agencies carry out their financial, management and program
responsibilities."[71]

Restrictions on GAO audit authority

An explanatory paragraph in the statutory compilation
prepared by the GAO affords a good summary of the statutory
constraints on audit authority of the Comptroller General:

> With certain exceptions, the audit authority
> and responsibility of the General Accounting
> Office extends to all activities, financial
> transactions, and accounts of the Federal
> Government. However, certain agencies and
> activities are not subject to audit by rea-
> son of specific statutory prohibitions and
> the type of funds involved. Where expend-
> itures are of a privileged or confidential
> or emergency nature accounted for solely
> on certificate of a designated Government
> official, the General Accounting Office
> audit function is restricted. . . . Cer-
> tain international organizations in which
> the United States contributes are exempt
> from the GAO audit.[72]

The compilation also directs attention to the fact
that GAO's audit authority does not -- in the absence of
special statutory provision -- extend to monies transferred
to states, instrumentalities, and local organizations "be-

cause such funds lose their identity as Federal funds when transferred."[73] However, the compilation also points out that "numerous laws enacted in recent years and authorizing Federal grants-in-aid, cost-sharing programs, and other financial assistance, specifically provide for GAO audit and access to records of recipients."

The Comptroller General's impact on the financial operations of state and local units of government has not, by any means, been dependent upon special statutory provisions relating to Federal funds received by such sub-national governmental entities. GAO, under Staats' aegis, took upon itself the task of promulgating audit standards that reach out beyond the Federal Government and that are designed to "be applicable to all levels of government in the United States."[74] Although it is obviously not legally incumbent upon other governmental levels to conform to such standards, the prestige which the Comptroller General has achieved in the auditing field per se makes for receptivity to auditing criteria he espouses. More recently, the GAO issued an exposure draft of "Audit Guidelines for Audits of Financial Operations of Federally Assisted Programs."[75] Manifestly, the Comptroller General has developed a momentum that, coupled with statutory mandates, has steadfastly been enhancing GAO's role in assuring effective accountability for Federal financial assistance to State and local governments and other non-Federal domestic organizations.

As shortcomings or abuse by Federal agencies in the use of funds not within the audit authority of GAO come to light, questions may be raised as to the possible elimination of such immunity from scrutiny by the Comptroller General. The disclosures of scandalous practices in connection with military club operations led to legislation making certain non-appropriated funds and related activities subject to review by the Comptroller General "in accordance with such principles and procedures and under such rules and regulations as he may prescribe."[76] Both Comptrollers General Warren[77] and Campbell[78] had recommended legislation dealing with such funds, but Congress dragged its feet. Staats was averse to GAO becoming deeply involved in this facet of financial operations. Responding to a subcommittee inquiry, GAO proposed that it review the systems of accounting and internal audit and the independent audits of nonappropriated fund activities. ". . . we would not at this time want to have responsibility for the direct review and audit of such activities, especially by legislative requirement."[79] Staats was apparently motivated, at least in part, by his general deemphasis of the strictly financial type of audit. When the General Accounting Office Act of 1974, which included this expansion

of GAO audit authority, was being considered, Staats made
certain that the primary responsibility for auditing non-
appropriated funds should rest with the operating agencies
and not be given to GAO,[80] which, as the statutory language
indicates, was given more of an overall responsibility.
In this way, Staats could defer to Congressional wishes
and yet not compromise his commitment to the broad-gauge
type of audit.

Reviews of program results (program evaluations)

With Staats' assumption of the Comptroller Generalship, the thrust for GAO audits penetrating deeply into
the substantive aspects of agency operations became even
stronger. Staats quickly made it evident that he conceived of GAO audits as having their primary focus on the
operational and program aspects of agencies. The term
"comprehensive audit" was largely replaced by new terminology such as "reviews of program results" and "evaluations
of program effectiveness." This changed nomenclature at
least had the merit of establishing unequivocally that the
GAO was increasingly conducting evaluations of management
and, even in some instances, the programs themselves. In
the House Appropriations Subcommittee hearings on his 1970
estimates, Staats informed the Subcommittee:

> To insure the most effective use of our staff
> and to assist the Congress in maintaining ef-
> fective legislative oversight of governmental
> programs and operations, we have increased
> our capability to examine the adequacy of
> program management and evaluate the effect-
> iveness or results of those programs of heavy
> dollar impact and congressional interest.[81]

The crescendo of GAO program evaluations increased
as the Comptroller General hammered away at this approach
to the audit function. This experience made GAO aware of
what is involved in a truly meaningful program evaluation
and enabled it to conceptualize such evaluations more
realistically than might otherwise have been the case.

Both the Legislative Reorganization Act of 1970 and
the Congressional Budget and Impoundment Control Act of
1974 gave a strong thrust to program evaluations. Congress patently had in mind that such evaluations would
serve as a vital tool in the implementation of the Congressional oversight function. The legislation requires
that the Comptroller General "develop and recommend to the
Congress methods for review and evaluation of Government
programs and activities carried on under existing law."
It also enjoins the Comptroller General to make such

176

evaluations when ordered by either House or upon his own
initiative or when requested by any committee of either
House or any joint committee of the two Houses, having
jurisdiction over the respective programs and activities.[82]
Subsequent to the 1970 enactment, the Comptroller General
opined that the legislation did not add anything to GAO's
legal authority that it did not have before. Staats has
been obdurate in his refusal to concede that the GAO's
mandate has moved far beyond what was articulated in its
original charter:

> The Budget and Accounting Act, 1921, gave
> GAO a base that has not been significantly
> broadened by subsequent legislation. Sub-
> sequent legislative delegations have, for
> the most part, evidenced current congres-
> sional interests and telegraphed to us the
> ways in which we could be of greatest ser-
> vice to the Congress.[83]

Staats adroitly sidesteps any reference to the extent to which he has inspired and even contributed to the
wording of such telegraphic messages!

The strong thrust for program evaluations

The GAO had been increasingly stressing reviews of
program results and effectiveness; it reported that the
portion of professional staff time involved in such reviews
increased from thirty-one per cent in fiscal year 1974 to
thirty-five per cent in fiscal 1975. Similarly, the GAO
stated that over fifty per cent of the self-initiated work
in fiscal year 1975 was in this category as compared to
forty-five per cent in the previous fiscal year.[84] Program evaluation has been defined by the GAO as follows:

> Program evaluation in a general sense is
> determining whether a program is effect-
> ively achieving the objectives intended
> and, in a more technical sense, determin-
> ing what has happened as a result of the
> program that would not have happened in
> its absence. Evaluation is concerned
> with questions of program effectiveness.
> In this respect, it is goal-oriented
> focusing on output as well as costs.[85]

The Comptroller General set forth specifically what
GAO had been doing to expand its program analysis and
evaluation.

> Providing GAO-wide assistance and co-
> ordination in identifying and analyzing

major program issues and alternatives and
furnishing this information to the Congress
in a timely manner.

Conducting special program analysis and
evaluation studies.

Developing analyses of the impact of (1)
Federal programs on the economy and (2)
changing economic conditions on those
programs.

Developing and coordinating GAO-wide
plans and efforts relating to reviews
of tax policy issues and to Federal
agency program-evaluation systems.

Synthesizing available evaluations and
analyses of program issues for use by
the Congress and GAO.

Developing and recommending to the Congress appropriate methods for evaluating and assisting the Congress in providing program-evaluation language in
legislation.[86]

From time to time, the Congress directs the Comptroller
General to make studies on the effectiveness or results of
legislation that it has enacted. For example, the Energy
Reorganization Act of 1974[87] requires the Comptroller General to evaluate the effectiveness of the programs and activities of the Nuclear Safety and Licensing Regulatory
Commission. Similarly, the National Productivity and
Quality of Working Life Act of 1975[88] directs the GAO to
evaluate the effectiveness of the activities of the Center
which is responsible for formulating a national productivity
policy and for reviewing and coordinating all Federal productivity activities. So long as the GAO's direct responsibility for conducting program evaluations is kept within
reasonable bounds, this type of involvement in the evaluative process has definite merit. Unquestionably, the experience which GAO builds up in the conduct of program
evaluations should be invaluable in enabling it to counsel
agencies as to evaluations which they conduct and to determine the quality of such evaluations. The report "Review
of the 1974 Project Independence Evaluation System"[89] is
illustrative of what GAO can do in reviewing a complex
evaluation, forecasting, and analysis system.

The Comptroller General is trying to stave off the
deluge of program evaluation studies that could result if

Congress construed the statutory provisions as making him
primarily responsible for conducting such evaluations. On
the other hand, he is seeking to provide the technical leadership that will be conducive to the soundness of evaluations undertaken by the agencies. Indicative of this thrust
on the part of GAO is the exposure draft of a document entitled "Evaluation and Analysis to Support Decision-making,"[90]
"intended to be of value to the novice and the experienced
practitioner whether engaged in financial audits, program
review or in program evaluation or analysis."

     Mindful of the fact that even those Members of Congress
who are proponents of program evaluation may not be fully
aware of what is entailed, the GAO prepared, in 1976, a
document entitled "Evaluating Federal Programs: An Overview for the Congressional User." Interestingly enough,
the booklet seeks to tell the legislators not only what
actually has happened as a result of past legislation and
why, but even refers to legislative inaction. This latter
is a discreet way to put Members of Congress on notice
that statutory recognition and even prescription of program evaluations, in themselves accomplish little. Such
a reminder is called for since there appears to be a propensity for legislative articulation of interest in a new
technique such as program evaluation which interest is not
followed by continuing Congressional effort to see that
such technique is actually employed in sound fashion and
the results utilized in the legislative process.

     The GAO booklet cautions the reader that, however use-
ful evaluative studies can be, the expectations as to what
can be expected of them must be realistic. It reminds
legislators that: program intent may be elusive; measurement of all program effects may be impossible; cause/
effect links may be difficult to establish; and the necessary time, talent, and resources are scarce. These observations underline the essentiality of a reasonable degree of Congressional sophistication as to the nature,
potentialities, limitations, and applicability of program
evaluation if it is to make a substantial contribution to
the oversight and legislative activities of the Congress.

              REVIEW OF THE POVERTY PROGRAM - A PIONEER
                 EFFORT IN PROGRAM EVALUATION

Initiation of economic opportunity review

     Despite his usual aplomb, Comptroller General Staats
must have experienced some trepidation when the Prouty
Amendment (Section 201 of the Economic Opportunity Amendments of 1967) directed the GAO to study the programs
and activities financed in whole or in part under the

Economic Opportunity Act of 1964. GAO was ordered to determine: (1) the efficiency of the administration of such programs and activities by OEO and by local public and private agencies carrying out such programs and activities, and (2) the extent to which such programs and activities achieved the objectives set forth in the Act of 1964.

The inception and prosecution of this study is one of the most significant milestones in GAO's history. GAO's repeated enunciation of the comprehensive audit concept had become even more pronounced with the advent of Staats. Frequent public utterances as to the operational and substantive nature of GAO's audits made it difficult for the Comptroller General to demur to the type of challenge presented by the Prouty Amendment. Although Staats was undoubtedly earnest in espousing audits that penetrate into agency programs and operations, he certainly was not ready for the herculean task that now confronted him.

The dimensions or boundaries of the GAO review of the poverty program were set by Congressional mandate as contrasted with GAO-initiated studies, in which the limits are delineated by the Comptroller General. It is true, as has been pointed out, that some reviews are made pursuant to requests by Congressional committees or individual Members who define the subject matter and, on occasion, prescribe certain specifications. However, such requests from committees or Members of Congress differ greatly from a statutory fiat. Moreover, the completion date of the project was fixed by statute and -- although some postponement was ultimately obtained -- this was a far more binding and psychologically demanding constraint than that to which the GAO ordinarily was accustomed.

But the most disconcerting aspect of the OEO review called for by the Prouty Amendment was the nature of the programs and activities that GAO was called upon to evaluate from the standpoint of both efficiency and effectiveness. Patently they were of a type distinctly elusive so far as measurement of results is concerned. Equally, if not more, discomfiting was the controversial nature of the program. Implicit in this assignment was the catapulting of GAO into the political front line.

Resources utilized for the OEO review

Venturing into a frontier area, the GAO found it necessary not only to mobilize a large segment of its regular staff resources but to supplement them with very substantial help from contractors and consultants. There

was a serious question as to whether the results were
commensurate with the required inputs. The latter should
be viewed not merely in terms of the contractual, consultant, and travel costs but also the diversion of a
significant portion of the agency's professional staff.
Comptroller General Staats reported to a House subcommittee that the estimated out-of-pocket costs for the OEO
study totalled $1,619,900.[91] Staats told the same sub-
committee that approximately 250 of GAO's staff had participated in individual reviews some time during the course
of the project.[92] The mobilization of so many professional
staff members to work on the study meant delaying or even
eliminating other projects some of which might have been
of at least equal urgency. The Prouty Amendment had the
effect of giving the OEO project top priority regardless
of the real merits of the case. The results according to
a top GAO executive, were an "imbalance in activities."

Outpouring of reports on OEO

The review regrettably resulted in an outpouring of
reports that could not but support the criticisms that
have been voiced as to GAO's proclivity for turning out
reports regardless of the interests and needs of Congress.[93]
The overall report, which was submitted to Congress
early in 1969, was followed by more than 50 supplementary
reports on the reviews or individual examinations made at
various program sites throughout the country. A motivating factor in this deluge of reports might have been a
phenomenon that has previously been pointed out, i.e.,
those GAO personnel who have worked assiduously on a project generally derive gratification from seeing their efforts reflected in a report submitted to the Congress.
In addition, the Comptroller General probably felt that
the record-breaking inputs required by this project and
the mass of data compiled in making the study called for
supporting the overall report with a series of individual
reports.

Tone of OEO report - agency and press reactions

In its summary of principal findings and recommendations, the overall report stated that "the accomplishments
achieved under the Economic Opportunity Act should be ap-
praised in the light of the difficulties encountered by
the agency (OEO) created to carry out the purposes of the
Act."[94] It then enumerated some of these difficulties.
Having at least mentioned a number of the obstacles such
a program encounters, the report goes on to say: "Our
review properly and inevitably focuses on problems, shortcomings, and recommended improvements."[95] In its response
to Chapter 2 of the report, OEO seized upon this statement:

The GAO thus confined itself largely to
areas of deficiencies, and while it lists
many of the factors that contributed to
the agency's problems, the overall result
is necessarily on the negative side.[96]

Those responsible for the administration of the program might have been rankled by what they considered to
be damning with faint praise. For example, commenting on
the Community Action Program, the report stated that it
"had achieved varying success in involving local residents
and poor people in approximately 1,000 communities," and
it cited other accomplishments. Having bestowed this accolade, the report went on to say:

However, CAP has achieved these ends in
lesser measure than was reasonable to
expect in relation to the magnitude of
the funds expended.[97]

Perhaps reflecting disappointment that the report
was not a blanket indictment of the poverty program, the
Washington Post story of March 24, 1969 carried the heading "Long Dreaded Report on OEO Finds Both Good and Bad"
and went on to say: "The report long touted as a scorch-
ing criticism of the Federal Anti-poverty program turned
out last week to be rather favorable - if confusing."
The story quoted one Congressional source as saying:
"If the GAO report is suppose [sic] to be an evaluation,
I am more worried about the GAO than I am about OEO."
The New York Times led off its first-page story with the
heading "Congress is Told Drive on Poverty is Badly Managed."[98]   The news story was supplemented by a profile on
Staats which had something of a snide quality!

Rarely has Mr. Staats been caught off-base
in the political jockeying that marks Washington Bureaucracy. Today was a good example of his technique. As the Controller
[sic] General, the head of the General Accounting Office, he issued a report on the
poverty program that was right down the
middle.

Staats felt that the press reactions in general had been
good. This evaluation on the Comptroller General's part
might reflect that he anticipated the press would pounce
upon the report much more vigorously than it did.

Mixed Congressional reactions to OEO report

Congressional reaction to the GAO report was understandably mixed, and the feelings of individual Members were influenced by their attitudes with respect to OEO and the specific facets of the program. Senator Prouty spoke of "the vast contributions of the General Accounting Office to our responsible legislative oversight;" he reminded his colleagues that the main document would be supplemented by more than 50 additional reports, and thanked the Comptroller General and his staff "for a job well done."[99] Senator Mondale, by contrast, was most severe in his judgment:

> But I have grave doubts that this is the role that the General Accounting Office should perform because these are political judgments. These are judgments in addition that require the sophistication of professionals in education, in health, in legal services, that involve a lifetime of the most rigorous sophisticated academic and practical background coupled with experience.[100]

In the hearings held by the Senate Subcommittee on Employment, Manpower, and Poverty on the closing of Job Corps centers, Senators Edward Kennedy and Gaylord Nelson sharply criticized the GAO sample of Job Corps centers and asserted that it did not afford a tenable basis for the conclusions that had been drawn.[101] At the same time, both Senators were careful to avoid the appearance of having a personal animus against Staats. Nelson referred to the Comptroller General as "a highly regarded man across this Nation,"[102] and Kennedy told Staats: "I think the group you represent, the GAO, is extremely important, and generally extremely helpful to the Members of the Congress."[103] In House hearings, Staats received personal praise from Chairman Carl D. Perkins of the Committee on Education and Labor. However, Perkins then said: "But I don't agree with the report."[104] He had already subjected Staats to a grilling so severe as to impel a minority Member to remind the Chairman of "fairplay."[105]

Unfavorable reaction of the House Appropriations Committee

The roughshod questioning to which Staats was subjected -- despite the personal esteem in which he was held by the Congress and despite the generally benign attitude of Congress toward the GAO -- brought out in bold relief the risks the Comptroller General assumed when he undertook studies that directly relate to Congressional decision-making on important controversial policies.

While the GAO study was under way, the House Approp-

riations Committee had stated there was a question as to
whether Congress, in future consideration of program authorization legislation, should follow the precedent that had
been established in the OEO Amendments of calling upon the
Comptroller General to make a program evaluation. It was
the Committee's feeling that to do so would tend to dim-
inish the flexibility of GAO in examining all programs
and expenditures of the Government. The Committee also
expressed concern that such action, if carried too far,
"would in substance considerably duplicate the expense of
oversight staffs and special 'investigative' Committee
expenditures."[106]

Following the submission of the poverty program report, the House Appropriations Committee commented even
more strongly and at greater length concerning the implications of such Congressional assignment. It pointed out
that the GAO "did not have the in-house capability for this
kind of policy examination" and was, therefore, required
to retain outside firms on a contractual basis at a substantial cost. An even more salient comment made by the
Committee was that the project "brought the GAO into the
business of making recommendations in controversial legislative policy areas." Expanding upon this issue, the Committee said:

> Calling on GAO to make detailed recommendations
> on pending policy legislation might well in time
> get them tangled - and mangled - politically, and
> thus in the long run risk impairing their ef-
> fectiveness as an impartial, unbiased, independ-
> ent arm of the Congress in examining and report-
> ing on the adequacy, efficiency and economy of
> management of the countless programs of govern-
> ment and the propriety of government expenditures.[107]

One of the spillover effects of the OEO study was
that of stimulating clarification of GAO's role with respect to the evaluation of programs and their implementation. It probably paved the way for the 1970 legitimization basis for the type of broader reviews which GAO was
already emphasizing. The admonitions of the House Appropriations Committee manifestly did not deter Staats from
full-blown implementation of the program evaluation role
for GAO. The Committee's skepticism was certainly not
shared generally by the Congress which has, if anything,
tended to indulge in unreasonable expectations as to the
extent of the program evaluations that can be undertaken
by GAO.

NONFINANCIAL CHARACTER OF MANY
GAO AUDITS RAISES AN ISSUE

The preceding discussion has brought out the fact that a great deal of the Comptroller General's audit work deals only incidentally with the strictly financial aspects of Government agencies. What are termed audits are in many instances actually reviews of operations and/or programs. The more orthodox type of financial audit made by the Comptroller General is conducted in connection with: (a) the discharge of GAO audit responsibilities under the Government Corporation Control Act; and (b) the conduct of financial examinations of Governmental activities that -- although not employing the corporate structure -- are of a commercial type. Such audits are, as already stated, of relatively nominal significance in the total GAO output.

Contract audits which also call for financial audit skill present more challenging assignments both because of Congressional and public interest in defense spending programs and the opportunities they offer for uncovering shortcomings in defense procurement and identifying overpayments which may be recouped in whole or in part by the Government. Yet there was a tendency, at least for a short period, for the GAO to relax its contract audit activities not only as a result of the Holifield hearings discussed in Chapter 8, but also the greater allure of the operational or program type of audit.

The Comptroller General's reports do not in most instances profess to deal with the strictly financial aspects of the Government. The Comptroller General's reports have concerned themselves increasingly with operational and program matters and have de-emphasized comprehensive treatment of financial operations and conditions. The very magnitude of the Federal Government and the intricacies of its financial operations might be a deterrent to the Comptroller General's dealing with the finances of the total Government. There is no specific statutory mandate for his making this type of analysis. Yet it does seem incongruous that the overall audit agency does not concern itself with the Government's financial condition.

Criticism has been leveled against the GAO failure to provide "government-wide views of agency financial operations."[108] The Comptroller General's annual reports afford no overall picture or analysis of the financial operations and condition of the Federal Government. This void in the output of the Government's auditor has become all the more serious in light of the mounting public and Congressional concern over the implications of the vast deficits entailed in the Federal budget. As is brought out in the concluding chapter, the Comptroller General agrees on the need for consolidated financial statements but passes the buck to the Treasury Department. But he even reacted negatively to a recommendation that the GAO "make the examination of agency reports submitted to the Treasury a part of its review of agency financial operations."[109] Staats was loath to divert much of his GAO resources to looking into the "fairness of financial reports." However, the GAO did not cavalierly brush aside its responsibility with respect to the quality of financial reports emanating from the agencies. An internal memorandum prepared as an aftermath of this exchange of views had this closing paragraph:

> We are not recommending any broad-scale audit program of examining financial statements but we do need to recognize that we have a responsibility in this area under our general audit responsibilities and that we should be registering some evaluation of the fairness, reliability, and credibility of agency financial reports.[110]

THE GAO APPROACH TO THE CONDUCT OF ITS AUDITS

Crucial impact of the audit approach

Whatever disagreement there may be as to the range of subject matter that appropriately comes within the scope of GAO's audit activity, a particularly sensitive aspect of GAO's reviews lies in the approach which the audits reflect. At least in the past, this frequently became a source of tension and recrimination between the agency and the GAO. It would be naive and completely unrealistic to expect that any incisive, thoroughgoing audit effort could be conducted without strain and some conflict in viewpoints. This, however, does not dispose of the question as to whether the approach that is followed tends to aggravate rather than minimize the irritation. Comptroller General Staats understandably expressed doubt that the Comptroller General could carry out his duties without some controversy developing. But, at the same time, he stated that he would try to keep the "fuss" on a high organization and low noise level "so that those that develop might appropriately be called differences of opinion or constructive suggestions.[111]

The GAO cannot afford to merely shrug off criticisms that might be directed at its audit approach. It needs to sensitize itself to such reactions and continually seek to determine the extent to which they might be reduced or even prevented entirely without in any way attenuating the effectiveness of GAO's audit efforts. The fact that criticisms,

such as those discussed below and in the following chapter, were often expressed by agencies is -- however one
may discount them -- significant, if only from the standpoint of the insights they afford into the GAO-agency relationships that affect the conduct and even the results
of GAO audit efforts. It is interesting that some GAO
executives who read the original draft of this manuscript
reacted with the same defensiveness and irritability as
that often shown by agencies in their review of GAO draft
reports. Patently, one is dealing here with the underlying
sensitivity to criticism, especially that which may affect
the public image.

Criticism of GAO's audit methodology

Agency reactions to GAO audits are more readily dis-
cernible when the Office reports its findings and recommendations. The GAO's reporting system and the responses
it evokes are the subject of the next chapter. Hence,
the discussion, at this juncture, of agency criticisms of
the approach GAO takes to its reviews and special studies
can be relatively brief.

The most repeated and basic criticism directed at the
GAO's audit approach was that noted in Chapter 3, i.e.,
that undue emphasis was placed upon the discovery and reporting of deficiencies. An Assistant Secretary, reflecting this view, contended that an audit should not be an
"adversary proceeding." It was further asserted that deficiencies are not placed in proper perspective because
they are not related to the more favorable features of the
operations or program and that, as a result, the audit yields
a distorted picture. A Bureau of the Budget official commented: "There is a tendency on the part of the GAO to
stress fault-finding because of their being in the Legislative Branch." Another Bureau executive, referring to
GAO's attempts to make a comprehensive audit of the Bureau,
remarked that the GAO staff "were out to get something."
A former GAO staff member, later a key official in an important Government agency, said he had left the GAO because
"at that time there was developing a tendency to slam the
agency no matter how hard they were working at their problems." Bearing out this criticism, a GAO executive said:
"We were perhaps inclined for a while to be too critical;
we were going overboard." He used the past tense because
it was his feeling that, with the change in Comptrollers
General, GAO was now less prone to be critical.

Commenting on the suggestion that GAO might do more
in the way of commending agencies for good performance,
a GAO official first referred to the very limited resources
of the Office. He then observed:

Giving an agency a citation for what it does
right requires as much effort as work in an
area where you come out with deficiencies. Can
we afford as an office to go much out of our
way to pat an agency on the back? We would
have to put an awful lot of work into it before we could send a report to the Comptroller
General putting our stamp of approval on what
an agency has been doing.

In fairness to the GAO, the question should be posed
as to whether the public and Congressional expectations
with respect to a central monitoring agency such as the GAO
are not that it will seek out the meritorious aspects of
governmental management but rather that it will ferret out
shortcomings. It might be felt that agencies are ordinarily
not diffident about proclaiming their accomplishments and
so the auditor should focus upon uncovering inadequacies.

A related criticism frequently voiced with respect to
GAO's audit approach and already alluded to earlier in this
study was that it had something of a picayunish quality in
that it emphasized trivia at the expense of more fundamental
issues or aspects. Thus, one agency official commented:
"Most GAO people strain at the gnats to demonstrate that
they are truly critical." Not only Executive agencies but
those within the Legislative Branch feel that GAO could be
more selective in its studies; and, as one committee staff
member expressed it, eliminate "the nickel and dime stuff."
Comptroller General Staats' emphasis on broad audit perspective has probably made the GAO less vulnerable on this
score.

There was a feeling, quite understandable, that GAO is
doing "Monday morning quarterbacking," that puts it in the
position of showing great perceptiveness and wisdom and
leaving the agency with the appearance of ineptness, if
not outright inefficiency. In other words, it was contended
that a serious weakness of GAO's audit approach is the failure to relate the analysis to the situation that existed at
the time a particular decision was made or the action taken.
In refutation of this criticism, a GAO audit supervisor
stated that the causal factor was more often the failure to
use or fully understand the information that was available,
rather than the lack of adequate information.

Other factors inimical to a good audit climate

Establishing good rapport with the agency to be audited
requires more than apprising the respective officials as to
the audit work that is contemplated; there must also be a
willingness to consider agency reactions and suggestions.

A departmental official told of suggesting to GAO that a study be deferred until the system which the department had set up to measure quality of service had been given an opportunity to work. He stated that the GAO went ahead despite this, claiming that they had already lined up the staff for the work. If such was the case, then GAO truly placed itself in an indefensible position.

One of the basic issues involved in the conduct of GAO audits insofar as agencies are concerned is whether the underlying objective is to produce a report or to effect improvements. The question has been raised as to whether the GAO representatives should establish and carry forward a working relationship in which shortcomings and possible corrective action will be discussed with the agency as the work progresses and the preparation of a report will be regarded as completely secondary. An agency official stated that a tremendous amount of time, in his opinion, was wasted by GAO because of its assumption that agency reactions would be negative and that the GAO would, therefore, have to make a very strong case in order to achieve its purpose. It was his feeling that GAO was not taking advantage of the opportunity to discuss matters frankly and freely with agency people.

How close should GAO audits be to the decision-making process?

A frequently expressed criticism of the GAO audits is that they are of an historical rather than of a current nature. Should GAO be entirely retrospective in its approach or should it increasingly concern itself with what is going on currently and even impinge upon the decision-making process more directly than by the evaluation of decisions after they have once been made? Such participation does, of course, take place when the Comptroller General's rulings influence and even inhibit agency action. But the issue presented at this point relates to the audit process as such. It has been observed by one agency official that for GAO to do a current audit means that "they have to know what is happening and that almost means participation. We have asked them to come in on several problem areas that we have had and participate with us." This official felt that GAO is somewhat "schizophrenic" on this score. "It is a matter of their saying: 'we'll come in and watch with you and, if you ask us, we will comment but really not participate.'" Referring to difficult decisions being made currently, this official stated that they needed GAO's views now rather than being told by GAO a year or two hence that what had been done was bad.

This line of reasoning poses underlying questions as

to the appropriate role of the agency responsible for
checking on accountability. Can participation in decision-making be consonant with the evaluative role
that the auditor is expected to perform? Does such collaboration entail a diffusion of responsibility for the
decision that is made or the action that is taken? Could
GAO's participation in decision-making within the Executive Branch be reconciled with its status as an instrumentality of the Legislative Branch?

One might expect that the thesis advanced with respect to GAO's becoming actively involved in agency decision process would be unpalatable to Executive agencies.
Yet the representative of another major agency was funda-
mentally in agreement with this point of view. He reported
that they had overcome GAO's reluctance by suggesting to
the staff of the very influential Congressional committee
within whose purview the agency came that the GAO look at
a problem at the same time that the agency was considering it. ". . .They are not so much smarter than we are
when the decision has to be made. They are much smarter
ten years later when something goes wrong; then things
crystallize."

At first blush, it might appear that the agencies
leaning in this direction are anxious to avail themselves
of the analytical skills and knowledge that GAO can contribute to problem-solving. However, another motivation
soon becomes manifest: that of precluding subsequent
criticism because the established critic has been co-opted
by the very agency which is subject to its scrutiny. In
short, it is possible that agencies may resort to the defensive tactic of welcoming rather than fending off GAO's
impinging upon their decision-making, simply to preclude
possible criticisms at a later stage. This attitude is
similar to that reflected at the time when agencies were
submitting vouchers for pre-audit by the GAO in order to
obviate disallowances by the Comptroller General.

Emphasis on savings

In his annual reports, the Comptroller General ap-
prises the Congress of the savings and collections directly attributable to GAO's work. Staats explained to
an appropriations subcommittee that the hundreds of millions of savings during the 15-month period ended September
30, 1976 resulted "from a wide variety of improvements in
the economy and efficiency of Government programs and operations," while the collections included collection of debts
that other Federal agencies were unable to collect and the
recovery of excessive or erroneous payments.[112] Staats
followed up these observations with the statement that

189

during this same period "GAO contributed directly and substantially to further Federal collections and savings of
$1.6 billion." In claiming such credit, the Comptroller
General referred to GAO contributions to such actions as
the termination and deactivation of major military weapons
systems and the consolidation of common agency support
activities. Then, making his case even more impressive,
Staats observed that: (a) "Federal agencies took many
actions in response to GAO recommendations to achieve
economies or make improvements in their operations which
cannot be accurately quantified into dollar savings," and
(b) "perhaps even more important than the collections and
monetary savings are the many recommendations we make
which, while not resulting in dollar savings, point out
ways to make Federal programs more effective."

Although ostensibly reluctant to emphasize unduly the
savings aspect of GAO operations,[113] the Comptroller General is understandably not completely averse to exploiting
the potentialities of such figures in winning Congressional
goodwill, particularly when the GAO appropriation requests
are under consideration. He is mindful of the fact that
savings figures impress Congress especially when they
are far in excess of the funds provided for GAO. One
writer, making an analytical study of the GAO, was impelled
to state that it was "one agency which puts into the Treasury more money than it takes out."[114] The savings claimed
by GAO tend to captivate the press; and, in the past, the
GAO has not been reluctant to exploit savings figures as a
basis for eliciting commendatory news stories.

There is undoubtedly something of a conflict between
the desire to make well-rounded, professional types of
audits and an almost built-in proclivity to uncover possibilities for effecting substantial savings. It would be
untenable to deprecate the relevance of potential saving
as a factor in the selection of audit projects and in determining directions which the audits are to take. However, emphasis upon the achievement of monetary savings,
if carried to an extreme, can distort the audit approach.

Agency stress and strain engendered by GAO audits

Even where a GAO audit discloses significant shortcomings and paves the way for corrective action, such
efforts are still subject to challenge if they cause such
disruption and tensions that the dysfunctional results
offset the gain derived from the studies. It is incumbent upon an independent audit agency such as the GAO to
minimize the interference with operations and the impair-
ment, however, temporarily, of a satisfactory working environment. A committee staff member who had extensive

background in the Executive Branch stated that a general criticism was the time wasted by both GAO and agency personnel in connection with GAO audits. Similarly, an agency official who formerly held a responsible post in the GAO observed: "Petty findings can divert scarce time from Government officials." He emphasized the amount of correspondence entailed in dealing with issues raised by the GAO. Still another individual complained that a great deal of work was involved in explaining to the GAO "why they are wrong about something."

In any confrontation between an agency and the GAO, each may be prone to regard the other as intransigent. There is an inevitable conflict between the pride of the analyst and the tendency of an official to minimize, if not refute in its entirety, any statement that he considers as impugning, the quality of his agency's performance. Expressions of dissatisfaction concerning the time and effort of agencies that must be diverted in connection with GAO audits generally reflect, in some measure, the general irascibility engendered by disagreement with the GAO's findings. At the same time, they cannot be dismissed summarily as being completely ill-founded. The exit interviews and agency clearance of draft reports to which reference is made at a later point in this study, may require significant time and effort on the part of the agencies. An agency can find itself in correspondence with the Office of Management and Budget and Congressional Committees concerning the report. It may be interrogated on the GAO report when it appears before the Appropriations Committee or its authorizing committee.

Agency personnel inevitably need to divert energies from regular operating responsibilities to dealing with matters that arise in connection with the GAO audit activities. However, one cannot regard the demands which GAO audits make upon the agencies as really extraneous to the discharge of the responsibilities vested in the particular agency. The basic rationale for GAO audits is that of serving as an instrumentality for seeing that the accountability of agencies and their personnel is properly discharged. In addition, the price which GAO audits exact in terms of the demands upon the agencies needs also to be viewed in light of the stimulus that these reviews afford to more effective management.

Agency cooperation in GAO audits

Aloofness or passivity on the part of the agency with respect to GAO's audits would ordinarily add to the time and effort required for such reviews. Whatever the difficulties created for GAO by agency "remoteness" or even

191

antipathy during the analytical stage of the audit, the lack of rapport becomes far more of a "drag" in obtaining implementation of the recommendations. The attitude which agency officials have concerning a GAO audit may not remain constant throughout the project. An initially skeptical or indifferent attitude may be changed because of the ability of the audit staff to convince the officials as to the merits of the audit. Conversely, developments during the course of the audit may cause an initially favorable attitude to be changed into one of suspicion or even hostility.

The receptivity of agency personnel to the study can have an important impact upon the degree to which GAO has ready access to information. The degree of cooperation which GAO is able to obtain also affects the facility with which the audit personnel can get an understanding of technical operations. An audit supervisor cited a case where the personnel engaged in a highly technical program were very proud of their operations and, therefore, most anxious that the GAO personnel understand them.

Tied in with agency cooperation is the use of the exit interview. This is a technique which GAO employs to make certain that, as an audit is drawing to completion, the factual findings are correct. This is effected through conferences with the appropriate agency personnel. To the extent that disagreements are ironed out during the exit interviews, there are commensurate reductions in the tensions and delays stemming from the GAO-agency interchanges in connection with agency review of draft reports. The usefulness of the exit interview in this regard is much greater if it is concerned with not only factual findings but also preliminary conclusions and recommendations.

Political realities in the audit process

The functioning of the GAO is inevitably conditioned by its political setting. GAO may feel that it cannot concern itself with the fact that, as one departmental executive pointed out, agency operations reflect, among other factors, pressures by both the Congress and the agency's constituency: "These are political realities. You really cannot trot these out to the auditors."

Yet there must be situations where, willingly or not, the GAO is constrained to recognize political realities in determining the particular audits to be undertaken and the approach to be followed. More specifically, there is the question as to the extent to which GAO might be inhibited in probing into or reporting upon, a particular matter if it is regarded as politically "hot." Another

relevant query is: Do preferences of Congressional committees or Members with whom GAO has built up unusually
good rapport influence at least subconsciously GAO's
stand on issues? Manifestly, one can merely conjecture
with respect to these matters. A key GAO official remarked:

> You must bear in mind that there are mixed
> feelings on the Hill. For example, pro-
> ponents of Foreign Aid do not want critical
> GAO reports while opponents are looking for
> critical findings. We must follow a middle
> of the course approach. Elmer is working
> very hard on this.

The Comptroller General cannot afford to be oblivious
of the political ramifications of the subject matter with
which he deals. But, at the same time, he must resist
pressures to compromise the established audit standards.
In fact, the Comptroller General could get himself into
an untenable position if he showed himself to be a
"political pragmatist."

GAO'S LEADERSHIP IN THE AUDITING FIELD

The credibility and acceptability of GAO's audits,
whether it be on the part of Congress, agencies, or the
relevant professions, needs to be perceived in the context of the recognition which the Comptroller General
has won for the GAO in the auditing field generally. With
the ascendancy of Comptroller General Staats, there was a
sharply stepped-up momentum within GAO for expanding the
horizons of governmental auditing. In enunciating the
broader audit standards which GAO presently espouses, Staats
has stated:

> This demand for information [about government
> programs] has widened the scope of government-
> al auditing so that such auditing no longer is
> a function concerned primarily with financial
> operations. Instead, governmental auditing
> now is also concerned with whether government-
> al organizations are achieving the purposes
> for which programs are authorized and funds
> are made available, are doing so economically
> and efficiently, and are complying with ap-
> plicable laws and regulations. The stand-
> ards contained in this statement were developed
> to apply to audits of this wider scope.[115]

GAO was the prime mover in a highly significant effort in the auditing area which entailed collaboration
with professional societies, representatives of Federal

agencies and state, county, and city governments; as well as public interest groups. The end product was the audit standards designed to be applicable to all levels of government in the U.S.[116]

The deference which the profession now accords GAO is reflected in the report which the American Institute's Committee on Relations with GAO prepared on the standards:

> The members of this Committee agree with the philosophy and objectives advocated by the GAO in its standards and believe that the GAO's broadened definition of auditing is a logical and worthwhile continuation of the evolution and growth of the auditing discipline.[117]

Also exemplifying GAO's role as a driving force in the rethinking of governmental auditing are its influence in the creation of eleven intergovernmental audit forums and the project it undertook with the International City Management Association to demonstrate the application of broad-scope auditing at the local government level.[118] The thrust underlying these developments stems from the enhanced prestige which the GAO enjoys in connection with serving as a Congressional resource and as the auditor of the performance of Federal departments and agencies. Thus the breadth of the audit function as now conceived and implemented by the Comptroller General and the stature that GAO has achieved within professional, governmental and academic circles are mutually reinforcing.

The Comptroller General has recognized that the sharp departure he has effected from the more orthodox audit approach to GAO's far-reaching reviews requires that the auditing personnel reflect a strong multidisciplinary mix. The GAO disavows that it makes technical judgments on the performance of weapons systems or other kinds of technologically complex systems. It points out, however, that it has a diversified staff and that it has access to outside experts and consultants in many fields. GAO feels that, in this way, it is able to understand technical judgments made by experts in a government agency and is in a position to call attention to factors or issues that may have been overlooked in making those judgments.[119]

Although the essentiality of a multidisciplinary staff is fully acknowledged by the Comptroller General, the transition from a staff dominated by the professional accountant has not kept pace with the rapid change in GAO's audit philosophy. As of September 30, 1976, of 4142 professional staff, there were 2701 classified as accountants and auditors.[120]

194

The significance of the fact that almost two-thirds of
GAO's professional staff consisted of accountants and
auditors is accentuated by the dominance of accountants
in the top echelons of the organization. Having committed the GAO to an audit concept of unusually wide
scope, the Comptroller General must perforce be certain
that all professional levels of the GAO have the mix of
talents essential to meet this more demanding challenge.

1. Comptroller General of the United States, 1976 Annual Report, p. 6.

2. Codification of Statements on Auditing Procedures, American Institute of Certified Public Accountants (1962), p. 11.

3. Comptroller General of the United States, 1975 Annual Report, p. 5.

4. 1976 Annual Report, op. cit., p. 7.

5. The Comptroller General reported that during the 15-month period ended September 30, 1976, GAO received 764 requests for audits or special studies. Ibid., p. 3.

6. Comptroller General Report, Review of Projects in Colombia Showing Need for Improvements in Planning and Supervision, B-161882, September 21, 1967.

7. Comptroller General Report, Review of Economic Assistance to Dominican Republic, B-161470, May 1, 1968.

8. House Appropriations Committee, Hearings Before A Subcommittee. Legislative Branch Appropriations for 1977, p. 314.

9. 1976 Annual Report, op. cit., p. 7.

10. Comptroller General's Memorandum to Heads of Divisions and Offices, September 16, 1975.

11. House, Committee on Government Operations, Forty-Second Report by the Committee on Government Operations, H. Rept. 2257, 89th Congress, 2nd Session, 1968, p. 45.

12. See Comptroller General Reports, Survey of Internal Audits and Inspections Relating to United States Activities in Vietnam, B-159451, July 18, 1966; Review of Audit and Inspection Programs Conducted by United States Agencies in Vietnam, B-159451, May 4, 1967; Report on United States Construction Activities in the Republic of Vietnam 1965-1966, B-195451, May 15, 1967.

13. Letter from Comptroller General Elmer B. Staats to Chairman William L. Dawson, July 8, 1969.

14. B-155817, June 16, 1969.

15. B-114808, June 30, 1969.

16. B-133044, June 30, 1969.

17. B-165683, June 30, 1969.

18. Comptroller General Report, Audit of the House Beauty Shop-Calendar Year 1976, GGD-77-54, June 8, 1977.

19. Comptroller General Report Government Regulatory Activity, Justifications, Processes, Impacts, and Alternatives, PAD-77-34, June 3, 1977.

20. 1976 Annual Report, op. cit., p. 74.

21. Comptroller General Report, Natural Energy Policy: An Agenda for Analysis, EMD-77-16, January 27, 1977.

22. Comptroller General Report, Energy: Issues Facing the 95th Congress, EMD-77-34, April 28, 1977.

23. Comptroller General Report, Assessment of U.S. and International Controls Over the Peaceful Uses of Nuclear Energy, ID-76-60, September 14, 1976.

24. Comptroller General Report, Alcohol Use is More Prevalent in the Military Than Drug Abuse, MWD-76-99, April 18, 1976.

25. Comptroller General Report, War on Organized Crime Faltering - Federal Strike Forces Not Getting the Job Done, GGD-77-17, March lu, 1977.

26. Comptroller General Report, Space Shuttle Facility Program: More Definitive Cost Information Needed, PSAD-77-17, May 9, 1977.

27. Comptroller General Report, The Long-Term Fiscal Outlook for New York City, PAD-77-1, April 4, 1977.

28. Comptroller General Report, Issues Surrounding the Management of Agricultural Exports (2 volumes), ID-76-87, May 2, 1977.

29. Comptroller General Report, Aircraft Midair Collisions: A Continuing Problem, October 23, 1974.

30. Comptroller General Report, Immigration -- Need to Reassess U.S. Policy, GGD-76-101, October 19, 1976.

31. An example is the Audit of Financial Statements of St. Lawrence Seaway Development Corporation, FOD-76-18, July 28, 1976.

32. ID-77-11, June 6, 1977.

33. GGD-76-97, March 4, 1977.

34. January 10, 1977. This unique report was issued over the signature of a division director rather than the Comptroller General.

35. GGD-76-87, May 27, 1976.

36. FOCD-76-64, January 7, 1977.

37. OCG-77-1, January 31, 1977.

38. Comptroller General Report, Greater U.S. Government Efforts Needed to Recruit Qualified Candidates for Employment by U.N. Organizations, ID-77-14, May 16, 1977.

39. Comptroller General Report, The World Food Program - How the U.S. Can Help Improve It, ID-77-16, May 16, 1977.

40. ID-77-27, April 20, 1977.

41. Comptroller General Report, Need to Resolve Safety Questions on Saccharin, HRD-76-156, August 16, 1976.

42. Congressional Record, July 29, 1976.

43. See letter from Assistant Comptroller General Phillip S. Hughes to Senator Abraham A. Ribicoff, Chairman, Senate Committee on Government Functions, March 31, 1975.

44. Letter from Senator O. Pastore, Chairman, and Congressman Chet Holifield, Vice Chairman, Joint Committee on Atomic Energy to Comptroller General Elmer B. Staats, April 29, 1968.

45. House, Appropriations Committee, Hearings Before a Subcommittee, Legislative Branch Appropriations for 1970, pp. 536-37.

46. Letter from Comptroller General Elmer B. Staats to Congressman Jack Brooks, September 10, 1974.

47. Letter from Comptroller General Elmer B. Staats to Senator Gaylord Nelson, June 30, 1970.

48. Letter from Comptroller General Elmer B. Staats to Congressman H.R. Gross, August 12, 1970.

49. The two communications from Comptroller General Staats to Senator Proxmire were dated April 15, 1975 and July 18, 1975, respectively.

50. Letter from Comptroller General Elmer B. Staats to Senator William Proxmire, May 1, 1975.

51. Letter from Comptroller General Elmer B. Staats to Congressman Dante B. Fascell, November 30, 1976.

52. Comptroller General Report, <u>Investigation in Thailand of the Systems for Distributing Petroleum, Oil, and Lubrications and for Processing Related Documentation</u>, B-163938, January 9, 1969.

53. B-156556, June 2, 1969.

54. Letter from Comptroller General Elmer B. Staats to Congressman Samuel S. Stratton, March 21, 1975.

55. Letter from Comptroller General Elmer B. Staats to Chairman, House Subcommittee on Fisheries and Wildlife Conservation and the Environment, September 10, 1976.

56. Letters from Comptroller General Elmer B. Staats to Congressman Charles B. Rangel, July 23, and November 21, 1974.

57. Letter from Comptroller General Elmer B. Staats to Congressman Joshua Eilberg, December 6, 1974.

58. Letter from Comptroller General Elmer B. Staats to Congressman H. John Heinz, III, October 18, 1976.

59. Letter from Comptroller General Elmer B. Staats to Congressmen William Lehman, Claude Pepper and Dante Fascell, April 3, 1975.

60. Comptroller General of the United States, <u>1927 Annual Report</u>, p. 42.

61. Memorandum from Comptroller General Lindsay C. Warren to Chief, Audit Division, GAO, January 3, 1942.

62. Public Law 93-604.

63. Comptroller General of the United States, <u>1975 Annual Report</u>, p. 8.

64. However, the theoretical liability of the accountable officer has meant relatively little in practice, and

an internal GAO memorandum, after referring to the few demands that had been made upon accountable officers for recovery of funds, said: ". . . under present conditions settling an account of a disbursing officer or issuing a certificate of settlement has relatively little practical meaning." Memorandum from Director, Office of Policy and Special Studies, GAO, to the Comptroller General, October 11, 1968.

65. Memorandum from Comptroller General Elmer B. Staats to Heads of Federal Departments and Agencies, B-161457, August 1, 1969.

66. House Subcommittee Hearings on Legislative Branch Appropriations for 1977, op. cit., p. 315.

67. Memorandum from Director, Office of Policy and Special Studies, GAO, to Directors, Civil, Defense, Field Operations and International Divisions, August 1, 1969.

68. Comptroller General of the United States, 1950 Annual Report, pp. 39 and 44.

69. Comptroller General of the United States, 1952 Annual Report, p. 21.

70. John C. Fenton, "The Corporation Audits Division - Its Legacy to the Seventies." The GAO Review, Summer 1971, p. 88.

71. Chapter 2, page 1 of the Manual.

72. Legislation Relating to the General Accounting Office, January 1975, p. C-i.

73. Ibid., p. D-i.

74. Comptroller General of the United States, Standards for Audit of Governmental Organizations, Programs, Activities, and Functions, 1972, p. I.

75. March 30, 1976.

76. Public Law 93-604.

77. Letter from Comptroller General Lindsay C. Warren to Chairman William L. Dawson, House Committee on Expenditures in the Executive Departments, October 25, 1949, and H. Rept. 6325, 81st Congress, 1st Session, 1949.

78. Letter from Comptroller General Joseph Campbell
    to Chairman William L. Dawson, House Committee
    on Government Operations, April 30, 1962.

79. GAO Congressional Contact File Memorandum of November 3, 1969.

80. House, Government Operations Committee, Hearings
    Before a Subcommittee, Bills Relating to the
    General Accounting Office, 93rd Congress, 2nd
    Session, 1974, p. 34.

81. House Appropriations Committee, Hearings Before Subcommittee on Legislative Branch Appropriation, 91st
    Congress, 1st Session, 1969, p. 533.

82. Public Law 93-344 Section 702. The 1970 Legislative Reorganization Act had called upon the
    Comptroller General to have available in the GAO
    employees expert in analyzing and conducting cost
    benefit studies of Government programs. It further provided that he should establish within the
    GAO such a unit as he considered necessary to
    carry out the functions and duties imposed upon
    him by Title II of the Act "Fiscal Controls."
    The 1974 legislation authorized the Comptroller
    General to establish an Office of Program Review
    and Evaluation within the GAO. As a result, GAO
    now has a Program Analysis Division.

83. Elmer B. Staats, "The Role of GAO During the 1980's,"
    The GAO Review, Spring 1977, p. 33.

84. Comptroller General of the U.S., The Congressional
    Budget and Impoundment Control Act of 1974: Its
    Impact on the Authorizing Committees and GAO,
    1976, p. 14.

85. Ibid.

86. Comptroller General of the United States, 1975 Annual Report, p. 88.

87. Public Law 93-438.

88. Public Law 94-136.

89. OPA-76-20, April 21, 1976.

90. OPA-76-9, December 9, 1975.

91. House Committee on Appropriations, Hearings Before a
    Subcommittee, Legislative Branch Appropriations for
    1970, 91st Congress, 1st Session, 1969, p. 566.

92. Ibid., p. 536.

93. Comptroller General Report, Review of Economic Opportunity Programs, B-130515, March 18, 1969.

94. Ibid., p. 7.

95. Ibid., p. 8.

96. Ibid., p. 19.

97. Ibid., p. 10.

98. New York Times, March 19, 1969.

99. Senate Committee on Labor and Public Welfare, Hearings Before a Subcommittee on Employment, Manpower, and Poverty, Economic Opportunity Amendments of 1969, 91st Congress, 1st Session, 1969, p. 354.

100. Ibid., p. 367.

101. Senate, Committee on Labor and Public Welfare, Hearings Before the Subcommittee on Employment, Manpower, and Poverty, Closing of Job Corps Centers, 91st Congress, 1st Session, 1969, p. 348 et seq.

102. Ibid., p. 353.

103. Ibid., p. 366.

104. House, Committee on Education and Labor, Hearings Before the Ad Hoc Hearing Task Force on Poverty, Economic Opportunity Amendments of 1969, 91st Congress, 1st Session, 1969, p. 2348.

105. Ibid., p. 2314.

106. House, Report of Appropriations Committee, Legislative Branch Appropriation Bill, 1969, 90th Congress, 2nd Session, H. Rept. 1576 (1968), p. 18.

107. House, Report of Appropriations Committee, Legislative Branch Appropriation Bill, 1970, 91st Congress, 1st Session, H. Rept. 91-487 (1969), p. 31.

108. Budgeting for National Objectives (New York: Committee for Economic Development, 1966), p. 56. The Committee raised pertinent questions concerning the fragmented nature of GAO financial audits viewed as a totality and the lack of periodic financial examination coverage encompassing all agencies. See also

Arthur Andersen and Co., <u>Sound Financial Reporting in the Public Sector - A Prerequisite to Fiscal Responsibility</u>, 1975.

109. Joint Financial Management Improvement Program, <u>Annual Report Fiscal Year 1967</u>, p. 79. See also, Letter from Phillip S. Hughes, Deputy Director, Bureau of the Budget, to Comptroller General Elmer B. Staats, June 24, 1968 and Comptroller General's reply addressed to Phillip S. Hughes, Deputy Director, Bureau of the Budget, July 31, 1968.

110. Memorandum from Director, Office of Policy and Special Studies, GAO, to the Directors of the Civil, Defense, and International Divisions, August 2, 1968.

111. Remarks of Comptroller General Elmer B. Staats before Committee of General Counsels of the Federal Bar Association, Washington, D.C., April 17, 1966.

112. Statement of Comptroller General Elmer B. Staats before the Legislative Subcommittee, House Appropriations Committee, on "Budget Estimates for Fiscal Year 1978," February 3, 1977.

113. In an internal GAO memorandum, the Comptroller General said:

> While appropriately recognizing non-monetary improvements, there is nevertheless value in continuing to point up the monetary savings whenever they can feasibly be estimated. In many instances, the possibility of a substantial saving may provide the very impetus which we are looking for to gain acceptances for a needed improvement. However, caution should be exercised in spending undue amounts of time and effort in estimating savings and benefits. (July 22, 1966.)

114. Eric Daenecke, <u>A Study of the United States General Accounting Office</u> (Unpublished Ph.D. dissertation, The American University, 1950), p. 257.

115. <u>Standards for Audit of Governmental Organizations, Programs, Activities, and Functions</u>, <u>op</u>. <u>cit</u>., p. I.

116. <u>Ibid</u>.

117. Quoted by Elmer B. Staats, "Governmental Auditing Yesterday, Today, and Tomorrow." The GAO Review, Spring 1976, p. 3.

118. Ibid., pp. 4 and 5.

119. General Accounting Office, Answers to Frequently Asked Questions, p. 23.

120. 1976 Annual Report, op. cit., p. 221.

Chapter 6

COMPTROLLER GENERAL'S REPORTS - THEIR
PRODUCTION AND IMPACT

It* is, by the most generous interpretation I can
muster, an exercise in _ex post facto_ diplomacy by
amateurs.[1]

With minor exceptions, we are in general agreement with the findings and recommendations of
the report** and share GAO's concern that organized crime still flourishes.[2]

These sharply contrasting examples of agency reactions
to Comptroller General's reports afford an appropriate backdrop for analysis of GAO's report preparation process as
well as the responses which the reports evoke.

THE BROAD SPECTRUM AND LARGE
VOLUME OF GAO REPORTS

The earlier discussion has brought out the wide range
of subject matter covered by the GAO in its audits and reviews. There is an almost staggering outpouring of reports
varying from those on relatively minor matters to those
that hit the headlines. Behind this output is a massive
effort directed to the production of these documents in a
manner that keeps possible error to an irreducible minimum.
Before a report is issued, it may have involved extended
delays and internal tensions. Once the report is released,
there may be strain between the GAO and the agency whose
operations and/or program have been reviewed. Whatever
their shortcomings, the GAO reports are an invaluable source
of information on the Federal Government's programs and activities. They can be effective vehicles for pinpointing
issues in situations calling for corrective action and may
even identify any corrective or other measures that are
indicated.

A distinctive feature of the reporting system employed
by the GAO to present its audit findings and recommendations
is reliance upon the use of individual reports dealing with
the specific reviews conducted by it. The Comptroller General issues a comprehensive annual report which comes out
approximately six months after the end of the fiscal year;
but it is the individual reports that serve as the basic
means for communicating GAO audit findings to the Congress
and agencies. The multiple channels of communication between the GAO and Congress, discussed in Chapter 2, also

*The GAO report on the Mayaguez incident.
**"War on Organized Crime Faltering."

place the Comptroller General's reporting in an entirely different frame of reference than that of other countries.

Types of reports

There are three basic types of reports prepared by the GAO: reports to the Congress; reports to Congressional committees, subcommittees and individual Members of Congress; and reports to agency officials.[3] The reports to Congress, with which this chapter is primarily concerned, are regarded as the keystone of the total reporting system since they are the medium through which the Comptroller General reports to the Congress as a body. The discretion that characterizes the transmittal of reports to Congress affords the Comptroller General a certain sanction in his dealings with agencies since officials are ordinarily hesitant about having Congress apprised as to shortcomings alleged by the Comptroller General. It is true that the distinction between reports to the Congress and those to agencies has been somewhat attenuated by the Legislative Reorganization Act of 1970 so far as apprising Congressional committees of GAO recommendations to agencies. Nevertheless, the more formal type of report tends to have greater compelling quality.

The GAO Report Manual states that individual reports to the Congress should be prepared if one or more of the following purposes would be served: comply with a specific statutory requirement; call attention to important matters requiring or warranting action by the Congress; communicate useful information on important matters of interest to the Congress.[4]

The determination of whether a report should be to the Congress

The actual application of these criteria still permits considerable leeway in the exercise of judgment as to whether such a report should be submitted. In some instances, the decision to issue a report to Congress may be made when the study is initially undertaken. Or developments since the inception of the project or circumstances existing at the time the report is ready for presentation may be the determining factors. It is obvious that different echelons within the GAO may have varying views as to the appropriate addressee of a particular report. GAO personnel frankly stated that there was a "push" to have a report go to Congress if the respective division so recommended, since this involved a morale element. One gets the feeling that the operating divisions look upon Congressional reports as the significant accomplishments of their respective units. Hence, they tend to be disappointed if reports they hope to have submitted to the Congress are "downgraded." Commenting on the propensity for turning out Congressional reports which, when unrestricted as to distribution, carry blue covers, one staff member said: "They have gone blue book happy;" others refer to this phenomenon as the "blue book syndrome." A followup -- several years later after the original study -- on this phenomenon indicated that the emphasis on blue-covered reports still persists. The reporting practice has a pragmatic quality and tends to be responsive to the attitudes and values of the Comptroller General and how he interprets the wishes of the Congress. The so-called "Holifield hearings" discussed in Chapter 8, subjected the Comptroller General's reporting practices to critical scrutiny. Although these hearings revolved around audits of defense contractors, they had a profound effect upon the totality of the GAO's auditing and reporting practices.

An underlying issue with respect to GAO's reporting is whether the report should be issued to the Congress if the agency and the GAO are in agreement and if the department or other establishment proceeds to take corrective action that is indicated. It was asserted by agencies that submitting reports to Congress when these circumstances are present serves no constructive purpose and merely produces irritation and resentment. Referring to this line of reasoning, a GAO executive pointed out that, when an agency says it has corrected an inadequacy, it frequently has not actually dealt or come to grips with the basic cause or difficulty.

Tone of reports

As is to be expected, the agencies are very much concerned with the tone of the GAO reports. The GAO Report Manual cautions staff to avoid language which unnecessarily generates defensiveness and opposition. It even admonishes that although criticism "often is necessary to demonstrate the need for some management improvements, our emphasis in the reports should be on the needed improvements rather than on criticism."[5] But such hortatory statements may not accord with realities. The faultfinding emphasis which agencies attribute to the audit carries forward, it is maintained, into the reports themselves. Comptroller General Campbell's memorandum that was presented in 1962 at the beginning of the Comprehensive Audit Manual, reflected a theme which might well have made agencies apprehensive as to what they might expect to find in GAO reports:

> Our experience with the committees and individual members of that body [Congress] has

been that they are interested in our findings relating to deficient performance and opportunities for improvement. This policy of emphasizing the examination into weaknesses in agency performance has been a basic one for some time. . . . we must guard against allocating too much of our effort to the less important, more easily examined, and less controversial Government activities.

One does not have to go beyond the confines of the GAO to confirm the fact that there was built into the organization a pronounced leaning towards stressing agency shortcomings in GAO reports. This proclivity militated against widespread acceptance of the more balanced tone now envisaged by the Manual. A GAO executive said: "I am not sure but that approbation and promotion are based upon the findings of the shortcomings." Another GAO official was frank enough to say: "No agency is impervious to publicity, and GAO has derived its publicity from the audit route." Still another top executive made this interesting observation, which ties in very well with the comment just cited: "Public reaction is generally in relation to the derogatory elements of our reports."

The "climate" that had -- at least until recently -- surrounded the shaping of GAO reports is reflected in a memorandum from a division director submitting a report to the Congress for the signature of the Comptroller General:

This report is unique in that it is a GAO presentation of facts and problems underlying a broad facet of a program rather than a critical evaluation.

I am prepared to defend our position if we have any adverse reaction on our submitting a non-critical report to the Congress in this particular case.

An agency official, commenting on the more typical report tone, said:

So far as GAO audits are concerned, one gets no concept of how well the program is managed. . . . Every year at Appropriations Committee time when we go up in front of Congress some Committee Member pulls out all the blue books and we catch hell.

Another agency executive remarked: "What I object to is the ungodly amount of effort that GAO puts into some of their reports that try to find something to criticize."

Illustrative of agency sensitivity is the umbrage which the Food and Nutrition Service of the Department of Agriculture took at the title of a Comptroller General report. In responding to the draft report, the Acting Administrator said:

> Our first comment concerns the title of the report itself -- Food Stamp Receipts -- Who's Watching the Money? The title implies that nothing is currently being done to monitor food stamp receipts. This . . . demonstrates a preliminary bias on the part of GAO. It also appears to us to be an editorial comment whose purpose is to impart a generally unfavorable opinion of the Agency prior to any review of the report itself.[6]

The Comptroller General's unresponsiveness to this protestation might have stemmed from the damning nature of the lead-off statement on the cover of the Report which read: "Misuses and mishandling of over $34 million in food stamps went undetected for extended periods because neither the Food and Nutrition Service nor the States were effectively monitoring the agents which sold food stamps." Once having hit upon an eye-catching title, the GAO was not receptive to changing it. Staats has sought to reduce the abrasive nature of GAO reports. However, a style that has been so firmly established within an organization cannot be summarily reversed.

One agency official, speaking of the tone and phraseology of GAO reports, pointed out that the difficulty might not lie so much in the manner in which GAO presented its material, but rather in the use which was made of it.

> I must admit that for many years this gave us a problem because the reports were inflammatory -- we don't have that any more. But when the final report is issued -- and it is no fault of GAO so far as I can see -- it depends on who gets the report and how they want to use it. The newspapers can pick it up and write the sensational stuff.

THE SLOW-MOVING REPORT PROCESS

Delays in reporting

A perennial and widespread complaint leveled, both within the Congress and the Executive Branch, against GAO relates to the extended period of time that ordinarily elapses between the initiation of a study and the issuance of a final report. The unfavorable reaction engendered by such delays is exacerbated by the fact that in many instances personnel and/or situations might have changed considerably since the particular study was launched. The problem of delays relates particularly to those reports that are based upon studies initiated by the Comptroller General, since reports prepared in response to requests by committees or individual Members of Congress were, until recently, given a top priority. However, even this type of report has not been prepared as expeditiously as those within the Congress expected.

This led Senator Lee Metcalf to include in a series of questions addressed to the Comptroller General an inquiry as to how that official was responding to "a frequent criticism that GAO takes an excessive length of time to complete tasks requested by the Congress." After explaining that some of the work GAO was asked to perform is very complex and entails a good deal of planning and field work, Staats apprised the Senator that: GAO (a) had provided for special handling of requests for information only; (b) was encouraging informal briefings of Congressional Members and staffs to provide information sooner than could be done in formal reports; and (c) was spending more time with the requestor before starting to work in order not to "waste time on tasks that may be of marginal interest to the committee or member."[7]

The reporting delays that have bedeviled GAO for many years should be particularly perturbing to GAO officials. The Office, which is on the <u>qui vive</u> to uncover shortcomings of other agencies, found itself ineffectual in coping with the problem of turning out reports in a reasonably expeditious manner. As long ago as 1955, the Planning Staff said:

> Whether our reports are to be effectively
> used is directly related to whether they
> are timely issued. Too often we fail in
> this respect. In some instances we have
> not met advanced commitments and in others
> we have not complied with statutory time
> requirements.[8]

It would seem that extended reporting delays were built into the operations of the GAO and that, despite efforts to speed up the process, the achievement of tangible improvement has been impeded by a feeling of futility. In

short, reporting delays became "institutionalized" so that
they tended to be the accepted norms rather than shortfalls
from established standards.

An interesting example of GAO report delay is found
in the report on the pricing of the contracts which the
Army Ammunition Procurement and Supply Agency of Joliet,
Illinois, had awarded to the Eureka Williams Company. The
field work in connection with this study was begun on January 4, 1967 and was completed in July 1967. An advance
copy of a proposed draft report was submitted to Washington
early in September of that year. The chronicle of subsequent steps affords a vivid case study of the vagaries of
report processing within the GAO. The saga finally ended
with the issuance of the report on July 15, 1969.[9] The
draft report had been addressed to the Secretary of Defense.
Subsequently it was decided to "upgrade" it to Congressional
report status. Then a decision was reached not to issue an
individual pricing report on the Eureka case but rather include it in an overall report to be submitted to the Congress. This was subsequently reversed, and the responsible
GAO executives decided to revert to a Congressional report
dealing only with the Eureka case. In the case of another
study, the preliminary exploration began as early as 1965,
and a preliminary draft of a report was ready by August
1966. The report itself was not issued until January 1968.[10]
Cases such as these occurring early in the Staats regime
must have sensitized him to the urgency of corrective action,
and he initiated a study of reporting delays.[11]

Adverse reactions to GAO's delayed reporting

Reference has already been made to criticism on the
Hill directed to reporting delays. A committee staff assistant
suggested an informal arrangement for making GAO's findings
quickly available to his committee "so that you do not have
to wait for some stinking blue book." The Staats reply to
Senator Metcalf already alluded to indicates that such a
step has been taken. The assistant chief clerk of a key
committee, who was prone to play down criticisms of the GAO,
nevertheless felt impelled to comment: "If a report gets
here after the hearings, it languishes. Reports are not
of a hell of a lot of use to us after hearings are over."

When the Government Operations Committee, in its 1956
Report on the GAO, criticized the protracted delays between
the initial preparation of reports and their ultimate trans-
mission to the Congress,[12] Comptroller General Campbell replied that this was "an operating problem about which we
are very much concerned."[13] He very correctly attributed
the delays to the GAO's careful review process and agency
clearance of reports, both of which are discussed subse-

quently in this chapter. The resistance of this serious
GAO weakness to remedial action may be regarded by GAO
critics as being symptomatic of bureaucratic inertia. It
unquestionably is incompatible with a viable process for
monitoring the Government's operations.

The delays in GAO reports are a prolific source of
vexation to the agencies:

> A general criticism I have of GAO, and I am
> sure common to everybody around the table,
> is the need to get more current attention and
> more current response from the GAO. We spend
> a hell of a lot of time answering questions
> about what we did about something two or
> three years ago, that has long since been
> cured because we learned about it at the
> time they were looking at it and corrected it.

An agency official, seeking to present a more sympathetic
viewpoint, observed:

> And it seems to me that -- whereas it is
> obviously useless from the agency viewpoint
> to get a final audit report where everything
> has been taken care of months or years be-
> fore -- in terms of establishing their re-
> cord I think the GAO still has to use that
> data. But I suspect the problem here is
> one perhaps primarily of presentation.

The representative of another agency pointed out that
although his organization would like to see the final report earlier -- more or less for internal use -- the GAO
does -- prior to the availability of the report -- bring
to the agency's attention matters on which corrective action should be taken. But agency consensus with respect
to what GAO reporting delays mean for the agencies is distinctly critical. The prevailing tenor is exemplified in
the following comment of an agency official:

> There is no excuse, regardless of policies
> around GAO, for a three-year old report.
> It serves no purpose. . . . I think that,
> if it is going to be an effective report,
> it must be a timely report; otherwise,
> some other device must be found to do the
> job they are trying to do.

An assistant secretary for administration, who was very
temperate in his criticism of the GAO's reporting practices, commented that the "total process means that the
administrator gets reports on the deeds of his predecessors."

    A Department of Agriculture official was less for-
giving on this score. Although the particular incident
occurred some years ago, it bears mention since a top GAO
executive, when interviewed about it, praised the report
about which the agency official was exercised. The report had disclosed that a house of ill fame had been located on national forest lands.[14] A court injunction
enjoining and restraining the claimant from operating
the house was obtained in December 1957. The Agriculture
Department official, taking the GAO to task for reporting
the matter so long after the fact, i.e., 1962, said:

> The case had been closed five years when GAO
> came along and dragged it out again. What
> the hell was the use of doing this. . . .
> This kind of thing destroys confidence in
> the GAO.

The delay in this case was probably compounded by another
factor that sometimes detracts from the timeliness of a
report: the elapse of time before the GAO even initiates
the study.

The quest for infallibility

    The underlying cause of these delays is the degree
of accuracy which GAO seeks to attain, or to put it otherwise, the extent of the calculated risk which it is willing to incur. What is involved is not merely a matter of
factual accuracy but also the interpretation of the findings and the formulation of recommendations for corrective
action. The preparation of reports is characterized by
what appears to be almost a phobia with respect to possible errors or weaknesses that might make the report
vulnerable to criticism or attack. An audit site supervisor said: "My head is on the chopping block if something gets into a report that is not factually correct."
An associate director, speaking of the report review process, which is discussed subsequently in this chapter,
commented: "If anybody's ass gets into a sling on the report, the OPSS[15] puts the onus on the operating division
and in turn the particular group." A key GAO executive
has said: "A few embarrassing errors can neutralize years
and years of good work." The Report Manual, explaining
the need for accuracy, states that "at stake is the professional reputation of the General Accounting Office."[16]
This hypersensitivity as to possible errors may also reflect a feeling that agencies and officials the GAO moni-
tors and who are frequently disconcerted by GAO reports
very much relish the opportunity to point out GAO's own
shortcomings in reporting on a particular matter.

In explaining the Office's almost frenetic efforts
to avoid possible errors, some GAO personnel refer to the
traumatic experience of the GAO when, in 1955, it was forced
to admit errors in a report that was the subject of Congressional hearings.[17] Internal GAO memoranda vividly convey the disconcerting effect that the disclosure of the in-
accuracies had upon the organization. Several months after Comptroller General Campbell acknowledged the blunders --
however grudgingly -- the head of the unit responsible for
the preparation of the report, resigned. The intense fear
of being proven wrong engendered by this incident apparently
worked itself into the GAO fabric.

Multiple layers of report review and the dysfunctional effects

Since the Comptroller General can, at best, give only
a cursory review to GAO reports calling for his signature,
the Office of Policy Acts as a surrogate for him in making
a top level review of the draft reports that will ultimately
require his signature. Yet, one must also be mindful of
the fact that this overall scrutiny is preceded by a series of reviews on the part of regional offices, the Washington audit group that has headquarters responsibility for the
project, and staff assistants to the heads of the respective
operating divisions. The reports that are to be signed by
the Comptroller General must also be submitted to the Office
of the General Counsel, which supposedly is concerned primarily with the legal aspects of the reports. However,
this ostensible legal review undoubtedly, at least on occasion, extends beyond the legal aspects of the report.
The Office of Congressional Relations "makes a quick review
of the report giving primary consideration to possible impact on congressional relationships."[18] A report which is
of a particularly delicate or controversial character will
be discussed with the Comptroller General at an intermediate stage in its preparation rather than await the completion of the preliminary draft. More than ten years ago,
the Task Force that studied the processing of audit reports
concluded that report processing time could "be shortened
by reducing the number of persons involved in the review
process and by reducing the number of reviews that are directed toward both the substantive content of the report
and the presentation and language used."[19]

The report review process militates against the timeliness and, in turn, the usefulness of GAO reports. At
least as equally disturbing is what the process exacts
not only in staff effort but also tensions within the organization itself as the report draft is shuttled back
and forth to iron out differences between various levels
of the organization involved in the preparation of the

particular report. The reactions of a former assistant director of GAO are germane: "I fled the GAO; I was totally frustrated. When I wrote a report in GAO, I had to go through the tortures of hell to get the report out. I was checked and double-checked. An almost interminable process."

Implicit in these multiple reviews is a diffusion of responsibility for the ultimate product. One might speculate as to whether those working on draft reports are less motivated to exert the maximum effort since they can anticipate that, regardless of the quality of their output, it will be subjected to extended and intensive review.

The tortuous internal review process also has a vital substantive effect on the end product. As the report flows through the review channels, the anonymity of those responsible for its preparation is accentuated, and the final result is a report that might be said to be of an institutional character. The participation of so many organizational elements in a report, it can be argued, inhibits both precipitate judgment and application of an unduly narrow perspective. Another argument that can be advanced in support of having such widespread participation in the preparation of reports is that it affords the means of bringing a composite of talents to bear upon a problem rather than relying upon the knowledge and competence of a few individuals.

The other side of the coin is that what is ultimately arrived at may be something of an imposed mix of ideas and values. Those on the higher echelons, who may be far removed from first-hand contacts with the programs or activities and their realities, may unduly influence the interpretation of the facts and the formulation of recommendations. A Congressman expressed concern "that the report that comes out is not the report of the auditor."

Agency review of draft reports and resultant delays

The problem of delay in the issuance of GAO reports is closely tied in with the GAO practice of clearing draft reports with the agencies and contractors so that they may have the opportunity to present their reactions to the GAO. The procedure, which had its inception in the audit of government corporations, was formalized, according to Comptroller General Staats, into written office policy in the middle 1950's. Staats explained to a subcommittee his position on this practice:

> When I took office in 1966, I carefully examined the existing policy and endorsed it.

215

I believe this procedure helps to assure
the factual accuracy of our reports. Moreover, when the agency disagrees with our
findings, conclusions, and recommendations,
the Congress is entitled to the agency's
position as well as our own. . . . We
sometimes encounter exceptional situations
in which it is appropriate to proceed without awaiting formal agency comments. . . .
Where our reports respond to requests of
committees and Members, we are frequently
asked not to obtain formal written comments.[20]

Earlier, in writing to a Congresswoman who like many
of her colleagues had taken issue with the report clearance process,[21] Staats referred to still another consideration, i.e., that agencies are much more willing to
provide the data, internal working documents, and other
materials requested by GAO "if they understand that any
difference they may have with GAO findings, conclusions,
and recommendations will be reflected in the report to
the Congress."[22]

The Report Manual recognizes that the period of time
constituting a reasonable opportunity for the agency submitting its comments may vary with the complexity of the
report and the physical dispersion of the agency's activities.[23] The Manual, which previously spoke of a four-
week period as the maximum permissible time, now allows
60 days.

Some might question how Staats' persuasive advocacy
of agency review can be reconciled with his deference to
committees and Members who request that reports be issued
without affording an opportunity for agency review. If
the Comptroller General has found that such reviews contribute significantly to accuracy, then it could be argued
he should not accede to Congressional requests for short-
cutting the report process in this manner unless he is
convinced that not only the accuracy but also fairness of
the report will not be undermined. The report on the
1976-77 swine flu program[24] was, "at the specific request
of several House committees," issued without written comments from HEW "because of the need for timely consideration of the issues." This is hardly a cogent reason.

Conflicting Congressional and agency reactions to advance
reviews

Agencies feel that the opportunity to review GAO draft
reports is an integral feature of what might be termed "due
process" in GAO reviews. The sensitivity of agencies with

216

respect to being subjected to the element of surprise in connection with GAO reports is illustrated in an incident in which the Department of Defense was involved. In this case, Defense officials were cross-examined before the Joint Economic Committee with respect to a GAO report the Department had not previously seen.[25] As one official put it:

> It was a bad situation. . . and it got a lot
> of people angry. I think some damage was done
> to some relationships that had been fostered
> under a very positive attitude that Secretary
> McNamara had taken toward audits in general and
> GAO in particular. It is difficult often to
> bring these positive relationships about, and
> I think damage was done and I regretted that.
> I think GAO also does, and, as far as I am
> concerned, they are going to be much more
> careful.

The fact that agencies strongly resent the issuance of any GAO reports without prior agency clearance should not be equated with a universal feeling of satisfaction with respect to GAO's handling of the reactions it receives to draft reports. One agency official asserted that, in connection with such clearances, auditors polish up weak points and buttress strong points and that the negative aspects of the reports are still retained. In short, it was his contention that the GAO interpreted the agency's reply in such a way that it strengthened GAO's findings, a practice that was deeply resented by the agency. This official had recommended that his department not comment on GAO draft copies, but his recommendation was not followed. Another official, commenting on the rigidity with which the GAO looked upon its draft reports, stated that such reports "seem to be written with the same type of concrete as the final reports. There is a great reluctance to make changes in draft reports."

In contradistinction to these observations, a Department of Agriculture official reported that he had found in his own dealings with the GAO that a draft report that is "cockeyed" can be changed on the basis of discussions with the GAO. "There can, of course, be honest differences."

The significance of agency and contractor review of draft reports is enhanced by the fact that the final reports include the comments of the respective agency or contractor to the extent that the GAO does not concur in them. Where the GAO agrees with a criticism or exception on the part of the reviewer, it merely makes the appropriate revision.

217

The calculated risks implicit in advance reviews

More than delay is involved in having draft reports
reviewed by agencies, contractors, and others deemed by
the Comptroller General to have a direct interest. There
is the probability of leaks, which have occasionally bedeviled the GAO. The Chairman of the House Government
Operations Committee once wrote the Comptroller General
concerning "premature disclosure of information from
drafts of your proposed reports" and cited two specific
cases.[28] Staats has played down the seriousness of the
problem; in his testimony at the House hearings on GAO's
1972 appropriation estimates, Staats stated that of the
900 reports submitted to Congress in the five years he
had been Comptroller General, there had been premature
discussion in the press in only about six or seven cases.[27]
More recently, a news story published at the close of 1976
on GAO's monumental study of Federal bank supervision[28]
was able to boast: "The 250 page GAO draft report, a
copy of which has been obtained by the Washington Post,
is not scheduled to be made public until spring 1977."[29]

Such clearances can also cause some to conjecture or
even allege that pressures brought to bear by those reviewing the drafts result in the GAO modifying a tenable
stance it has taken in the document being processed. Thus,
when the Comptroller General issued his final draft of the
study on defense industry profits, it was asserted in some
quarters that the GAO had capitulated to industry pressures
that resulted from distribution of a preliminary draft.[30]
The Comptroller General had to work assiduously to counter
this imputation.[31] In light of this consideration, as
well as the inevitable delays and the possibility of premature disclosures, it is not surprising that within the
GAO itself conflicting viewpoints were expressed as to
the merits of the advance review policy.

Readability of reports

Since Staats' advent, there has been sustained emphasis on making GAO reports more readable. His appointment
of GAO's first information officer evidenced Staats' desire to establish better communication between GAO and
its clientele. Staats' efforts to increase the readability
of GAO reports have encompassed not only style but also
physical layout and the use of visual materials such as
maps, pictures, and charts. One interesting innovation
designed to facilitate use of the reports has been the inclusion of succinct summaries that can be detached and
filed separately. This answers at least in part the criticisms of those within the Congress who have complained of
being inundated by GAO reports and being unable, because
of time constraints, to do anything but file them away.

The previous chapter told of the savings which the
Comptroller General claims are attributable directly to
GAO efforts as well as the even larger savings which he
attributes to the combined efforts of GAO and others.
Undoubtedly, reports are an important tool in effecting
these savings as well as in achieving economies and improvements which, according to the Comptroller General,
"cannot be accurately quantified into dollar savings."
This chapter deals with the impact of reports in a context in which their specific financial implications are
only incidental.

Varying reactions to GAO findings and recommendations

The discussion of specific case studies that follows
shortly brings out something of the flavor of responses
to the findings and recommendations formulated by the GAO
on the basis of reviews initiated by the Comptroller General. At this juncture of the discussion, it will, therefore, suffice to discuss in more general terms the reactions that are evoked by such reports. Agency reactions
are affected by a number of variables which, in turn, interact: the general posture of the agency vis-a-vis the
GAO, the relative significance of the subject matter of
the report, the extent to which the report sets forth deficiencies, absence or presence of difficulties being experienced by the agency in its relations with Congress
and/or the public, GAO-agency negotiations preceding the
issuance of the final report, and agency stance on previous GAO reports dealing with the same or related subjects.

An official subsequently elevated to Cabinet rank
made some candid observations as to how a department head
might react to the reports he receives from the GAO. He
stated that one factor was how early in his tenure the
secretary received the report -- intimating that a certain
tolerance develops with the passage of time. Even more
significant was his comment that the reaction was affected
by whether or not the secretary happens to have political
aspirations.

> If he is a political figure expecting to run
> for office sometime . . . and GAO reports
> come in during the first month or two, the
> first thing he says: "Christ Almighty, what
> is this?" A secretary who is not a political
> figure and maybe is a management man will
> take his first report and say: "This is
> very interesting; this might help you do a

better job." . . . I think the receptivity
to what GAO does varies differently with
secretaries, depending upon who they are
and what they think their present and future roles may be.

Congressional staff comments shed some interesting
sidelights on how some committee personnel respond to the
materials prepared by the GAO. A key staff member of an
important committee observed that he had learned that one
could not take a GAO report without checking it out:
"All sides of the issue might not have been studied or
the report might reflect predilections or prejudices of
the GAO." A subcommittee staff director made this interesting observation: "You have to hit the GAO reports right
on the head - neither underestimate nor overestimate them.
Very few people understand this." As is demonstrated subsequently, GAO reports play a significant role in the
legislative process and may even be the catalyst for Congressional enactments. On the other hand, an individual
Member's reaction is sometimes determined by whether a report is or is not supportive of a position which has already crystallized.

Far East supply system responsiveness study -- a non-Congressional report of singular significance

This study, which began shortly after Staats assumed
the office of Comptroller General, represents an unusual
case of (a) intensive collaboration between the GAO and
an agency in the conduct of a review; (b) the willingness
of the Comptroller General to forego the issuance of a report to Congress despite the fact that the study, which
involved considerable staff effort, was one of pronounced
moment.

A Dear Bob-Elmer letter dated July 27, 1966, which
the Comptroller General sent Secretary McNamara, referred
to several discussions which they had concerning the study
of "Defense supply management in the Pacific area," which
the GAO was initiating. Staats expressed a desire that the
review be carried out insofar as practicable on a cooperative basis. As to submitting a report to Congress, the
Comptroller General said that, aside from possibly reporting to a subcommittee of the Joint Economic Committee on
improvements made in Defense supply systems since his last
appearance before the subcommittee, "there is no request
from the Congress or commitment on my part to report to
Congress on the present study." This reassurance by the
Comptroller General is most significant; a GAO staff member commented: "Staats felt we should not in time of war
be harassing the Department of Defense."

220

Leading up to the initiation of the study was the fact that, when Staats came to the GAO, he found that GAO personnel had uncovered what they considered to be many serious inadequacies in the Far East Supply setup of the Department of Defense. The Secretary, who reportedly was exercised about the possibility of GAO "prying" into a combat area, was mollified when he was apprised of GAO's view of the situation and when Staats told him of the basis upon which he was willing to proceed. The Secretary, not surprisingly, expressed his concurrence with the "cooperative basis" which Staats proposed and stated that as the study progressed he would look forward to meeting with the Comptroller General regularly to review progress.[32] Somewhat atypical in GAO's conduct of the study was the participation of DOD staff in the conference that was held for regional personnel who were to work on the review. McNamara stated that some of the items that could be brought out by the study would be of sufficient overall importance to merit joint personal attention of the Comptroller General and himself. He coupled this with a reference to "our regular meetings as the review progresses."[33]

A series of exit conferences were held in Honolulu in October 1966 with CINCPAC military component commanders and Washington representatives of the Department of Defense. Following the conferences, Secretary McNamara wrote Staats expressing his gratification with the substantial agreement that had been reached with respect to the items identified for review at the Hawaii meetings. As to those items on which agreement was not reached, McNamara expressed the hope that "the development of additional information and continued cooperative analysis may lead to even further convergence of views." He also arranged for submittal of progress reports on the implementation of the recommendations and the development of necessary additional data and analyses. These reports were to be made available to the Comptroller General.[34]

A GAO executive, commenting on what this review meant in terms of the GAO said:

> The whole effort enhanced the image and influence of GAO in the military. It demonstrated the competence and expertise of the GAO. . . The experience showed GAO can be aboveboard without compromising independence.

The experience with the Far East Supply Responsiveness Study demonstrated that, in appropriate situations, reporting only to the agency may be the most effective means for working out solutions to even major problems. But the underlying reporting thrust -- at least insofar as significant

221

matters are concerned -- appears to be that of providing
documents for Congress. Such reports make GAO's output
more visible to Congress, the news media, and the public;
they are generally more gratifying to the staff and also
put greater pressure on agencies to accept GAO recommendations.

Agency disagreements with GAO reports

The quotations at the beginning of this chapter reflect
the range of agency reactions to the reports which the Comptroller General submits to Congress. The State Department's
bitter denunciation of the Mayaguez report characterizing
it as "totally inadequate and misleading"[35] was atypical as
was GAO's penetration into an unusually sensitive area. The
State Department's reply went so far as to be accusatory:
"We often make mistakes, but in my opinion the GAO has failed --
despite its best efforts -- to find any substantial failures
in the handling of the Mayaguez incident." The tone of the
Defense Department's comments were far milder: "There are
a few areas in the report which contain speculative conclusions on the part of the GAO which are based upon a too-rigid
interpretation of the facts."[36] Even when expressed in a
restrained manner, agency reactions can still indicate strong
opposition to a Comptroller General's report. Having reviewed the draft report on Federal proposals to finance the
commercialization of advanced energy technologies, the Administrator of the Energy Research and Development Administration expressed deep concern "because it presents strong
conclusions and recommendations to the Congress without a
sound underlying basis of analysis supporting them."[37]

An agency may implement a GAO recommendation despite
disagreement with it. The Comptroller General submitted
to the Department of the Treasury a draft report in which
GAO recommended that the agreement for compensating Washington, D.C. area banks for cashing Government salary checks
be terminated. The reply from the Treasury Department was
terse:

> The Department does not agree with all the
> reasoning in your draft report as to why
> the arrangement should be discontinued.
> I wish to advise you, however, that should
> your final report to Congress contain a
> recommendation that the arrangement be dis-
> continued, this Department will comply with
> the recommendation.[38]

The final report[39] did include such a recommendation, and
the Comptroller General later reported that the Treasury
Department had discontinued the check-cashing agreement.[40]

The Treasury's obstinacy hardly reflected credit upon the Department. If Treasury felt that it had a tenable basis for challenging the GAO recommendation, then it surely should not have gone along with it simply because the Comptroller General was including such a recommendation in his report to the Congress. One can assume that whatever criticisms the Treasury had of the GAO's reasoning were not very persuasive and that the Department's reaction stemmed from chagrin over the fact that the GAO had uncovered a recurrent unnecessary expenditure on the part of the Treasury. This case indicates that, where a vital issue is not involved, an agency may go along, albeit reluctantly, with a GAO recommendation unless it can develop very convincing reasons for rejecting what has been proposed.

After stating that discussions between staff members of the National Aeronautics and Space Administration and those of GAO had resulted in "the resolution of a number of issues and in clarification of the respective positions on other matters," NASA expressed its disagreement with the recommendations set forth in the GAO report dealing with space shuttle facilities.[41] The conflict in positions was handled graciously.

What could be considered sheer stubbornness on the part of GAO evoked strong negative response by the Defense Department to GAO's report on a technical procurement matter. This report contended that savings of about $4.4 million could have been effected in the procurement, maintenance, and supply support costs for fiscal years 1964 through 1969 if a domestically produced ejection seat system (instead of a foreign purchased system) had been used in the F-4C aircraft.[42] GAO argued that, in addition to higher costs which the procurement of the foreign produced ejection seats incurred, there were other considerations that weighed against this purchase contract.

In commenting on the draft report, the Department of Defense maintained that the substitution suggested by GAO would have resulted in a net increase of $511,000 rather than the saving indicated by the GAO. Moreover, DOD pointed out that a decision in May 1962 to effect replacement such as had been suggested by the GAO would have "resulted in an unacceptable delay in F-4 deliveries."[43] The GAO conceded in its report that: "At this time no overall benefits could be obtained through the use of domestically designed ejection seats in the F-4C aircraft since over two-thirds of the seats required for this aircraft have already been purchased."[44] However, it stood by the position that it had taken and issued a final report. DOD subsequently wrote the Comptroller General reaffirming its disagreement with the GAO's findings and attached a 13-page single-

spaced document that had been prepared by the Navy on the
subject. Later, in explaining why GAO had submitted a
Congressional report after receiving such negative and
pertinent comments from the Department of Defense, the
Comptroller General said:

> We considered these comments in the light
> of the information of record and concluded
> that the circumstances surrounding the con-
> tinued procurement of the foreign system
> would be of interest to the Congress.[45]

One can only speculate as to what was accomplished through
such a stalemate.

Favorable agency reactions to GAO reports

Agencies may not only concur in GAO reports but even
make laudatory comments and/or indicate that action is
being taken to effect the recommendations. Responding to
a report on aircraft midair collisions, the Department of
Transportation stated that the report presented "a fair
and reasonable assessment of the situation;" the Department also apprised GAO that the "Federal Aviation Administration is proceeding with efforts and a priority consistent
with the General Accounting Office recommendations."[46]

The report, "Nuclear or Conventional Power for Surface Combatant Ships?" elicited a very favorable response
from the Defense Department: "The Draft Report is a com-
mendably objective treatment of all sides of this complex
and often emotional issue. We anticipate that the Final
Report will serve as a vehicle to clarify and structure
the debate among the parties involved."[47] There have been
many such affirmative DOD reactions to reports submitted
by the Comptroller General. In its 1972 report on "Acquisition of Major Weapon Systems"[48] the GAO was able to inform Congress that DOD was in general agreement with its
findings, conclusions, and recommendations and that Defense
had taken corrective actions. This gratifying reaction
was probably attributable, at least in part, to the depth
and continuity with which GAO studied this subject and the
vulnerability that DOD had shown in this aspect of its
operations. The GAO report on "Combat Readiness of the
Strategic Air Command,"[49] not surprisingly, evoked a
pleased response by the Air Force; the GAO stated that
it was impressed with the management emphasis and techniques employed by the Strategic Air Command and believed
that other military services could profitably adopt some
of the procedures. The report on "Alcoholism Among Military Personnel" was an instance in which Defense agreed
with some GAO recommendations and took issue with another.

The disagreement related to the proposal that alcoholism
be considered a disease rather than misconduct.[50]

Both the Defense and State Departments agreed with
recommendations reflected in the title of the report "The
United States and Japan Should Seek a More Equitable Defense Cost-Sharing Arrangement."[51] The Department of Justice expressed "general accord" with the report "Immigration -- Need to Reassess U.S. Policy;"[52] its reaction was
undoubtedly influenced in some measure by the fact that
the report cited "the need for additional personnel and
resources to enforce immigration laws."

In his presentation of GAO's financial requirements
for fiscal year 1978, Comptroller General Staats gave a
subcommittee some examples of how GAO reports "often
directly affect the well-being of individual citizens."
He cited the fact that, as a result of GAO recommendations, the National Highway Safety Administration established a followup procedure to help insure that dealers
did not sell defective vehicles in inventory until they
corrected the defects. Other examples which Staats gave
of the effectiveness of GAO recommendations were the Food
and Drug Administration ban on the use of Red No. 2 color
additive in foods, drugs, and cosmetics and the issuance
of instructions by the Federal Highway Administration and
the Federal Aviation Administration "which should result
in more direct citizen involvement in Government financed
highways and construction projects."[53]

An agency receptive to a Comptroller General's recommendation may find that Congress demurs to such action.
Following a study of the dairy farm at the United States
Naval Academy, the Comptroller General recommended that
this farm be discontinued. After the Department of the
Navy had reviewed a copy of the draft report, it informed
the Comptroller General that it was developing a plan to
phase out the Naval Academy dairy.[54] A strongly negative
Congressional reaction to the proposed discontinuation of[55]
the farm resulted in the Navy's countermanding the order.

Similarly, the thrust of GAO recommendations for
savings in rural postal operations,[56] which had been cited
by the Postmaster General in issuing guidelines for closing
rural post offices, incurred some strong Congressional displeasure. Senator Randolph, for example, "pictured small
post offices as centers of rural life that often represented
a community's only contact with the federal government. 'I
think that when such offices are closed,' he said, 'the
American flag really comes down.'"[57]

The Justice Department made an unusual comment in re-

225

sponding to the draft report on organized crime. After
expressing general agreement with the findings and recommendations, the Department indicated some disagreement
with portions of the draft report but then went on to say:
"It is important to point out that we have gained considerable insights ourselves from the report and, more import-
antly, from the discussions held with the GAO staff responsible for its preparation."[58] This accolade indicates
the highly constructive ancillary effects that can come
from a GAO study.

Impact of reports upon Congress

Congressional utilization of GAO reports was considered generally in Chapter 2; at this point in the analysis, it would be appropriate to explore specific instances
of the response which Congress accords the reports it receives from the Comptroller General.

In his annual reports, the Comptroller General lists
those legislative recommendations included in the GAO reports that have been acted upon by the Congress.[59] Thus,
the 1975 Report cites such enactments as the establishment of the Commodity Futures Trading Commission[60] and the
passage of two provisions restricting the use of excess
defense articles in the Military Assistance Program.[61]
The 1976 Report states that the enactment dealing with
the U.S. grain inspection system[62] "was heavily influenced
by our report and should accomplish the general intent of
our recommendations." Similarly, the Comptroller General
pointed out that the 1976 extension of the Revenue Sharing
Program[63] "made certain changes that we had recommended
in testimony and reports to Congress."

The fact that Congress may not act forthwith on a GAO
recommendation for legislative action is not tantamount to
such GAO effort being completely abortive. The Comptroller
General is persevering on that score and uses both his
annual reports and a special report to remind the Congress
regularly of "open GAO recommendations for legislative
action."[64]

The many references in the Congressional Record to
the Comptroller General's reports -- whether commendatory
or critical -- are indicative of Congressional awareness
of GAO findings and recommendations. These references undoubtedly reflect GAO contacts with Congressional staff,
committees, and individual Members as well as the attention
which the media give the more newsworthy reports. A Senator or Representative who might ordinarily be indifferent
to, or even oblivious of, a GAO report may have his interest stimulated by such headline mention as: "$1 Billion

226

U.S. Overpayments Found,"[65] "GAO Urges Curb on FBI Control
Over Dissidents,"[66] "Booze in the Military,"[67] "GAO Report
is Said to Criticize Methods of Bank Regulators,"[68] and
"Still in a Rut - Education for Work."[69] If the report
is one initiated in response to a committee, subcommittee,
or Member's request, then, as is explained in Chapter 2,
the use made of the report is very much dependent upon
the initiator.

Problems posed by reports including classified data

The inclusion of classified data in GAO reports has
so many implications as to necessitate devoting a complete
chapter in the Report Manual (Chapter 18) to this facet of
the reporting process. The Manual states: "To make our
reports as useful to the Congress as possible, we should
not include classified information whenever our reporting
responsibilities can be satisfied without it."[70] Classified information obtained from any agency must be handled
in the manner prescribed by that agency's regulations,
Executive order, or pertinent legislation.

The report "Seizure of the Mayaguez,"[71] to which several references have been made in this study, demonstrated
the difficulties that can arise when a GAO report involves
classified material. The report was classified secret by
the President's Advisor for National Security Affairs even
though the State and Defense Departments, which provided
the information on which the report was based, had no objection to releasing the report as an unclassified document. In submitting the report to the House Subcommittee
on International Political and Military Affairs, the Comptroller General commented: "We believe that all information
in the report is unclassified but since GAO neither classifies nor declassifies documents, we have abided by the
National Security Council's request." Subsequent negotiations between the Subcommittee and the Special Advisor "led
to agreement that substantial portions of the report could
be declassified and released."[72] The GAO, when feasible,
prepares unclassified digests of classified reports or issues an "unclassified report and a separate classified
supplement containing the necessary classified information."[73]

A magazine article "Some of Our Plutonium is Missing"[74]
described the harassments that can beset those seeking to
effectively use a classified report. At the request of
the House Subcommittee on Energy and Environment, the GAO
prepared a report on shortcomings in the systems used to
control and protect highly dangerous nuclear material.[75]
The report, which was classified secret by the Energy and
Research Administration, was, according to the article,
"highly critical of Congressional oversight for counten-

227

ancing inadequate nuclear safeguards." The article goes on to say that the Joint Committee on Atomic Energy

> . . . attempted to muzzle this criticism by issuing a sanitized press release on the GAO report; it did not mention the huge amount of unaccounted for nuclear material; nor did it contain the criticism of Congressional oversight. Representative Dingell [the subcommittee chairman] was furious at what he interpreted as a conscious effort to distort the substance of the GAO report. Blocked in his desire to release the report in its entirety because of the secret classification affixed to it by ERDA, Dingell ordered his staff on the Energy and Environmental Subcommittee to prepare its own summary. He said, "I issued the report to give a more accurate view of the GAO findings."

It is interesting that the Joint Atomic Energy Committee, which some characterized as "probably the most powerful congressional committee in the history of the nation," was ultimately abolished in 1977.[76]

Justice Douglas, dissenting from a Supreme Court ruling, made an observation that is most apposite to discussion of the manner in which agencies can hamstring GAO reporting through insisting that particular reports be classified.

> Yet, anyone who has ever been in the Executive Branch knows how convenient the "Top Secret" or "Secret" stamp is, how easy it is to use, and how it covers perhaps for decades the footprints of a nervous bureaucrat or a wary executive.[77]

AN OVERVIEW OF GAO'S REPORTING

One can only conjecture whether the massive effort entailed in the tremendous outpouring of GAO reports is commensurate with the benefits derived from such reports. Any evaluation needs to weigh not only the utility of the reports to Congress but also their effectiveness in uncovering shortcomings in agency performance and stimulating both managerial and program improvements. Furthermore, the reports are an important vehicle for public dissemination of (a) information on issues with which the National Government is dealing, and (b) insights into

228

how well accountability -- both narrowly and broadly conceived -- for the expenditure of Federal funds is being
discharged.

In view of the staggering volume of reports, it be-
hooves the Comptroller General to reflect increased awareness that the aggregate of information which he addresses
to the Congress may overburden communication channels with
that body, particularly as materials flowing from the other
supportive agencies increase in volume. The steps which
the Comptroller General has taken to deemphasize formal
reports by making use of such media as staff and issue
papers,[78] offers promise of expediting the availability
of GAO findings and recommendations with resultant increased timeliness and usefulness. This study has already directed attention to the desirability of the Comptroller General establishing a more visible balance between assurance as to accuracy of reports and the delays
this entails in their completion. There is still a need
for the Comptroller General to counteract GAO staff perception of the formal reports as a prime means for winning
recognition within the organization.

GAO's reporting system should be viewed in light of
the vastness of the Federal Government and the multiplicity and diversity of its separate agencies and programs.
What may be feasible for a central monitoring agency in
most other governments may not be suited to the realities
of the governmental monolith that confronts the Comptroller General. Furthermore, the reporting practices
must be geared to the political system within which the
GAO functions. In any event, one should not lose sight
of the fact that the production of reports, however vital
an activity of the GAO, is only one facet of the aggregate of responsibilities vested in the Comptroller General. Hence, the interaction between the reports and
the other tasks GAO performs and the attendant powers it
exercises must constantly be borne in mind.

1. Letter from Lawrence S. Eagleburger, Deputy Under
    Secretary of State to Elmer B. Staats, Comptroller
    General of the United States, March 15, 1976.

2. Letter from Glen E. Pommerening, Assistant Attorney
    General for Administration to Victor S. Lowe, Dir-
    ector, General Government Division, GAO, January
    14, 1977.

3. During the 15-month period ended September 30, 1976,
    the GAO's output of reports is tabulated in the
    1976 Annual Report (p. 2) as follows:

    Congressional reports:
    To the Congress   301
    To Congressional committees   343
    To Members of Congress   295
                                      ───
                                      939
    Reports addressed to Federal
      agency officials   441
                                      ───
                       Total   1380

4. General Accounting Office, Report Manual, Chapter 1,
    p. 3.

5. Ibid., Chapter 4, p. 8.

6. Letter from P. Royal Shipp, Acting Administrator,
    Food and Nutrition Service, U.S. Department of
    Agriculture to Henry Eschwege, Community and
    Economic Development Division, GAO, June 6, 1977.
    The report (CED-77-76) was dated June 15, 1977.

7. Letter from Comptroller General Elmer B. Staats to
    Senator Lee Metcalf, Chairman, Joint Committee
    on Congressional Operations, August 8, 1974.

8. GAO Planning Staff, Review of the Comprehensive Audit
    Activities, February 1955, p. 5.

9. Comptroller General Report, Reasonableness of Prices
    Questioned for Bomb and Hand Grenade Fuses Under
    Three Negotiated Contracts, B-164784, July 15, 1969.

10. Comptroller General Report, Review of Loans to Graz-
    ing Associations, B-114873, January 4, 1968.

11. Task Force designated by the Comptroller General of the United States, Observations and Recommendations Relating to Processing of Audit Reports, January 1967.

12. House, Committee on Government Operations, Seventeenth Intermediate Report, 85th Congress, 2nd Session, 1956, p. 18.

13. Comments of the Comptroller General of the United States on Report of the Committee on Government Operations, p. 5.

14. Comptroller General Report, Review of Administration of Mining Claims Located on National Forest Lands Reserved From the Public Domain - Forest Service, B-215053, May 29, 1962.

15. Office of Policy and Special Studies, which was superseded by the Office of Policy.

16. General Accounting Office Report Manual, Chapter 4, p. 3.

17. GAO, Report of Investigations of the Program for Development and Expansion of Strategic and Critical Materials in the Interest of National Defense, June 1955.

18. General Accounting Office Report Manual, Chapter 8, p. 3.

19. Task Force Report, op. cit., p. 20.

20. House, Government Operations Committee, Hearing Before a Subcommittee, Review of the Powers, Procedures, and Policies of the General Accounting Office, 94th Congress, 1st Session, December 10, 1975, p. 6.

21. The House Government Operations Committee had said: " . . . too much consideration may have been given to revision of draft reports in response to the views of the agencies before the reports are issued and transmitted to the Congress." Seventeenth Intermediate Report, op. cit., p. 3.

22. Letter from Comptroller General Elmer B. Staats to Honorable Edith Green, May 8, 1969.

23. Report Manual, op. cit., Chapter 6, p. 9.

24. Comptroller General Report, The Swine Flu Program: An Unprecedented Venture in Preventive Medicine, HRD 77-115, June 27, 1977.

25. Joint Economic Committee, Report of the Subcommittee on Economy in Government, 90th Congress, 1st Session, 1967.

26. Letter from Chairman William L. Dawson to Comptroller General Elmer B. Staats, February 5, 1970.

27. House Appropriations Committee, Hearings Before Subcommittee on Legislative Branch Appropriations, 92nd Congress, 1st Session, 1971, p. 62.

28. Comptroller General Report, Federal Supervision of State and National Banks, OCG-77-1, January 31, 1977.

29. Washington Post, December 27, 1976.

30. Washington Post, March 27, 1971.

31. House Government Operations Committee, Hearing Before Legislation and Military Operations Subcommittee on Defense Profit Study of the General Accounting Office, 92nd Congress, 1st Session, March 26, 1971.

32. Letter from Secretary of Defense Robert McNamara to Comptroller General Elmer B. Staats, August 3, 1966.

33. Letter from the Secretary of Defense Robert McNamara to Comptroller General Elmer B. Staats, August 12, 1966.

34. Letter from the Secretary of Defense Robert McNamara to Comptroller General Elmer B. Staats, December 12, 1966.

35. Lawrence S. Eagleburger letter of March 15, 1976, op. cit.

36. Letter from Harry E. Bergold, Acting Assistant Secretary, International Security Affairs, Defense Department to J. Kenneth Fasick, Director, International Division, GAO, March 16, 1976.

37. Letter from Robert C. Seamans, Jr., Administrator, Energy Research and Development Administrator to Elmer B. Staats, Comptroller General of the United States, August 19, 1976.

38. Letter from John K. Carlock, Fiscal Assistant Secretary, Treasury Department, to Max A. Neuwirth, Assistant Director, GAO, December 1, 1966.

39. Comptroller General Report, Unnecessary Compensation to Washington, D.C. Area Banks for Cashing Government Checks, Treasury Department, B-115776, March 19, 1965.

40. Comptroller General of the United States, 1965 Annual Report, p. 268.

41. Comptroller General Report, Space Shuttle Facility Program: More Definitive Cost Information Needed, PSAD-77-17, May 9, 1977, p. 19.

42. Comptroller General Report, Review of Procurement of Foreign-Produced Aircraft Ejection-Seat Systems - Department of Defense, B-146778, January 18, 1967.

43. Ibid., p. 46.

44. Ibid., p. 33.

45. Comptroller General of the United States, 1967 Annual Report, p. 259.

46. Comptroller General Report, Aircraft Midair Collisions: A Continuing Problem, B-164497(1), October 23, 1974, p. 33.

47. PSAD-77-44, March 21, 1977, p. 31.

48. B-163058, July 17, 1972.

49. B-146896, March 9, 1970.

50. B-K4031(2), November 2, 1971. Several years later, the Comptroller General's report, Alcohol Abuse is More Prevalent in the Military than Drug Abuse (MWD-76-99, April 8, 1976), received general DOD agreement as to the thrust of its recommendations, with certain exceptions.

51. ID-77-8, June 15, 1977, pp. 19 and 20.

52. GCD-76-101, October 19, 1976.

53. Statement of Comptroller General Elmer B. Staats Before the Legislative Subcommittee, House Appropriations Committee on Budget Estimate for Fiscal Year 1978, February 3, 1977.

54. Letter from Victor M. Longstreeet, Assistant Secretary of the Navy (Financial Management), to Mr. J.K. Fasick, Associate Director, Defense Accounting and Auditing Division, GAO, October 25, 1965.

55. Letter from Charles A. Bowsher, Assistant Secretary of the Navy (Financial Management), to Comptroller General Elmer B. Staats, December 21, 1967. The letter tells of a statutory provision enacted after the Navy had decided to implement the GAO recommendation:

> The Military Construction Authorization Act, 1968, Public Law 90-110, Section 810(b), provides that this facility "shall not be determined excess to the needs of the holding agency or transferred, reassigned, or otherwise disposed of by such agency, nor shall any action be taken by the Navy to close, dispose of or phase out the Naval Academy Dairy Farm unless specifically authorized by an Act of Congress."

56. Comptroller General Report, $100 Million Could be Saved in Postal Operations in Rural America Without Affecting the Quality of Service, GCD-75-87, June 4, 1975.

57. Congressional Quarterly Weekly Report, August 28, 1976, p. 2349. See also critical remarks of Congressman Baucus, Congressional Record, March 9, 1976.

58. Comptroller General Report, War on Organized Crime Faltering - Federal Strike Forces not Getting the Job Done, GGD-77-17, March 17, 1977, p. 45.

59. See Chapter 3 in the 1975 and 1976 Annual Reports entitled "Legislative Recommendations."

60. Public Law 93-463.

61. Included in Foreign Assistance Act of 1974.

62. Public Law 94-582.

63. Public Law 94-488.

64. An example is Summary of Open GAO Recommendations for Legislative Action as of December 31, 1976, OCR-77-1002, February 16, 1977.

65. New York Times, November 21, 1976.

66. New York Times, February 24, 1976.

67. Washington Star, April 14, 1976.

68. *Wall Street Journal*, December 27, 1976.

69. *Philadelphia Evening Bulletin*, January 21, 1975.

70. General Accounting Office, *Report Manual*, Chapter 18, p. 1.

71. Comptroller General Report, *The Seizure of the Maya-guez - A Case Study of Crisis Management*, B-133001, May 11, 1976.

72. Letter from Dante B. Fascell, Chairman, Subcommittee on International Political and Military Affairs to Thomas E. Morgan, Chairman, Committee on International Relations, U.S. House of Representatives, October 4, 1976.

73. *Report Manual*, Chapter 18, p. 2. An example of an unclassified digest is that entitled "Another Look at the Readiness of Strategic Army Forces." LCI-76-457, June 9, 1977.

74. Barbara P. Newman in *The Nation*, October 23, 1976.

75. Comptroller General Report, *Shortcomings in the Systems Used to Control and Protect Highly Dangerous Nuclear Material*, EMD-76-3, July 23, 1976.

76. *Congressional Quarterly Weekly Report*, January 8, 1977, p. 44.

77. *Environmental Protection Agency vs. Mink*. 410 U.S. 73 (1973).

78. The release of staff studies carrying the signatures of the directors of the respective GAO divisions is growing. They deal with such subjects as: "*Food and Agriculture Issues for Planning* (April 22, 1977), *Management of Airline Personnel in the Federal Government: The Present Situations and Proposals for Improvements* (June 6, 1977), and *Environmental Protection Issues Facing the Nation* (July 8, 1977)."

235

Chapter 7

JUDICIAL AND LEGAL COUNSELOR ROLES
OF THE COMPTROLLER GENERAL

". . . the chairman of this committee is
absolutely right when he says that judicial
powers reside here and must be exercised by
the Comptroller General."[1]

"Our written decisions affected the rights
and obligations of agency heads, disbursing
and certifying officers, and individual
claimants."[2]

The term "General Accounting Office" and -- to a lesser degree -- the title "Comptroller General" obscure the[3]
fact that this agency has important adjudicatory powers.
The fountainhead of the power wielded by the GAO is not
so much the audits it conducts but rather the exercise of
its adjudicatory authority.

Yet this aspect of the Comptroller General's activities comes into the public limelight only occasionally, as
when an especially controversial issue such as President
Nixon's pension rights or the Philadelphia Plan is involved.
Even within the GAO itself, those chiefly concerned with
agency audits and reviews have limited awareness of the far-
reaching power stemming from the aggregate of the Comptroller
General's decision-rendering authority, the GAO's resolution
of bid protests, and the settlement of claims. The fact
that these activities of the Office come within the domain
of the lawyer sets them apart from those in which the accountant, social scientist, and those from other disciplines
hold sway.

SCOPE AND BASIS OF THE
COMPTROLLER GENERAL'S JUDICIAL ROLE

The decisions rendered by the Comptroller General
cover a broad spectrum of subjects and profoundly affect
operations within the Executive Branch. The impact of the
Comptroller General's legal rulings has become even more
pronounced because of his increasing responsiveness to Congressional requests for legal advice. As is brought out
subsequently, the line of demarcation between Comptroller
General decisions and counselling Congressional committees
and Members on legal matters has become hazy. In fact,
the analysis indicates that many of the more vital legal
matters with which the Comptroller General deals are the
subjects of opinions in response to Congressional requests.

The procedures which the GAO has established for the disposition of protests from dissatisfied bidders for Government contracts are a vehicle for the Office playing a pivotal role in the Government's procurement process, and, at the same time, affording a remedy that complements the regular judicial procedures.

Finally, the authority which statutes have vested in the Comptroller General with respect to the settlement of claims by and against the Government rounds out the imposing array of judicial-like tasks performed by this official.

Statutory basis for the Comptroller General's decisions

The Comptroller General's settlement and decision-rendering authority, which is the keystone for his adjudicative role, has a long background that began with the Act of March 3, 1817,[4] which provided that "all claims and demands whatever by the United States or against them and all accounts whatever in which the United States are concerned, either as debtors or creditors, shall be settled and adjusted in the Treasury Department." This provision was implemented through auditors whose findings were then reviewed by comptrollers. Because departments did not accept the finality of such determinations, the Act of March 30, 1868[5] specifically mandated that "balances, when stated by the auditor and properly certified by the comptroller -- shall be taken and considered as final and conclusive upon the Executive Branch of the Government, and be subject to revision only by the Congress or the proper courts." The Dockery Act of 1894[6] abolished the several separate comptrollers and centralized their responsibilities in a single Comptroller of the Treasury. This official was vested with dual authority: resolving appeals from the account settlements made by the auditors and rendering advance rulings (upon questions involving payments) in response to requests by disbursing officers and heads of departments. Such decisions were made binding in the subsequent settlement of the transactions. Since Section 304 of the Budget and Accounting Act transferred the powers and duties of the Comptroller of the Treasury and the six Treasury auditors to the GAO, the result was to vest this decision-making authority in the GAO. As a result, the United States Code contains the following provision:

> Disbursing officers, or the head of any executive department, or other establishment not under any of the executive departments, may apply for and the Comptroller General shall render his decision upon any question involving a payment to be made by them or under them, which decision, when rendered,

238

shall govern the General Accounting Office
in passing upon the account containing said
disbursement.[7]

A similar provision was subsequently adopted for certifying officers or employees although the wording is somewhat narrower and refers to "any question of law involved
in a payment on any vouchers presented to them for certification."[8] Apparently when impelled to rule on a question
submitted to him, the Comptroller General will treat a submission as a request from a department head even though the
requestor is actually at a subordinate level in the departmental hierarchy.[9]

Extracts from the House proceedings, at the time the
Budget and Accounting Act of 1921 was being considered, indicate that some of the Members of Congress explicitly attributed a judicial aspect to the role envisaged for the
Comptroller General.[10] One Congressman referred to the Office as "a semi-judicial one." Another spoke of giving it
a "judicial status" and of its examining questions "as the
court examines questions, upon the law and upon evidence."
Still another remark, although focused upon the authority of
the Comptroller General with respect to the settlement of
claims, brings out the stress placed upon the judicial
character of the Office which was being established.

> Neither the President of the United States,
> a member of his Cabinet, nor anyone that
> has a claim before the Comptroller General,
> has any right to dictate to him what his
> decision shall be upon the law and the facts
> involved in the case. It is a judicial de-
> termination, just as clear and distinct as
> any question in court - - -

Power afforded by settlement function

The significance and impact of the Comptroller General's decisions are dependent in large measure upon the
authority which he possesses for the settlement of public
accounts. This authority is also the basis for his passing
upon bid protests. Section 304 of the Budget and Accounting Act of 1921 provides: "The balances certified by the
Comptroller General shall be final and conclusive upon the
executive branch of the Government."

The United States Supreme Court has stated: "The
word 'settlement' in connection with public transactions
and accounts has been used from the beginning to describe
administrative determination of the amount due. . ."[11]
One writer has stated that settlement "in the technical

239

jargon of the Treasury, has always meant (and still means)
the final administrative determination of the balances due
to or from the United States on accounts between itself
and its debtors or creditors."[12] The settlement authority
of the Comptroller General, including as it does the power
to disallow expenditures, "permits the Comptroller General
to exert a strong influence upon the policies and programs
of governmental agencies."[13]

There are relatively few instances in which the Comptroller General actually seeks to recover, from accountable
officers or payees, disbursements which he deems illegal or
improper; hence, some might assume that the accounts settlement function is of little moment as a deterrent upon
the Executive Branch. Furthermore, the fact that the Comptroller General must look to the Department of Justice for
conducting litigation required to implement the decisions
as to the amounts due from accountable officers would appear to eliminate the Comptroller General's settlement
authority as any real threat to the Executive Branch. Yet
the very multiplicity of requests for the Comptroller General's decisions demonstrates that those accountable for
the expenditure of Federal funds are reluctant to be parties
to transactions that might subsequently be frowned upon by
the Comptroller General. In addition to the psychological
factor that has been so well described by Mansfield,[14]
there is a down-to-earth consideration in connection with
Government contracts. Contractors, especially those involved in very substantial undertakings with the Government,
are not prone to treat lightly the possibility that the
Comptroller General may disallow payments made to them.

In short, even though the ultimate sanction of re-
couping payments made by the Government is invoked infrequently, it can cast a cloud over a transaction deemed
questionable by the Comptroller General. This makes both
officials and contractors take pause. The Federal establishment has been so conditioned by the Comptroller General's
settlement authority that, except for unusual confrontations
such as those discussed later in this chapter, day-to-day
operations are conducted within the limitations established
by Comptroller General's decisions.

The influence which the GAO can bring to bear upon
agencies by invoking its settlement authority is demonstrated
in the communication the Acting Comptroller General addressed
to the Secretary of HEW informing him that the GAO would "disallow Medicaid payments for long-term care in institutions
made in the quarter beginning July 1, 1976, to those states
that have not submitted the required certifications and show-
ings which are satisfactory to you of compliance with the
utilization review requirements."[15] Since HEW had not re-

duced payments to non-complying states, both the Secretary
of HEW and the Secretary of the Treasury were put on notice
that "the appropriate accountable officer or officers of
the Government" would be held responsible for future improper payments. Copies of the letter were sent to "appropriate congressional committees, the SRS [Social and Re-
habilitation Service], Regional Commissioners, the Governors
of the States and jurisdictions, the appropriate HEW certifying officers and the Secretary of the Treasury."

The GAO had been asked by the Chairman of the Subcommittee on Oversight and Investigations, House Committee on
Interstate and Foreign Commerce to take this action. Previously, the Chairman had requested GAO to monitor the Department's progress in implementing the Social Security Act
provision invoked in this confrontation. Some months later,[16]
the Acting Comptroller General sent a thirteen page response
to a request by the Subcommittee Chairman that he report on
the status of the implementation of the provision in question.
The response not only reflected the positive impact which
GAO's monitoring had upon HEW's enforcement of the statutory
requirement, but also set forth recommendations to the Secretary of HEW and the Subcommittee. The incident shows how
the settlement authority of the Comptroller General can
complement Congressional oversight.

Mindful of the extent to which his power is dependent
upon the settlement function, the Comptroller General has
avoided any relinquishment of his settlement authority, although, as already discussed in Chapter 5, he has taken
steps to reduce the amount of detailed checking done by the
GAO in discharging this task. There is little predisposi-
tion to go along with the recommendation which the President's
Committee on Administrative Management made for transferring[17]
the settlement authority to the Treasury Department.

THE COMPTROLLER GENERAL'S BROAD INTERPRETATION
OF HIS DECISION-RENDERING AUTHORITY

Volume and form of Comptroller General's decisions

The very number of decisions rendered by the Comptroller
General is indicative of the broad-gauged approach which
this official has taken with respect to his authority to render decisions. The House Government Operations Committee, in
its 1956 report on the GAO, criticized the volume of Comptroller General's decisions and stated that many dealt with
relatively minor matters. The Committee felt that this indicated "an avoidance of responsibility on the part of disbursing and certifying officers and the need for more clearcut definitions, whenever possible."[18] Replying to this observation and the complementary recommendation for reducing

such decisions to a more reasonable number, the Comptroller
General countered with the argument that the largest single
class of cases which were handled represented appeals of
claimants from disallowances by GAO's Claims Division.[19]
He avoided dealing with the more fundamental issue as to
what might be done to reduce the outpouring of decisions.

Apropos of Comptroller General Campbell's reference
to decisions in connection with claims, it bears mention
that these do not fall technically within the statutory
provision for decisions. For that matter the distinction
between a decision proper and other types of legal rulings
is fuzzy at best. As is brought out at a later point in
this chapter, the Philadelphia Plan controversy presented
an example of the Comptroller General himself losing sight
of the supposed difference between a decision and an advisory legal opinion to a Member or committee of the Congress.

During the 15-month period ended September 30, 1976,
the Comptroller General rendered 4067 decisions of which
943 were to heads of departments and agencies, 260 to
certifying, disbursing and contracting officers, and 2864
to individual claimants.[20] The decisions appearing in the
published volumes, "representing about 10 per cent of the
total annual output, are considered to be of the greatest
interest from the standpoint of general application and
precedent."[21]

Comptroller General's assertiveness as to his authority

Very early in the history of the GAO the Comptroller
General took a hard-nosed stance with respect to his decision-making authority. When, in 1924, the Secretary of
the Navy demurred to a ruling by the Comptroller General
with respect to an overpayment by a Navy disbursing officer, the Comptroller General let it be known that he would
not tolerate any questioning of his rulings. He was apparently irked by the following statement in the concluding
paragraph of the Secretary's letter:

> . . . this department has no alternative but
> to obey the law as expounded by the Supreme
> Court and by the Attorney General.

This impelled Comptroller General McCarl to retort:

> I have to advise that neither the Supreme
> Court nor the Attorney General has rendered
> an opinion in this case. Neither is the
> matter here involved proper for submission
> either to the Supreme Court or the Attorney
> General.

After pointing out that the GAO had decided and certified that an overpayment had been made, McCarl concluded his decision as follows:

> . . . and the law has made such decision and certification final and conclusive upon the Executive Branch of the Government. In view of such finality the question of "no alternative" does not appear as stated in the concluding paragraph of the letter.[22]

Less than two months before the decision addressed to the Secretary of the Navy, the Comptroller General in very cutting tones had let the Employees' Compensation Commission know that he would not brook any impinging upon his decision-making authority.[23] McCarl was nettled by the Commission's suggestion that "friendly action" be taken to obtain a judicial resolution of the question that was involved. He stated that the question as to whether certain expenditures could be charged to the Commission's appropriations was one "for determination solely by the Comptroller General of the United States and may not be adjudicated by any court."

Legislative Reorganization Act of 1970 used to buttress decision authority

The GAO quickly pounced upon the Legislative Reorganization Act of 1970 to afford added assurance as to agency receptivity to Comptroller General decisions. The General Counsel broadly construed Section 234 of the Act;[24] he ruled that decisions "which contain recommendations or instructions addressed to the head of a department or agency will be included in the monthly lists." Then, on the basis of the 1970 Act's requirement of agency statements as to their action on GAO recommendations,[25] the General Counsel directed that in each such decision the agency shall be notified that it is required to report to "certain committees of the Congress as to the action taken with respect thereto." This questionable interpretation, however it has worked out in practice, demonstrates that the Comptroller General is constantly on the alert to buttress his decision-rendering function.

Issue of finality of Comptroller General's decisions

Early in the history of the GAO, the Comptroller General made assertions as to the finality of his decisions which have injected confusion that still exists at the present time. As has previously been pointed out, Section 304 of the Budget and Accounting Act, 1921, states that balances certified by the Comptroller General "shall be final and con-

clusive upon the executive branch of the Government." It
has already been noted that the statutes provide that a
Comptroller General's decision upon a question involving
payment to be made by the officer requesting it "shall
govern the General Accounting Office in passing upon the
account containing said disbursement."[26] This appears to
distinguish the binding nature of the settlement of an account from that which should be accorded a decision. The
former is binding upon the Executive Branch while the latter is conclusive with respect to only the Comptroller
General. However, McCarl ruled that the pertinent statutory provisions "make the decisions of this office on a
submission by a head of a department or disbursing officer
concerned final and conclusive upon the Executive branch
of the Government. . . "[27] Whether it be confusion in
the interpretation of the statutory language or simply reluctance to challenge the contentions of the GAO, the pronouncements which the Comptrollers General have made as
to the finality of their decisions have generally gone
unquestioned.

Comptroller General undeterred by challenges to his de-
cision-making prerogative

Comptroller General McCarl was uninhibited in his
responses to what he considered to be challenges to the
Comptroller General's decision-making authority as he envisaged it. In 1935, he got into an imbroglio with the
Secretary of the Navy. The vitriolic approach which he
took was undoubtedly evoked in large measure by the fact
that the Secretary of the Navy had the temerity to direct
accountable officers under his control that, notwithstanding the Comptroller General's decision as to the unavail-
ability of an appropriation for a particular purpose, they
should thereafter follow Attorney General's opinions and
Court of Claims decisions. The Comptroller General was in
no way daunted by the Secretary falling back upon the Attorney General, and he proceeded to cut that official
down to size.

Referring to the opinions of the Attorney General, the
Comptroller General said:

> There exists no law giving such opinions
> determinative effect or providing pro-
> tection for public officials who adopt
> such opinions in the discharge of their
> public duties. They are merely advisory
> and necessarily so else an Attorney Gen-
> eral could become effectively dominant
> in the affairs of all departments.[28]

244

McCarl warned of the baleful consequences if questions as to the use of appropriations were left to determination by any agency of the Executive Branch.[29]

Although many years have elapsed since this decision was handed down by the Comptroller General and although markedly different personalities have occupied the Office since then, the underlying philosophy with respect to decisions still bears at least the vestiges of the McCarl approach. In fact, the confrontation between the Comptroller General and the Attorney General in connection with the Philadelphia Plan, discussed at length subsequently, is reminiscent of McCarl's encounters with the Attorney General. For that matter, the Comptroller General's sensitivity as to the Attorney General impinging upon his prerogatives has intensified rather than abated.

Broad spectrum of Comptroller General's decisions

The subjects covered by the Comptroller General's decisions run the gamut from determinations of a highly specialized nature that are frequently of relatively limited significance to those involving important policy considerations. Comptroller General Campbell pointed out that the variety of legal matters which are presented for decision during any one fiscal year "is limited only by the extent of present day Government activity."[30] In a later report, he gave examples to illustrate the diversity of legal questions handled in a single year: an Area Redevelopment Administrator requested advice as to whether he could reimburse Defense Department cost-plus contractors for expenses incident to participation in exhibits in labor surplus areas; the Secretary of the Navy inquired if he had authority to transfer excess legal property in Guam to other Federal agencies without reimbursement; the Secretary of Defense requested a decision as to forfeitures in connection with overlapping court-martial sentences; the Administrator of the Federal Aviation Agency requested a ruling as to the propriety of the inclusion of a contingent liability provision in jet aircraft rental agreements.[31]

More recently, Congressional junketeers must have been jolted by the ruling that "the tab for foreign travel costs of lawmakers no longer may be picked up by the State Department, as has been the case for more than 20 years. Instead, each congressional committee will have to pay for its members' foreign trips out of its own budget."[32]

Exemplifying still further the diversity of problems covered by the Comptroller General's decisions are his rulings on: (a) the Agriculture Department's authority to indemnify turkey growers for losses sustained in connection with the Department's eradication of exotic Newcastle disease[33] and (b) an indemnification question raised by the State Department in connection with the exhibit of an archaeological collection sent to this country by the People's Republic of China.[34]

The tightrope which the Comptroller General walks on occasion in connection with his decisions is illustrated in a lengthy ruling which he made in response to a request from the Secretary of Transportation that he consider the question raised with respect to approving as a Federal Aid Highway Project a proposal made by the State of West Virginia. The Comptroller General's decision stated that the circumstances were such that GAO believed some indication of Congressional approval should be obtained. The Comptroller General, therefore, apprised the Secretary of Transportation that the GAO would not object to implementing the proposal in question "provided the Committees on Public Works of both the Senate and House of Representatives are given an opportunity to review the proposal and indicate their agreement therewith."[35]

The Comptroller General has utilized his decision-rendering to back up a GAO report, as when he affirmed the position taken in a report concerning the computation of charges for certain services of Customs officers.[36]

The preponderance of the decisions involve claims with respect to civil pay, military pay, transportation, and contracts. While most of these are run-of-the-mine, some -- particularly contracts -- can present important issues. The contract area, by its very nature embraces a diversity of subject matter that varies from contractual details that are plainly of limited significance to the application of Governmental procurement principles to a matter of considerable consequence as, for example, the Honeywell case[37] discussed later in this chapter in connection with bid protests. Another bid protest decision had important budgetary implications: the Comptroller General held that -- notwithstanding a conference committee report on the appropriation -- the Navy was not required as a matter of law to expend lump sum appropriations for a specific purpose when the statute did not so require.[38]

The fact that a decision is included in a printed volume is not indicative of it being of great moment. For example, one of the published decisions let it be known that the GAO "will not object to the United States Secret Service paying the rental charges on formal dress attire for the agents in question whenever a written determination is made by a proper official of the Service that the utilization of such formal attire is necessary for the proper performance of the duty to which the agent is as-

signed."[39]   A more recent published decision ruled that the
cost of decorative key chains given to educators attending
Forest Service-sponsored seminars does not "constitute a[40]
necessary and proper use of public funds."

      The Comptroller General's unpublished decisions, as
was observed earlier in this chapter, focus on matters that
appear, at least for the moment, to be of lesser consequence.
For instance, one such decision ruled that an offer to settle the Government's claim for $7,642.80, representing the
value of two truckloads of lettuce that had been rejected[41]
because of deterioration in transit, should be accepted.
The pay and allowances of the uniformed services necessitate the interpretation of a myriad of statutes and regulations that are in a constant state of flux. Often, these
rulings involve relatively nominal amounts: a decision involving the taxi fare allowable an officer and his depend-
ents came to the conclusion that he was entitled to $15
for taxi and a baggage charge of $3 in New York, plus a
similar amount in Chicago.[42]   The compensation of civilian
employees can involve rulings having important financial
implications; but, more frequently, the decisions deal
with relative minutiae. Thus, one decision ruled that
guard-chauffeurs who reported each day 15 minutes prior to
beginning their regular tour of duty were not entitled to
overtime since the free lunch period of equal time given[43]
these employees offset the early reporting time.   The
fact that a ruling involves a claim of only a nominal
amount can be deceptive since it can serve as a precedent
for future determinations that individually or cumulatively
prove to be of unquestioned importance. While readily conceding that some of the rulings in response to issues raised
by employees are manifestly not of an earth-shaking nature,
a GAO attorney observed that one justification for considering such matters and issuing decisions thereon was that
such a practice afforded the employees "an independent forum."

Legal opinions furnished committees and Members of Congress

      Coupled with the Comptroller General's decisions are
the legal opinions furnished Congressional committees and
individual Members; these often involve questions that are
in the limelight and/or are of considerable Congressional
concern. The 1975 Annual Report of the Comptroller General[44]
tells of opinions given on legal questions raised by President Nixon's resignation. One such opinion that received
much coverage by the media held that a President who resigned
prior to conviction would receive his pension; Senator
Philip Hart had requested the GAO to study the question.[45]
The Comptroller General furnished a very lengthy opinion to
Senator Thomas F. Eagleton, in response to his inquiries,
concerning the legality of the expenditure of funds involved

in the use of U.S. Armed Forces to evacuate Americans
and foreign nationals from South Vietnam and in the res-
cue of the American merchant ship Mayaguez.[46] Senator
Eagleton then requested a legal analysis of the Comptroller
General's opinion from the Legislative Counsel of the U.S.
Senate and Professor Raoul Berger; he directed the Senate's
attention to the differences in the views received from the
three sources.[47]

Senator Schweiker was able to inform the Senate that
a ruling furnished him by the GAO held that the Export-Im-
port Bank had not acted in compliance with existing law
when it extended credit to the U.S.S.R. in the absence of
individual Presidential determinations submitted to Congress to the effect that each such transaction was in the
national interest.[48] Responding to another "Congressional
request," the Comptroller General tackled the question of
whether the incumbent Federal Insurance Administrator had
been validly appointed by the Secretary of HUD. He concluded that such was not the case since there should have
been a Presidential nomination and Senate confirmation.[49]

Following a request from the Chairman of the House
Subcommittee on Executive and Legislative Reorganization,
the Comptroller General gave his opinion on three legal
questions that had arisen in the course of the Subcommittee's
hearings on Reorganization Plan No. 2 of 1970. This was
the Plan that established the Office of Management and Budget in lieu of the Bureau of the Budget and also created
the Domestic Council. The Comptroller General ruled that
some features of the Plan conflicted with the underlying
statute.[50] The Comptroller General's ruling was quickly
followed by an opinion from the Attorney General stating
that he strongly disagreed with Staats' views.[51] The two
legal adversaries had once more arrived at sharply divergent conclusions! The House Government Operations Committee
recommended disapproval of the Plan,[52] but the House did not
go along with this recommendation, and the Plan became effective. This was a vivid instance of the Comptroller General's willingness to counsel Congress on legal issues
even when they are remotely related, at best, to the legality of expenditures.

When, in 1971, the Department of Health, Education
and Welfare considered the closing of Public Health Service
hospitals and clinics throughout the country, the Chairman
of the House Committee on Merchant Marine and Fisheries
called upon the GAO for an expression of its views. The
Chairman referred to a 1965 Comptroller General's decision
which had held that the closing of all Public Health Service
hospitals was beyond the discretionary authority of the Department. In his 1972 ruling, the Comptroller General said:

"We find nothing in the HEW memorandum that would persuade us to reach a contrary view at this time."[53] The manner in which such a ruling may be construed is reflected in the heading of one news story: "Staats Opposes HEW on Hospital Closings."[54]

The semantic distinction that the GAO draws between decisions and legal advice given to Congressional committees or individual Members is nebulous and still leaves open the question as to the soundness and propriety of the Comptroller General serving in the capacity of legal adviser to the Legislative Branch. This issue is explored at a later point in this chapter.

Challenges directed at Comptroller General's decision-rendering

It is evident that the Comptroller General's decisions have far-reaching implications in terms of the decision-making entailed in the formulation and implementation of the programs and policies for which the Executive agencies are responsible. The President's Committee on Administrative Management felt that the Comptroller General's decision-making role made for divided authority and responsibility for the proper expenditures of public funds, deprived the President of power essential to the discharge of his major executive responsibility, and at the same time deprived Congress of a truly independent audit and review of the Government's fiscal affairs.[55] One writer feels that the result is "a serious limitation on administrative discretion, approaching a transgression on the constitutional authority of the Executive Branch."[56] Comptroller General Campbell, who was probably stimulated by the criticisms in the House Government Operations Committee Report of 1955, presented a rationale for his decision-making authority:

> Unlike the courts and other tribunals which
> have authority only to render decisions after
> the fact, the Office, through the statutory
> authority to render advance decisions, can
> prevent the starting of unauthorized programs,
> the making of illegal contracts, the expend-
> iture of Federal funds without regard to the
> law.[57]

Then, in an apparent attempt to establish that agencies were not resistant to the Comptroller General's decision-making role, Campbell referred to a significant trend on the part of Government officials to obtain advance decisions prior to the disbursement of public monies. Obviously, the requests for such decisions might be impelled by considerations of expediency rather than because the agencies lean toward Comptroller General decisions as the preferred means for resolving questions.

The decision-making role of the Comptroller General affords the advantage of having questions arising in connection with the Government's financial management resolved by an independent agency, which reflects expertise developed over many years. The resultant case law is unquestionably helpful for those who must deal with problems relating to the limitations applicable to expending public funds. There is an underlying question, however, as to whether the Comptroller General's exercise of his decision-making authority is prone to get out of bounds and, as one critic has contended, substitute that official's judgment for that of "the responsible administrators, even on matters about which the administrators are best situated to judge."[58] As the discussion that follows brings out, one disturbing result of the present arrangement is the spectacle of the Comptroller General and Attorney General locking horns on important public matters.

One can surmise that the decision-rendering process has become institutionalized as an integral component of the GAO and that the procedures for the formulation and reporting of such decisions have achieved such stature and have been so built into the modus operandi of the GAO and agencies that attempts to curtail this facet of the Comptroller General's responsibilities will continue to encounter marked resistance.

COMPTROLLER GENERAL'S DECISIONS VERSUS ATTORNEY GENERAL'S OPINIONS

The preceding discussion depicted the aloof, if not antagonistic, posture that the first Comptroller General, McCarl, took with respect to the opinions of the Attorney General. Notwithstanding that McCarl's successors may not have been so abrasive in expressing their positions, they have, as already indicated, adhered to the tenet that the Comptroller General does not defer to the Attorney General in ruling on matters which he feels come within his purview.

Although this discussion is focused upon the Comptroller General's decisions, clashes of viewpoints between these two officials may occur even in the absence of a formal decision by the Comptroller General. Thus, in the Foreign Aid controversy of 1960 -- described in Chapter 4 "Comptroller General's Access To Information" -- the Attorney General contradicted the Comptroller General's interpretation of the relevant statutory provisions: his opinion was the basis for Presidential action that completely nullified the punitive measures which the Comptroller

sought to invoke. The end result was very similar to what
happened when the Attorney General disputed the Comptroller
General's decision concerning the Philadelphia Plan, described subsequently.

A classic case of confrontation between the Comptroller General and Attorney General occurred in 1966 in
connection with the interpretation of the so-called Findlay
Amendment to the Department of Agriculture and Related Agencies Appropriation Act of 1967.[59] The Yugoslav Coordinating
Committee had sent medical supplies to North Vietnam; this
raised the question as to whether such action came within
the Amendment's prohibition of the use of the appropriated
funds for the sale of agricultural commodities "to any
nation which sells or furnishes or which permits ships or
aircraft under its registry to transport to North Vietnam
any equipment, materials, or commodities, so long as North
Vietnam is governed by a communist regime."

In response to an inquiry from the Department of State,
the Department of Justice agreed with the Legal Adviser of
the State Department that "this provision should be construed
as being applicable only to those cases where the government
of a country sells or furnishes products to North Vietnam."[60]
The General Counsel of the Department of Agriculture had previously expressed the view that the proviso used the term
"nation" to include private citizens of a country.

The GAO looked into the matter at the request of Congressman Findlay, who had already taken the position that
such shipments would be illegal. The culmination of this
dispute took the form of a 13-page ruling by the Comptroller
General.[61] The upshot of this lengthy analysis was a conclusion that, in view of the ambiguity of the language used
in the proviso, the funds in question "should not be used
to formulate or administer programs for the sale of agriculture commodities to Yugoslavia, under Title IV of Public Law 480 until legislative clarification of the proviso
is obtained."

A Department of Justice spokesman, who later discussed
this case, cited it as illustrating the problem of: "Who
is the Government's lawyer?" He expressed the feeling that
there has to be one final legal voice within the Government
and that, short of the courts, this has to be the Attorney
General. The smoldering adversary relationship between the
Comptroller General and Attorney General reached the boiling point in connection with the so-called "Philadelphia
Plan."

Inception of Philadelphia Plan confrontation

The public and possibly many Members of Congress are not ordinarily aware of the head-on clashes between the Comptroller General and the Attorney General. The confrontation in connection with the so-called "Philadelphia Plan" catapulted the conflict into the halls of Congress and the public limelight. It dramatically brought out the untenable state of affairs created by a situation in which the Comptroller General and the Attorney General take completely irreconcilable points of view with respect to an important issue. This clash between these two officials merits careful examination because its vestiges are evident in the Comptroller General's proposal, discussed at a later point, to strengthen his position vis-a-vis the Attorney General. What transpired also affords invaluable insights into the strategy and tactics employed by the Comptroller General in eliciting Congressional support for actions taken by him.

On May 22, 1968, the Comptroller General addressed a decision[62] to Representative William C. Cramer, who had requested his opinion as to the propriety of requiring a low bidder and its subcontractors to submit -- before award of the contract -- acceptable affirmative action programs to assure equal employment opportunities. Such a requirement was contemplated by the Department of Labor under a proposed order which had been submitted for comment within the Department. The order was designed to implement the equal employment opportunity provisions of Executive Order 11246, that had been issued by President Johnson in 1965. It is important to note that the decision was in response to a request by a Member of Congress, not the Secretary of Labor, and dealt with a proposal still under consideration within the Labor Department. The decision stated that the Secretary of Labor was being advised by the GAO that, if the proposed order was adopted, it should, before becoming effective, be implemented by regulations setting forth minimum requirements to be met by the bidder's program and any other standards or criteria by which the acceptability of the program would be judged.

In November, the GAO heard from Congressman Cramer that the Philadelphia Executive Board had established a so-called "Philadelphia Pre-Award Plan" which seemed to be inconsistent with the principles enunciated in the Comptroller General's decision of May 22. The Comptroller General, responding to the Congressman's letter reaffirmed in a second decision the position he had taken previously.[63]

Comptroller General caught in Congressional maelstrom

Several months later, the Comptroller General wrote the Secretary of Health, Education, and Welfare requesting that, if the circumstances were as alleged by a contractors'

252

organization, the Department of Health, Education, and Welfare "withhold approving such contracts, or the expenditures of any Federal funds for such contracts, until such time as this office is able to decide the propriety of such expenditure."[64] By now, the Comptroller General found himself in the unenviable position of having to rule further on a subject that was evoking mounting Congressional controversy. Senator Javits stated that the original Philadelphia Plan had been revised to meet the objections voiced by the Comptroller General. The Senator expressed the belief that it would be entirely proper for the Comptroller General to defer to what he termed "the primary authority and responsibility of the Labor and Justice Departments" especially since the revised Plan did not appear to entail additional cost to the Government and met the Comptroller General's own requirements for bids on Government construction projects.[65]

The Philadelphia Plan decision and reactions it evoked

On August 5, 1969 the Comptroller General addressed a 17-page letter to the Secretary of Labor in which he concluded that conditions of the type proposed by the revised Philadelphia Plan were in conflict with the Civil Rights Act of 1964, "and we will necessarily have to so construe and apply the act in passing upon the legality of matters involving expenditures of appropriated funds for Federal or federally assisted construction projects."[66] The letter, interestingly enough, informed the Secretary of Labor of questions that had been submitted to the GAO by Members of Congress with respect to this matter. The Comptroller General stated that the GAO realized that its conclusions might disrupt the program and objectives of the Labor Department and cause concern among members of minority groups.

Secretary of Labor Schultz' reaction to Staats' decision not only reflected sharp disagreement with the stand taken by the Comptroller General but also expressed determination to proceed with the effectuation of the Plan regardless of the adverse ruling. In a press statement released on August 6, Secretary Schultz made several salient points. He took issue with the basis for the Comptroller General making such a ruling:

> The Comptroller General is the agent of Congress, not a part of the Executive Branch. His opinion was not solicited by the Labor Department. He has authority to pass on matters of procurement law and concedes that the Philadelphia Plan is consistent with procurement law. His objection to the Plan is based on his interpretation of the law unrelated to procurement.

The tempo of Congressional discussion of the issues
posed by the Philadelphia Plan increased as proponents and
critics of the Plan expressed their views. Senator Javits
expressed the belief that the Comptroller General's ruling
was erroneous and premised on a misconception of his authority in this area. This challenge of the Comptroller General's authority is significant particularly since the
Senator went on to say:

> Since the Justice Department through Attorney
> General Mitchell has expressed the opinion
> that the revised Philadelphia Plan is legal,
> clearly any issues concerning it should be
> resolved in the courts, not in the Comptroller
> General's office.[67]

Javits further stated that he fully supported the decision
of the Secretary of Labor to go ahead with the Plan.

The Senator had inserted in the Congressional Record
an editorial that had been in the Washington Post of August 10, and which said that there was "a smell of sheer
capriciousness in the Comptroller General's ruling." The
editorial referred to Comptroller General Staats being
"goaded by Senators Dirksen, Fannin, and McClellan." It
asserted that the Comptroller General's opinion bordered on
absurdity and that Secretary Schultz was thoroughly justified in relying on the Attorney General's view and in continuing with the program.

The stance taken by Secretary Schultz was criticized
by Senator McClellan on the Senate floor. Directing attention to Secretary Schultz' announced intention to continue
with the implementation of the Plan, McClellan referred to
"those in the Executive Branch who presume to take the laws
into their own hands."[68] In his remarks to the Senate,
McClellan made a statement identical to that included in
the material which the Comptroller General had submitted
to him:

> By law, the decisions of the Comptroller Gen-
> eral are final and conclusive on the execu-
> tive branch of the Government and establish
> the validity of the individual payments and,
> in some instances, the legality of entire
> programs.

The question has already been raised in this chapter as to
the basis for the assertion that the Comptroller General's
decisions have the finality which statements such as this
attribute to them.

The Attorney General's opinion on the Philadelphia Plan

On September 22, Attorney General Mitchell responded
to the request of the Secretary of Labor for an opinion
as to the legality of the Department of Labor's order
with respect to the revised Philadelphia Plan.[69] The Attorney General stated that he concluded the Plan was not
in conflict with any provision of the Civil Rights Act
and that it was a lawful implementation of the provisions
of Executive Order 11246. The aspect of the Attorney
General's opinion that undoubtedly was the most disconcerting to the Comptroller General was the pronouncement
made in the concluding sentence:

> I hardly need add that the conclusions ex-
> pressed herein may be relied on by your De-
> partment and other contracting agencies and
> their accountable officers in the administra-
> tion of Executive Order 11246.

The following day, the Secretary of Labor ordered
the Philadelphia Plan into effect.[70]

Senate Subcommittee on Separation of Powers becomes involved in dispute

The Philadelphia Plan controversy became so acute
that the Senate Subcommittee on Separation of Powers
held a hearing on the Plan. The Comptroller General appeared before the Subcommittee and explained the position
which he had taken. Staats addressed himself to that feature of the Comptroller General's opinion which obviously
rankled him most, i.e., the concluding sentence in which
Mitchell had given the Department of Labor and other contracting agencies and their accountable officers carte
blanche to proceed with the implementation of the Plan:

> In this connection, I would like to point out
> as emphatically as I can that I believe that
> one of the most serious questions for the
> subcommittee's consideration is whether the
> executive branch of the Government has the
> right to act upon its own interpretation of
> the laws enacted by the Congres, and to ex-
> pend and obligate funds appropriated by the
> Congress in a manner which my Office, as the
> designated agent of the Congress, has found
> to be contrary to law.[71]

Immediately preceding this statement by Staats was his
comment that the Attorney General appeared to have ig-
nored completely Section 304 of the Budget and Accounting

Act, 1921, which provides that balances certified by the Comptroller General shall be final and conclusive upon the Executive Branch of the Government.[72] Striving almost desperately to mobilize Congressional support for the GAO, the Comptroller General told the Subcommittee:

> We believe the actions of officials of the executive branch in this matter present such serious challenges to the authority vested in the General Accounting Office by the Congress as to present a substantial threat to the maintenance of effective legislative control of the expenditure of Government funds.[73]

Following Staats' appearance before his Subcommittee, Senator Ervin told the Senate that there was nothing in the Budget and Accounting Act which permitted a department disagreeing with the Comptroller General's legal reasoning on which a decision was predicated to disregard the decision. He also observed: "I would remind the Senate that the Comptroller General is an arm of the Congress. An affront to him is an affront to us all."[74]

The Subcommittee came out with a finding that the Plan was invalid and that "if the remedies available to the Comptroller General are inadequate and if judicial action thwarts the will of Congress, legislation must be enacted to protect against this usurpation of Congress' constitutional function."[75]

Comptroller General seeks to effect compliance with decision

Having been sharply rebuffed by the Executive Branch, the Comptroller General sought to head off a course of action on the part of that Branch that could well make a shambles of his decision authority at least insofar as matters of great moment are concerned. On November 12, 1969, he sent each department head a letter together with copies of his August 5, 1969 decision and the statement which he had presented in October before the Senate Subcommittee on Separation of Powers.

Staats underlined portions of his statement which he felt required "serious consideration" by agency officials "particularly construction contracting officers, certifying and/or disbursing officers, before taking actions involving the obligation or expenditure of public funds in connection with Federal or federally assisted construction projects." He directed their special attention to that paragraph of the decision which said that the GAO would regard the use of the Plan as a violation of the Civil Rights Act of 1964, in passing upon the legality of matters

256

involving expenditures of appropriated funds for Federal
or federally-assisted construction projects. The Comptroller General also called the attention of department
heads to the comments which he had made in his statement
to the Senate Subcommittee including the following:

> Basically, it has been our position that the
> law is to be construed as written and enforced
> in accordance with the legislative intent when
> it was enacted. We believe this is what the
> law requires. Also, we are part of the legis-
> lative branch of the Government and we think
> this approach is the only proper one we can take.

This last sentence illustrates how the Comptroller General
can envelop himself with the cloak of the Congress and
maintain that a particular position which he has taken is
inevitable if he is to function as a surrogate for the
Legislative Branch in seeing that its mandates are not
contravened.

Attempt to vest Comptroller General with sanctions for enforcing decisions

The controversy raging around the Philadelphia Plan
and the Comptroller General's decision reached a boiling
point when the Senate inserted in the Supplemental Appropriations Act 1971 (H.R. 15209), which had been passed
by the House, a provision that "no part of the funds appropriated or otherwise made available by this or any
other Act shall be available to finance, either directly
or through any Federal aid or grant, any contractor agreement which the Comptroller General of the United States
holds to be a contravention of any Federal statute."
The Comptroller General was a strong advocate of such a
provision and had, in fact -- prior to the Senate's action -- suggested statutory language for this purpose
that was specifically tied in with the Philadelphia Plan.[76]

The House conferees refused to accept the rider the
Senate had inserted, and the conferees filed a report on
their differences. The battle lines were drawn. Secretary Schultz was reported as saying that the upcoming vote
on the rider was "the most important civil rights vote in
a long, long time."[77] The intercession of President Nixon
into the controversy indicated the importance attributed
to the issue. What had begun as a disagreement between
the Comptroller General and two cabinet members had become
a confrontation between the Congress and the Executive
Branch as a totality. The day following the Senate's
adoption of the rider, President Nixon had urged the Senate and House conferees to "permit the continued implemen-

tation of the Philadelphia Plan while the courts resolve
this difference between congressional and executive legal
opinions."[78]

On the very day that the House was to act on the conference report, a Presidential statement was issued which
began: "The House of Representatives now faces an historic
and critical civil rights vote." The President went on to
"assure Congress and the public of this Nation that I consider the independence of the Comptroller General of the
United States of the utmost importance in the separation
of powers in our Federal system." Nixon said that he was
taking the position that "the amendment need not be stricken
but that it should be modified to permit prompt court review
of any difference between legal opinions of the Comptroller
General and those of the Executive, and to permit the Comptroller General to have his own counsel [rather than the
Attorney General] to represent him in such cases." The
President followed these conciliatory overtures with the
statement that he shared the Attorney General's doubts as
to the constitutionality of the proposed amendment and that
he might have to withhold his approval of any legislation
containing it.[79]

The House insisted on elimination of the rider, and
the Senate concurred. This result had required intensive
Presidential effort. The Administration put "considerable
muscle"[80] into heading off the effort to strengthen the
Comptroller General's hands in the implementation of his
decisions.

Judicial overruling of Comptroller General's decision

This rejection of the rider did not, of course, dispose
of the underlying legal issue. An association of contractors challenged the Philadelphia Plan in the Federal District
Court. The Court held that the Plan did not conflict with
the Civil Rights Act and that the Executive Branch did not
lack the power to issue the order in question.[81]

This decision denying the plaintiffs' motion for an injunction probably was not completely unwelcome to the GAO.
The Comptroller General was now able to declare a "cessation of hostilities" and extricate the GAO from what must
have been an increasingly embarrassing impasse. Staats
wrote those directly interested or concerned that the Congressional action and court rulings "preclude further action by us at this time to question payments made under
contracts incorporating the provisions of the revised
Philadelphia Plan."[82]

Implications of the Philadelphia Plan controversy

The Philadelphia Plan dispute brought the Comptroller General into a sensitive policy area and subjected him to criticism from which he had been relatively immune for many years. A New York Times editorial was hardly flattering in its description of the Comptroller General's decision-making on this issue: "The unions, with strong support from Southern segregationists on Capitol Hill succeeded in persuading Controller [sic] General Staats that the Philadelphia Plan violated the ban on racial quotas under the Civil Rights Act."[83]

The Philadelphia Plan chronology supports the concern of those who are fearful that the Comptroller General's decisions enable him as a Legislative Branch official to exercise a tight grip upon the Executive Branch and that this is not only incompatible with the doctrine of separation of powers but shackles the vigorous implementation of policies. Even some of those sympathetic to the Comptroller General having responsibility for rendering de-decisions with respect to proposed or consummated financial transactions may feel that the authority should be exercised with such restraint that the Comptroller General does not appear to preempt decision-making that appropriately falls within the domain of the Executive Branch. The Philadelphia Plan controversy demonstrated that department heads and the Chief Executive will react with firm resistance -- and even bitterness -- to what they consider to be an intrusion by the Comptroller General into Executive policy formulation and implementation. The resolute rejection of a Comptroller General's decision -- such as that by Secretary Schultz[84] -- can militate against the acceptance generally accorded these decisions. Entirely apart from this consideration, the Comptroller General needs to be highly judicious in decisions involving controversial areas lest the objectivity of the GAO be impugned and its stature undermined.

Although the statutory provision favored by Staats was defeated, the legislative battle that revolved around it proved that the Comptroller General can mobilize strong support within the Congress, particularly when the position he takes ties in with the interests or philosophy of more influential members of that body. Moreover, the Comptroller General came out of the confrontation with Presidential re-affirmation of his independence and an expression of the Chief Executive's willingness to permit the Comptroller General to be represented by his own counsel, rather than the Attorney General, in the courts. The latter commitment was especially significant in light of the tensions and confusion engendered over the years by the conflicting rulings of the Attorney General and those of the Comptroller General. As is brought out subsequently, the Comptroller

General currently alludes to the concession by President
Nixon in his efforts to obtain such authority from the
Congress.

COMPTROLLER GENERAL AS A LEGAL
ADVISER TO THE CONGRESS

Rationale for legal advice to Congressional Committees and members

The Philadelphia Plan involved a secondary issue: the
propriety of the Comptroller General issuing legal rulings
in response to inquiries from Members of Congress. The
statutes specifically provide only for decisions that dispose of questions raised by certifying and disbursing officers and heads of departments. Yet the Comptroller General submitted his initial decisions in connection with
the Philadelphia Plan to a Member of Congress; in fact,
these are included in the published decisions. Other
rulings cited earlier in this chapter demonstrate that,
over the years, the precedent had been established for
the Comptroller General to answer legal questions posed
by committees and individual Members of Congress. An internal GAO memorandum has attempted to rationalize this
practice through the following reasoning:

> Though our conclusions and opinions expressed
> to Members of the Congress are advisory in
> nature and not binding and though they do not
> stem from any statutory injunction, we have
> always construed it our duty as an arm of the
> Congress to provide for its Members as much
> assistance as we are able within the limits
> of our staff resources. Any request from a
> Member of Congress for information or advice
> will be promptly considered, and all pertin-
> ent information will be furnished him.

One might have expected that the Philadelphia Plan
experience would have deterred the Comptroller General
from playing the part of legal counsel to the Congress.
But apparently the Comptroller General either feels --
as the internal memorandum intimates -- that it is incumbent upon the GAO to give such legal advice or deems
it expedient for GAO to accede to these requests regardless of whether they are compatible with the organization's role. Thus Staats reported that, during the 15-
month period ended September 30, 1976, 513 opinions had
been submitted in response to Congressional requests.[85]
These were entirely apart from the 426 reports on pending
legislation.

A COMPTROLLER GENERAL'S DECISION HELPFUL TO
PRESIDENT TRUMAN BUT EMBARRASSING TO THE GAO

During President Truman's administration, an incident
occurred which involved the antithesis of the approach
the Comptroller General took in connection with the Philadelphia Plan. Although the incident occurred some years
ago, it is still remembered by some in the GAO as a case
study of the risk the Comptroller General incurs if he
lays himself open to the allegations that extraneous
factors entered into a decision rendered by him.

Comptroller General agreed to questionable appropriation transfer

President Truman in 1947 set up the Citizens Food Committee, but initially there were no funds available for it.
Hence, the Administration decided that $500,000 should be[86]
allocated to the Committee from appropriated funds.
Comptroller General Lindsay Warren personally countersigned
the warrant which transferred $500,000 to the Citizens Food
Committee from the $350 million appropriated for the pro-
vision of relief assistance to the people of countries de-
vastated by war. Notwithstanding the Comptroller General
had not rendered a formal decision, his signature on the
document effecting the transfer in question was deemed
"equivalent to a decision by the Comptroller General that
the proposed use of the funds is a legal use. . ."[87] The
transaction was looked upon by some of the Republican Members of Congress with a jaundiced eye; and the State Department Subcommittee of the House Committee on Expenditures
in the Executive Departments held hearings on this matter.

The Bureau of the Budget had acted as an intermediary
between the White House and the GAO in obtaining the Comptroller General's acquiescence in the transfer of funds.
But the Comptroller General had to bear the complete onus
for the unusual deference which his Office had shown to
the Executive Branch. The State Department, which carried
out the mechanics for effecting the transfer, stated that
it had acted in reliance upon the Comptroller General's[88]
approval.

Ineffectual attempts to defend the transfer

Frank Weitzel, Assistant to the Comptroller General,
who subsequently served as Assistant Comptroller General,
and E.L. Fisher, the General Counsel of the GAO, appeared
before the Subcommittee on behalf of the Comptroller General: they were hard pressed to present a convincing defense of Warren's action. Even a more sympathetic committee might have found it difficult to be persuaded by

the line of reasoning taken by the two GAO witnesses.
Fisher tried valiantly, however ineffectually.

At one point in the hearings, the following dialogue
occurred between Fisher, who had advised the Comptroller
General that the proposed expenditure was proper, and [89]
Francis T. O'Donnell, Counsel for the Subcommittee.

> Mr. O'Donnell: Did you tell anyone that this
> transfer was approved because you could not
> very well tell the President he was nuts?

> Mr. Fisher: That he was nuts?

> Mr. O'Donnell: Yes.

> Mr. Fisher: No, sir.

A short time later, O'Donnell asked Fisher whether
subsequent to the approval of the transfer, he had told
anyone that a matter like this put the GAO "behind the
8 ball." Fisher's reply was:

> If I did, I am sure from your question that it
> was misinterpreted. I meant exactly what I
> told you a while ago, that unless we can show
> that the President's determination was wrong,
> we can't attack it. To that extent, we would
> be behind the 8 ball when he makes this deter-
> mination if we want to turn it down without
> some excuse.

House Committee's condemnation of decision

In its report which was approved and adopted as the
report of the full Committee on Expenditures in the Executive Departments, the Subcommittee concluded that the
transfer of funds was not authorized by law. [90] The Committee was of the opinion that there was more than reasonable doubt of the intent of Congress and there was sufficient doubt to warrant the Comptroller General to withhold his approval of the transfer.

The report concluded with a comment which, although
it might appear to be relatively mildly critical, was
actually a sharp rebuke to the GAO when considered in
light of the fine rapport which Comptroller General Warren was able to establish with the Congress on the basis
of his many years of service in the House of Representatives.

The General Accounting Office must have the complete confidence of Congress. It is hoped that

262

future decisions in cases of this kind will
justify that confidence.[91]

Even assuming that partisanship strongly influenced
the majority of the Subcommittee, the evidence adduced
during the hearings cast a cloud on the manner in which
the Comptroller General exercised his judgment with respect to the Luckman Committee issue. This is not to
gainsay the desirability and even essentiality of the
Comptroller General avoiding the obstructionistic and
narrowly legalistic approach that too frequently characterized decisions during the McCarl era. Certainly the
Comptroller General should be expected to reflect perceptiveness as to the realities that confront Governmental
agencies and be willing to resolve reasonable doubts in
favor of those responsible for the implementation of programs. Yet, the judicious resolution of questions presented to the Comptroller General should not be equated
with submissiveness to the wishes of the Executive Branch
or, for that matter, those of Members of the Congress.

THE GAO'S SETTLEMENT OF CLAIMS
BY OR AGAINST THE GOVERNMENT

The responsibilities vested in the GAO for the settlement of claims are closely related to the decision-rendering facet of the Comptroller General's activities.
This analysis has alluded to the fact that many of the
Comptroller General's decisions are issued in connection
with the adjudication of claims.

Section 305 of the Budget and Accounting Act, 1921,
provides that "all claims and demands whatever by the
Government of the United States or against it . . .
shall be settled and adjusted in the General Accounting
Office." Since the Dockery Act provision with respect
to the recovery of debts owing the Government was made
applicable by Section 304 of the 1921 Act to the GAO,
this agency has the responsibility "to superintend the
recovery of all debts finally certified by it to be due
to the United States." These broad statutory definitions
of the GAO's responsibilities with respect to claims have
been narrowed by various statutory measures giving Executive Branch agencies authority with respect to such
matters.

Claims against the Government

The Comptroller General has described in the following manner those GAO activities that relate to claims
against the United States:

263

Claims against the United States that are referred to the General Accounting Office for
settlement are usually limited to those acquired by statute to be paid on settlement
of this Office and those involving doubtful
questions of law or fact as to the validity
or amount of the claim or the entitlement
of the claimants. They arise from virtually
any transaction of the Government and are
received from individuals, business entities,[92]
and foreign, State, or municipal governments.

The element of doubt is apparently a major factor in
the submission of claims to the GAO.[93] "There is no statutory limit on the size of a claim against the Government
which may be settled by the General Accounting Office."[94]

The Comptroller General has pointed out that the settlement of claims by the GAO affords claimants the opportunity to have claims reviewed and acted upon without resorting to more formal remedies. By this means, a claim
may be settled in a less costly and more expeditious manner than if the individual went to court.[95] Staats has
also directed attention to the advantage the Government
derives from the GAO claims function:

. . . it reduces significantly the number of
claims that otherwise would be the subject of
formal legal proceedings instituted by claimants with the attendant expense, delays, and
overcrowding of court dockets. Similarly,
GAO's claims settlement function is beneficial to the United States in that it reduces
significantly the number of requests that
otherwise would be made upon the Congress or
individual Members thereof for the enactment
of private legislation.[96]

Since the determinations made by the Comptroller General are binding upon neither the Congress nor the courts,
claimants are not precluded from resorting to other available courses of action.

In one of his decisions, the Comptroller General
pointed out that the statutory provision with respect to
his settlement of claims does not describe what evidence
shall be the basis of the allowance of a claim and that
this is left to the discretion of the GAO.[97] The Comptroller General has held that, in a case with respect to
which there is no controlling judicial precedent and as
to which substantial doubt exists as to the action which
a court of competent jurisdiction might take, it was his

duty to deny the claim and leave the claimant to his
remedy in the courts.[98] In a later decision, the Comptroller General reaffirmed this position and, citing a
Court of Claims ruling, stated that it was not only the
right but the duty of the GAO to deny the claim when it
believed that there might be substantial defenses in law.[99]

The Comptroller General reported that, during the 15-
month period ended September 30, 1976, GAO had settled
11,314 claims for $155.1 million.[100]

Debt claims by the Government

The function which the GAO discharges in connection
with the so-called "debt claims," involves amounts that
it is contended are owing to the Government. The Comptroller General has given a succinct explanation of this
activity:

> The subject matter of these debt claims is as
> varied as that of claims against the United
> States. We examine and adjudicate the claims
> referred here because of administrative doubt
> so that action to collect the amounts found
> due the United States may be taken if approp-
> riate. In other debt claims we examine and
> develop the claims and take whatever steps
> may be necessary to collect. Our collection
> actions include demands for payment, locator
> actions, development to ascertain the finan-
> cial status of the debtors, and the issuance
> of proofs of claim in bankruptcy and deceased
> debtor cases.[101]

If the GAO is unsuccessful in its efforts to recover
amounts which it deems are due the Government, it may
transfer them to the Department of Justice for collection
provided that the debtor's financial circumstances warrant this action.

During the 15-month period ended September 30, 1976,
GAO disposed of 66,646 debt cases and collected over
$7.5 million.[102]

GAO - A FORUM FOR BID PROTESTS

A large and very significant part of the GAO's legal
work in the contract area involves the handling of bid
protests. "Any interested party may file a protest with
GAO. Usually protests are filed by disappointed bidders
or offerors or by potential bidders or offerors. However, GAO will also consider protests filed by others

who have some legitimate interest in the particular action."[103]
The review of bidder protests applies to both negotiated
contracts as well as those involving formally advertised invitations to bid. As a result, GAO has a much broader area
than is available to it in connection with the audit of
contract performance.

The Comptroller General has stated that the objectives
of GAO bid protest procedure are: "to provide an informal
and impartial forum for the timely and inexpensive resolution of complaints by parties aggrieved by agency procurement actions" and "to provide an added discipline upon the
operation of the Federal procurement agencies."[104]

Legal basis for GAO handling bid protests

The GAO predicates its right to hear bid protest cases
upon its authority to review expenditures and to disallow
payments if the expenditures are not legally proper. It
follows the line of reasoning that, if a contract is awarded
that is not in conformity with the pertinent statutory and
other legal requirements, it is illegal and, hence, payments
made pursuant to it are subject to disallowance.

The implications of the Comptroller General's handling
of bid protests impelled a Washington legal practitioner
to write:

>The role of the Comptroller General as a source
>of recourse for the contractor is one of the
>most perplexing things that any lawyer or any
>contractor in the field of public contracts
>has to face. At times, this role is omnip-
>otent. Certainly it is vast, obviously vague,
>and plainly it is obscure. Patently, it is
>rarely fully understood.[105]

Until 1970, the GAO could also contend that, since
judicial relief was not available to an unsuccessful bidder, the Office's bid protest procedure afforded him the
only remedy. But a 1970 court ruling eliminated GAO's
claim to being the exclusive medium for giving relief to
aggrieved bidders. The U.S. Court of Appeals for the
District of Columbia, early in that year, held in the
much cited Scanwell case that an unsuccessful bidder
did have standing to sue and that the doctrine of sov-
ereign immunity had no application in light of the Administrative Procedure Act. Apparently unaware of the
fact that the appellant had been before the GAO, the
Court also held that a bidder who challenges the legality
of an agency action in awarding a contract is not required
to protest to the GAO before availing himself of his

judicial remedies.[106] The GAO had upheld the award of the
contract in question despite the protestor's contention
that the low bid was unresponsive.[107]

The aftermath of the Scanwell ruling

Since the Scanwell ruling, the Circuit Court, obviously mindful of the plethora of bidder appeals that
might seek judicial intervention, has sought to point up
the availability and merits of the remedy offered by the
GAO. Thus, while reversing a lower court that had granted
a temporary injunction so that the Comptroller General
might first render a decision on the bidder's appeal, the
Circuit Court went to some length to describe the GAO procedure in a commendatory manner.[108] In another opinion
delivered at the same time, the Court expressed concern
over the fact that the District Court "did not even consider the opinion of the Comptroller General denying the
protests." It went on to comment: "A Court's reluctance
to interfere with the executive procurement process should
be especially strong where, as here, the General Accounting Office has made a determination upholding the procurement officials on the merits."[109] Ordinarily, the GAO
will not rule in a protest "where the matter involved is
the subject of litigation before a court of competent
jurisdiction." However, the Bid Protest Procedure makes
an exception "where the court requests, expects, or otherwise expresses interest in the Comptroller General's decision."[110] Such expression of interest manifestly reflects a desire on the part of the courts to avail themselves of the expertise which GAO has in procurement law.

Despite the fact that a dissatisfied bidder may now
go into court, the number of bid protests handled by the
GAO is still impressive.[111] This is not surprising in
light of the fact that the GAO procedure is more expeditious and less costly than invoking the judicial remedy
and since a protestor who is not satisfied with the Comptroller General's decision can still resort to the courts.

Bid protest procedures

Until 1971, GAO protest procedures were of an informal
character. This approach on the part of the GAO might
have been encouraged by the reluctance that the courts had
manifested until the Scanwell ruling to intervene in such
matters, thus obviating the possibility that the GAO handling of bidders' appeals would be subjected to judicial
scrutiny. Under Congressional prodding,[112] the GAO formulated and adopted regulations defining the procedures for
the filing and hearing of bid protests. The regulations
initially issued were revised in response to criticisms
by the Subcommittee. Since then further changes were made

to achieve "speedier disposition of bid protests by the imposition of time limits on all parties involved, including the contracting agencies and the General Accounting Office."[113]

The GAO may intervene not only before an award is actually made but also after a contract has been entered into and even after its performance has begun. However, in directing cancellation of contracts, the GAO is mindful of the fact that the Court of Claims may allow damages in such cases.[114] Hence, as the Comptroller General pointed out, if an award had already been made and any substantial amount of work has been done by the time the GAO receives the protest, the protestant has little, if any, chance of remedial action.[115] In such a situation the bidder whose protest had been upheld could find himself with a Pyrrhic victory.

Honeywell and other bid protests

The ramifications of the bid appeal procedure were brought out dramatically by the protest of Honeywell, Inc. against the selection of IBM as the source for furnishing electronic data processing equipment required by the Air Force.[116] Proposals had been submitted by four companies: Burroughs, Honeywell, IBM, and RCA. It was determined that only IBM met all the requirements of the request for proposals. In light of this finding, the other offerors were not considered further.

Honeywell lodged a protest with the GAO. The Comptroller General, upholding the underlying contention of Honeywell, said: "Under the circumstances, further written or oral discussions should be held with Honeywell as well as with other offerors whom you consider to be within a competitive range." As a result, the selection of IBM was reversed and there was a resolicitation of contract proposals, the award going to Burroughs. The GAO reported that the contract awarded on the basis of this resolicitation resulted in a saving of $36 million.[117]

In another case also involving IBM, the GAO held that the Army had acted without requisite authorization from the General Services Administration in the procurement of data processing systems.[118] "As a result of this decision, the program cost will be reduced by approximately $10,000,000."[119]

The GAO reviewed an award in connection with the Space Shuttle Program involving an estimated $800 million over a 15-year period. It recommended that NASA determine whether in view of substantial net decrease between the two lowest proposers, the selection decision should be reconsidered.[120]

The viability of the bid protest procedure

There has been agency recognition of the utility of the GAO bid protest function. The General Counsel of one large Government agency, who mentioned the possibility of dissatisfied bidders bringing their grievances to the attention of their Representatives or Senators, stated that he preferred their going to the GAO since Congressional intervention might inject irrelevant considerations into the resolution of the issue. The General Counsel of one of the military departments felt that, in handling such appeals, the GAO was in position "to take off a lot of Congressional heat." However, top levels of the Executive Branch have perceived the Comptroller General's approach to bid protests as an encroachment upon executive decision-making. The Office of Federal Procurement Policy proposed changes in the procurement regulations that would make procurement agencies free to accept, reject, or ignore GAO rulings on bid protests. This challenge is all the more significant in light of the fact that Attorney General Bell subscribed to the position which Attorney General Mitchell had taken in 1971 to the effect that the Comptroller General's decisions on bid protests are purely advisory. Hence, the GAO has supported a legislative proposal to provide specific statutory authority for its bid protest function.[121]

Not only is the Comptroller General firmly resistant to any undermining of his authority to deal with bid protests, but he has also given the function broader dimensions. Citing the large Federal expenditures for grants and the wide variety of recipients, the Comptroller General decided to expand the scope of GAO bid protest activities to include complaints by prospective contractors concerning the propriety of contract awards made by Federal grantees in furtherance of grant purposes.[122] This development is still another demonstration of the GAO thrust to become more deeply involved in the subnational levels of government as well as the private sector.

The primacy which the GAO has assumed in connection with this aspect of Governmental procurement has placed it in a pivotal position to develop what one Government lawyer called a "procurement common law." The Comptroller General may treasure the bid protest function as highly supportive of the judicial character of his office. His leanings in this respect are reflected in the fact that the GAO booklet on bid protests opens with a quotation from James Madison concerning the judicial nature of the Office of the Comptroller under the Act of 1789 establishing the Department of the Treasury.[123]

COMPTROLLER GENERAL'S ASSERTION OF AUTHORITY TO
REVIEW BOARDS OF CONTRACT APPEALS' DECISIONS

Basic questions as to the scope of the Comptroller
General's adjudicatory powers were raised by two decisions
handed down by that official within a few days of each
other in December 1966. These involved the Comptroller
General's authority with respect to decisions of Boards
of Contract Appeals. The resultant controversies, one
of which culminated in a determination by the Supreme
Court, are illustrative of the aggressiveness and tenacity
with which the Comptroller General is prone to approach
his oversight of governmental expenditures.

The disputes clause and its implementation

The Boards, which are established by their respective
Governmental agencies rather than by statute, are concerned primarily with adjudicating disputes that arise in
connection with contracts entered into by Government departments and other agencies.[124] The standard disputes
clause[125] found in Government contracts provides that any
dispute concerning a question of fact arising under a
contract which is not disposed of by agreement shall be
decided by the contracting officer whose decision is final
and conclusive unless an appeal is addressed to the Secretary. The decision of the Secretary or his duly authorized
representative is, under the standard disputes clause,
made final and conclusive "unless determined by a court of
competent jurisdiction to have been fraudulent or capricious, or arbitrary, or so grossly erroneous as necessarily
to imply bad faith, or not supported by substantial evidence."
The clause further provides that it does not preclude consideration of legal questions in connection with such decisions but that nothing in the contract shall be construed
as making final the decision of the official or board on
a question of law. The language of this clause closely
follows the phraseology of the so-called Wunderlich Act.[126]
This legislation was an aftermath of the Supreme Court decision in United States vs. Wunderlich,[127] in which the scope
of judicial review of a contracting officer's final decision
was limited to one ground: allegation and proof of actual
fraud.

S and E case - overruling Board decision favorable to contractor

The first of the two landmark decisions of the Comptroller General with respect to the review of agency decisions on contract appeals involved S&E Contractors, Inc.[128]
The certifying officer submitted to the GAO an Atomic Energy
Commission voucher based upon a decision of a hearing exam-

iner (the AEC did not have a contracts appeal board at
that time); the decision had been reviewed and sustained
in part by the Commission. In a decision of prodigious
length (102 pages), the Comptroller General overruled
the hearing examiner and informed the certifying officer
that the voucher could not be certified for payment.

The almost overwhelming length of the decision is attributable, in part, to its effort to dispose definitively
of objections which had been raised by the contractor's
attorneys against the GAO injecting itself into this matter. The contractor contended that it was improper for
the GAO to enter into this proceeding "where the terms
pertaining to settlement of disputes arising under a Government contract had been fully complied with by both the
contractor and the Government agency, and where further
recourse lies for both in the courts. . ."[129] With this
as a point of departure, the contractor stated that GAO's
action constituted a breach of contract and was "an un-
warranted attempt to usurp power granted by law and contract to the AEC" and injected GAO into a proceeding in
which it had no position.

The Comptroller General, in responding to this challenge
as to his authority, fell back, as he is wont to do, upon
the provisions of the Budget and Accounting Act of 1921
with respect to the GAO's settlement and adjustment of
claims and demands by or against the Government. He also
cited the statutory provisions for the Comptroller General
rendering decisions on legal questions involved in vouchers
presented for certification and went on to say: ". . .
payments made by public officers in the transaction of the
Government's business are not final until settled by the
General Accounting Office."[130]

The contractor further contended that the disputes
clause -- described earlier in this discussion -- provided
for finality of the agency's determination unless a court
of competent jurisdiction determined it to be fraudulent,
capricious, etc. Since the GAO is not such a court, the
contractor contended it was without authority to review
the examiner's decision,[131] but the Comptroller General rejected this contention.

The Comptroller General took the occasion to indicate
the breadth of the review which the GAO claimed with respect to decisions by contracting agencies rendered under
the disputes clause. He stated that such review was not
limited to legal questions but extended also the questions[132]
of fact and so-called mixed questions of law and fact.
In his S&E decision, the Comptroller General fully exploited
the opportunity to argue for the desirability of the GAO

reviewing administrative determinations of appeals from
decisions made by contracting officers.[133]

Judicial rebuff to the GAO

The AEC having refused, in light of the Comptroller
General's decision, to take any further action on the contractor's claim, the contractor took his case to the Court
of Claims. The Court held "that the Comptroller's powers
of decision and settlement, though great, may be assumed
to lapse and fail at the Court House door." It, therefore,
concluded it was unnecessary for the Court "to determine
what decisions he might make or what finality they might
have in cases not brought before" the Court.[134] The Court
proceeded on the basis that it was considering -- not the
Comptroller General's ruling -- but rather the Justice Department's contention that the AEC decision was erroneous
on matters of law and unsupported by substantial evidence.
It remanded the case to a Commissioner for review under
Wunderlich Act standards.

S and E Contractors appealed their case to the U.S.
Supreme Court, which in a five to three decision, decis-
ively disposed of GAO's contention as to its broad authority to intervene in disputes clause cases. The Court held
that, in the absence of fraud or bad faith, a Federal agency's settlement under the disputes clause is binding on
the Government and "there is not another tier of administrative review."[135] The majority opinion concluded with
this statement:

> If the General Accounting Office or the De-
> partment of Justice is to be an ombudsman
> reviewing each and every decision rendered
> by the coordinate branches of the Government,
> that mandate should come from Congress, not
> from the Court.

The very lengthy dissenting opinion, which is highly
critical of the majority holding, makes this noteworthy
observation:

> The Court's bete noire, then, is primarily
> the General Accounting Office with a side-
> swipe at the Department of Justice.

The Comptroller General finally capitulated on this issue
and withdrew his objection to the payment of a contractor's
claim (allowed by a board of contract appeals) in light of
the Supreme Court ruling.[136]

272

Southside Plumbing Case - overruling board decision favorable to Government

A few days after his S&E ruling, the Comptroller General again interposed himself in the contract appeals process, but this time he dealt with a board ruling favorable to the Government. He reversed in part a decision by the Armed Services Board of Contract Appeals, which had denied the appeal of Southside Plumbing Co., Inc. Attorneys for the contractor had requested the GAO to review the Board's decision, and the Comptroller General held that the contractor was "entitled to an equitable adjustment" for the work in question. The GAO returned the record of the Board proceedings and file to the Secretary of the Air Force with the request that the claim be referred to the Armed Services Board of Contract Appeals so that the Board might take appropriate steps to have the contracting officer determine the amount which the contractor was entitled to receive as equitable adjustment. The decision closed with the statement that the GAO did not anticipate taking any further action with regard to the claim "in the absence of receiving a request from the claimant that we do so, following the exhaustion of the remedies afforded to it under the Disputes clause."[137] The Air Force declined to abide by the GAO decision and requested a ruling from the Attorney General.

In the brief it submitted to the Attorney General, the GAO maintained that it had the clear duty to allow a claim, if in reviewing the Board's decision, the conclusion was reached that the facts found by the Board did not in law justify the denial of the claim or that the record on which the Board's decision was based did not contain substantial evidence to support its factual conclusions. Then, indicating the ultimate sanction it might have in such a case, the GAO brief said:

> If in exercising the authority to allow we
> certify a voucher for payment or issue a
> warrant on the Treasury for payment, we be-
> lieve that payment thereof would become a
> purely ministerial act enforceable by judi-
> cial action by proceedings in the nature
> of mandamus.[138]

Attorney General rules against the GAO

The Attorney General was apparently most reluctant to be drawn into this controversy: and he delayed giving an opinion until January 16, 1969, only a few days before the change in Administration. He informed the Secretary of the Air Force that he had concluded that the Secretary was not required to remand Southside's claim to the Board for[139] further proceedings in accordance with GAO's opinion.

The Comptroller General, writing to the new Attorney General (John N. Mitchell), expressed "complete disagreement" with the conclusion reached in his predecessor's opinion. Staats stated that the GAO would, however, take no further action in the particular case. At the same time, to indicate that he was not capitulating to the stand taken by the Department of Justice, the Comptroller General said:

> . . . we must advise that in the future we intend to consider on the merits any claims which may be presented to us without regard to the views stated in the opinion of your predecessor.[140]

The Attorney General, responding to Staats' statement, made the following suggestion to which the Comptroller General agreed:

> I trust that you . . . will afford this Department an opportunity for discussion before taking any action that would be prejudicial to the government's litigating position in future cases.[141]

Although the Southside case raised a highly controversial issue as to the Comptroller General's authority in the area of the review of Board of Contract Appeals determinations, the case itself was terminated rather smoothly. The claimant submitted an offer in compromise, which the Department of Justice, after consulting the GAO, accepted.

The implications of the disputes clause issue

The Supreme Court ruling in the S&E case was a crucial setback to the GAO in its efforts to establish a pivotal role for itself in the resolution of disputes clause cases. The negative reaction of the Attorney General in Southside Plumbing to the GAO assertion of authority to reverse or modify disputes clause decisions unfavorable to a contractor inhibited the Comptroller General from pushing very hard on this front. The stance of the Comptroller General in the S&E and Southside Plumbing cases vividly demonstrates that GAO is not prone to accede readily to any contraction of surveillance it deems to be "a desirable check and safeguard against administrative action that may be illegal, arbitrary, capricious, or grossly erroneous in derogation of the Government's and the taxpayers' best interests."[142]

However, even before the Supreme Court handed down its decision, there were expressions of concern about GAO's position as to the review of disputes clause decisions. Professor Petrowitz, whom the Supreme Court described as "our leading authority on these problems," sounded a cautionary note:

> If the ability of the boards to render ex-
> peditious decisions having reasonable fin-
> ality is seriously impaired by second guess-
> ing, their effectiveness and efficiency will
> be largely destroyed.[143]

Cibinic and Lasken, in their incisive analysis of the Comptroller General's role in connection with Government contracts, expressed the belief that "GAO review of board of contract appeals decisions should be stopped. The present stance of the Southside Plumbing and S&E Contractors cases indicates that the GAO is little more than a way station to the courts when it rules on a board of contract appeals decision."[144] In his study of the GAO, Professor Morgan subsequently observed: "The General Accounting Office can perform some roles well, but claims settlements in the disputes context is not one of them."[145]

COMPTROLLER GENERAL'S PROPOSAL FOR RESOLVING IMPASSE WITH ATTORNEY GENERAL

Whether it be the Philadelphia Plan disagreements, the conflict of views concerning finality of board of contract appeals decisions, or other irreconcilable differences between the Comptroller General and the Attorney General, the resultant impasses are inimical to the smooth functioning of the Executive Branch. The spectacle of the Attorney General and Comptroller General being adversaries is bound to be confusing and even disconcerting to individuals or organizations that have a direct interest in the subject matter involved in such disputes. Since there is a tendency for the Comptroller General to become more assertive as to his adjudicative role, there is increasing probability of further confrontations such as those that have been discussed herein.

Rather than being deterred by the Philadelphia Plan and other setbacks, the Comptroller General has been calling upon Congress to provide him with authority to bring suit in the U.S. District Court for declaratory relief in the event that he has "reasonable cause to believe that any officer or employee of the executive board is about to expand, obligate, or authorize the expenditure or obligation of public funds in an illegal manner."[146] This authority could be exercised only in connection with

accounts over which the Comptroller General has settlement
authority. While conceding that differences between the
Comptroller General and the Attorney General have been rare,
Staats argues: "Under the present system, the Attorney General generally has the final word, since unlike the Attorney
General, the Comptroller has no present authority to appeal
to the courts to resolve the dispute --."[147] Indicative of
the Comptroller General's astute advocacy of the GAO cause
is his reliance upon President Nixon's proposed compromise
in the Philadelphia Plan dispute in support of his proposal.
Another strategem employed by the Comptroller General to
bestir the Congress to accept his proposal is to contend
that under the existing arrangement the Attorney General,
an officer of the Executive Branch, can negate the GAO's
determination that an expenditure is illegal. When pressed
by interrogating members on the fact that there had been
only three "disputes" between the Comptroller General and
Attorney General during the nine year period 1966-75,
Staats countered with the statement that "the fact that
we know that the Attorney General can override us may
well have some bearing upon our willingness to be 'tough.'"[148]
Such legislation would at least have the merit of permitting
the systematic resolution of issues that otherwise are left
to the "flexing of muscles" by the Attorney General and the
Comptroller General and their protagonists in the respective branches.

ISSUES POSED BY GAO'S EXPANDING ADJUDICATIVE AND LEGAL COUNSELLING FUNCTIONS

So far as both the public and the Congress are concerned, the very title, "General Accounting Office" tends
to obscure the extent to which the GAO has already acquired far-reaching adjudicative and legal counselling
functions -- whether based upon statute, the Comptroller
General's interpretation of his authority, or Congressional practice. The Comptroller General is in a strong
strategic position to importune the Congress to strengthen
still further GAO's role in this area. His arguments become even more persuasive to the Congress when he contends
that such additional authority is essential to the effective discharge of the tasks he performs as a surrogate for
that body.

However, as the Comptroller General presses for additional authority such as that just discussed, and as there
is greater perception of the aggregate of power he exercises, there are indications that Congress has become
more inquiring as to the ramifications of the adjudicative
and legal counselling functions performed by the GAO.
These activities need to be perceived as a totality in
the context of not only the other responsibilities en-

trusted to the Comptroller General but also the relations between the Executive and Legislative Branches. Furthermore, any steps directed to the resolution of problems raised by the relations between GAO and the Department of Justice should consider the role of that Department within the Executive Branch and also its relation to the Congress.

Footnotes - Chapter 7

1. Remarks of Congressman Andrews during the 1919 House discussions of the proposed Budget and Accounting Act, quoted in Financial Management in the Federal Government, 87th Congress, 1st Session, Senate Document No. 11, February 13, 1961, p. 303.

2. Comptroller General of the United States, 1975 Annual Report, p. 59.

3. Eli Baer, "Practice Before the General Accounting Office," 19 Federal Bar Journal 275 (July 1959, V. 19, No. 3). This writer commented that few lawyers realize the opportunities afforded by practice of law before the GAO.

4. 3 Stat. 366.

5. 15 Stat. 54.

6. 28 Stat. 206. The developments prior to the Dockery Act are described in Harvey Mansfield, The Comptroller General. (New Haven: Yale University Press, 1939) and Cibinic and Lasken, "The Comptroller General and Government Contracts," 38 George Washington Law Review 349 (March 1970).

7. 31 U.S.C. 74.

8. 31 U.S.C. 82d.

9. 41 Comp. Gen. 767 (1962).

10. Financial Management in the Federal Government, op. cit., pp. 300-303.

11. The Illinois Surety Co. vs. United States ex. rel. Peeler, 240 U.S. 214 (1915), p. 219.

12. Lucius Wilmerding, Jr., The Spending Power, A History of the Efforts of Congress to Control Expenditures (New Haven: Yale University Press, 1943), p. 259.

13. "The Comptroller General of the United States: The Broad Power to Adjust All Claims and Accounts," 70 Harvard Law Review 350 (1956), p. 352.

14. "The fact is that disallowances are effective deterrents whether or not they are collected. As the

quest for marital felicity requires more than keeping out of the divorce court, so here the compelling standards of conduct are not fixed by the judiciary. Administrative officers with jobs to finish cannot afford much time or energy for jurisdictional controversy. They want to avoid disallowances, rather than win lawsuits." Mansfield, op. cit., p. 116.

15. Letter from R.F. Keller, Acting Comptroller General of the United States to the Secretary of Health, Education, and Welfare, June 1, 1976.

16. Letter from R.F. Keller, Acting Comptroller General of the United States to Honorable John E. Moss, Chairman, Subcommittee on Oversight and Investigations, Committee on Interstate and Foreign Commerce, House of Representatives, March 1, 1977.

17. Report of President's Commission on Administrative Management (Washington, D.C.: Government Printing Office, 1973). See also Joseph P. Harris, Congressional Control of Administration (Garden City, N.Y.: Doubleday & Co., 1964), p. 158.

18. House, Government Operations Committee, "The General Accounting Office, Seventeenth Intermediate Report," 84th Congress, 2nd Session, 1956, p. 38.

19. Comments of the Comptroller General on Report of House Government Operations Committee, "General Accounting Office" (1956), p. 64.

20. Comptroller General of the United States, 1976 Annual Report, p. 52.

21. 54 Comp. Gen. VII (1975).

22. 3 Comp. Gen. 771 (1924).

23. 3 Comp. Gen. 545 (1924).

24. 31 U.S.C. 1174.

25. 31 U.S.C. 1176.

26. 31 U.S.C. 74.

27. 5 Comp. Gen. 822 (1926), p. 824. Staats has taken the same position; see 1976 Annual Report, p. 6; but he does say: "Private firms and individuals have further recourse to the courts in most instances."

28. 14 Comp. Gen. 648 (1935), p. 649.

29. Ibid., p. 651.

30. Comptroller General of the United States, 1958 Annual Report, p. 211.

31. Comptroller General of the United States, 1963 Annual Report, p. 240 et. seq.

32. Wall Street Journal, June 17, 1977.

33. 52 Comp. Gen. 519 (1973).

34. 54 Comp. Gen. 807 (1975).

35. Letter from Comptroller General Elmer B. Staats to the Secretary of Transportation, B-149811, December 22, 1967.

36. B-114898, November 13, 1975.

37. 47 Comp. Gen. 29 (1968).

38. Matter of LTV Aerospace Corporation, October 1, 1975.

39. 48 Comp. Gen. 48 (1969), p. 49.

40. 54 Comp. Gen. 976 (1975).

41. United States Comptroller General, Digests of Unpublished Decisions; Transportation, Vol. XI, No. 1 (1967), p. 3, G-159553.

42. United States Comptroller General, Digests of Unpublished Decisions; Pay and Allowances of the Uniformed Services, Vol. XI, No. 3 (1968), p. 1, B-162524.

43. United States Comptroller General, Digests of Unpublished Decisions; Civilian Personnel, Vol. X, No. 4 (1967), p. 3, B-160508.

44. Page 61.

45. New York Times, August 4, 1974.

46. Letter from Comptroller General Elmer B. Staats to Senator Thomas F. Eagleton, December 8, 1975. In earlier opinions furnished Senators on international matters, the Comptroller General (a) advised that there was no basis for raising legal objections

concerning AID expenditures for the support of
the American University in Cairo (Letter from
Comptroller General Elmer B. Staats to Senator
Ernest Gruening, B-156766, September 18, 1969);
(b) gave an opinion concerning the legality of
allowing United States naval vessels to remain
on loan to certain foreign countries after expiration of the covering agreements (Letter from
Comptroller General Elmer B. Staats to Senator
J.W. Fulbright, Chairman, Committee on Foreign
Relations, B-163943, April 29, 1968).

47. *Congressional Record*, May 12, 1976.

48. *Congressional Record*, March 8, 1974.

49. B-183012, December 9, 1976.

50. Letter from Comptroller General Elmer B. Staats to
the Honorable John A. Blatnick, Chairman, Subcommittee on Executive and Legislative Reorganization, Committee on Government Operations, House
of Representatives, May 4, 1970.

51. Letter from Attorney General John W. Mitchell to the
Honorable John A. Blatnick, May 6, 1970.

52. House, Government Operations Committee, *Disapproving
Reorganization Plan No. 2 of 1970*, H. Rept. 91-1066,
91st Congress, 2nd Session, 1970. See also Hearings Before Executive and Legislative Reorganization
Subcommittee on this Plan.

53. Letter from Comptroller General Elmer B. Staats to
the Honorable Edward A. Garmatz, Chairman, Committee
on Merchant Marine and Fisheries, House of Representatives, February 23, 1972.

54. *Washington Star*, February 25, 1971.

55. *Report of President's Committee on Administrative
Management*, op. cit., p. 22.

56. Harris, op. cit., p. 160. See also *70 Harvard Law
Review 350* (1956), p. 353.

57. Comptroller General of the United States, *1957 Annual Report*, p. 215.

58. Harris, op. cit., p. 160.

59. Public Law 89-556.

60. Letter from Frank W. Wozencraft, Assistant Attorney General, Office of Legal Counsel, Department of Justice, to Leonard C. Meeker, the Legal Adviser, Department of State, November 18, 1966.

61. Letter from Comptroller General Elmer B. Staats to the Secretary of Agriculture, February 2, 1967.

62. 47 Comp. Gen. 666 (1968).

63. 48 Comp. Gen. 326 (1969).

64. Letter from Comptroller General Elmer B. Staats to the Secretary of Health, Education, and Welfare, February 25, 1969.

65. Congressional Record, July 30, 1969.

66. 49 Comp. Gen. 59 (1970), p. 71.

67. Congressional Record, August 11, 1969.

68. Congressional Record, August 13, 1969.

69. Letter from Attorney General John N. Mitchell to the Secretary of Labor, Setember 22, 1969.

70. New York Times, September 24, 1969.

71. Senate, Committee on the Judiciary, Hearings Before the Subcommittee on Separation of Powers, The Philadelphia Plan, 91st Congress, 1st Session, 1969, p. 147.

72. Ibid., p. 146.

73. Ibid., p. 147.

74. Congressional Record, November 3, 1969.

75. Senate Committee on the Judiciary, Report by the Subcommittee on Separation of Powers, The Philadelphia Plan, 92nd Congress, 1st Session (1971).

76. Letter from Comptroller General Elmer B. Staats to the Honorable George H. Mahon, Chairman, Committee on Appropriations, House of Representatives, December 19, 1969.

77. New York Times, December 21, 1969.

78. Weekly Compilation of Presidential Documents (December 22, 1969).

79. Weekly Compilation of Presidential Documents (December 27, 1969).

80. Time Magazine, December 27, 1969, p. 48. See also "Philadelphia Plan: How White House Engineered Major Victory," New York Times, December 28, 1969.

81. Contractors Association of Eastern Pennsylvania et al. vs. The Secretary of Labor et al., 311 F.Supp. 1002 (E.D. Pa. 1970). The U.S. Circuit Court of Appeals for the Third Circuit affirmed the judgment of the District Court, 442 F.2d 159 (3d Cir. 1971). Senator Javits considered this to be so significant that he had the rather lengthy opinion of the Court printed in the Congressional Record (April 30, 1971). Subsequently, the Supreme Court refused to review the ruling of the Circuit Court, 404 U.S. 854 (1971).

82. Letter from Comptroller General Elmer B. Staats to the Honorable Robert G. Bartlett, Secretary of Highways, Commonwealth of Pennsylvania, April 28, 1970.

83. New York Times, December 22, 1969.

84. Schultz later became Director of the Office of Management and Budget and then Secretary of the Treasury.

85. Comptroller General of the United States, 1976 Annual Report, p. 52.

86. Letter from President Truman to the Secretary of State, October 17, 1947.

87. House, Committee on Expenditures in the Executive Departments, Hearings Before State Department Subcommittee, Investigation of the State Department Subcommittee, Investigation of the State Department Transfer of Relief Funds to the (Luckman) Citizens' Food Committee, 80th Congress, 2nd Session, 1948, p. 45.

88. Ibid., p. 5.

89. Ibid., p. 68 et seq.

90. Tenth Intermediate Report of the Committee on Expenditures in the Executive Department. Investigation of the State Department of Relief Funds to the (Luckman) Citizens' Food Committee, 80th Congress, 2nd Session, House Report No. 1722 (1948), p. 5.

91. Ibid., p. 6.

92. Comptroller General of the United States, 1969 Annual Report, p. 246.

93. For definition of doubtful claim see Comptroller General of the United States, General Accounting Office Policy and Procedures Manual For Guidance Of Federal Agencies, Title 4, p. 4-4.

94. Letter from Paul G. Dembling, General Counsel, GAO to author, August 10, 1972.

95. Settlement and Adjustment of Accounts of Executive Departments and Government Agencies, 70 Harvard Law Review 351 (1956) op. cit., 355.

96. Comptroller General of the United States, 1971 Annual Report, pp. 123-124.

97. 22 Comp. Gen. 269 (1942), p. 270.

98. 33 Comp. Gen. 394 (1954).

99. 42 Comp. Gen. 124 (1962).

100. 1976 Annual Report, p. 211.

101. Comptroller General of the United States, 1969 Annual Report, pp. 246-247.

102. 1976 Annual Report, p. 212.

103. General Accounting Office, Bid Protests at GAO - A Descriptive Guide, p. 6.

104. Hearings Before a Subcommittee of the Committee on Government Operations, House of Representatives, Review of the Powers, Procedures, and Policies of the General Accounting Office, 94th Congress, 1st Session, December 10, 1975, p. 8.

105. Geoffrey Creyke, Jr., in The Government Contractor and the General Accounting Office (Washington, D.C.: Machinery and Allied Products Institute, 1966), p. 49.

106. Scanwell Laboratories vs. John H. Shaffer, 424 F.2d 859 (1970). See also Ballerina Pen Company et al. vs. Robert L. Kunzig et al., 433 F.2d 1204 (1970).

107. 49 Comp. Gen. 9 (1969).

108. Wheelabrator Corporation vs. Chaffee, 455 F.2d 1306 (1971).

109. Steinthal and Co. vs. Seamans, 455 F.2d 1289 (1971).

110. GAO Bid Protest Procedures, Sec. 20.10. See also 54 Comp. Gen. 1009 (1975).

111. During the 15-month period ended September 30, 1976, the GAO decided 978 bid protests and disposed of 807 protests without formal decision, most of which were withdrawn before decision.

112. House, Committee on Government Operations, "GAO Bid Protest Procedures," Eighteenth Report, H. Rept. 1134, 90th Congress, 2nd Session, 1968.

113. Federal Register, Vol. 36, No. 247, December 23, 1971, pp. 24791-92 effective February 7, 1972. Superseded by revised procedures dated April 24 and effective June 2, 1975, Federal Register, Vol. 40, No. 80, pp. 17979-80. See also Joel S. Rubinstein, "The Anatomy of a Bid Protest," Federal Bar Journal, Vol. 34, No. 3, p. 252 (1975).

114. Coastal Cargo vs. The United States, 173 Ct. Cl. 259 (1965); Warren Bros. Roads Co. vs. The United States, 173 Ct. Cl. 714 (1965).

115. Hearings Before the Senate Government Operations Committee on S.1707, 91st Congress, 1st Session, 1969, p. 24. See also Bid Protests at GAO, op. cit., p. 14.

116. 47 Comp. Gen. 29 (1967).

117. Comptroller General of the United States, 1968 Annual Report, p. 344. The 1976 Annual Report (pp. 54-56) gives examples of the kinds and issues considered and resolved in bid protest cases; the report states: "Because of our expertise in bid protests, the Federal judiciary requests our services in court actions brought against contracting agencies by disappointed bidders."

118. 54 Comp. Gen. 196 (1975).

119. 1975 Annual Report, p. 62.

120. 53 Comp. Gen. 977 (1974).

121. These developments are described in the statement
which Paul G. Dembling presented on July 27, 1977
before the Committee on Governmental Affairs Subcommittee in Federal Spending Practices and Open
Government, U.S. Senate. Mr. Dembling went to
great length to refute the "impression that our
decisions are purely advisory." Citing various
cases, Dembling concluded: "Clearly, therefore,
the courts must consider that the ultimate trib-
unal in the vast majority of bid protest cases
will be the GAO. . ."

122. "Review of Complaints Concerning Contracts Under
Federal Grants," Federal Register, Vol. 40, No.
170, September 12, 1975, pp. 42406-07.

123. The quotation in the booklet reads: "It seems to me
that they partake of a judiciary quality as well
as executive. . . The principal duty seems to be
deciding upon the lawfulness and justice of the
claims and accounts subsisting between the United
States and particular citizens: this partakes
strongly of the judicial character. . ."

124. Senate, Select Committee on Small Business, United
States Senate, Report Prepared by Professor Harold
C. Petrowitz, 89th Congress, 2nd Session, Sen. Doc.
No. 99 (1966), pp. 20-21.

125. "This clause is not required by statute but is a
creation of the executive branch of the Government."
Nash and Cibinic, Federal Procurement Law (Washington, D.C.: The George Washington Press, 1969), p. 848.

126. 68 Stat. 81.

127. 342 U.S. 98 (1951).

128. 46 Comp. Gen. 441 (1966).

129. Ibid., p. 451.

130. Ibid., p. 453.

131. Ibid., p. 457.

132. Ibid., p. 453.

133. Ibid., p. 458.

134. S&E Contractors, Inc. vs. The United States, 193
Ct. Cl. 335 (1970).

135. S&E Contractors, Inc. vs. United States, 406 U.S. 1 (1972).

136. 52 Comp. Gen. 63 (1973).

137. Letter from Assistant Comptroller General Frank H. Weitzel to the Secretary of the Air Force, B-156192, December 8, 1966.

138. Brief on the Jurisdiction of the General Accounting Office in Contract Disputes with Special Reference to B-156192, December 11, 1967.

139. Letter from Attorney General Ramsey Clark to the Secretary of the Air Force, January 16, 1969.

140. Letter from Comptroller General Elmer B. Staats to the Attorney General, John N. Mitchell, February 7, 1969.

141. Letter from Attorney General John N. Mitchell to Comptroller General Elmer B. Staats, March 10, 1969 and Letter from Comptroller General Elmer B. Staats to the Attorney General, John N. Mitchell, April 16, 1969.

142. Letter from R.F. Keller, General Counsel, GAO, to Peter Tierney, Virginia Law Review Association, December 23, 1968.

143. Senate, Select Committee on Small Business, Petrowitz Report, op. cit., 159.

144. Cibinic and Lasken, op. cit., p. 394.

145. Thomas D. Morgan, The General Accounting Office: One Hope for Congress to Regain Parity of Power With the President," 54 North Carolina Law Review 1279 (October 1973), p. 1328.

146. Sec. 101, S.2268, 94th Congress, 1st Session (1975).

147. Hearing Before the Subcommittee on Reports, Accounting, and Management of the Committee on Government Operations, U.S. Senate, October 2, 1975, Part 1, p. 31.

148. Ibid., p. 32.

Chapter 8

THE COMPTROLLER GENERAL'S ROLE IN GOVERNMENT
PROCUREMENT INCLUDING WEAPONS ACQUISITIONS

Although the GAO has no function in negotiating
or executing public contracts or otherwise obli-
gating the Government or private individuals except in its own internal operations, under its
authority to settle and adjust accounts it has
become the most influential force in the gov-
ernment-contract field.[1]

PROCUREMENT SURVEILLANCE - A VITAL
ASPECT OF GAO'S OPERATIONS

The Government's procurement activities may appear
lackluster as compared with the more substantive program
functions. Yet many of the crucial issues that Congress
has raised with respect to the defense establishment have
revolved around the acquisition of weapon systems. The
challenge which Congressional committees and individual
Members have directed at the Defense Department's procurement programs and practices as well as specific transactions have led the Legislative Branch to look to the
GAO for closer scrutiny and incisive analyses of weapons
acquisitions. The increased Congressional concern with
procurement throughout the Government is evidenced in
the establishment of the Commission on Government Procurement in 1969, and the legislative actions that are
being taken to implement the recommendations of that Commission. The thrust is for Congress to expand the constraints upon contracting officers.[2] This is hardly surprising in light of the fact that the Comptroller General
has estimated that Federal procurement for the fiscal year
1974 totalled at least $54.3 billion. He also estimated
that the cost of 115 major systems being acquired by the
Defense Department at the beginning of fiscal year 1975
was $193 billion and that the 300 acquisitions by civil
departments and agencies would cost more than $130 billion.[3]
But the implications of the manner in which the Federal
establishment procures materiel and services are more far-
reaching than might be assumed. A legal scholar has pointed
out that the procurement process, through the imposition of
special requirements upon contractors and grantees "may
be a particularly important vehicle for trying to achieve
public policy objectives during the 1970's."[4] Within the
GAO itself, it is noteworthy that one of the most significant crises in its history arose in connection with its
audits of contract performance.

Analysis of the GAO's activities in the procurement area yields insights that make for a better understanding of the manner in which it responds to the pressures converging upon it. One perceives the forces that come into play when the Comptroller General's scrutiny is brought to bear upon matters that vitally affect the financial interests of major corporate enterprise. It is evident that Congressional and public expectations as to the GAO role in the oversight of procurement are intertwined with the changing concept of the Government contractor, especially those whose economic destinies are primarily or significantly dependent upon Government business.[5] Monitoring Government procurement affords the Comptroller General unusual opportunities to dramatize how he serves as a Congressional surrogate in checking on possible waste and impropriety in spending. GAO disclosures of short-comings in the award or performance of contracts strike a far more responsive chord than findings to the contrary. As the sequence of events in connection with the Holifield Hearings brings out, what the GAO does in connection with procurement interacts with other facets of the operations. We are not dealing with an array of the Office's tasks that are entirely separate and apart from the surveillance of other Governmental activities.

THE VARIOUS FACETS OF GAO'S PROCUREMENT ACTIVITIES

The GAO views its procurement responsibilities broadly and goes far beyond the contractual and other strictly procurement procedures as vital and far-reaching as these may be. It concerns itself as well with the decision-making that precedes the initiation of the procurement process. The GAO's role in the procurement process has been viewed as having three major facets:

1. Evaluating: (a) the effectiveness with which Government agencies determine their procurement needs, and (b) the manner in which agencies enter into and administer contracts directed to meeting such needs.

2. Checking on conformity of contractual performance with stipulated conditions and standards.

3. Affording bidders and contractors an administrative means for resolving their grievances and claims.

GAO reviews in the procurement area "include major weapon system acquisitions, as well as comparable systems in the civilian agencies; research and development projects, and automatic data processing equipment acquisitions."[6]

290

The subsequent discussion brings out GAO's deep penetration into weapons acquisition with resultant involvement of the Comptroller General in issues and problems that reach beyond what many would regard as strictly procurement matters.[7]

The 149 recommendations which the Commission on Government Procurement[8] published early in 1973 afforded the GAO a springboard for a macro approach to the Federal Government's procurement, particularly since the House Government Operations Committee requested GAO to check on the progress of the program formulated by the Commission. Congress established the Office of Federal Procurement Policy in OMB -- pursuant to the Commission's first recommendation -- and made it responsible for providing overall direction of procurement policy. The creation of such a focal point for basic procurement matters should facilitate Congressional oversight of this area, a result that has significant implications for the GAO.[9]

The discussion of the adjudicative aspects of the Comptroller General's activities brought out how his statutory authority with respect to settlement of accounts and claims has afforded him a basis for handling appeals of dissatisfied bidders. The Comptroller General has directed attention to the fact that an important aspect of the review of the bid protests is "the pointing up of problem areas which should be corrected."[10] Agencies may be apprised of shortcomings in the steps taken towards the award of a contract and be advised to revise their procedures or practices accordingly, even though the GAO determines that cancellation of the particular transaction might not be in the best interests of the public.

The Comptroller General's decisions, it has been noted, have been an important and potent vehicle for that official placing his imprint upon agency procurement practices and entering into the decision-making attendant upon the contracting for goods and services. But the role which the GAO performs in connection with procurement encompasses far more than actions of an adjudicative character. The Office's activities in the procurement area increasingly represent a blend of the examination of individual cases and a critique of the system or subsystems within which the particular transactions are consummated. GAO reviews of the formulation and implementation of the agency procurement programs are an increasingly important means for identifying problems that call for agency action and perhaps even Congressional intervention. Contract audits enable the GAO to present specific cases that are symptomatic of procurement shortcomings and the disclosure of which may also lead to the recoupment of monies previously paid out by the Government. Moreover, as brought out later in this discussion, special tasks assigned by the Congress or individual committees afford the Comptroller General an excellent opportunity to come to grips with the more substantive features of Government's procurement and to suggest changes that appear to be indicated. As it deals with procurement in greater depth, the GAO impinges on agency decision-making and is prone to touch the "nerve center."

The GAO activities with respect to procurement differ markedly as between those involving defense and those relating to the civil activities of Government. This is due not only to differences in the character of the purchases involved but also to the fact that there are separate statutory provisions governing the two types of procurement. The Armed Services Procurement Act of 1947[11] applies to the military departments, the Coast Guard, and the National Aeronautics and Space Administration. The Armed Services Procurement Regulations (ASPR) are a very important means for the implementation of the statute insofar as the defense establishment is concerned. The Federal Property and Administrative Services Act of 1949[12] applies to procurement effected by the General Services Administration and other agencies not coming within the purview of the Armed Services Procurement Act.

GAO CONCERNS WITH PROCUREMENT
DURING WORLD WAR II

Decentralization of audit activities

During World War II, the GAO separated the audit of cost-plus-fixed-fee and certain other war contracts from the regular audit work in Washington. At the same time, it decentralized such activities so that in 1944 there were 256 localities in which the field audit of such contracts was being carried on.[13] As has been indicated earlier in this study, this decentralization was an important factor in moving the GAO away from its previous rigid adherence to the highly centralized approach to the discharge of its audit responsibilities. The Comptroller General was gratified with the results which were achieved through audits at the sites of the particular activities. He pointed out that this type of audit eliminated the necessity for voluminous correspondence requesting documents and supporting details. Moreover, questions raised by the project site auditors obviated the need for issuance of many formal exceptions. Another advantage mentioned by the Comptroller General, which undoubtedly did much to make the GAO receptive to the decentralization of its activities, was the opportunity which on-site audits afforded auditors to familiarize themselves with the facts and circumstances surrounding transactions and thereby "to make a much more comprehensive audit than would otherwise be possible."[14] This reference to "comprehensive audit" is noteworthy in light of the subsequent enunciation of the comprehensive audit approach as the basic motif for GAO reviews.

Comptroller General Warren made it clear that, in its audit of cost-plus-fixed-fee contracts, the GAO had no authority to disallow expenditures under such contracts merely because they were unwise or in excess of those dictated by sound business judgment, provided they were approved by the contracting officer and supported by evidence of the expenditures. However, the Comptroller General pointed out that the GAO could and did question expenditures not within the scope of the contract as well as those that were contrary to law.[15]

Limited audit authority of GAO concerning World War II contract termination-claims

Despite the excellent rapport which Comptroller General Warren had with the Congress, he was rebuffed in his attempts to have the Congress enact legislation which would authorize the GAO to make an independent audit of settlements of claims arising from the termination of war contracts.[16] Warren was deeply stung by Congressional refusal to give him the broad authority which he had requested with respect to a review of contract settlements prior to final payment. He stated that failure to vest him with the authority he had requested had "paved the way for the improper payment of many millions of dollars of public funds through fraud, collusion, ignorance, inadvertence, or overliberality in effecting termination settlements."[17] He further pointed out that the examinations made for the purpose of detecting cases of fraud had brought to light many instances of payments to contractors in excess of amounts due but which could not be said with any certainty to have been induced by fraud.[18] However one may view the merits of the position taken by Comptroller General Warren, the experience with the World War II contract settlements demonstrated that sometimes even a Comptroller General of unusual acceptability to the Congress cannot prevail over countervailing forces opposed to efforts directed to tighter control in connection with such vast spending programs as those involved in defense.

293

POST WORLD WAR II DEFENSE CONTRACTS - THE
IMPETUS FOR GAO PROCUREMENT REVIEWS

Contract audits

The House Government Operations Committee pointed
out that neither the Budget and Accounting Act, 1921,
nor the Budget and Accounting Procedures Act, 1950 says[19]
anything about the GAO auditing Government contractors.
The Comptroller General's authority to settle accounts
and to look into the disbursement of public funds do afford him the basis for reviewing contractual payments insofar as the respective agencies are concerned. However,
legislation which Congress enacted in 1951 at the time of
the Korean conflict and which is discussed subsequently
in this chapter required that negotiated contracts (explained in the next section) include a clause giving the
Comptroller General access to books and records of contractors. The obvious implication of this measure was
that the Comptroller General would conduct audits in connection with negotiated contracts.

Although GAO contract audits are focused upon negotiated contracts, the Comptroller General views his responsibility in the procurement area as encompassing all types
of contracting. The GAO has stated that underlying all of
its contract audits "is the overall objective of testing
the effectiveness of the Federal agency management controls
which should be operating to safeguard the Government's
interests." The GAO, in effect, contends that, in order
for it to perform the task of determining how effectively
Government agencies discharge their financial responsibilities, it must concern itself generally with the manner in
which agencies award and administer contracts. However,
since the statutory provision for the Comptroller General
having access to contractors' records is limited to negotiated contracts, this means that, in the case of other
contracts, i.e., those based on advertised solicitation
of bids, the Comptroller General's reviews must be confined to the agencies themselves.

The primary responsibility for auditing a negotiated
contract is that of the agency which has awarded the contract, rather than that of the GAO. The GAO stresses
that its contract audit work is of necessity selective in
its application. It states that, in determining the work
to be done, consideration is given to such factors as
the size or type of contract, the basis for award, the
nature of cost or pricing data furnished or the lack of
such data and "a wide variety of other factors affecting
the Government's interests."[20] In its listing of the
factors that may lead to the initiation of a contract

audit, the GAO includes, among other items, requests for
information from Congressional committees or Members of
Congress; information coming to the attention of the GAO
from previous or current audit work or from other sources;
and the fact that a contractor is participating in a new
program or one of unusual importance.

Magnitude of negotiated contracts and possible abuses

The so-called "negotiated procurement refers to any
method of contracting without use of formal advertisement
and award procedures;" that is, without issuing invitations
to bid, followed by public openings and the award of the
contract to the lowest responsible offeror.

The magnitude of Government procurements effected
through negotiated contracts can be perceived from the
fact that during fiscal years 1971-75, "DOD noncompetitive
procurements accounted for about 58 per cent of its total
procurement dollars spent."[21] "Negotiation is usually
necessary when there is a lack of a sufficient number of
potential sources of supply vigorously competing for the
business or when the item being procured cannot be defined
with sufficient specification to enable meaningful competition on a fixed-price basis."[22] Both the Armed Services Procurement Act and the Federal Property and Administrative Services Act set forth specific exemptions
to the general requirement that all contracts subject to
the respective Act be formally advertised. In a recent
examination of contracts negotiated by five central agencies, the GAO found "many unjustified noncompetitive awards."[23]

The possibility of the Government losing out because
of relaxation of the normal procedural safeguards surrounding the award of public business is readily apparent. Responding to the increasing volume of defense spending for
goods and services and the expanding use of negotiated
contracts, the GAO began to concentrate attention on negotiated contracts. The Comptroller General apprised Congress of agency shortcomings in connection with such contracts:

> We have found that such weaknesses in agency
> techniques for evaluating contractors' price
> proposals have resulted, in some cases, in
> contractors realizing profits substantially
> in excess of those contemplated during nego-
> tiations.[24]

Citing specific cases of overpricing that involved
large amounts, Comptroller General Campbell stressed to
both the Defense Establishment and the Congress the im-

portance of handling the negotiation of contracts in a manner that adequately protected the interests of the Government.[25] Such revelations by the Comptroller General were an important factor in stimulating the sequence of events that led to the enactment of the so-called Truth-in-Negotiations Act discussed in the following section. During the fiscal years 1957 through 1965, the GAO reported to the Congress findings of excessive prices and other costs totalling over $125 million incurred under contracts negotiated by the military departments. About $69 million of this amount had been recovered through June 30, 1965.[26]

Increased breadth of GAO defense reviews

The intensification of the GAO audit activities in connection with defense procurement assumed added meaning because of the increased breadth of the GAO's reviews in the defense establishment.

> While we have continued to devote our efforts mainly in the areas involving procurement, supply management functions and operations, and the military assistance program, we are increasing our efforts in these areas upon such vital matters as modern weapons systems, and the determination of requirements, with special emphasis on important end items such as jet engines and missiles.[27]

In 1962, the Comptroller General informed Congress that DOD audits completed during the year and in progress at the close of the year included reviews of:

> (1) the determination of requirements for equipment and supplies, (2) the management and operation of supply systems, (3) the negotiation of contract prices, (4) the development and procurement of new types of equipment and systems, (5) the maintenance, repair, and overhaul of equipment, (6) the military assistance program, (7) the utilization of manpower, and (8) the use of commercial air transportation.

The perspective which the GAO acquired through the greater breadth and depth of its reviews in the Defense Department increased its capability to deal with defense procurement problems in a far more substantive manner than would otherwise have been possible.

TRUTH-IN-NEGOTIATIONS ACT - A
RESPONSE TO GAO DISCLOSURES

GAO the catalyst in enactment of the legislation

The shortcomings which the GAO had found in the cost-pricing data which contractors and subcontractors submitted in support of their price proposals undoubtedly were a major motivation for the Department of Defense adopting a regulation in 1959, stating that, where the negotiated price for procurement was expected to exceed $100,000, contractors and subcontractors should certify that such data were current, complete, and correct. Later, in 1961, the regulation was revised "to require inclusion of a 'price reduction for defective pricing data' clause in all negotiated fixed-price contracts or subcontracts which are expected to exceed $100,000 and where adequate price competition is lacking."[29]

GAO reviews revealed that, in a significant number of instances, the Army and Navy failed to obtain the required certifications from prime contractors and that the prime contractors of the three military departments failed to obtain certifications from their subcontractors. The GAO felt that administration of the regulation with respect to cost and pricing data would be more effective if there were a statutory requirement for such certifications in connection with negotiated contracts.[30] Hence, the Comptroller General played a very active part in securing the ultimate enactment of such legislation.

Basically, the Truth-in-Negotiations Act,[31] which was adopted in 1962, enacted into law what previously had been only a Defense Department regulation. The statute was described as "without question the most controversial development in the area of Government contracts in the last 20 years."[32] Contrariwise, Comptroller General Staats contended that the law "is based on a sound legal concept" and that it "provides a reasonable and practical solution" to the problem of how the Government can "procure its needs at fair prices in those areas where the normal forces of the market are not operating."[33]

GAO follow-up on the Act

The history of the Truth-in-Negotiations Act demonstrates that the GAO cannot only be a potent force in the enactment of legislation coming within its sphere of interest but can also use such laws as a springboard for stimulating continued Congressional concern about the subject matter that is involved. Uncovering apparent deficiencies with respect to contracting officials obtaining accurate,

current, and complete cost-pricing data for the establishment of fair and reasonable prices became very much the
frame of reference for the contract audit activities that
are discussed at a later point in this analysis.

Strain engendered by checking on compliance with the Act

The controversial nature of the Truth-in-Negotiations
Act would in itself have made for difficulties in monitoring
observance of its requirements. However, sensitivities were
increased still further by GAO's having been the prime mover
in the enactment of this legislation and by the Joint Economic Committee's intensive follow-up on the Act's implementation. Contractors complained that there was doubt as to
the meaning of the statutory requirements. Some claimed
that there was considerable uncertainty in industry and in
the Government as to what constituted adequate disclosures
of cost and pricing data.[34]

It would be naive to expect that contracting agencies
or contractors would respond with marked receptivity to
audits directed to effecting compliance with a statutory
requirement of this type. On the other hand, it appears
that excessive irritation was engendered by efforts directed towards the implementation of the statute. Even
within the GAO, there was some feeling that the earlier
comments of Comptroller General Staats as to the extent of
Defense Department's noncompliance with the statute reflected something of a blunderbuss approach. The irritation caused by what struck Defense Department officials
as carping criticism was intensified by Senator Proxmire's
indictment of the Defense Department on the basis of the
Comptroller General's findings.

There is much to be said for having the continuity
of interest and extensive follow-up such as that shown by
the Joint Economic Committee with respect to the Comptroller General's analyses and evaluations. But one must
realistically recognize that there is always the possibility
that a committee or individual Member may perceive the
issue in far different dimensions than that envisaged by
the Comptroller General or may pursue it with an intensity
not contemplated by that official and which, much to his
dismay, makes his findings anathema to the agency concerned.
Staats ultimately changed his tune and sought to develop a
more amicable relationship with the Defense Department insofar as GAO's checking on compliance with this Act is concerned; he reported to Congress:

> We believe that the Department of Defense has
> made real progress in achieving the intent and
> purpose of Public Law 87-653. Continued emphasis

298

by the Department of Defense on appropriate
implementation of this law should go far in
achieving the benefits intended by its enactment.[35]

Early in 1977, the Comptroller General reported: "Generally, Department of Defense procurement staff are effectively carrying out the system established for pricing noncompetitive contracts."[36] However, the report
also apprised Congress that the GAO continued to identify
overpriced contracts. This should have alerted DOD that
it was not to rest on the laurels bestowed by GAO!

COMPTROLLER GENERAL'S ACCESS TO CONTRACTORS' RECORDS

Chapter 4, Comptroller General's Access to Information, discusses the problems which the GAO has experienced
in obtaining agency data which it deems necessary for
carrying out its audit activities. Access to records has
also evoked controversy in connection with the audits of
negotiated contracts.

The 1951 statute provided that all contracts negotiated without advertising

. . . shall include a clause to the effect
that the Comptroller General of the United
States or any of his duly authorized representatives shall until the expiration of
three years after final payment have access
to and the right to examine any directly
pertinent books, documents, papers, and
records of the contractor or any of his subcontractors engaged in the performance of
and involving transactions related to such
contracts or subcontracts.[37]

Judicial interpretation of GAO access authority

A 1967 ruling of the United States Circuit Court of
Appeals for the Ninth District gave a broad interpretation to the authority granted the Comptroller General by
this statutory provision. This ruling, which the United
States Supreme Court refused to review, placed the GAO
in an unusually strategic position to insist upon having
access to information in the possession of Government
contractors.[38] The district court had held for the Government in a suit brought to enforce the right to examine[39]
certain books and records of the Hewlett-Packard Company.
The Comptroller General's representatives had been permitted access to books and records relating to sales prices
of the items sold under the four contracts involved but

had been refused cost of production information. The Company contended that such information was not directly pertinent to the contracts since the contract prices had been determined upon the basis of the listed catalog prices and since the Company did not supply to the Government any information as to the costs of production or profit margins upon any of the items covered by the contract. The trial court "declared that the company's costs of direct material, direct labor and overhead costs in producing the items furnished under the contracts, directly pertain to, and involve transactions relating to, the contracts." The Circuit Court of Appeals said:

> . . . the word "contract," as used in this statute is intended to have a broader meaning, embracing not only the specific terms and conditions of the agreement, but also the general subject matter. The subject matter of these four contracts is the procurement of described property by the Government.

It is significant that the Circuit Court explicitly recognized that, in making contract audits, the GAO is concerned not merely with checking or verifying data as to the particular transaction but also in obtaining information which might lead to a reexamination and subsequent modification of the procurement practices. But, as will be brought out shortly, the Circuit Court ruling has not afforded a complete solution to the Comptroller General's problems with respect to obtaining information from contractors. A U.S. District Court was far less sympathetic to the GAO when it ruled favorably on the complaint of Eli Lilly and Company, a leading drug manufacturer, asking that the Court declare that a request by the Comptroller General to examine certain records of Lilly exceeded his legal authority and to enjoin him from examining or attempting to examine such records.[40] The Court observed that the prices in each of the seven contracts involved were identical to those initially offered by Lilly and were not actually negotiated and that, because of the way in which the prices were determined, Lilly was not required to submit cost or pricing data to the contracting agencies prior to the award of any of the contracts.

The Government admitted that: (a) the sole purpose of GAO's requested access was not to audit Lilly's negotiations and contract performance, and (b) one purpose was to have a better public and legislative understanding of the economics of the industry. The Court noted that GAO's study had its inception in the concern which the Subcommittee on Monopoly of the Senate Select Committee

on Small Business had about competition in the pharma-
ceutical industry and the costs of drugs procured by
the government. It was obvious that GAO's role was essentially that of a handmaid to the Subcommittee; this
ploy apparently incurred the displeasure of the Court,
which held that "the Comptroller General's authority
must be narrowly construed to limit the right of access
to the purpose for which the right was granted, namely,
to audit particular negotiated contracts." Thus at this
juncture, the judicial stance on the Comptroller General's
access in connection with negotiated contracts reflects a
sharp conflict of views.

Comptroller General's request for subpoena authority with respect to contractors' records

The difficulties GAO has experienced in getting access to contractors' records involved in negotiated contracts impelled the Comptroller General in 1969 to suggest
to the Senate Committee on Executive Reorganization that
the GAO be given still further powers to obtain information from contractors.[41] As to reliance upon the procedure followed in the Hewlett-Packard case, Staats
pointed out that obtaining judicial resolution of such
disputes meant several years loss of time as well as much
effort on the part of the Department of Justice. Having
portrayed the roadblocks sometimes confronted by the GAO,
Staats proposed that Congress grant the Comptroller General "the authority to compel by judicially enforceable
subpoena the production of those books, accounts, and
other contractor records covered under the examination
of records clause now required in negotiated contracts."

Congressional reluctance to grant the Comptroller
General the power to subpoena contractors' records was
demonstrated in the fate of the provisions in the 1970
Military Procurement Authorization Bill, which would
have permitted the Comptroller General to issue subpoenas
in connection with the study which that bill called upon
him to make of contractors' and subcontractors' profits
on negotiated contracts. The Conference Committee set
up to reconcile the differences between the Senate and the
House agreed that, since the GAO was an arm of the Legislative Branch of the Government which has subpoena power,
it was not necessary to grant additional subpoena power
to "a subordinate Agency of the legislative branch."[42]

But Comptroller General Staats has been persevering
in his efforts to obtain the authority to issue subpoenas
"requiring the production of negotiated contract and sub-
contract records and records of other non-Federal persons
or organizations to which he has a right of access by law

301

or agreement."[43] In support of the bill vesting him with
such authority, the Comptroller General gave a Senate Committee specific examples of problems the GAO had encountered in obtaining access to records of non-federal organizations; these involved: major suppliers of meat to the
military; major defense contractors such as Boeing Aircraft Corporation, Minnesota Mining and Manufacturing Company, and General Electric; a National Park Service contractor; and several drug firms.[44] Staats argues that,
if he had subpoena authority, many of such delays in complying with his requests would probably not occur and that
there would be a quicker resolution in the courts of any
disputes over his right to access.[45] The case for giving
the Comptroller General this additional muscle needs to be
viewed not by itself but from the standpoint of the totality of GAO prerogatives and the thrust for their expansion.

THE HOLIFIELD HEARINGS - CRITICAL CONFRONTATION BE-
    TWEEN THE GAO AND THE MILITARY INDUSTRIAL COMPLEX

The reports which Comptroller General Campbell prepared on the basis of his contract audits aroused a welter
of criticism by contractors and Defense Department officials. The protestations reached such a crescendo that the
Military Operations Subcommittee of the House Committee on
Government Operations held extensive hearings in 1965 on
the audit of defense contracts. The Subcommittee was
chaired by Congressman Chet Holifield; and the hearings,
are, therefore, more popularly known as the Holifield
Hearings.

Criticisms levelled at the GAO

Opening the hearings, Chairman Holifield referred to
the "necessary and useful work" of the GAO in identifying
illegal, improper, or unnecessary expenditures and in suggesting improvements in Governmental operations. Having
bestowed this accolade, Congressman Holifield then defined
the problem with which the Subcommittee was seeking to deal:

> Resentment often arises over what the agencies
> believe to be invasion of their management pre-
> rogatives, and over reports which do not give a
> balanced account of their achievements as well
> as their deficiencies. And where contractors
> are involved, often they believe that the GAO
> reports invade their privacy, prematurely pub-
> licize issues still under administrative re-
> view, and place the companies in a derogatory
> position which they believe is unjustified.
> The Government agencies and the contractors
> both point to the fact that GAO reports often

deal with matters and events which are years
old, difficult to reconstruct, and occurring
in situations and circumstances which hindsight robs of perspective and understanding.[46]

The challenges directed at the audits of defense contracts had implications that extended to the totality of
the GAO's audit activities. Although ostensibly dealing
only with defense contract audits, the hearings crystallized issues as to the manner in which the GAO conducted
its reviews generally, the approach reflected in its
analyses, and the practices employed in reporting findings
and recommendations on the basis of audits. The outpouring of criticisms reflected pent-up resentment for which
the hearings served as a release.

The underlying allegation made during the hearings
was that of rigidity on the part of the GAO and an inability to engage in meaningful dialogues with agencies
on matters of mutual concern. Another criticism which
Comptroller General Campbell recognized and to which he
sought to respond was that the GAO was said to be "exercising 20-20 hindsight without adequate recognition of
the circumstances and conditions existing at the time of
negotiations." The Comptroller General retorted with the
statement that the GAO did "go to great lengths in our reviews to determine these factors at the date of negotiation."[47]

Representatives of industry presented some telling arguments in support of their position vis-a-vis the GAO. One
asserted that the GAO had become "unduly involved in the
exercise of managerial opinion both as to management judgments by the procuring agencies and management judgments
by industry." This witness also stated that the headline
character of GAO reports give that agency great power.[48]
The Chairman of United Aircraft Corporation told the Subcommittee that the GAO had overstepped the boundaries of
its functions and had engaged in practices and procedures
which were beyond the scope and ability of its personnel
and which were detrimental to the efficient execution of
Government procurement operations. He went on to say:

It seeks out only what it regards as errors,
illegalities, and inefficiencies. It files
reports only on subjects which it considers
wrong. . . It pays little or no attention
to the quality of the product delivered under the contracts it reviews nor to the effect on quality or delivery schedules which
might result from yielding to its recommendations. The result is that a reading of GAO
audit reports leads to a badly distorted im-

pression that most military procurement is
unsound. This distortion is accentuated by
the GAO's practice of loading its reports
with colorful language bordering on the sen-
sational and apparently intended to appeal
to the public and to others not intimately[49]
acquainted with the facts.

Traumatic impact of Holifield Hearings - GAO capitulation

The Holifield Subcommittee hearings had a marked effect on not only the GAO's contract audit work, but also --
as has been previously intimated -- the entirety of GAO
audit activities. The sharp and repeated criticisms directed at the GAO during these hearings placed the office
in a relatively submissive and placatory mood, more particularly since matters came to a head just about the time
Comptroller General Campbell was relinquishing his office.

The Committee report[50] prepared on the basis of the
hearings was quite different from what might have been expected. The fact that Elmer Staats had, in the meantime,
been appointed Comptroller General undoubtedly made the
Committee less prone to severely denigrate the GAO. Another significant factor accounting for the relative mild-
ness of the report was the letter[51] which Frank Weitzel,
in his capacity as Acting Comptroller General, addressed
to Congressman Holifield shortly before the House Government Operations Committee received the Subcommittee report. The Weitzel letter had overtones of administrative
self-flagellation, in the course of which the erring
agency expressed its contrition and committed itself to
a course of corrective action. Responding to the criticism that the GAO reports had concentrated on the castigation of agencies, Weitzel conceded that many of the
audit reports had not included enough information about
the overall aspects of the respective operations or their
size and nature to provide an adequate perspective against
which the significance of reported weaknesses could be
fairly judged. He stated that steps had been taken to
have the GAO reports include more information about the
activities that were examined.

The Weitzel letter informed Congressman Holifield
that the GAO was further modifying its practices to provide that the titles of its reports to the Congress "be
couched in constructive terms rather than in terms of
the deficiencies being reported. We plan also to present detailed text comments of our reports in as constructive a vein as possible."

The GAO, according to Weitzel, intended to reduce
the number of audit reports presented to the Congress

by having reports of broader scope in which individual examples of waste or inefficiency would be used as illustrations of the need for management improvements, rather than being made the subjects of individual Congressional reports. The rationale for the change was that more-inclusive reports would have a greater impact on promoting improvements in agency management policies and methods and would provide "greater assistance to congressional committees in carrying out their legislative and oversight responsibilities." Weitzel strove earnestly to present a cogent rationale for each switchover in GAO practice to avoid the appearance of abject capitulation by the Office.[52]

The Committee report and its aftermath

It is impossible to determine precisely what took place behind the scenes during the months that elapsed between the time the Subcommittee hearings closed in July 1965 and when the Committee Report was issued in March of the following year. One official described the initial draft as "blistering" and said that it was "softened down" considerably. The final draft concerned itself in large measure with commenting on the changes set forth in the Weitzel letter. Referring to the criticisms that had been voiced during the hearings, the Committee said that not all were supported but "some appeared to have merit."[53] It could hardly have been more restrained in evaluating the charges directed against the GAO. After stating that GAO reporting practices had been substantially improved, the Committee very significantly indicated that this was "a direct result of matters brought up at the hearings and discussed further in subsequent informal conferences with the Comptroller General and his associates."

There was not complete Committee unanimity on the report; and Congressman Jack Brooks, a very active member of the Committee, expressed strong dissent. In light of subsequent developments and his continuing interest in the GAO, Brooks' reactions are very pertinent:

Essentially, it is the function of the GAO to discover and report deficiencies. Hence, I do not believe that fewer GAO reports, giving less emphasis to deficiencies, constitutes an improvement.

The recommendations and conclusions in this report can only intensify the difficulties confronting the GAO in maintaining an effective contract audit system and in carrying out many other vitally important responsibilities for the Congress of the United States.[54]

One Committee staff member was vitriolic in his condemna-
tion of the Holifield Subcommittee: "Industry got to the
Holifield Subcommittee, which cut the guts out of the GAO."

The Holifield Subcommittee hearings and the resultant
steps taken by the GAO to mollify its critics brought about
some needed improvements. On the other hand, the whole experience was so demeaning for the GAO that, at least temporarily, it injected an inhibiting element into the contract audit program. As the pendulum swung the other way
to more intensive scrutiny of defense contracts, the constraints stemming from the Holifield Hearings were increasingly dispelled, but significant vestiges still remain. A staff member of the Joint Economic Committee,
writing some years later on the GAO, referred to the
hearings as an "inquisition" and contended that they "had
whacked the GAO in the head, and in some ways it has still
not recovered."[55]

A postscript on the Holifield Hearings report

Several years after the Holifield hearings, the writer
conferred with officers of industry associations and executives of various large Government contractors in order to
obtain firsthand impressions of their attitudes toward
the GAO. It was apparent that the feelings of these representatives of the private sector were still characterized by resentment towards the GAO and a proclivity for
taking it to task. The essentiality of an agency such as
the GAO was readily admitted; but they reiterated criticisms that had been voiced at the Holifield hearings.

In expressing their views, industry representatives
were very much influenced by the image of power that the
GAO had in the eyes of the corporate sector. There was
an obvious reluctance to say anything that might result
in incurring the disfavor of the GAO and which might lead
to retaliatory measures on its part. The power which industry attributed to the GAO stemmed not so much from the
legal sanctions which it might invoke but the influence
it has with the Congress.

There was generally a feeling that the GAO personnel
performed their tasks competently so long as they confined
their efforts to the more strictly auditing sphere. In
fact, some commended the high degree of accounting accuracy reflected in the GAO reports. As was the case with
Government executives, contractors were inclined to feel
that GAO auditors win advancement and recognition on the
basis of inadequacies discovered by them.

An industry association raised, in effect, the same
underlying issue posed by those who challenge the complex

of powers vested in the Comptroller General:

> We have said before - and it bears repeat-
> ing - that a principal, if not the chief,
> source of problems arising from the GAO
> contract audit program is the fact of the
> unusual combination of governmental powers
> vested in the Comptroller General. His
> office exercises a legislative power of
> investigation - or audit - and a variety
> of executive powers such as the power to
> suspend or disallow payments and thus to
> strike down a procurement arrangement on
> grounds of illegality or error. It seems
> doubtful if the organizational conflicts
> revealed by the Holifield Subcommittee
> hearings can be overcome so long as this
> combination of powers exists or at least
> so long as it is administered as it has
> been in the past.[56]

THE F-111 INVESTIGATIONS - A FORERUNNER OF GAO DEEPER INVOLVEMENT IN DOD PROCUREMENT

Congressional use of GAO stimulated by costliness and complexities of weapon systems

The vast sums ordinarily entailed in the acquisition
of a weapon system focus Congressional and public attention
on such programs, particularly when there are evidences
of constantly mounting costs and/or disconcerting failure
of the system to come up to original expectations. The
GAO is a key resource to which Congressional committees
and individual Members look when they seek to explore
such developments, that -- because of the technical nature
and complexity of the subject matter -- challenge the best
of analytical skills.

GAO's experience with the F-111 studies demonstrates
how time consuming such reviews can be and how the completion of the Office's tasks can be impeded, if not stalemated, by resistance on the part of both the agency and contractor. It is also illustrative of how an important and
demanding analysis can have little visibility outside of
the committee for which it is conducted.

The studies which the GAO initiated in 1963 in response to Congressional interest in, and concern about,
the F-111 were the forerunner of the thrust for deeper
GAO involvement in analyses with respect to weapons systems. The discussion of the Comptroller General's access

to information (Chapter 4) described some of the difficulties which the GAO experienced in seeking to discharge
the tasks imposed by the Senate Permanent Committee on Investigations and later the House Appropriations Committee.

McNamara's F-111 tribulations

The F-111 or TFX was conceived by Secretary McNamara
as the fighter-bomber plane that would serve the needs of
both the Air Force and the Navy.[57] The woes which first
beset McNamara in the implementation of the F-111 program
were recounted several years later in a newspaper article:

> The TFX was McNamara's first genuinely bruising
> encounter with Congress. . . The issue then
> was McNamara's award of the contract to the
> General Dynamics Corp. which had been vetoed
> by four military source selection boards in
> favor of the Boeing Corp. The overriding
> implication of the McClellan inquiry was that
> the $6 billion TFX award to a Texas plant was
> a political fix on the part of the Kennedy
> Administration then looking forward to the
> 1964 Presidential race.[58]

This inauspicious beginning of the F-111 project was
followed by questions as to the basic merit of such a
plane and criticisms of the mounting costs. The problem
of cost overruns in connection with the F-111 assumes
added interest in light of the spate of criticism that
was set off by the C-5A disclosures, which were discussed
earlier.

Committee interest in the F-111 impelled the GAO to
do considerable analytical work on this weapons system.
Relatively little of this effort was visible insofar as
the public is concerned -- or, for that matter, most Members of Congress. This was so because of the classified
character of the subject matter and also the fact that
the results of such analyses were submitted to committees,
which, in accordance with the practices already explained,
could determine the extent to which GAO reports should be
made available outside the respective committees that requested them.

GAO's input and output on F-111 analyses

The input required to prepare the F-111 analyses
could presumably have been reduced considerably had the
GAO been accorded readier access to the pertinent records.
Even when information was obtained after considerable delay, its usefulness for effective Congressional oversight

was impaired by the staleness of the data. The departmental
defensiveness engendered by the mounting criticisms directed
at the F-lll made GAO's task all the more difficult.

The grave concern which Secretary McNamara felt about
the F-lll difficulties that began to evidence themselves
was reflected in his initiation, during the summer of 1966,
of weekly meetings to discuss F-lll problems. These meetings were attended by top Defense Department personnel and
key officials of General Dynamics Corporation and Pratt
and Whitney. The meetings came to be known -- rather omin-
ously -- as "Project Icarus." At the September 10, 1966
meeting, McNamara reportedly noted that the F-lll program
was being investigated by GAO on behalf of the Senate Subcommittee chaired by Senator McClellan. The summary of
this meeting indicated that a General Dynamics official
"observed that Service plant representatives have been in-
structed on what to divulge and what not to divulge."[59]

However useful the formal reports furnished the two
Committees, the continuing consultations between GAO representatives and Committee staff members were unquestionably an invaluable source of information and ideas for
the Committees. Facts and suggestions furnished by the
GAO helped to crystallize questions raised by the Committees
at their hearings. The information compiled by the GAO and
the insights which its auditors acquired concerning the F-lll
program facilitated continuing Committee inquiry into the
program.

1969 - THE WATERSHED OF EXPANDED GAO
ROLE IN DEFENSE PROCUREMENT

Pressures for more intensive scrutiny of procurement

Whatever the constraints emanating from the Holifield
Hearings, there developed -- as previously observed -- a
strong thrust for GAO allocating more of its resources
for the analysis of the acquisition of defense materiel.
The very magnitude of defense outlays and their policy
implications dollarwise would in themselves impel Congress and the public to call upon the Government's central
monitoring agency to give this segment of Federal spending
a top priority. The fact that such expenditures mean cur-
tailment of vital social and economic programs evoked increasingly critical, and even hostile, scrutiny on the part
of those concerned about inadequate financing of such programs. The so-called military-industrial complex and the
profits that corporate enterprise derives from defense procurement have disturbing overtones for many people and
elicit feelings of concern, uneasiness, and even suspicion.
The concentration of much of this business in a relatively

small number of companies compounds the misgivings. The
criticisms as to looseness in the award and administration of contracts add to the pressures for independent
surveillance of defense procurement. The impact of technological obsolescence and the abandonment of weapons
systems upon which large sums have already been expended
give rise to a questioning attitude on the part of Congress and the public. Substantial differences between
original estimates and actual costs, however they may be
explained, exacerbate the situation, particularly when
the general "climate" is one of increasing concern about
defense spending.

Impact of mounting criticism of military procurement upon the GAO

Congressional and public criticism of weapon systems
procurement reached something of a zenith in 1969. The
Military Procurement Authorization Bill, 1970, the hearings of the Senate Subcommittee on Economy in Government,
disclosures as to large overruns by defense contractors,
and challenges directed within the Congress to those who
ordinarily shepherded defense spending measures in rather
cavalier fashion gave rise to a cascade of proposals for
Congressional analysis and oversight of weapons systems
programs. In light of these developments it is not surprising that the Comptroller General refers to 1970 as
the year when GAO became "deeply involved in reviews of
the acquisition of major weapon systems -- growing out of
the interest of Congress in independently developed data
on the cost, schedule and performance of systems for
which funding was being requested."[60]

Reflecting the spreading concern over shortcomings
in defense procurement, the House Committee on Appropriations commented: "Whether it is termed cost overrun, or
cost growth, or cost increase, fiscal year 1969 can well
be characterized as the 'Year of the Cost Overrun.'"[61]
An even more significant and disturbing observation by
the Committee was that it feared that low standards of
weapon system reliability "have resulted in reduced effectiveness of our military forces."[62]

These developments had a two-fold effect insofar as
the GAO was concerned. There were some intimations that
the GAO had not been as effective as it might have been
in bringing to light shortcomings in the implementation
of the defense procurement programs. The other aspect
was a tendency to assign additional responsibilities to
the GAO with a view to having it furnish information that
would enable the Congress to have a tighter grip on the
spending for weapon systems. The information gap, as
Senator Ribicoff pointed out, was especially acute in

the case of those Members of Congress who were actively
opposed to current military policy but who were not members of the committees within whose purview such decision-
making came.[63] "To acquire the needed data, Senators turned
to the GAO."[63]

Congressional consideration of the Military Procurement Authorization Bill for the fiscal year 1970 gave
rise to extended discussions of the role of the GAO. The
submission of several far-reaching amendments while the
bill was before the Senate crystallized issues as to the
breadth and depth of the GAO's analytical responsibilities.
The resultant formulation and strenuous advocacy of proposals for expanding GAO's role in the defense procurement
area, although focused on military spending, had important
implications with respect to the totality of GAO's functions.

Senator Eagleton's proposal for GAO study of MBT-70 tank

A prime example of such moves was the attempt by Senator Thomas F. Eagleton to amend the Military Procurement
Authorization Bill so as to preclude availability of funds
for the MBT-70 tank until after the Comptroller General
had submitted to the Congress a comprehensive study "of
the past and projected costs of such tank and a thorough
review of the consideration which went into the decision
to produce such tank."[64] The problem, as is noted later,
has proven to be perennial.

In arguing for the bill, which he introduced on behalf of Senator Hatfield and himself, Eagleton stated that
he did not pretend to have the technical competence to
judge the ultimate effectiveness of the MBT-70.[65] Very
significantly, Senator Eagleton contended that the Comptroller General can and should render to Members of Congress "that which the Bureau of the Budget renders unto
the President of the United States and the Executive Branch."
Senator Proxmire, agreeing with Senator Eagleton, commented:

> I do not think the GAO would presume to tell
> us whether the MBT-70 is the most effective
> weapon to meet the contingency for which it
> was planned. That is not their job. Again
> and again they have been reluctant to do that.
> But they will give us facts and information
> and cost effectiveness, and we make up our
> own minds, as the Senator knows.

After considerable discussion of the Eagleton proposal,
Senator Stennis informed the Senate that "an around-the-
table gentleman's understanding" had been reached and that
the Armed Services Subcommittee, of which he was Chairman,

would request the GAO to make a study of the MBT-70. Senator Eagleton then withdrew his amendment "without prejudice." The GAO submitted its report by the established deadline and issued an unclassified version.[66] The Armed Services Committee, after receiving the GAO Report, voted unanimously to retain $55.4 million for the MBT-70 in the Military Procurement Authorization Bill. This disposed of the matter so far as the Senate was concerned; but, the MBT program was subsequently killed by Congress. However, the Defense Department effort to develop and produce a new main battle tank has continued, and Senator Eagleton's interest in the subject has apparently remained unabated. Thus, in 1976, following requests from the Senator and Representative Les Aspen, the Comptroller General prepared a secret report on the subject, which was then followed by an unclassified version.[67] The report covered requirements for a new main battle tank; combat effectiveness and survival as well as costs of a new tank, the XM-1, and a comparison between it and a German version.

Schweiker and Podell proposals for reports on defense contracts

Proposals of Senator Schweiker and Representative Podell with respect to weapons systems contracts, although ultimately defeated, had a significant impact on GAO's activities in the procurement area. Senator Schweiker introduced an amendment that would have required the Secretary of Defense, in cooperation with the Comptroller General, to develop a system for reporting on major contracts for weapon systems.[68] The Comptroller General was to be responsible for auditing the reporting system and would also have been required to make audits of major contracts where he deemed such audits to be warranted. An especially significant feature of the Schweiker amendment was that it would have vested the Comptroller General with subpoena authority vis-a-vis contractors, subcontractors, and procuring agencies. This was a precursor of the strenuous efforts by the Comptroller General to buttress GAO access to contractors' records. A proposal by Congressman Podell called for the Comptroller General reporting annually on contract overruns and delays in contract completion.[69]

These developments prompted the Comptroller General to write Senator Stennis, as Chairman of the Armed Services Committee, describing in some detail the status reports on major weapons systems that the GAO was planning to submit to Congress at the beginning of each session. As to the legislative proposals that had been advanced for various types of reports and reviews by the GAO with respect to defense procurement, Staats recommended that "the most careful consideration be given" to such legislation before

312

it was enacted. The Comptroller General expressed the belief that the basic authority of the GAO was adequate to carry out the program which he had outlined. Similarly, while indicating agreement with the objective of the Podell bill, Staats questioned whether it provided "the most practical approach to the problem of reporting on contracts."[71]

Staats was manifestly loath to disagree with Senator Stennis, who strongly opposed vesting the Comptroller General with subpoena power. Senator Schweiker was surprised to find that the Comptroller General did not support such a move; he related that, when he had questioned Staats concerning this question, the Comptroller General had said that this was a matter of basic policy for the Congress itself to decide.[72] Staats' ambivalence on this issue is further evidenced by his affirmative response to the question posed by a Representative as to whether he felt that "the lack of subpoena power, particularly in the area of defense, has caused problems for the General Accounting Office in obtaining necessary information?"[73]

Staats' position is more understandable when viewed in the context of not only deference to Senator Stennis but also his almost desperate efforts to stave off the attempts to prescribe by statute specific analytical and reporting responsibilities in connection with defense procurement. He took every opportunity to convince the Congress that the GAO was redirecting its efforts so as to give greater priority and emphasis to Government procurement, especially that relating to defense.

The position taken by the Comptroller General might also have been influenced by considerations of strategy in dealing with Congressional committees. The Schweiker amendment was something of a threat to the two Armed Services Committees, especially since it attempted to effect an important change without obtaining the blessing of these two powerful committees. Additionally, since the Comptroller General was not fully prepared to present a legislative program, he might have felt that prudence dictated his opposition to a proposal such as that submitted by Senator Schweiker. The strenuous efforts by Senator Schweiker and supporters of his viewpoint proved to be abortive when the Conference Committee considered the Military Procurement Authorization Bill.[74]

Senator Proxmire's proposal for GAO study of defense profits

Senator Proxmire proposed an amendment to the Military Procurement Authorization Bill designed to carry out the recommendation which the Senate Subcommittee on Economy in Government had made for the GAO conducting a comprehensive study of profitability of defense contracting. The Proxmire amendment called for the Comptroller General conducting a study and review, on a selective basis, of the profits made by contractors and subcontractors on defense contracts. In view of the great reluctance which Staats had previously expressed as to the GAO conducting such a study of defense contract profits, it is noteworthy that Senator Proxmire was now able to inform the Senate that [75] his proposal had the support of the Comptroller General. The Senator observed: "It is precisely the kind of work the GAO is equipped to do. Let no one argue that the watchdog agency of the Congress of the United States is not equipped to determine the rate of return on costs and investments of defense contractors."

The ensuing series of events with respect to the Proxmire amendment contrasted sharply with those relating to the Schweiker amendment. Unlike the close vote on the Schweiker proposal, the Proxmire amendment was carried by a vote of 85 to 0. The Conference Committee accepted the Proxmire amendment with a modification of the subpoena provision that placed the two Armed Services Committees in a pivotal position to determine the extent to which the subpoena power would be available to implement the amendment. The Proxmire amendment, unlike the Schweiker amendment, was of a one-time character and, therefore, more readily acceptable. It afforded members an opportunity to show that they were concerned about defense contractor profits without their making any definitive commitment as to continuing scrutiny.

The stance of the Comptroller General with respect to the Proxmire proposal unquestionably reflected a pragmatic approach. Apparently sensing that Proxmire had a good chance of obtaining Congressional adoption of his proposal and also having experienced the abrasive quality of the Senator's displeasure -- as was brought out previously -- the Comptroller General decided to join forces with him.

Staats has turned full circle on the desirability of GAO conducting studies of contractors' profits and has been importuning Congress for authority to make selective studies of the profits of contractors and subcontractors whose Government contracts aggregated $1 million or more in their most recent fiscal year. [76] Such studies would be made at least once in each five-year period, and the reports on the results of each study be submitted promptly to Congress. The Comptroller General would be empowered to require contractors to submit information to him, and he would have access to their records. In his advocacy of this measure, Staats has referred to the 1969 Act and the resultant report to the Congress. He has argued that permanent authority for such studies on a periodic basis is preferable to one-time studies, the initiation of which can engender "added controversy." Another argument advanced by Staats is that "an independent study by GAO of profits is a greater value to the Congress than studies performed by the contracting agencies in the executive branch."[77]

GAO institutes status report on weapon system acquisitions

Early in 1970, the Comptroller General issued his promised report on the status of selected major weapon systems.[78] The Report covered 57 major systems as of June 30, 1969; these involved total estimated completion costs of $113.7 billion. A major weapon system acquisition was defined as one "expected to require cumulative research, development test, and evaluation (RDT and E) financing in excess of $25 million, or which were estimated to require cumulative production investment in excess of $100 million." The GAO was able to obtain sufficient detail on only 38 of the weapon systems to permit a comparison of cost estimates at different points in time. In addition to the report made available to the public, there were 10 separate classified reports dealing with the status of the 57 individual programs. Apart from its own findings, the GAO evaluated the Defense Department's Selected Acquisition Reporting System.

The Report showed that 38 weapon systems that had planning cost estimates of $42.0 billion had completion costs of $62.9 billion as of June 30, 1969. The GAO also disclosed that 34 of the 57 systems reviewed "either had experienced or were expected to experience slippage in the originally established program schedules of from 6 months to more than 3 years." GAO was now probing far more deeply into the military procurement area. Even before the Report was issued, the Subcommittee on Economy in Government had been told by the Assistant Comptroller General that "additional work will continue to more fully develop the underlying causes of problem areas identified and proposed solutions."[79] The following year, the Comptroller General followed up his initial effort with a report "Acquisition of Major Weapon Systems," which was described as the first of "a continuing series of appraisals of those factors most closely related to effective performance in procuring major weapons."[80]

The reporting on weapon system acquisitions continued on a periodic basis and was the medium for GAO informing Congress as to both changes in planned performance and increases in estimated costs, such as that of a $30 billion increase for 50 major weapon systems for the year ended December 31, 1974.[81] The overall reporting system was

315

then changed so as to combine in one report the status of major weapons systems with the status of major civil acquisitions. Thus, the Comptroller General, in his report, "Financial Status of Major Federal Acquisitions September 30, 1977,"[82] disclosed that 808 civil and military acquisitions expected to cost $281 billion at their early or developmental stages were now, according to agency estimates, to cost $482 billion. "Inflation, engineering, and quantity changes were identified as the major causes of cost growth."

In addition to the more comprehensive type of report, the GAO prepares individual reports on the status of major systems being acquired. For example, he recently presented Congress with a report, "Status of the F-16 Aircraft Program."[83] Similarly, the Comptroller General reported on the Trident submarine and missile programs.[84] Entirely apart are the reports on procurement practices and special audits, investigations, and reviews in connection with procurement.[85]

GAO'S DEEP INVOLVEMENT IN SUBSTANTIVE WEAPONS ACQUISITION ISSUES

Variety and depth of GAO reviews

The scope of GAO reviews of weapon acquisitions has gone far beyond the procurement process per se and has concerned itself with the more substantive aspects. Hence, we find the Comptroller General reporting to Congress on a review of the controversy over whether the Navy's major surface combatant ships should be all nuclear-powered, all conventionally-powered, or a mix of both.[86] His report on the F-16, which has been alluded to, not only recommended that the Secretary of Defense reassess the F-16 survivability features but that he also not allow European pressure to hamper performance of testing necessary to justify a full production decision.[87] The report on the acquisition of a new main battle tank previously mentioned -- to which the Secretary of Defense was unreceptive -- recommended to the Secretary that he "accelerate ongoing studies which should consider the cost-effectiveness of an alternative armored force not wholly dependent on the use of costly heavy tanks."[88]

The questions raised by the GAO concerning a new eight-inch gun proposed by the Navy evoked such reaction that the Navy decided to delay full-scale production of the gun until it could gain further information about the accuracy and effectiveness of the weapon.[89] The GAO had contended that the gun was "so inaccurate at longer ranges that it would use about all its ammunition before hitting

a target."[90] This same news story reported that the GAO
letter to Defense Secretary Rumsfeld had "also suggested
that Navy officials had given 'possibly misleading testimony' about the gun to Congress."

The B-1 was the subject of continuing study by the
GAO, which looked into and reported to Congress on the
aspects of the "alternative candidate for the strategic
manned bomber mission . . . survivability, penetrability,
range, payload, target coverage, and cost."[91] At the same
time, he made this reference to GAO's activities in the
weapons systems area, Staats told of GAO reports and testimony to the Congress dealing with the airborne warning
and control system (AWACS).

The depth of GAO's approach to weapons acquisitions
is reflected in the Comptroller General's announcement in
1974 that one of GAO's new approaches was the study of mission areas and families of weapons system. "We believe
the Congress needs a better understanding of the interre-
lationships of enemy threat, mission requirements, and
the role that individual weapons systems play in the ac-
complishment of missions."[92] In light of the broad ambit
which Staats has established for GAO in defense procurement, it is not surprising to find the Comptroller General
submitting a classified report on how two coproduction
programs (F-5E Aircraft in Taiwan and the M-16 Rifle in
the Philippines) were "meeting their objectives, including[93]
expansion of technical and military support capabilities."

One of the latest aspects of GAO's increasingly deep
involvement in analyses relating to the acquisition of major
weapon systems is the effort to demonstrate, through a
number of reports, the nature of the data which it feels
Congress should have as to overall objectives, systems already in the inventory or development, and long-range budget implications. In undertaking this task, the Comptroller
General maintained that the Defense Department had not been
responsive to such needs. He cited three reports which the
GAO had issued and which dealt with requirements for additional strategic airlift, field army air defense, and sea
control. Probably anticipating that some might speculate
as to whether GAO was not overreaching itself, Staats re-
assured a Subcommittee that "our aim in this type of reporting is not to make military judgments, but to help assure that the information furnished to the Congress is complete, objective, and in the proper perspective."[94]

The Gamma Goat - a case study of GAO impact on weapon
acquisition

GAO's studies of the Army cargo truck referred to

317

as the Gamma Goat reflect GAO perseverance and also demonstrate the influence which such analyses can have upon
Congressional thinking with respect to materiel matters.
At the same time, the position taken by the Army is illustrative of how an agency can proceed counter to a GAO
recommendation even when that Office has Congressional
backing. A 1971 report had expressed the opinion that
the Army should not enter full-scale production in light
of shortcomings identified by GAO. A follow-up report
in 1975 questioned whether the vehicle could successfully
perform its mission in combat without major and costly
modifications. The Comptroller General recommended that
the vehicle be tested under simulated combat conditions
under the supervision of an independent testing organization to determine whether to proceed with the program or
whether to replace the vehicle.[95]

In reporting on the Defense Appropriations bill, the
House Appropriations Committee concurred in the GAO recommendation; and the Senate Appropriations Committee in its
report, agreed with the House Committee and recommended
that no funds be obligated for improvement of the vehicle
until the testing was completed. Subsequently, the Comptroller General reported to Chairmen of both these Committees and also the Chairmen of the Armed Services Committees of both Houses that the Army was not complying[96]
with the intent of the two Appropriations Committees.
According to the Comptroller General, Army officials had
interpreted the language in the committee reports as being a recommendation rather than a specific directive!

CONGRESSIONAL INITIATION OF UNIFORM COST ACCOUNTING STAND-
ARDS FOR DEFENSE CONTRACTORS

Even before the 1969 "push," Congress took the first
step towards subjecting the cost data of defense contractors
to unprecedented control. In acting to extend the Defense
Product Act of 1950 two years beyond the then expiration
date of June 30, 1968, Congress -- contrary to the wishes
of the Comptroller General -- added a provision that reflected the pressure to use the GAO as an instrumentality
for tightening up defense procurement:

> The Comptroller General, in cooperation with
> the Secretary of Defense and the Director of
> the Bureau of the Budget, shall undertake a
> study to determine the feasibility of apply-
> ing uniform cost accounting standards to be
> used in all negotiated prime contract and sub-
> contract defense procurements of $100,000
> or more.[97]

In discharging this responsibility, the Comptroller General
was to consult with representatives of the accounting profession and of "that segment of American industry which is
actively engaged in defense contracting." Senator Proxmire,
who introduced this amendment, had once more given the GAO
a task that it did not welcome at the time.

The study's conclusions and their controversial implemen-
tation

The study undertaken by the Comptroller General with
reluctance and even misgivings came out with the finding:
"It is feasible to establish and apply cost-accounting
standards to provide a greater degree of uniformity and
consistency in cost accounting as a basis for negotiating[98]
and administering procurement contracts."[98] Having taken
the plunge, the GAO went on to state that the cost-accounting standards should be made applicable Government-wide to
negotiated procurement contracts and subcontracts. Aware
of the highly controversial character of this subject, at[99]
least from the standpoint of industry,[99] the Comptroller
General was careful to support his position with extensive
analyses.

The climate of concern about defense costs and apparent shortcomings in the procurement of weapon systems
made it fairly certain that there would be favorable public and Congressional reaction to the GAO's findings. A
New York Times editorial said: "The recommendation of
the General Accounting Office that all defense contractors
follow uniform accounting procedures should be translated[100]
into law."[100] Congress proceeded to implement the GAO
proposal that "new machinery shall be installed for the
development of cost accounting standards." The Comptroller
General expressed his preference for the establishment of
an independent board selected by the President to promul-[101]
gate the standards.[101] The alternative suggested by the
GAO was to vest the Comptroller General with this responsibility; an advisory board would, under this setup,
have been provided to assist the Comptroller General, who
would appoint the Board. The Congress leaned to giving
the basic responsibility to the Comptroller General and,
therefore, established the Cost-Accounting Standards Board
"which shall be independent of the executive departments
and shall consist of the Comptroller General of the United
States who shall serve as Chairman of the Board and four[102]
members to be appointed by the Comptroller General."[102]

In signing the bill which extended the Defense Production Act until June 30, 1972, and which included the
provision for the Cost-Accounting Standards Board, President Nixon stated that this was one of three provisions in

the bill which he found objectionable and which would
have impelled him to withhold his approval were it not
for the need to extend the basic law.[103]   The President
saw no objection to such a board but expressed his opposition to having it independent of the Executive Branch:

> . . . the establishment of these standards
> will necessarily affect the negotiation and
> administration of Government contracts.
> Those functions are the responsibility of
> the Executive Branch under the Constitution.

Nixon called attention to the fact that the Comptroller
General and the American Institute of Certified Public Accountants had testified in favor of establishing an independent board within the Executive Branch. Expressing his
agreement with this approach, the President requested Congress "to enact an amendment as soon as the House returns
from its recess to place the functions of the Board in the
Executive Branch." But Congress did not recede from the
position it had taken.

The Chief Executive cogently argued that the Board's
task is one that vitally affects, and is inextricably related to, the procurement activities of the Executive
Branch. Although the Board is set up separate and apart
from the GAO, the pervasive role of the Comptroller General makes this distinction more theoretical than real.
It bears mention that the Comptroller General, once the
Board had gotten under way, receded from his original
position and told a Subcommittee considering a bill to
abolish the existing board and establish a new Cost Accounting Standards Board within the Executive Branch:

> In summary, I strongly favor the Board's re-
> maining as the Congress established it. . .
> an agent of the Congress, independent of the
> Executive Branch, with appropriate Congres-
> sional authority and control over its issuances. . .[104]

The Comptroller General's dominant role in the Cost
Accounting Standards Board is still another facet of his
authority that raises a question as to the tenability of
the mix of responsibilities vested in him. One might well
speculate as to whether the Comptroller General did not
feel awkward in presenting to the Congress a report commending the Board, in which he is the ruling figure.[105]

COMPTROLLER GENERAL'S ROLE IN DETERMINING
AGENCY USE OF COMMERCIAL SOURCES

Two distinct aspects of the commercial source problem

The Comptroller General has stated that the GAO has
a two-fold concern with agency decision-making as to whether products or services should be obtained through private suppliers or from within the Government itself. On
the one hand, the GAO has a responsibility for seeing
that applicable laws and regulations are observed. The
other aspect of the GAO's interest in this area relates
to what might be termed the economics of outside contractual arrangements as compared with the use of in-
house sources.[106]   The two factors which the GAO considers
must be viewed against the backdrop of the Presidential
policy to rely upon private enterprise for products and
services obtainable from commercial sources except where
it is otherwise in the national interest. Guidelines for
the implementation of this policy are presented in Budget Bureau Circular A-76, which sets forth the circumstances under which it is appropriate for the Government
to provide a commercial or industrial product or service
for its own use.[107]

The Comptroller General has stated that GAO supports
the policy enunciated in this circular and that it "has a
long history of working cooperatively with OMB to clarify
the policy statement and strengthen implementing guidance."[108]
The Commission on Government Procurement, in its report of
December 1972, recommended five basic changes in this policy
including the enactment of a national policy to rely on
private enterprise for needed goods and services to the
maximum extent feasible within the framework of procurement
at reasonable prices. These recommendations, with which
the GAO fully concurs, afford the Comptroller General additional justification for intensifying GAO efforts in
this facet of procurement. In fact, Staats established
a GAO task force "to review the overall effectiveness of
the executive agencies' policies and program for acquiring
commercial or industrial products for commercial use."[109]

With the Government's undertaking many new programs
requiring skills that may be in short supply, contractual
arrangements can appeal to the administrator as the simpler
and more expeditious approach for obtaining such talent.
Moreover, the contractual basis obviates the need for the
administrator to concern himself with Civil Service complexities, rigidities, and limitations. He is relieved
of direct responsibility for dealing with labor relations
problems. In addition, the contractual basis permits
greater flexibility in phasing out programs since the
termination of a contract can ordinarily be done more
speedily and with far less complications than in closing
out an operation that is handled directly by the Government.

Comptroller General's rulings on specific contracts

The Comptroller General seeks to prevent the use of
contracts to make what he regards as unjustifiable inroads
into civil service employment. He may not only advise the
agency of his interpretation of the applicable statute but
also specifically direct the agency as to the corrective
action to be taken. The Comptroller General's position
on this issue was reflected -- early in his tenure -- in
his referring to the Civil Service Commission the question
as to the legality of contracts that had been used at the
Air Force Base at Fuchu, Japan, for obtaining the services
primarily of electronics technicians.

> . . . it was observed that they worked in
> positions similar to those held as civilian
> employees and military personnel, that they
> worked under the supervision of Government
> personnel, and that the Government retained
> final control over their employment and dis-
> missal.[110]

The Commission held that the contract violated the law
and the Comptroller General expressed general agreement
with the Commission's conclusions.

The National Aeronautics and Space Administration
found itself under challenge with respect to its use of
contractor-furnished personnel to perform engineering
and related technical support services at the Goddard
and Marshall Space Flight Centers. The GAO had prepared
a Congressional report showing that estimated annual savings of as much as $5.3 million could have been achieved
had these services been performed by Civil Service employees rather than on a contractual basis.[111] The report
referred to "possible violations of the applicable laws"
by the Goddard Center but made no definitive finding on
that score, stating that the matter had been brought to
the attention of the Civil Service Commission.

Following hearings by the Special Studies Subcommittee
of the House Government Operations Committee on the subject
of support service contracts,[112] the General Counsel of
the Civil Service Commission held that the Goddard Space
Flight Center contracts were a violation of the applicable
personnel laws.[113] The Comptroller General wrote the
Chairman of the Civil Service Commission that, just as
the GAO had concurred in the action taken in connection
with the Fuchu Air Force Base contract, so it now concurred in "the action now indicated."[114]

Whatever the differences in perspective, the Civil Service Commission is very much dependent upon the GAO in obtaining agency acceptance of the restrictions on their resorting to contractual arrangements in lieu of sources within Government. The Comptroller General has recognized that both the GAO and the Commission have a continuing responsibility to assure that the applicable laws are not by-passed.[115] But Staats expressed a caveat to the effect that the GAO, in discharging its responsibilities in this area, would also "continue to undertake to determine whether agencies are operating in an economical and efficient manner in carrying out their functions." In other words, the Comptroller General did not recede from GAO's position as to the relevance of costs in evaluating specific situations. Subsequently, in testifying before the House Military Operations Subcommittee, the Comptroller General stated that the GAO felt that the decision as to whether something should be secured in-house or from an outside source should be made after agency management has made an analysis of the cost.[116]

Requests from several Subcommittee Chairmen led the GAO to review certain aspects of a management support contract which the Energy Research and Development Administration had awarded for various energy-related planning and analysis services. The GAO concluded that ERDA should reduce its dependence on such contracts, and the officials involved stated they were doing so by increasing their staffing.[117] In making this analysis, the Comptroller General identified another consideration in comparing in-house performance with contracting out, i.e., the retention of essential managerial control.

In stressing the importance of complete and accurate cost comparisons, the Comptroller General has expressed the belief that "obtaining needed goods and services at the lowest possible cost is a sound public policy that must be given equal consideration to the policy of placing reliance on the private sector."[118]

COMPTROLLER GENERAL'S PERVASIVE ROLE IN GOVERNMENT PROCUREMENT

It is evident from the discussion in this and preceding chapters that the Comptroller General's role in the Government's acquisition of goods, services, and facilities embraces far more than the determination of whether this task is performed economically and whether contractors conform with stipulated conditions and standards.

While such monitoring of procurement activities through operational reviews and contract audits is vital, an equally, if not even more significant aspect of the Comptroller General's involvement in this facet of Government operations is the more direct impact he has upon the formulation and implementation of procurement objectives and policies.[119] This influence is wielded through the processing of bidder appeals and other legal matters involving procurement; follow-up on the outcome of the recommendations of the Commission on Government Procurement; analyses of major civil and defense system acquisitions including their effectiveness; settlement of contractors' claims; checking on the implementation of the policy for maximizing utilization of private enterprise as a source of goods and services; and conducting special studies such as those of Government contractors' profits. Although the Cost Accounting Standards Board is a separate legal entity, the fact that the Comptroller General not only serves as its chairman but also appoints the other four members adds still further to the broad aggregate of power which the Comptroller General and, in turn, the GAO have in the procurement area.

The desirability and essentiality of the Comptroller General's in-depth monitoring of the Government's procurement operations are unassailable. Furthermore, the multidisciplinary talents which the Comptroller General is marshalling to cope with the demands of GAO's expanded overall role have greatly strengthened the Office's capability to deal with substantive procurement matters. However, the very fact that the Comptroller General's procurement activities are so varied and far-reaching accentuates the need for a well defined framework for this phase of his operations. This assumes added urgency in light of the Comptroller General's proposals for expanded authority with respect to this facet of the Government.

Footnotes - Chapter 8

1. Settlement and Adjustment of Accounts of Executive Departments and Government Agencies, 70 Harvard Law Review 350 (1956) 357.

2. Robert Sheriffs Moss, "Government Contracts: Nature, Scope and Types," Corporate Practice Commentator, 67-68 Annual, pp. 1-28.

3. Comptroller General of the United States, 1975 Annual Report, p. 107.

4. Thomas D. Morgan, "Achieving National Goals Through Federal Contracts: Giving Form to an Unconstrained Administrative Process," 1974 Wisconsin Law Review, 301-348.

5. See Murray Weidenbaum, The Modern Public Sector (New York: Basic Books, 1969); also Bruce L.R. Smith and D.C. Hague, ed., The Dilemma of Accountability in Modern Government (New York: St. Martin's Press, 1971). Bruce L.R. Smith, ed., The New Political Economy: The Public Use of the Private Sector (London: The Macmillan Press, 1975).

6. Seymour Efros, "A Primer on Government Procurement," The GAO Review, Winter 1976, p. 23.

7. The Comptroller General, in apprising Congress of work in process as of the beginning of the 1977 fiscal year, cited "reviews of (1) the detailed status (cost, schedule, and performance) and financial status of major civil and defense systems; (2) the effectiveness of various systems; (3) the mission capability and existence of technical problems with the F-15 aircraft; (4) overall airlift requirements; (5) strategic nuclear possibilities and capabilities; (6) problems in achieving major weapon system standardization in the North Atlantic Treaty Organization (NATO). . ." 1976 Annual Report, p. 110.

8. The Commission on Government Procurement was established by Public Law 91-129 (1969) with the Comptroller General as a member.

9. 88 Stat. 796. See Comptroller General Report, Executive Branch Actions on Recommendations of the Commission on Government Procurement, PSAD-76-39, December 19, 1975.

10. Comptroller General of the United States, 1967 Annual Report, p. 128.

11. 62 Stat. 21.

12. 63 Stat. 377.

13. Comptroller General of the United States, 1944 Annual Report, p. II.

14. Comptroller General, 1943 Annual Report, p. 72.

15. 1944 Annual Report, p. 71.

16. Ibid., p. 4.

17. Senate, Report of the Activities of the General Accounting Office Under Section 16 of the Contract Settlement Act of 1944, 81st Congress, 1st Session, Sen. Doc. No. 108, 1949, p. 1.

18. Ibid., p. 3.

19. House, Committee on Government Operations, Defense Contract Audits, Sixteenth Reports, H. Rept. 1132, 90th Congress, 2nd Session, 1968, p. 8.

20. General Accounting Office, Audits of Government Contracts (Washington, D.C.: Government Printing Office, 1966), p. 11.

21. Comptroller General Report, Pricing of Noncompetitive Contracts Subject to the Truth-in-Negotiations Act, PSAD-77-91, April 11, 1977, p. 1.

22. General Accounting Office, Comprehensive Audit Manual, Part V, p. 6-1.

23. Comptroller General Report, Competition for Negotiated Government Procurement Can and Should be Improved. PSAD-77-152, September 15, 1977.

24. Comptroller General, 1957 Annual Report, p. 74.

25. Comptroller General, 1960 Annual Report, p. 100.

26. Comptroller General, 1965 Annual Report, p. 66.

27. Comptroller General, 1958 Annual Report, p. 73.

28. Comptroller General, 1962 Annual Report, p. 75.

29. Comptroller General, 1961 Annual Report, p. 104.

30. Comptroller General, 1962 Annual Report, p. 93.

31. 76 Stat. 528.

32. Cibinic and Lasken, "The Comptroller General and Government Contracts," 30 George Washington Law Review 350, 391, March 1970.

33. Elmer B. Staats, "The Truth-in-Negotiations Act in Perspective," in The Truth-in-Negotiations Act, Machinery and Allied Products Institute and Council for Technological Advancement (Washington, D.C., 1969), pp. 8-9.

34. House, Committee on Government Operations, Hearings Before Military Operations Subcommittee on H.R. 474 (1969), Part 9, p. 2449.

35. Comptroller General, 1969 Annual Report, p. 178. See also 1971 Annual Report, Appendix, p. 72.

36. Pricing of Noncompetitive Contracts, op. cit.

37. 65 Stat. 700.

38. Hewlett-Packard Co. vs. United States, 385 F.2d 1013, (9th Cir. 1967), Cert. Denied 390 U.S. 988 (1968).

39. During the Senate Armed Services Committee hearings on his nomination as Deputy Secretary of Defense, David Packard, head of Hewlett-Packard, attributed his original position to apprehension that the GAO might disclose its findings to competitors. Packard said he felt that Staats had "corrected" the applicable procedures and that he "would stand firmly behind the Congress in supporting the right of the GAO to see whatever records they thought appropriate." Senate, Committee on Armed Services, Hearings on Nominations of Laird, Packard, and Darden, 91st Congress, 1st Session, 1969, p. 56.

40. Eli Lilly and Company vs. Elmer B. Staats, U.S. District Court, S.D. Indiana, No. IP75-72-C, November 30, 1976.

41. Senate, Committee on Government Operations, Hearings Before Subcommittee on Executive Reorganization, Capability of GAO to Analyze and Audit Defense Expenditures, 91st Congress, 1st Session, 1969, p. 36.

42. House, H. Rept. 91-607, 91st Congress, 1st Session, 1969, p. 21. The conferees agreed that, in lieu of vesting the Comptroller General with the right to issue subpoenas, the Committee on Armed Services of the House of Representatives or the Committee on Armed Services of the Senate could, upon the request of the Comptroller General, "issue subpoenas requiring the production of such books, accounts, or other records as may be material to the study and review carried out by the Comptroller General under this section."

43. Title II, S.2268, 94th Congress, 1st Session, 1975.

44. Hearing Before the Subcommittee on Reports, Accounting and Management of the Committee on Government Operations, U.S. Senate, 94th Congress, 1st Session, October 2, 1977, GAO Legislation, Part 1, p. 36.

45. Ibid., p. 34-35.

46. House, Hearings Before a Subcommittee of the Committee on Government Operations, Comptroller General Reports to Congress on Audits of Defense Contracts, 89th Congress, 1st Session, 1965, p. 2.

47. Ibid., p. 628.

48. Ibid., pp. 412-413.

49. Ibid., p. 426.

50. House, Committee on Government Operations; Defense Contract Audits, H. Rept. 13444, 89th Congress, 2nd Session, 1966.

51. Ibid., Weitzel letter is included as Appendix 1 to the Committee Report, pp. 19-24.

52. Some of the other changes mentioned in the Weitzel letter were:

    1. Establishing, as a uniform practice, the inclusion of comments on draft reports by agencies, contractors and others as appendices to the final reports.

    2. Discontinuing the practice of (a) disclosing in reports the identities of individuals immediately responsible for actions or operations criticized by the GAO and (b) including in the reports recommendations for disciplinary or other personnel action.

3. Omitting from reports to the Congress mention of the fact that GAO had referred the report to the Department of Justice.

4. Institution of procedure for insuring delivery of reports to the Congress and to the agencies and contractors concerned before distribution to others.

53. Committee Report on Defense Contract Audits, op. cit., p. 2.

54. Ibid., pp. 27-28.

55. Richard F. Kaufman, "The One-Eyed Watchdog of Congress," The Washington Monthly, February 1971, pp. 55-59.

56. The Government Contractor and the General Accounting Office (Washington, D.C., Machinery and Allied Products Institute, 1966), p. 163.

57. Tom Alexander, "McNamara's Expensive Economy Plane," FORTUNE, Vol. 75, No. 6, June 1967, p. 89.

58. "Robert S. McNamara: The Storm Continues," Washington Post, June 15, 1967.

59. Senate, Committee on Government Operations, Hearings Before the Permanent Subcommittee on Investigations, F-111 Aircraft Program, 91st Congress, 2nd Session, 1970.

60. Statement of Comptroller General Elmer B. Staats Before the Subcommittee on Priorities and Economy in Government, Joint Economic Committee, June 8, 1976.

61. House, Committee on Appropriations, Report on Department of Defense Appropriations Bill, 1970, H. Rept. 91-698, 91st Congress, 1st Session, 1969, p. 47.

62. Ibid., p. 69.

63. Abraham Ribicoff, "Military Spending and an Expanded Role for the General Accounting Office," Harvard Journal on Legislation, Vol. 7 (May 1970), p. 495.

64. S2546, 91st Congress, 1st Session, July 18, 1969.

65. Congressional Record, August 8, 1969.

66. Comptroller General Report to the Senate Committee
    on Armed Services, Study of the MBT-70 Program,
    Department of the Army, B-163058, September 2, 1969.

67. Comptroller General Report, Critical Considerations
    in the Acquisition of a New Main Battle Tank, PSAD-
    76-113A, July 22, 1976. Subsequently, in a report
    dated December 12, 1977, the Comptroller General
    contended that there were incompatibilities be-
    tween the XM-1 tank and the infantry fighting ve-
    hicle that the Army was developing.

68. Congressional Record, August 7, 1969.

69. H.R. 11493, 91st Congress, 1st Session, 1969.

70. Letter from Comptroller General Elmer B. Staats to
    Senator John C. Stennis, August 1, 1969. A simi-
    lar letter was sent to the Chairman of the House
    Armed Services Committee.

71. Letter from Comptroller General Elmer B. Staats to
    Chairman William L. Dawson, House Committee on
    Government Operations, July 14, 1969.

72. Congressional Record, August 7, 1969.

73. Letter from Comptroller General Elmer B. Staats to
    the Honorable John B. Anderson, September 30, 1969.

74. H. Rept. 91-607, 91st Congress, 1st Session, 1969,
    p. 25.

75. Congressional Record, September 17, 1969. The De-
    fense Industry Profit Study, B-159896 was issued
    by the Comptroller General on March 17, 1971.

76. Title IV, S.2268, op. cit.

77. GAO Legislation, op. cit., p. 39.

78. Comptroller General Report, Status of the Acquisition
    of Selected Major Weapon Systems - Department of
    Defense, B-163058, February 6, 1970.

79. Congress, Joint Economic Committee, Subcommittee on
    Economy in Government, Hearings, The Acquisition
    of Weapon Systems, 91st Congress, 1st Session,
    1969, Part 1, p. 6.

80. B-165058, March 18, 1971. See also the later report
    dated July 17, 1972 which showed that for 77 sys-

tems the estimated cost through completion was
$28.7 billion or 31 per cent in excess of the
original estimate.

81. 1975 Annual Report, op. cit., p. 117.

82. PSAD-78-60, January 20, 1978. Senator Stennis was
    pleased when, in 1975, Staats expanded his report-
    ing to include the status of major civil acquisi-
    tions. As a steadfast protagonist of defense
    spending, the Senator was quick to point out,
    in connection with the Senate's annual floor
    debate on the weapons authorization bill, that
    this new information "should underscore the sober
    reality that the cost problem is not a unique dis-
    ease of the military weapons programs." Congres-
    sional Record, March 20, 1975.

83. PSAD 77-41, April 1, 1977.

84. Comptroller General Report, Status of the Trident
    Submarine and Missile Programs, PSAD-77-34, March
    8, 1977. In the previous year, GAO had furnished
    Congress with a staff study on the Patrol Combat-
    ant Missile (Hydrofoil) Ship to provide "informa-
    tion on the cost, schedule, and testing of the
    ship and its major subsystems." PSAD 76-117,
    March 16, 1976.

85. 1975 Annual Report, op. cit., p. 107, et seq.

86. Comptroller General Report, Nuclear or Conventional
    Power for Surface Combatant Ships, PSAD 77-74,
    March 21, 1977.

87. Status of the F-16 Aircraft Program, op. cit., pp.
    11 and 21.

88. Critical Considerations in the Acquisition of a New
    Main Battle Tank, op. cit., p. 52.

89. New York Times, December 27, 1976.

90. New York Times, November 22, 1976.

91. Address of Elmer B. Staats, Comptroller General of
    the United States, Naval Post-Graduate School
    Bannerman Lecture Series, Monterey, California,
    November 12, 1974.

92. Ibid.

93. An unclassified digest of the Report (ID-76-84) was released on June 6, 1977. The digest defines co-production as "a program wherein the United States enables an eligible country or international organization to acquire the expertise to manufacture, assemble, repair, and maintain a specific weapon, support system, or individual military item."

94. June 8, 1976 Statement Before Senate Subcommittee on Priorities and Economy in Government, op. cit.

95. Comptroller General Report, Should the Gamma Goat be Improved or Replaced? PSAD-76-48, December 8, 1975. Another example of the GAO getting into the specifics of the decision-making process is the report Selection of a Machine Gun for Armored Vehicles, PSAD-76-112, March 23, 1976. The report concluded that the "Army should not rely too heavily on its cost-effectiveness analysis because of questionable assumptions made" but instead should consider the factors identified by the GAO.

96. Letters were dated November 13, 1976.

97. 82 Stat. 279.

98. Comptroller General Report, Feasibility of Applying Uniform Cost-Accounting Standards to Negotiated Defense Contracts, B-39995(1), January 19, 1970, p. 22.

99. See Forrest L. Heuser, "The Question of Uniform Accounting Standards," Management Accounting, July 1969, pp. 20-23; "Financial Executive Institute Comments on GAO UCAS Draft Report," The Federal Accountant, Vol. XIX, No. 1 (March 1970), pp. 21-33.

100. New York Times, January 27, 1970.

101. Senate Committee on Banking and Currency, Subcommittee on Production and Stabilization, Hearings, Extension of the Defense Production Act and Uniform Cost-Accounting Standards, 91st Congress, 2nd Session, 1970, p. 15.

102. 84 Stat. 796.

103. Statement by the President on Signing S.3302, The White House, August 17, 1970.

104. Statement of Elmer B. Staats in S.1901 before the Senate Subcommittee on Production and Stabilization, April 12, 1972.

105. Comptroller General Report, Status Report on the Cost-Accounting Standards Program Accomplishments and Problems, PSAD-76-154, August 20, 1976.

106. House, Government Operations Committee, Hearings on Support Service Contracts, Special Studies Committee, 90th Congress, 1st Session, 1967, p. 3.

107. Bureau of the Budget Circular A-76, Revised, August 30, 1967, and President's Memorandum of March 3, 1966 to the Heads of Departments and Agencies.

108. Statement of Elmer B. Staats, Comptroller General of the United States Before the Subcommittee on Manpower and Personnel, Senate Committee on Armed Services, July 12, 1972.

109. Ibid. At the same time that Staats reported this action to the Subcommittee, he also apprised it that, since January 1, 1972, GAO had issued 30 reports which directly or indirectly concerned OMB's and DOD's implementation of the A-76 policy.

110. House, Committee on Post Office and Civil Service, Decision of the Comptroller General of the United States Regarding Contractor Technical Services, H. Rept. 188, 89th Congress, 1st Session, 1965, p. 1.

111. Comptroller General Report, Potential Savings Available Through Use of Civil Service Rather Than Contractor-Furnished Employees for Certain Support Services, National Aeronautics and Space Administration, B-133394, June 9, 1967.

112. House Committee on Government Operations, Hearings on Support Service Contracts, op. cit.

113. Opinion of the General Counsel, United States Civil Service Commission, Legality of Selected Contracts - Goddard Space Flight Center - National Aeronautics and Space Administration, November 1, 1967. A supplement to this opinion was issued on July 8, 1968.

114. Letter from Comptroller General Elmer B. Staats to Chairman John W. Macy, Jr., United States Civil Service Commission, November 1, 1967.

115. Ibid.

116. House, Committee on Government Operations, Hearings on H.R. 474, op. cit., Part 3, p. 720.

117. Letter of September 21, 1976 addressed by Comptroller General Elmer B. Staats to various Subcommittee Chairmen.

118. Letter from Comptroller General Elmer B. Staats to Congressman Clarence J. Brown, February 14, 1977.

119. Recent examples of the Comptroller General's deep penetration into the procurement area are his testimony of December 22, 1977 on "Economic Issues in Military Airlift" presented to the Senate Subcommittee on Priorities and Economy in Government and his report A Critique of the Performance of the Defense Systems Acquisition Review Council; Billions in Public Funds Involved, PSAD-78-44, January 30, 1978.

Chapter 9

THE COMPTROLLER GENERAL'S EXPANDING ROLE IN THE
GOVERNMENT'S FINANCIAL MANAGEMENT

. . . the Accounting and Auditing Act of 1950
stressed the role that GAO should play in fos-
tering improved budgeting, accounting, and auditing in the Federal Government. The Legislative Reorganization Act of 1970 emphasized the
GAO role in cost-benefit analysis, and the Congressional Budget and Impoundment Control Act
of 1974 again stressed the contribution that
GAO should make to improve Federal program evaluation; to meet the fiscal, program and budgetary information needs of Congress; and to
assist it in exercising its own new budgetary
approaches and concepts.[1]

The initial GAO legislation and the steady enlargement of the Comptroller General's responsibilities, to
which Staats refers in the foregoing statement, have given
him a key position in the Government's budgetary process
as well as other phases of its financial management.
The impressive ascendancy of the GAO in the fiscal area
has -- as is observed in Chapter 5 -- been accompanied
by the agency becoming the driving force for the rethinking of governmental auditing at all levels of the public
sector.

In his prepared statement on GAO budget estimates
for fiscal year 1978,[2] Staats distinguished between those
GAO activities primarily directed to financial accountability and those concerned with improving financial management in Government. Staats explained that the first
category "emphasizes the completeness and accuracy of accounting records and statements, the validity of financial
transactions, and the timeliness and usefulness of reports."
Specific activities so classified are, according to the
Comptroller General, the review of accounting systems actually in operation, the audit and settlement of the accounts
of accountable officers, and the audits of Government corporations.

As to GAO work that would in fiscal year 1978 be directed to improving financial management, the Comptroller
General enumerated:

(a) Continued participation in the Joint Financial
    Management Improvement Program.

(b) Helping Federal, state, and local governments

to improve their accounting, auditing, and
program evaluation standards and methods.

    (c)   Reviewing and approving agency accounting
            systems.

    (d)   Helping committees to get the fiscal, budget-
            ary, and program information they need to
            effectively use the information they get.

GAO IMPACT UPON THE BUDGET PROCESS

In the remarks just cited, the Comptroller General
seemed restrained in his reference to the GAO activities
in the budgetary area, although he did say: "This is an
increasingly important part of our work -- one which got
particular emphasis as a result of the Budget and Impoundment Control Act of 1974." Perhaps, Staats was mindful of
the risk of stirring unrealistic Congressional expectations,
which, as is described in Chapter 5, had happened in connection with program evaluations.

GAO's budgetary involvement of long standing

The antecedents of the Comptroller General's present
deep involvement in the Government's budgeting date from
the enactment of the legislation founding the GAO. The
monitoring and investigative functions enunciated in the
1921 Act are bound to yield information that can be utilized by the Congress in its review of budget proposals
and the follow-through on appropriations made available
to the agencies. Moreover, the Comptroller General's
authority to settle accounts and to rule on the legality
of proposed expenditures make him an important participant
in the execution phase of the budget process. Finally,
the much debated authority of the Comptroller General to
pass upon agency accounting systems enables him to make
significant input into the accounting aspects of the Government's budgeting. For that matter, the accounting system prerogative has, as the discussion that follows brings
out, been the fulcrum for the Comptroller General assuming
leadership in the totality of the Government's financial
management.

Long before Watergate, Congress had become increasingly
concerned about its relatively weak budgetary posture vis-a-
vis the Executive Branch, a feeling that was accentuated by
the prestigious and influential position of OMB and its predecessor, the Bureau of the Budget.[3] In 1966, the Joint
Committee on the Organization of the Congress concluded that
Congress "must equip itself to insure effective and meaningful exercise of its constitutional responsibilities in the

budgetary field."[4] In reaching this conclusion, the Joint
Committee referred to "the development of more sophisticated
techniques of budget analysis" which was taking place. The
Committee identified the need for making better use of the
GAO "as an arm of Congress in the budget evaluation process
as well as in the postaudit function."

The advent of the planning-programming-budgeting approach, including cost-effectiveness analysis, had a sin-
gular effect in bestirring Congress to reevaluate and
strengthen its resources for coping with the demands which
the budgetary process imposes upon it. Congress showed
increasing awareness of the implications which not only
PPB but also new management technology, including system
analysis, have for the Government, as well as legislative
decision-making. The Joint Committee's concern about Congressional ability to deal with more advanced budgetary
techniques was kept very much alive in subsequent discussions within the Congress.

The Legislative Reorganization Act of 1970[5] carried
forward the thrust to strengthen Congressional capability
to discharge its budgetary and oversight functions. A
particularly salient feature, insofar as GAO was concerned,
was that squarely placing upon the Comptroller General the
responsibility for reviewing and analyzing the results of
Government programs and activities, including the making
of cost benefit studies. This mandate manifestly had important budgetary implications. The collaborative tasks
which the Act assigned to the Comptroller General concerning the system for budgetary and fiscal data and standard
budget classifications further reinforced the Comptroller
General's influence in the Federal budget process.

GAO implications of the Congressional Budget and Impound-
ment Control Act of 1974

The Congressional Budget and Impoundment Control
Act of 1974[6] has far-reaching ramifications for the GAO,
especially with respect to the manner in which it serves
the budgetary needs of Congress. Title VIII-Fiscal and
Budgetary Information and Controls, expanding upon the
Legislative Reorganization Act of 1970, further defines
and strengthens the collaborative role which the Comptroller General is to play in cooperation with the Secretary of the Treasury, the Director of the Office of Management and Budget, and the Director of the newly-created
Congressional Budget Office in developing, establishing,
maintaining, and publishing standard terminology, definitions, classifications, and codes for Federal fiscal,[7]
budgetary, and program-related data and information.

337

The 1974 legislation requires the Comptroller General to conduct and report annually on a continuing program to identify and specify the needs of the committees and Members of the Congress for fiscal, budgetary, and program-related information. In the third such report, the GAO stated that it had made considerable progress during the past year in defining and developing information requirements of the Congress but that "much improvement is needed in existing information and its presentation to the Congress."[8] The Comptroller General is also given the task of assisting committees in developing their information needs; moreover, he is required to critique the recurring reporting requirements of the Congress and its committees. In responding to these statutory mandates, the Comptroller General has many opportunities to place his imprimatur upon the mechanics of the budget process.

As contrasted with these continuing or recurring occasions for GAO involvement in Congress' budgetary activities, the Comptroller General assisted in effecting the changeover to the immediate rearrangements which the 1974 Act required within the Congress.[9] Illustrative of how the committees looked to the GAO for assistance in implementing their responsibilities under the 1974 Act was GAO's response to the request of the Chairman of the Senate Committee on Agriculture and Forestry that it study the Act's "impact on GAO and the authorizing committees." The resultant information apparently elicited so much interest that the GAO issued a booklet for the purpose of expanding the distribution of this information.[10]

The enlarged GAO program evaluation role set forth in Title VII, which is discussed in Chapter 5, represents a formidable enhancement of GAO's responsibilities in connection with the substantive aspects of the budgetary process, particularly as it relates to the Congress. In seeking to achieve more effective participation in budgetary decision making, Congress manifestly looked to the GAO as an agency having the expertise that could aid immeasurably in carrying this thrust to a successful conclusion.

Title X of the 1974 Act -- Impoundment Control, a reaction to what Congress considered to be Presidential abuse of the impoundment of appropriations,[11] vested the Comptroller General with responsibility to monitor particular budgetary actions of the Chief Executive. The Comptroller General is required to review all deferrals and rescissions of budget authority which the President proposes and to advise the Congress as to their legality and impact. He is empowered to bring suit to effect the freeing of budget authority. This pivotal responsibility of the Comptroller General in the implementation of the

highly significant Congressional constraint on Presidential
control of governmental expenditures bespeaks the fact
that Congress attributes to the GAO a role far more encompassing than that ordinarily associated with an audit agency.
It also reflects a propensity on the part of Congress to
look to the Comptroller General when it needs a surrogate
to effectuate its edicts.

Chapter 3 alludes to the confrontation between Comptroller General Staats and President Ford in connection
with such litigation. A detailed chronology of this lawsuit is presented in an appendix to the lengthy GAO report[12]
on impoundments during the fiscal years 1975 and 1976.
The report afforded the Comptroller General the opportunity
to comment on the manner in which the Chief Executive had
performed one facet of his responsibilities: "On balance,
GAO feels that the President has done a good job of implementing the Impoundment Control Act."

Continued expansion of GAO's budgetary role

The proposed Government Economy and Spending Reform
Act of 1976[13] presents an example of how the enlargement
of GAO's budgetary role tends to be a concomitant of Congressional action to strengthen its control of government
expenditures. The Act had, as the Comptroller General
pointed out, many significant implications for the GAO.
This bill would have required enactment of new budget
authority for Government programs and activities at least
every four years and sought to establish a procedure for
zero-base review and evaluation of Government programs
and activities every four years. It provided for the use
of GAO audits and reviews in implementing the added Congressional control over Federal programs. The Comptroller
General, who expressed agreement with the underlying purpose of the bill, suggested that it "be amended to require
that during its reviews GAO give special priority to the
identification of problems resulting from Federal programs
and activities having similar objectives and report its
findings and recommendations to the Congress and cognizant
committees as promptly as possible."[14]

GAO input into Congressional budgetary action is increasingly reinforced by the mass of both program and fis-
cally-related material that flows from the GAO to Congress.
For example, in the House discussion of the Defense Appropriations Bill for 1976, attention was directed to the
acknowledgement by the Appropriations Committee that its
"evaluation of the Defense budget proposal was materially
assisted by the General Accounting Office studies of various DOD programs and activities. A total of 97 reports
and 44 staff studies on selected major weapons systems --

were made available to the Committee by the GAO during the period July 1, 1974 through July 1, 1975."[15] The Comptroller General may respond to specific Congressional requests as to agency budget estimates, viz., that it "review the Navy's appropriation request for fiscal year 1977 to construct support facilities for Trident submarines"[16] or that it "review the Department of Defense's effort to reexamine its fiscal year 1978 budget request as it relates to reimbursements for activities which support foreign military sales."[17] GAO assistance to Congress on budgetary matters also includes responding to inquiries involving specific expenditures of appropriated funds.[18]

President Carter's adoption of zero-base budgeting for the Federal Government[19] appears to have engendered an even stronger thrust for GAO penetration into the Government's budget system including both its executive and legislative branch facets. It has recommended that "the Congress begin to experiment with mission budgeting" which it explains "assembles and groups various kinds of expenditures according to their end purpose" and which it feels can serve "as a structural foundation for 'zero-base' and 'sunset' reviews as well as governmental reorganization."[20] In its advocacy of this budgetary approach, the Comptroller General contends that it has potential for not only strengthening Congressional policy review and program oversight but also helping Executive agencies formulate more meaningful budgets. Especially significant is the Comptroller General's reference to "providing one budget system oriented to both executive and congressional needs."

Apparently anticipating some questions as to why he took this task upon himself, the Comptroller General fell back on: (a) the Congressional request that GAO follow up on the recommendations of the Commission on Government Procurement, which had proposed mission budgeting and (b) the mandate of the 1974 budget legislation calling upon the GAO to help Congress meet its budgetary information needs. Patently, Comptroller General Staats, who had been for many years a key executive in the Bureau of the Budget (OMB's predecessor), was hardly reluctant to have GAO advance a proposal that goes to the fundamentals of the budget system viewed as a totality.

The Comptroller General's observations on mission budgeting were followed shortly thereafter by his testimony before a House Budget Committee task force on the use of productivity data in the Federal budget process.[21] Staats stated that such data could and should be used much more for budgetary purposes. He took a sideswipe at OMB, whose use of productivity data, according to the Comptroller General, is "uneven" and whose focus, he contended, "is

often on whether a program should be funded at all instead
of on productivity questions." Staats addressed his criticisms not only to OMB but also maintained that Congress
and agency top management have to be more supportive of
increased utilization of productivity data.[22]

The increasing thrust for GAO participation in the bud-
get process

GAO has both the capability and willingness to buttress Congress' role in the budget process, and Congress
is manifesting a propensity for availing itself more intensively of the assistance which GAO can render in this
sphere. The budgetary area, which is inextricably related to oversight, is one in which the GAO can perhaps
be of the greatest service to the Congress.

Comptroller General Staats, earlier in his term, had
been relatively restrained in envisaging GAO's role in
the program and budget areas. He had eschewed GAO making recommendations for the adoption of particular programs since he deemed this to be incompatible with "our
responsibility for subsequent independent reviews of the
implementation of programs which may be authorized."[23]
Staats, at that time, disavowed either having the authority or seeking "to become a congressional bureau of the
budget with responsibility for the review of departmental
budget requests --"[24] From the developments that have
been depicted, it is obvious that the passage of time together with expanded Congressional demands upon the GAO
have effected a sharp divergence from this earlier diffi-
dence.[25] Staats' budgetary expertise, acquired during
his many years of Budget Bureau experience, placed him
in a strategic position to implement a broad budgetary
role for GAO. Now that the previous constraints have
been modified drastically, the GAO, under Staats' direction, has been moving ahead with steadily increasing
momentum in the budget area.

The complex, sensitive, and varied nature of GAO's
budgetary tasks accentuates the importance of its bringing to bear upon such activities savoir faire in relations
with Congress and agencies, multidisciplinary competence
to deal with a broad range of problems, and restraint as
to the capabilities claimed for the GAO. There are
countervailing forces to any GAO tendency to overreach
itself in the budgetary area, particularly insofar as
substantive matters are concerned. As the Congressional
Budget Office develops, it will provide an inhibiting
factor in GAO's expansion as a supportive facility for
Congressional budgetary reviews and controls. In fact,
it is essential that there be effective coordination of

GAO efforts with those of CBO. The Congressional Research Service will also tend to reduce dependence upon the GAO in discharging the more active budgetary role which the 1974 Act articulated for the Congress. Finally, the Office of Technology Assessment may become a more formidable "competitor" of GAO in serving as a budgetary resource of Congress insofar as highly technical programs are concerned.

COMPTROLLER GENERAL - ARBITER OF AGENCY ACCOUNTING SYSTEMS

At least until recently, the Comptroller General's authority over agency accounting systems was the source of considerable friction between the Executive Branch and the GAO. Vesting the Comptroller General with such a responsibility was challenged repeatedly by students of government as an intrusion upon the prerogatives of the Executive Branch.

Far-reaching implications of the accounting systems issue

What, at first blush, may appear to be a lacklustre function of interest primarily to the professional accountant entails significant issues as to the appropriate role of the Government's auditor. As the subsequent analysis brings out, the accounting systems facet of GAO activities underpins the leadership the Comptroller General has assumed in the Government's financial management. The events surrounding this aspect of the GAO shed additional light on Congressional conceptualization of the Comptroller General's role. They also demonstrate how a Congressional committee may make a cause celebre out of Executive agency unresponsiveness to GAO efforts. Analysis of the GAO efforts in connection with accounting systems affords invaluable insights into how the Office handles relations with Executive agencies and how its priorities change from time to time. Finally, this aspect of the Comptroller General's operations has important implications in terms of the interrelations between the GAO and the Office of Management and Budget.

Congressional rejection of attempts to divest Comptroller General of accounting systems authority

As has been pointed out previously, the President's Committee on Administrative Management had recommended, in 1937, that the "authority to prescribe and supervise accounting systems, forms, and procedures in the Federal establishments should be transferred to and vested in the Secretary of the Treasury."[26] The Committee directed attention to the fact that, in 1932, President Hoover had recommended a similar reallocation of this responsibility. In support of its recommendation, the Committee argued that having such authority vested in the Comptroller General had tended "to deprive the Executive of adequate accounting machinery, or even authority to develop this important instrument of financial direction."[27]

The opening chapter of this study incorporates a recital of the efforts to divest the Comptroller General of his authority over agency accounting systems and to place this responsibility in the Executive Branch. It points out that the first Hoover Commission, which was generally successful in having the Congress adopt recommendations with respect to budgeting and accounting, was rebuffed sharply with respect to its proposal that an Accountant General with the rank of assistant secretary be set up in the Treasury Department and that he be responsible for developing accounting systems and procedures, subject to approval of the Comptroller General. This proposal, which sought to effect a compromise, proved to be anathema to the Congress.

The Congress appears to be well-wedded to the concept that the Comptroller General's authority over accounting systems is a sine qua non of effective legislative oversight of expenditures. It is either unable or refuses to see how intimately accounting systems are interwoven with administration and is unresponsive to the arguments against having such a vital managerial and budgeting tool subject to control by an agency of the Legislative Branch.[28]

The Accounting and Auditing Act of 1950 (part of the Budget and Accounting Procedures Act of 1950) sought to place the Comptroller General's accounting systems authority in broader perspective and at the same time to make it less abrasive. It injected a collaborative element into the Comptroller General-agency relationship as to accounting systems. Section 112(a) of that Act calls for the Comptroller General consulting the Secretary of the Treasury and the Director of the Bureau of the Budget and for considering the needs of the other executive agencies before prescribing the "principles, standards, and related requirements, for accounting to be observed by each executive agency." The 1950 Act also provides for the GAO cooperating with Executive agencies in the development of their accounting systems. The concept of the agencies having the primary responsibility for the formulation of systems is reaffirmed by Section 113(a), which requires the head of each Executive agency to establish and maintain systems of accounting and internal control designed to provide the several types of information set forth in that provision. However, the Section

112(b) requirement that agency accounting systems be approved by the Comptroller General was for many years a prolific source of irritation between that official and Executive agencies.

The Joint Financial Management Improvement Program -- discussed at some length later in this chapter -- has helped to assuage the ruffled feelings that had often evidenced themselves in negotiations between the GAO and individual agencies for obtaining the Comptroller General's approval of the latter's accounting systems. The continuing collaboration of the Comptroller General, the Secretary of the Treasury, and the Director of the Office of Management and Budget tends to make the Executive Branch more receptive to the Comptroller General's efforts and to reduce the authoritarian overtones of the GAO program in this area.

Agency criticism of GAO accounting systems authority

Government agencies were often rankled by the need to conform to the criteria which the Comptroller General applies in approving accounting systems. An agency official epitomized the feelings of many administrators within the Executive Branch when he said that the determination of the system that provides accounting for executive management should be the responsibility of the executive and that the authority of the auditor should be confined to reviewing the system. This statement reflected a widespread feeling within departments and other agencies that GAO's appropriate role would be the auditing of the accounting systems that are developed and installed by those in the Executive Branch.[29]

The view that accounting systems approval is an inappropriate responsibility for the Comptroller General is not confined to those within the Executive Branch or students of government. Within the GAO itself some personnel expressed doubts as to the soundness of the present statutory provision.

Congressional pressures for implementation of Comptroller General's authority

The installation of accounting systems bearing the Comptroller General's approval became a fetish in the eyes of the House Government Operations Committee. The latter's intensive follow-up on the implementation of Section 112(b) of the Accounting and Auditing Act of 1950 provided a potent sanction for the accounting systems program but, at the same time, generated considerable resentment on the part of Executive Branch agencies. The so-called "score card" approach of the House Government Operations Committee, which the GAO condoned for some years, resulted in what some agencies considered harassment.

A letter which Comptroller General Campbell had addressed in 1964 to the heads of Federal departments and agencies, seeking to stimulate increased accounting system effort apparently was the catalyst for initiation of hearings by the House Executive and Legislative Reorganization Subcommittee for considering progress in the development of financial management systems in the Federal Government.[30] The Committee recommended that the heads of departments and agencies take immediate action to see that their subordinates concerned with financial management proceeded with dispatch to institute accounting systems in accordance with standards prescribed by the Comptroller General and to submit such systems to him for approval. A further recommendation was that target dates agreeable to the Comptroller General be proposed and adhered to. At the same time, the Committee recommended more intensive efforts not only by the Comptroller General but also the Bureau of the Budget and the Treasury Department.[31]

The House Government Operations Committee did not relax its efforts in pressuring agencies to install accounting systems acceptable to the Comptroller General. In 1967, its Special Studies Subcommittee held hearings on the subject; Congressman Porter Hardy, the Acting Chairman, expressing amazement that "agencies would in effect seem to just flout the law," threw down the gauntlet: " -- if I can continue, or my chairman continues to let me pursue this subject, we are going to ride herd on a few folks to see if they won't do something about it."[32] Apparently mindful of the possibility that such irascibility might complicate what was already a difficult situation, Comptroller General Staats sought to reassure the Subcommittee by informing it that there had been "a definite general increase in activity in the executive agencies directed toward this area during the past year. I would say perhaps even more so during the last few weeks."[33] But the Comptroller General's reassurance did not inhibit the Committee from badgering the Director of Finance of the Department of Agriculture on the basis of what were ill-founded assumptions as to the panacea nature of accounting systems. Such an experience must have left the departmental representative with the impression that, if further castigation by the Committee was to be headed off, the Department should place itself in a position to report significant progress in obtaining approval of its accounting systems regardless of whether the Department felt that such changes had a great deal of merit.

While indicating satisfaction with the recent progress that had been made the Committee felt that sterner
attitudes toward "foot dragging" agencies might be required and indicated that the imposition of sanctions
against slow-moving agencies might be necessary.[34]   One
can only speculate as to the extent to which Congressional
concern about accounting systems was motivated entirely by
a conviction as to the essentiality of these systems for
effective administration. Certainly to some degree this
dialogue between the Congress and the Executive Branch reflected the use of the accounting system issue as a means
for the assertion of Congressional power over the Executive
agencies.

Unrealistic and dysfunctional nature of Committee approach

Manifestly, accounting systems are highly useful, if
not indispensable, managerial tools. However, they can
hardly be regarded as correctives for all operational shortcomings. Neither can they be viewed as being of equal importance in connection with all functions and programs regardless of the nature or size. It was perturbing to read
the House Government Operations Committee's high-flown
statement of benefits that are supposedly derived from
such systems:

> Good accounting will pinpoint costs, identify
> weak and wasteful operations, provide compara-
> tive cost data, relate costs to program ac-
> tivities, reflect promptly the results of
> management and other improvements, point out
> areas for concentrated attention, and in many
> other ways show the way to economical and ef-
> ficient operations.[35]

A more restrained, balanced, and realistic approach
would have made the Committee's efforts less irksome without necessarily militating against its effectiveness in
stimulating agency efforts directed to the improvement of
their accounting system. In fact, there was a real danger
that relentless prodding by the Committee resulted in agencies developing and installing systems primarily to win
the Comptroller General's approval and thereby placate the
Committee, even though the agency saw little, if any, merit
in the system. One device that the agencies employed to
convince the House Government Operations Committee that
they are earnest in their efforts to develop and install
systems conforming to the Comptroller General's criteria
was that of retaining outside experts. The fact that the
retention of such consultants had tactical advantages in
dealing with the House Government Operations Committee
undoubtedly made agencies more receptive to the services

offered by consultants. The Subcommittee did not demur
in the slightest when informed that a Labor Department
contract stipulated a ceiling price of more than $1 mil-
lion for a public accounting firm's development of accounting systems.[36]

The following year, the Subcommittee held a hearing
on what was termed "A Review of Labor Department Accounting Systems."[37] Congressman Hardy, citing the progress
that had been made by the Department of Labor, indulged
in an invidious comparison and the threat of punitive
action:

> You are undoubtedly aware of considerable
> congressional suggestion for the imposition
> of penalties against those who are dragging
> their feet and putting off modernizing their
> accounting systems. If this attitude per-
> sists, I think a legislative approach may
> be forthcoming. And some of you won't like
> it. When the 91st Congress meets in Jan-
> uary, I think you all had better be prepared
> to give an accounting of how you are doing
> with your accounting systems.[38]

In his testimony at this hearing, Staats was very
mindful of the hard-hitting tactics of the House Government Operations Committee with respect to the agencies
and the resultant resentment of the Government establishments; he adroitly steered a careful course. While seeking to show he was appreciative of the Committee's efforts,
he, at the same time, tried to reassure the agencies that
systems would not be arbitrarily imposed upon them.
Staats stated that, if the GAO's efforts were to be truly
worthwhile, they had to have the active support and participation of management officials in each agency.

COMPTROLLER GENERAL'S EMPHASIS ON
ACCOUNTING SYSTEMS FUNCTION

The accounting systems activity of GAO reached a
high point under Comptroller General Warren; but, during the tenure of Comptroller General Campbell, this facet
of the GAO operations lost much of its dynamism. Under
Comptroller General Staats, there has been a renascence.
This is not at all surprising since the Budget Bureau,
in which Staats occupied key posts for many years, held
itself forth as a strong advocate of improved financial
management in the Federal Government.

An early Staats directive stated that the satisfactory discharge of the GAO accounting responsibilities was
just as important as the discharge of any of its other

347

assigned responsibilities.[39] While stressing cooperative assistance to the agencies, Staats, at the same time, made it clear that such assistance was not intended to replace agency staffs in the design, development, and revision of their systems for which they were primarily responsible. "We should not write their manuals or procedural instructions for them."

The Comptroller General used identical phraseology in several of his annual reports to convey the importance of accounting systems.[40] In his statement to the Senate Subcommittee on Executive Reorganization, the Comptroller General presented a rationale for GAO's accounting system activities:

> The degree to which agency accounting and other information systems provide adequate and reliable information on costs and accomplishments is particularly important in our reviews of the results of programs. Such information is essential for management at all levels, including the Congress, in evaluating program results, making adjustments in operations, and planning for the future.[41]

The objective of having in each Government agency an accounting system that fully and accurately discloses the financial data needed for both accountability and managerial purposes is obviously sound. In light of his statutory responsibility, the Comptroller General is constrained to play a major part in the efforts directed towards the attainment of this objective. But, at the same time, it is incumbent upon him to see that his efforts do not result in exaggerated impressions as to either shortcomings in the agencies or potentialities of accounting systems within the Government.

In announcing changes in GAO's approach to accounting systems review, Staats took the occasion to state that the GAO would continue to emphasize "that it is the primary responsibility of each executive agency to install and maintain accounting systems which are adequate and in accordance with the principles, standards, and related requirements and the proposed designs which we approve."[42] No agency would disagree that the installation and maintenance of adequate accounting systems is a managerial responsibility. However, they can contend that, under existing statutes, their role has been very much watered down by the ultimate authority which the Comptroller General exercises over their systems.

348

Simplification of system approval procedure

Bedeviled by the extended delays in the definitive approval of agency accounting systems, the Comptroller General simplified the system review process so that some kind of approval could be given by the GAO at an earlier stage than was possible under the original procedure. Before Staats changed the practice, no final system approval was given an agency until representatives of the GAO reviewed and tested the operation of the system to determine whether it conformed to the prescribed principles and standards.[43] This meant that, until the system was actually installed, it could not be evaluated by the GAO as to its acceptability and no progress could be reflected in reports on the status of the accounting system program. It was all or nothing.

Under the change effected by Staats, the Comptroller General's approval consists of two stages, i.e., (a) agency statements of principles and standards established to govern their accounting systems, and (b) proposed general designs of those systems. Concurrently, the Comptroller General announced that the GAO would no longer undertake to formally approve accounting systems in actual operation.[44] The GAO was to "devote more effort to conducting reviews of agency accounting operations from time to time, as now required by law, and provide reports to agency officials and to the Congress setting forth our evaluation and recommendations." It appears that, within the constraints imposed by the Budget and Accounting Procedures Act of 1950, the Comptroller General sought to make the accounting system role of GAO more comparable to that of the auditor in the private sector, i.e., evaluating the accounting system in operation and bringing any shortcomings to the attention of responsible executives.

In announcing this change, the Comptroller General stated that it did not signify any diminution in the degree of importance which the GAO attached to this phase of its responsibilities or any reduction in the amount of effort to be devoted to it. "It does mean some shift in the nature of our efforts, particularly in providing for more evaluations of agency accounting operations." Staats also made it known that the GAO planned to keep Congress and agencies informed on the status of Federal agency accounting systems by preparing "an annual report summarizing the progress and status in each agency of accounting systems improvement efforts." These annual reports are undoubtedly intended to spur agency efforts in developing systems that meet the Comptroller General's standards.

The change in review process, coupled with the reestablishment of a centralized accounting systems staff,

349

afford a tenable basis for the Comptroller General maintaining that he is striving to make the GAO's accounting system program more acceptable, less demanding, and more fruitful insofar as the agencies are concerned.

GAO's broader concept of its accounting system function

The program's dimensions have been broadened by relating it to the settlement of accounts and internal audit, aspects of financial management discussed in Chapter 5 dealing with the Comptroller General's reviews. The Comptroller General announced that tests in several departments had demonstrated the feasibility of "settling the accounts of all accountable affairs in a department on the basis of our overall evaluation of the effectiveness of systems of accounting and internal controls, including internal audit."[45] The GAO recommended to heads of agency audit units that there be increased emphasis on internal audits of accounting systems and accounting reports sent to the Treasury.[46] The increasing agency involvement espoused by GAO will not only buttress its accounting systems program and lighten its workload but also should help to make GAO's dominance in this area more palatable to the agencies.

The stature of the systems program has been enhanced by GAO's expression of concern that the systems not merely produce accurate data in accordance with prescribed principles and standards but that the information which is generated be accepted and used by operating managers.[47] This broader perspective ties in with GAO's concern with agency information systems, which in turn involve the extensive use of computers in which the GAO is deeply interested. The depth of this latter interest is reflected in the 175 reports on data processing that the GAO issued in the 11 years following the enactment in 1965 of the Brooks Act dealing with problems stemming from the Government's expanding use of computer technology.[48] An internal booklet defines GAO's automatic data processing objective as:

> To strengthen the use and management of ADP techniques so that information produced by ADP systems - much of which is supplied to the Congress in its oversight role - will be reliable, useful, and cost effective.
>
> To recommend (to the Congress and the departments and agencies) ways of using automated systems to make Federal programs work better.[49]

Outcome of Comptroller General's push for systems approvals

The Comptroller General reported that as of September 30, 1976 it had taken 26 years to get 52 per cent of the 338 accounting systems subject to his review approved.[50] While specifically commending the Departments of Labor, Treasury, Commerce, and Transportation for working hard to establish good accounting systems, the Comptroller General took to task the Departments of Interior, Health, Education and Welfare, and State for having progressed so little "that we are concerned whether they will have approved accounting systems in the near future." The Defense Department had made little progress until recently but in the last 4 years had shown "remarkable progress." Whatever the other reasons for agency foot-dragging in designing systems that receive the GAO imprimatur, the vestiges of Executive Branch resistance to the Comptroller General's authority over this aspect of agency management must be an element.[51] During the early part of Staats' regime, an agency official commented: "We are one of the few agencies whose total financial system bears the blessing of GAO; and I am not sure whether that's good or bad, to tell the truth."

The Comptroller General has set up the objective of completing the initial review of all Executive Branch accounting systems by the end of fiscal year 1980. He is striving to convince Congress, OMB, and Executive agencies that in the allocation of resources, qualifying accounting systems for GAO approval merits the same high priority he accords it. Staats even resorted to invoking the financial plight of New York City and observing that "the contribution of poor accounting practices to that situation are well known."

The GAO is cognizant of the fact that the installation of effective accounting systems does not in itself suffice to assure that accounting operations are of high quality, that internal controls are effective, and that the information provided by the systems are responsive to managerial needs. Citing the responsibility imposed upon it by the Accounting and Auditing Act of 1950, the GAO reviews both approved and unapproved accounting systems of the Executive agencies. As indicated earlier, such reviews, unlike the approval of the systems, are completely consonant with the generally accepted role of the auditor.

ACCOUNTING SYSTEMS ROLE OF OFFICE
OF MANAGEMENT AND BUDGET

Essentiality of OMB participation

The Comptroller General's statutory responsibility

for the approval of accounting systems does not obviate the
need for, nor preclude the feasibility of, having within
the Executive Branch a strong, central facility for identifying the accounting system needs of individual agencies
and the Federal establishment as a whole and collaborating
with the GAO to see that these needs are met. Such a task
was integral to the full sweep of Budget Bureau responsibilities and is even more relevant to the role envisaged
for the Office of Management and Budget, which replaced the
Bureau and whose managerial mission was stressed by President Nixon when he proposed its establishment. Because of
its prestige and power, the Office of Management and Budget
is in an unusually strategic position to spearhead Executive
Branch accounting activities. Although the frame of reference for accounting systems is determined by the Comptroller
General, there still remains a broad area in which the Budget
Bureau's successor can make substantial contributions.

Budget Bureau lackadaisical with respect to accounting systems

For many years the Bureau had an Office of Financial
Management, which had the primary responsibility for following through on accounting systems within the Executive
Branch. However, the Bureau's impact was not as forceful
as it undoubtedly could well have been and, in fact, the
second Hoover Commission commented on the inadequacy of
the Bureau's efforts in this area.[52]

In justifying to a House subcommittee the limited
character of the Bureau's activities in this area, Philip
S. Hughes, then Deputy Director of the Bureau of the Budget and subsequently an Assistant Comptroller General,
observed:

> The Bureau of the Budget's limited size and
> diverse responsibilities require that our
> role be primarily one of leadership, stimu-
> lation, and periodic reviews of status. The
> major credit for progress made should go to
> the staff of the GAO and of the operating
> agencies directly involved.[53]

Although Hughes contended that the Bureau had maintained
"steady pressure for accounting systems improvement,"[54]
Executive Branch agencies generally felt that the Bureau's
activities in this area were relatively nominal. In its
report, the House Government Operations Committee indicated its dissatisfaction within the Budget Bureau efforts.
"There is still too much generalization within the Bureau
as to its activities in this direction and not enough dis-
cernible results."[55]

There were those in the Bureau itself who felt that
it would have "to put more steam behind the financial
management program." A former Bureau director attributed
the Bureau's lessened interest in financial systems to
the shift in the underlying motif of the agency. "You
transferred from the accountants and bankers to the econ-
omists, and you have different philosophies."

Renascence of Budget interest in improvement of financial management

The Nixon Administration evidenced strong support of
the Financial Management Improvement Program described in
the next section. This was apparently one facet of a broader
development, namely, greater interest on the part of the Bureau of the Budget in executive management as such. Additionally, the implementation of the accrual concept of accounting and, perhaps, greater awareness of the accounting
implications of PPB approach to budgeting appeared to
have infused the Bureau of the Budget with new vitality
so far as the Government's financial processes are concerned.

The resurgence of the Budget Bureau's interest was reflected in the letters which the Director of the Bureau addressed to various members of the Cabinet in the early part
of 1969 directing their attention to those provisions of
the Budget and Accounting Procedures Act of 1950 that define the financial system responsibilities of the heads of
Executive agencies. The letters also reminded the addressees
of the statutory mandate that agency accounting systems conform to the principles, standards, and related requirements
prescribed by the Comptroller General and provision for such
systems being subject to that official's approval. They
then went on to say:

> In the executive branch as a whole, progress
> towards the development of accounting systems
> that meet the approval of the Comptroller Gen-
> eral has been very disappointing. After al-
> most 19 years, the majority of the accounting
> systems have not been approved.

The Budget Director not only sought to stimulate the
top departmental officials to accelerate their accounting
system efforts but also to convince them that the systems
were worth the cost and effort. The recipients of the
letter were informed that the Bureau planned to devote
greater effort, in collaboration with the GAO, toward
the more rapid development of effective financial management systems throughout the Executive Branch. But the
letter was not just hortatory in nature. It requested
each department head to review the current status of plans
for the systems work in his department and to let the Bud-

get Director know by a designated date the plans which the secretary had for moving such work forward as well as any specific problems which were impeding progress.

The Director of the Bureau of the Budget was persevering; and he later announced that, during 1970, the Bureau was "launching a more intensive effort to support the Joint Financial Management Improvement Program objective of bringing all departmental and agency financial systems up to higher standards and levels of performance."[56]

But this thrust was not long-lived. In 1973, President Nixon transferred the responsibility for financial management systems development together with other functions to the General Services Administration.[57] If one accepts the premise that accounting is a vital managerial tool, this move seemed incompatible with the increased managerial emphasis that the President had ostensibly envisaged in replacing the Budget Bureau with OMB. Less than three years later, President Ford reversed the action taken by President Nixon.[58]

JOINT FINANCIAL MANAGEMENT IMPROVEMENT PROGRAM - A
VEHICLE FOR GAO-EXECUTIVE BRANCH COLLABORATION

Inception and legitimization of joint program

The Joint Financial Management Improvement Program had its inception in 1948 when Comptroller General Warren addressed a letter to the heads of all Government departments and agencies for the purpose of acquainting them "with a broad program which is under way in the General Accounting Office with active participation by the Bureau of the Budget and the Treasury Department, for improving accounting in the Federal Government."[59] In addition to stating the basic features of the Government's accounting as envisaged by this program, the letter emphasized the cooperative relationship that had been established by the Comptroller General with the Secretary of the Treasury and the Director of the Bureau of the Budget. Warren explained that the Treasury Department had a vital interest in the results to be achieved "in terms of fulfilling its fiscal responsibilities and providing current financial information regarding the operations of the Government as a whole based on integration of accounting results." The collaboration of the Bureau of the Budget was deemed by the Comptroller General to be of importance because "with participation of the Bureau, improvements in accounting will go hand in hand with improvement in budget processes." The first Hoover Commission was impressed with what had been accomplished through this

354

Joint Program and referred to "the admirable work of the
Secretary of the Treasury, the Comptroller General, and
the Director of the Bureau of the Budget."[60]

The Budget and Accounting Procedures Act of 1950
(Section 111(f)) gave statutory recognition to the Joint
Program by stating that the Comptroller General, the
Secretary of the Treasury, and the Director of the Bureau
of the Budget should "conduct a continuous program for the
improvement of accounting and financial reporting in the
Government." Both the House and Senate Committees, in reporting on the proposed legislation, stated that it em-
bodied the principles and objectives of the cooperative
program.[61] It is obvious that Congress, rather than effecting any reallocation of the Comptroller General's
authority over Executive Branch accounting systems, has
preferred to rely upon the Joint Program as an answer to
the criticisms that have been leveled at the control which
the GAO exercises over Executive Branch accounting systems.

Benefits of Joint Program

However skeptical one may be of this device to overcome the shortcomings inherent in the present statutory
arrangement, one cannot dismiss the benefits that have
been derived from the Joint Financial Management Improvement Program (JFMIP). Comptroller General Warren looked
upon the Joint Program as one of his major accomplishments
as Comptroller General.[62]

The continuing collaboration between the Government's
three top fiscal officials has apparently reduced conflicts
of viewpoint which might have triggered off confrontations
as to jurisdiction; it has kept the Comptroller General
apprised of accounting needs and problems as perceived by
the Executive Branch. The fact that, during 1966, the
Civil Service Commission became an active participant has
enabled the Joint Program to serve as a vehicle for stimulating efforts directed to meeting the personnel needs in
the financial management area.

The Joint Program gradually assumed much greater breadth
than was originally contemplated:

The program was originally conceived as an accounting improvement program that would strengthen the interrelated functions of the central
agencies and better coordinate these efforts
with the improvement activities of the operating agencies. The greater potential of improvement efforts directed at the broader field of
financial management soon became apparent. The

program since has been associated with improvements on many fronts -- legislation, budgeting, accounting, auditing, central financial operations, cash management, strengthening staff resources, and improvements in individual agency operations.[63]

The broad gauge approach of JFMIP is reflected in its sponsorship of an annual Financial Management Conference, the purpose of which is to "stimulate the development and widespread use of good financial management practices."[64] The 1977 Conference had workshops dealing with such variegated subjects as cash management, Federal consolidated finance statements, intergovernmental auditing, and zero-base budgeting.[65]

The Joint Program has also served as a means for the Chief Executive expressing his support of improved financial management. Using the Program as a frame of reference, the Presidential directives have not only reminded the agencies of their financial management responsibilities but have also underlined the fact that agency systems should be fitted into an overall pattern in which each of the three central fiscal agencies has an important role. President Johnson, in 1965, wrote to heads of departments and agencies to tell them of his "strong and continuing interest in the development of business-like financial systems throughout the Federal Government."[66] President Nixon also expressed full support of the Joint Financial Management Improvement Program, which he described as "an indispensable project with a charter to sharpen some of the tools of management."[67]

Joint Program's advantages for Comptroller General

This significant buttressing and even revitalization of the Joint Program strengthens the position of the Comptroller General in the financial system area. It serves to deemphasize his authoritarian role in connection with accounting systems and accentuates his serving as a resource for improving the management information essential to the effective functioning of the Executive Branch. The reiteration of Presidential support of the program places department and agency heads in a less tenable position to treat the Comptroller General as an interloper from the Legislative Branch and to utter anguished cries as to his poaching upon preserves that appropriately lie entirely within the domain of the Executive Branch. Although one would be unfair in assuming that Warren thought of the program primarily as a gambit for making the Comptroller General's accounting systems authority more palatable to the Executive Branch, it is apparent that he was

356

not unmindful of its potentialities on that score:

> This approach makes possible a continuation
> of the policy of Congress that the establish-
> ment of basic accounting requirements be re-
> garded as a vital adjunct of congressional
> control over the funds which it provides for
> the executive branch through appropriations
> or otherwise. At the same time, the exer-
> cise of this function has, under the joint
> program, been consistent with the revised
> concepts of responsibilities of executive
> agencies for accounting as prescribed by law.[68]

The JFMIP has implications for GAO that extend beyond
reinforcing the Comptroller General's accounting system
role and strengthening his credentials for concerning himself with the totality of the Government's financial management -- highly significant impacts in themselves. The
program, in which the Comptroller General tends to be a
driving force, can also be supportive of GAO efforts that
are not strictly of a financial nature. Thus, for about
three years, JFMIP participated actively in the interagency
(Civil Service Commission, GAO, and Treasury) project for
measuring and enhancing Federal productivity, a subject
patently germane to GAO concern with the efficiency and[69]
economy of operations.

GAO'S POSITION OF POWER IN
GOVERNMENT'S FINANCIAL MANAGEMENT

Its activities in connection with the budgetary process and agency accounting systems afford the GAO a pivotal
role in the Government's financial management -- a role
which the Comptroller General has firmly embraced. This
position is enhanced by GAO's responsibility for the settlement of the accounts of accountable officers and its rendering of decisions in the legality of expenditures. Finally, the Joint Financial Management Program has afforded
the Comptroller General an invaluable vehicle for solidifying his profound influence on this aspect of the Government's management.

Some might feel that this aggregate of responsibilities means an untenable intrusion of a Congressional facility into the Executive Branch; they might even focus
their criticisms on the Comptroller General's authority
over agency accounting systems, an issue which, as previously noted, was highly controversial at one time. One,
however, has to consider realities. Despite the blunders
committed and the antagonisms evoked, GAO's efforts in
the accounting system area have been a significant stimulus

in directing agency attention and tangible recognition to the essentiality of well-conceived accounting tools. It might be argued that the Budget Bureau would have been far more active in this area were it not for the legal authority vested in the GAO. But it can reasonably be contended that the Bureau's increasing concern with the broad implications of the Government's programs would have inhibited its interest in agency accounting, particularly with the ascendancy of the economist in the Bureau's leadership. In fact, the statutory role of the Comptroller General in connection with this facet of executive agency management might have made the Bureau and its successor, OMB, more responsive than they otherwise would have been to the challenge of improving the Government's financial management. Similarly, agency progress in the installation of adequate accounting systems might have been even more agonizing were it not for the constant prodding by GAO, which, in turn, has had Congressional backing.

The question of whether the GAO has impinged unduly upon Executive Branch prerogatives in financial management needs to be perceived in the context of the capacity and interest which that Branch has demonstrated in this facet of its operations. The statutory allocation of the accounting systems authority to GAO need not have precluded the Executive Branch from showing far more dynamism in strengthening this phase of its management. Especially under Staats, who entered the Comptrollership post with an imposing background in the Bureau of the Budget, the GAO has been in a highly strategic position to fill in financial management voids of the Executive Branch.

GAO's ascendancy in this phase of the Government's affairs has become less dependent upon its authority to review agency accounting systems or to disallow expenditures in settling accounts of accountable officers. It increasingly revolves around the assistance which the Comptroller General renders Congress in the implementation of the more vital budgetary role which the Legislative Reorganization Act of 1970 and the far-reaching Congressional Budget and Impoundment Control Act of 1974 envisaged for the Legislative Branch. Whether it be in working with Executive agencies to improve the program and budget information available to the Congress, conducting reviews or special analyses having budgetary significance, or checking on Presidential observance of the Impoundment Control Act, the Comptroller General's imprint on Congressional review, enactment, and follow-through of the Federal budget has been growing steadily. The result may well be a reordering of GAO priorities in the area of financial management.

1. Elmer B. Staats, "The Role of GAO During the 1980's,"
   The GAO Review (Spring 1977), p. 33.

2. Statement of Elmer B. Staats, Comptroller General of
   the United States Before the Legislative Subcommittee,
   House Appropriations Committee on Budget Estimates
   for Fiscal Year 1978, February 3, 1977.

3. See Jeffrey L. Pressman, House vs. Senate, Conflict
   in the Appropriation Process (New Haven: Yale
   University Press, 1966), p. 20, and Richard F. Fenno,
   Jr., The Power of the Purse - Appropriations Politics
   in Congress (Boston and Toronto: Little, Brown &
   Company, 1966), p. 101.

4. Final Report of the Joint Committee on the Organization of Congress, 89th Congress, 2nd Session, 1966,
   p. 26.

5. Public Law 91-510.

6. Public Law 93-344.

7. The Act required the Comptroller General to submit
   to the Congress, on or before June 30, 1975, a
   report containing the initial standard terminology,
   definitions, classifications and codes. (See ACG-
   75-29 dated 6/30/75.)   Late in 1975, the GAO published a glossary entitled "Budgetary Definitions."
   (OPA 76-8, November 1975.) Pursuant to the statutory provision calling upon the Comptroller General to submit additional reports "as he may think
   advisable," he subsequently presented to the Congress a proposed revision of the Federal Budget's
   function/subfunction classifications. (PAD-76-49,
   August 20, 1976.)

8. Comptroller General Report, Progress in Improving
   Fiscal, Budgetary, and Program-Related Information
   for the Congress, PAD-76-64, August 30, 1976. One
   year later, the Comptroller General reported:
   ". . . improvement is still needed in existing information and its presentation to the Congress.
   The long process of improving information has begun and will continue." PSAD-77-73, August 30, 1977.

9. The GAO worked intensively with twenty-five standing
   committees to enable them to identify, section by
   section, in the authorizing language what their

association was with appropriations. The new legislation had involved the standing committees of both Houses much more directly in the appropriation process than had been the case theretofore. Each committee must submit to its respective Budget Committee "the estimate of the total amounts of new budget authority, and budget outlays resulting therefrom, to be provided or authorized in all bills and resolutions within the jurisdiction of such committee which such committee intends to be effective during the fiscal year beginning on October 1 of such year." (Section 310(c).) The GAO helped the committees bridge the gap between authorizations and the appropriations predicated upon the authorizations.

10. Comptroller General Report, The Congressional Budget and Impoundment Control Act of 1974: Its Impact on the Authorizing Committees and GAO, OPA-76-29, April 21, 1976.

11. "Used with restraint and circumspection, impoundment has been used for decades without precipitating a major crisis. But during the Nixon years restraint was replaced by abandon, precedent stretched past the breaking point, and statutory authority pushed beyond legislative intent." Louis Fisher, Presidential Spending Power (Princeton: Princeton University Press, 1975), p. 201.

12. Comptroller General Report, Review of the Impoundment Control Act of 1974 After 2 Years, OGC-77-20, June 3, 1977.

13. S.2925, 94th Congress, Second Session.

14. March 19, 1976 Statement of Comptroller General Before the Subcommittee on Intergovernmental Relations, Senate Committee on Government Operations, p. 6.

15. Congressional Record, September 30, 1975.

16. Letter from Acting Comptroller General R.F. Keller to Chairman George H. Mahon, House Committee on Appropriations, September 20, 1976.

17. Letter from Acting Comptroller General Paul G. Dembling to Chairman George H. Mahon, House Committee on Appropriations, May 6, 1977.

18. Thus, Senator Percy was furnished information on the extent to which Federal funds or resources had been applied to the Chicago Police Department's intelligence operations. Letter from Comptroller General Elmer B. Staats to Senator Charles H. Percy, May 29, 1975.

19. Presidential Memorandum for the Heads of Executive Departments and Agencies, February 14, 1977. See also OMB Bulletin No. 77-9, April 19, 1977. Zero-Base Budgeting.

20. Comptroller General Report, Mission Budgeting: Discussion and Illustration of the Concept in Research and Development Programs, PSAD-77-124, July 27, 1977, pp. 8 and 28.

21. February 14, 1978 Statement of Comptroller General Before the Task Force on Expenditures, Regulations and Reorganization. House Budget Committee.

22. A less far-reaching, but nevertheless significant, example of GAO's efforts to improve the budget system is its criticism of the exclusion of the Federal Financing Bank from Federal budget totals as well as "other questionable budget practices." Comptroller General Report, Government Agency Transactions with the Federal Financing Bank Should be Included in the Budget, PSAD-77-70, August 3, 1977.

23. Senate, Committee on Government Operations, Hearings Before Subcommittee on Executive Reorganization, Capability of GAO to Analyze and Audit Defense Expenditures, 91st Congress, 1st Session, 1969, p. 7.

24. Ibid., p. 30.

25. Although not directly focused on budgeting per se, GAO's review of long-range analysis systems certainly has implications for budgetary planning. See Comptroller General Report, Long-Range Analysis Activities in Seven Federal Agencies, PAD-77-18, December 3, 1976.

26. Report of the President's Committee on Administrative Management (Washington, D.C.: Government Printing Office, 1937), p. 24.

27. Ibid., p. 21.

28. A House Appropriations Committee staff report (1971), that apparently had little impact, made this salient

comment: "Consideration should be given to assigning the responsibility for the approval of financial management systems to the Bureau of the Budget." The report also stated that "if the approval concept is retained, it should be applied at the financial management system level either in addition to or in lieu of the accounting system level." House Appropriations Committee, Hearings Before Subcommittee on Legislative Branch Appropriations, 92nd Congress, 1st Session, 1971, p. 766.

29. A somewhat atypical reaction was voiced by an Executive agency official who developed a line of reasoning that made the existing allocation of accounting system authority compatible with the doctrine of separation of powers. He pointed out that Congress could by statute set up very detailed procedures for the consummation of agency financial transactions. Hence, he did not subscribe to the thesis that it is untenable to have a legislative agency prescribe the essentials of accounting systems.

30. House, Committee on Government Operations, Hearings Before a Subcommittee of the Committee on Government Operations, Submissions of Agency Accounting Systems for GAO Approval, 88th Congress, 2nd Session, 1964.

31. House, Committee on Government Operations, Third Report, Submission of Agency Accounting Systems for GAO Approval, House Report 179, 89th Congress, 1st Session (1965), p. 9.

32. House, Committee on Government Operations, Hearings Before Subcommittee, Rate of Progress Being Made by Government Agencies in the Requirements of the Budget and Accounting Procedures Act of 1950, 90th Congress, 1st Session, 1967, p. 2.

33. Ibid., p. 3.

34. House, Committee on Government Operations, Twenty-Second Report: Submission of Agency Accounting Systems for GAO Approval (Second Review), H. Rept. 1159, 90th Congress, 2nd Session, 1968, p. 3.

35. Ibid., p. 5.

36. Rate of Progress Being Made by Government Agencies in the Requirements of the Budget and Accounting Procedures Act of 1950, op. cit., p. 55.

37. House, Committee on Government Operations, Hearings Before Special Studies Subcommittee, A Review of Labor Department Accounting Systems, 90th Congress, 2nd Session, 1968.

38. Ibid., p. 2.

39. Memorandum from Comptroller General Elmer B. Staats to Heads of Divisions and Offices, GAO, June 3, 1966.

40. Comptroller General, 1969 Annual Report, p. 53. See for similar statements, p. 32 of the 1966 Annual Report; p. 47 of the 1967 Annual Report; and p. 47 of the 1968 Annual Report.

41. Senate, Committee on Government Operations, Hearings Before Subcommittee on Executive Reorganization, Capability of GAO to Analyze and Audit Defense Expenditures, 91st Congress, 1st Session, 1969, p. 34.

42. Memorandum from Comptroller General Elmer B. Staats to Heads of Federal Departments and Agencies, October 16, 1969.

43. Comptroller General of the United States, Accounting Principles and Standards for Federal Agencies (1965), pp. 2-76 and 77.

44. Comptroller General's Memorandum of October 16, 1969.

45. Comptroller General Report, Status, Progress, and Problems in Federal Agency Accounting During Fiscal Year 1974, B-115398, November 12, 1974, p. 30.

46. Comptroller General Report, Status, Progress, and Problems in Federal Agency Accounting During 15 Months Ended September 30, 1976, FGMSD 77-21, August 24, 1977, p. 31.

47. Comptroller General, Lessons Learned About Acquiring Financial Management and Other Information Systems, August 1976.

48. Comptroller General Report, Problems Found with Government Acquisition and Use of Computers from November 1965 to December 1976, FGMSD 77-14, March 15, 1977.

49. What GAO is Doing in the Area of Automatic Data Processing. Financial and General Management Studies Division, September 1974.

50. August 24, 1977 Report, op. cit., p. 3. The 26 years cited by the Comptroller General began in 1950 with the Accounting and Auditing Act which, as already explained, requires the head of each executive agency to establish and maintain accounting systems that "conform to the principles, standards, and related requirements prescribed by the Comptroller General." This requirement was, of course, antedated by the provision in the Budget and Accounting Act of 1921 that the Comptroller General prescribe the forms, systems, and procedures for administrative appropriations and fund accounting in the several departments and establishments.

51. One of the causes of this recalcitrance was agency opposition to the implementation of the accrual basis of accounting which, in the words of the GAO, "consists of recognizing in the books and records of account the significant and accountable aspects of financial transactions as they occur" as distinguished from the cash basis "under which financial transactions are recorded in accounts only when cash is received or disbursed." GAO Policy and Procedures Manual for Guidance of Federal Agencies, Title 2, p. 18.

52. Commission on Organization of the Executive Branch of the Government, Budgeting and Accounting, A Report to the Congress (Washington, D.C.: Government Printing Office, 1955), p. 31.

53. House, Committee on Government Operations, Hearings Before Subcommittee, op. cit., 1967, p. 36.

54. Ibid., p. 37.

55. House, Committee on Government Operations, Submission of Agency Accounting Systems for GAO Approval, (Second Review), op. cit., p. 4.

56. Memorandum from Robert P. Mayo, Director, Bureau of the Budget, to Heads of Executive Departments and Agencies, January 30, 1970.

57. Executive Order 11717, May 9, 1973.

58. Executive Order 11893, January 2, 1976.

59. Letter from Comptroller General Lindsay C. Warren to Heads of Departments and Agencies, October 20, 1948.

60. Commission on Reorganization of the Executive Branch of the Government, Report on Budgeting and Accounting in the Executive Branch (Washington, D.C.: Government Printing Office, 1949), p. 38.

61. S. Rept. 2031, 81st Congress, 2nd Session (1950), p. 9. H. Rept. 2556, 81st Congress, 2nd Session (1950), p. 8.

62. Letter from Comptroller General Lindsay C. Warren to Members of Congress, March 31, 1954, in which Warren expressed the view that continuance of the program was vitally necessary.

63. Joint Financial Management Improvement Program, 20th Annual Financial Report (Washington, D.C.: Superintendent of Documents, 1968), p. 2.

64. JFMIP Annual Report for 1976, p. 5.

65. JFMIP Principal Addresses Presented at the Sixth Financial Management Conference (1977).

66. Memorandum from President Lyndon B. Johnson to Heads of Departments and Agencies, May 24, 1966.

67. Memorandum from President Richard M. Nixon to Heads of Departments and Agencies, August 12, 1969.

68. Comptroller General, 1950 Annual Report, p. 6.

69. JFMIP Annual Report for 1976, pp. 17-21. See also Implementing a Productivity Program: Points to Answer, March 1977. In 1976, the responsibility for general direction of the internal Federal productivity program was assumed by the National Center for Productivity and Quality of Working Life established by P.L. 94-136.

Chapter 10

A TIME FOR REEXAMINATION OF THE
GENERAL ACCOUNTING OFFICE

Sometimes you say you are an independent agency
and sometimes you say you are a branch of the
Executive and sometimes you say you are an arm
of Congress, and sometimes you say you are none
of these.[1]

From time to time, the Congress, for good and
sufficient reasons, has assigned additional
duties to the GAO. In some instances these new
responsibilities appear to deviate from the
purposes originally conceived for the office.
It is the position of some authorities that the
original mission may have become adversely affected by, and possibly subordinated to, these
other duties.[2]

The foregoing remarks made by Senator Lee Metcalf
and Representative Jack Brooks respectively in the course
of Senate and House subcommittee hearings on the GAO were
sparked by the crystallization of a more questioning, albeit not hostile, Congressional attitude as to the role
and status of the Comptroller General.

Even those critical of the GAO are quick to agree on
the essentiality of a central monitoring agency for the
Federal Government. There is also widespread acceptance
of the fact that the GAO has had a very salutary effect
upon the Government and that, whatever its shortcomings,
the GAO has produced studies and effected changes that
have had a profound and constructive impact upon the
operations of the Federal establishment. But the height-
ening momentum with which the Comptroller General's domain
has expanded calls for more than an overall reaction to
his performance. The need for searching examination is
all the greater because of the lack of awareness by the
public and even within the Congress as to the total
spectrum of powers wielded by the Comptroller General.
Furthermore, the phenomenal growth in the staff and other
supportive services (in addition to the GAO) available
to Congress as well as the statutory establishment of
independent monitoring units within Executive agencies
have vital implications for the Comptroller General that
have not been fully recognized.[3]

THE FOUNTAINHEAD OF THE COMPTROLLER
GENERAL'S FAR-REACHING POWER

What emerges from an in-depth analysis of the Comptroller General of the United States and the General Accounting Office, which he heads, is the image of a legislative agency that has assumed a position of almost awesome power in not only the Federal Government's operations but also the formulation of national policies and programs. The influence which the Comptroller General derives from serving as the Government's auditor and reporting findings and recommendations to the Congress is in itself vast, particularly since the Comptroller General has adopted a broad concept of auditing that encompasses not only financial accountability but also the efficiency and economy of operations and the results achieved. This influence is reinforced by the direct assistance rendered Congress in the implementation of its oversight and budgetary responsibilities. Reports in response to specific requests are only one facet of this assistance, that enhances GAO's position. Counselling Congressional committees on proposed legislation and furnishing both committees and Members legal opinions and advice are still other aspects. But the bulwark of the Comptroller General's power is the composite of his authority to: disallow expenditures, render decisions as to availability of appropriations, pass upon appeals of bidders for Government contracts, settle and adjudicate claims by or against the United States, and approve the accounting systems of Government agencies. The expanding authority of the Comptroller General reached something of a zenith in 1974, when Congress vested him with the responsibility to monitor compliance with the restrictions it had placed upon Presidential and other Executive Branch action to defer or rescind budget authority that had been enacted by Congress. The Comptroller General was also empowered to initiate litigation to compel the release of funds.

The power base enjoyed by the Comptroller General is not predicated entirely on statutory enactments but reflects, to a surprising degree, the freedom which that official has exercised in interpreting the GAO mission and determining how best to implement it. Hence, under the rubric "audits," GAO conducts reviews and studies that go far beyond what would be embraced by the most liberal construction of that term. The Comptroller General has increasingly involved himself in critical areas of national policy and seems to welcome a foray with the White House on proposals it initiates. As a result, headlines such as the following occur with great frequency: [4]"Carter Energy Plan Called Overstated in a Report by GAO."[4] "GAO Says Ship-Preference Bill Would Add $240 Million to Oil Cost."[5] Similarly, a newspaper article leads off with the statement: "Comptroller General Elmer B. Staats has told the Carter Administration that it cannot legally phase out the controversial Clinch River breeder reactor and that any government official who approves spending to terminate the project will be held personally liable for the debt."[6]

One finds the Comptroller General issuing a voluminous report that purports to "summarize available knowledge on U.S. coal development and seeks to identify the major policy issues that must be considered -- especially if we are to achieve the coal production and use goals in the Administration's Natural Energy Plan."[7] The Comptroller General stated that this review was made pursuant to the Budget and Accounting Act of 1921 and the Accounting and Auditing Act of 1950, which have apparently become "umbrella authority" for analyses that may stray far afield but that challenge the GAO. Without impugning the value of such studies, one may still speculate as to their congruence with the fundamental motif of the Government's audit agency and how well they fit into a rational scheme for the effective utilization of the burgeoning supportive services now available to the Congress. As the Comptroller General takes on a more active role in the decision-making process, he may compromise his credibility as the auditor of the programs, activities, and financial operations involved in the implementation of the resultant decisions.

Entirely apart from the expanded scope of the Comptroller General's activities within the Federal Government per se, the dependence of state and local units of Government upon Federal fiscal assistance has made for growing GAO impact upon the financial and managerial practices of the sub-national levels of Government. His sponsorship of intergovernmental audit forums together with his formulation of audit standards having general applicability to governmental entities have buttressed this impact. GAO's far-reaching inquiries into the Government's procurement programs and practices as well as the performance of individual contractors have significant implications for the private sector, especially because of the magnitude of funds which the Government expends for the acquisition of goods, services, and facilities. The Comptroller General's "outreach" beyond the boundaries of the Federal Government also manifests itself in the influence which the auditing philosophy enunciated by the Comptroller General has had upon the public accounting profession.

COMPTROLLER GENERAL'S FUNCTIONS ARE AN UNUSUAL MIX

An earlier chapter brought out that, when Comptroller General Staats brought a suit against President Ford pursuant to the Impoundment Control Act of 1974, his contention

369

that he was acting in this respect "as an independent officer who performs non-legislative functions" impelled
long-overdue Congressional inquiries as to the underlying
nature of the Comptroller General's role in the political
process. The Comptroller General had explicitly stated
that he was neither an executive nor legislative officer
and that his "historically executive duties are to be
'exercised without direction from any other officer.'"
Such statements emanating from the Comptroller General
have underlined the issue as to the tenability of the unusual mix of responsibilities vested in that official.
The blend of functions which at one time was challenged
sharply by students of government has become even more
complex as, in the absence of a well-conceived frame of
reference for its tasks, there has been a tendency to
add to GAO responsibilities because of exigencies and
pressures extant at particular points of time. For example, there was little reason for the Comptroller General to be assigned responsibilities under the 1971 Acts
relating to the financial disclosure of campaign expenditures for Federal elections; the subsequent transfer
of these duties was most appropriate. Similarly, the
Comptroller General has been burdened with review and
clearance functions in connection with the information-
gathering practices of fourteen independent regulatory
agencies; he himself has recommended the reassignment
of the clearance function to an Executive agency, preferably the Office of Management and Budget.[8] Although
the Comptroller General, originally reluctant, is now
happy to serve as chairman of the Cost Accounting Standards Board and appoints its members, one can still question the compatibility of this responsibility with his
basic mission. More recently, the spectacle of the Comptroller General, invoking the Impoundment Control Act,
to bring a suit against the President dramatically posed
the query as to whether Congress had not seriously compounded the confusion as to what properly comes within
the purview of the Comptroller.

If responsibilities continue to be allocated to the
Comptroller General on an ad hoc basis, the inevitable
result will be a potpourri of functions that will militate against the GAO's effectiveness in discharging the
role which it has as the Government's central audit agency
for assuring accountability of Federal agencies and their
personnel. The Comptroller General has appropriately observed that the GAO "has the biggest audit, monitoring
and oversight job in the world." The ramifications of
this herculean task should be overriding in assaying the
soundness of superimposing other responsibilities upon it.

As the Comptroller General becomes enamored with par-

ticipating in the resolution of vital and intriguing
policy issues, he may tend to gloss over less glamorous,
albeit vital, aspects of the auditing function. For example, a leading public accounting firm recommended that
the Federal Government prepare and publish consolidated
financial statements, the lack of which is a significant
void in the Government's fiscal management.[9] The Comptroller General agreed as to the need for "better overall financial reports that show clearly for the benefit
of the Congress and the public the major aspects of its
financial position and operations," but felt that the
recommendation fell within the jurisdiction of the Treasury Department.[10] Granting that this identification of
Treasury's responsibility is correct, one may still question why the Comptroller General, as the Government's
auditor, had not much earlier pushed vigorously for the
availability of such financial statements, which would
then be subject to his review. This lowering of priorities accorded the less dramatic tasks undoubtedly accounted for the Comptroller General's initiation of the
legislation enacted in 1975 changing the frequency with
which the GAO is required to audit Government corporations from annually to at least once in every three years.[11]

ACCOUNTABILITY VERSUS INDEPENDENCE
OF THE COMPTROLLER GENERAL

The implications of the steady and marked accretion
in the power of the Comptroller General need to be perceived in light of the fact that he has been relatively
immune from systematic review and evaluation of his operations. Carrying the escutcheon of the valiant de-
fender of the Federal Treasury and the detector of inept-
itude and even rascality in the management of the Government's affairs, the Comptroller General has rarely been
subjected to more than benign and/or disjointed Congressional scrutiny even at the hearings on the GAO's estimates
of its budgetary needs. Continuing and sophisticated
evaluation of GAO performance would identify shortcomings,
make for optimal allocation of resources, and inhibit any
proclivity to kick over the traces. Regularly recurring
reviews of the Comptroller General's activities, accomplishments, and problems would make for greater awareness
of the vital role that this official plays in the political process. The outside reviews to which public accounting firms are subjecting themselves underscores the
tenability of requiring that those exercising the audit
prerogative undergo similar scrutiny. The case for such
an outside review of GAO operations is all the more persuasive because of their variegated nature.

But any review mechanism that is set up for the Comptroller General must not derogate from the independence that is indispensable if the GAO is to discharge its audit responsibilities in a manner conducive to the objectivity, credibility, and forthrightness of its reviews. However, the very mix of functions which the Comptroller General cited in the impoundment control case and which extend the GAO's activities far beyond the auditing area complicates the independence issue. Staats argues that the functions GAO performs are so interrelated that there is no "practical way" to split them.[12]

Rather belatedly, Comptroller General Staats acted to avoid an imbalance between responsiveness to Congressional needs for assistance and the other GAO responsibilities. The differentiation between the various GAO tasks has to be carried further so that there is full recognition that the strictly auditing aspects impose an overriding obligation to the public that transcends the other GAO activities insofar as independence, priorities, and allocation of resources are concerned.

But it was not only the allocation of staff resources that reflected the Comptroller General's ambivalence in maintaining a balance between his vaunted independence and GAO's direct assistance to the Congress. Independence was clearly compromised by the practice of permitting committees and individual Members to determine the distribution of reports prepared in response to their requests. This obeisance to Congressional wishes, which this author consistently criticized,[13] was finally modified in June 1977 by a directive stating: "Request assignment reports will generally be made available for unrestricted distribution no later than 30 days after their issue dates."[14]

Apparently the Comptroller General had come to the realization that he had unduly circumscribed his freedom of action in the discharge of his underlying responsibility. This awareness might have been stimulated by the inquiries which Members of Congress addressed to him as to the nature of the independence he claimed in his impoundment suit against the President as well as by a proposal to change the provisions for the appointment, term, and removal of the Comptroller General and his deputy.

RECONSIDERATION OF COMPTROLLER GENERAL'S
ROLE HAS ASSUMED INCREASED URGENCY

Incisive reexamination of the totality of the Comptroller General's authority is especially appropriate in light of the persevering efforts of that official to obtain legislation strengthening his access to the records of Federal agencies and "non-Federal persons and

372

organizations" and permitting him to institute court action to stop the incurring of obligations or expenditures
"in an illegal manner."[15] Whereas access to essential
information is manifestly vital to the performance of
the audit component of the Comptroller General's multi-
faceted role, the authority to invoke judicial intervention to head off agency expenditures which that official
alleges to be illegal strikes at the nagging question as
to the extent to which the Government's auditor should
be vested with authority to control the actions of those
he audits. Perhaps pragmatic considerations negate theoretical objections, but the resolution of such issues
should be predicated on a complete overview of the spectrum
of the Comptroller General's tasks with particular emphasis
on their interaction.

Questions that have arisen in connection with the
preparation and transmittal of Comptroller General reports
to the Congress, which is the centrality of GAO operations,
present another reason for reconsidering the Comptroller
General's role and the manner in which it is implemented.
One may conjecture as to how effectively Congress was able
to utilize the 939 reports which were submitted directly
to it or to its committees and Members during the 15-month
period ended September 30, 1976.[16] This almost staggering
volume was entirely apart from the 441 reports addressed
to Federal agency officials; copies of many of these reports, the Comptroller General informs us, were also sent
to "interested committees and Members of Congress." The
possibility that this reporting contributes to an informational overload is heightened by the output emanating from
the three other Congressional support agencies (Congressional Budget Office, Congressional Research Service, and
the Office of Technology Assessment), as well as the Congressional staff. Fortunately, as the analysis brings
out, the GAO is seeking to deemphasize its dependence upon
formal reports as a means for communicating findings and
recommendations to the Congress and its committees. It
will be necessary for the Comptroller General to counteract GAO staff perception of formal or "blue cover" reports
as an important means for winning recognition with the
organization. A more fundamental problem is that of forestalling unnecessary overlap between the GAO and the three
other support agencies which, unlike the GAO, essentially
have the single mission of serving the Congress in a supportive or informational capacity.

The need for reexamining the Comptroller General's
role and operations has currently become even more pressing
because of the steps Congress has been taking to establish
Presidentially-appointed inspectors general in Executive
agencies.[17] The legislation is designed to "create inde-

pendent and objective units" one function of which is "to conduct and supervise audits and investigations relating to programs and operations" of their respective agencies. Since each such official is to report to not only the head of his establishment but also the Congress and its appropriate committees and subcommittees, there is bound to be an important interface with the Comptroller General. Recognizing that the duties and responsibilities of the inspectors general impinge upon those of the Comptroller General, the legislation requires each inspector general to "give particular regard to the activities of the Comptroller General of the United States with a view to avoiding duplication and incurring effective coordination and cooperation."

The widening application of the inspector general concept, if coupled with its effective implementation, portends significant recasting of the Comptroller General's role and operations. Whether or not impelled by the move for inspectors general or by the other persuasive considerations, such a change should not be left to chance but rather stem from Congressional in-depth inquiry into the aggregate of responsibilities and powers vested in the Comptroller General. Such an analysis should address itself to the compatability between the different functions presently performed by the Comptroller General, their interplay with the activities of other monitoring and Congressional support agencies, and their impact both constructive and otherwise, upon the Executive Branch. Finally, Congress should recognize that the independence indispensable to the Comptroller General in his capacity as the Government's auditor is not to be equated with immunity from regular evaluations of his performance.

Entirely apart from any rethinking of the Comptroller General's mission, there is a need for him and his staff to be mindful of the sensitivities of those whose activities are audited and to minimize tensions attendant upon GAO efforts. At the same time, the Comptroller General cannot be deterred from dealing with problems in a forthright manner because particular findings or recommendations might embarrass or irk those concerned. The expanding scope and depth of its reviews has added to the essentiality of the GAO reflecting restraint and an awareness of its own limitations. The discretion and independence which the Comptroller General rightly claims makes it all the more incumbent upon him to continually maintain appropriate balance between results achieved through GAO's activities and not only the resources they require but also the attendant stress and strain upon the Government's operations.

Footnotes - Chapter 10

1. Senate, Hearing Before the Subcommittee on Reports, Accounting, and Management of the Committee on Government Operations, GAO Legislation, 94th Congress, 1st Session, October 2, 1975, p. 25.

2. House, Hearing Before a Subcommittee of the Committee on Government Operations, Review of the Powers, Procedures, and Policies of the General Accounting Office, 94th Congress, 1st Session, December 10, 1975, p. 2.

3. See Commission on the Operation of the Senate, Congressional Support Agencies, 94th Congress, 2nd Session, 1976, to which this author contributed a paper.

4. New York Times, July 29, 1977.

5. New York Times, August 26, 1977. The ship preference proposal came from the White House, and, when it was defeated in the House, the Times (October 20, 1977) reported that the opponents had cited the GAO report. Costs of Cargo Preference, USAD 77-82, September 9, 1977.

6. New York Times, March 13, 1978.

7. Comptroller General Report, U.S. Coal Development -- Promises, Uncertainties, EMD-77-43, September 22, 1977.

8. Comptroller General, 1976 Annual Report, p. 8.

9. Arthur Andersen and Co., Sound Financial Reporting in the Public Sector - A Prerequisite to Fiscal Responsibility, 1975.

10. Review of the Powers, Procedures, and Policies of the General Accounting Office, op. cit., p. 43.

11. Public Law 93-604.

12. GAO Legislation, op. cit., p. 27.

13. "The General Accounting Office as a Congressional Resource," in Congressional Support Agencies, op. cit., pp. 48-49. The author's criticism of this practice had also been expressed much earlier.

14. June 1, 1977 Memorandum of the Director of Planning of GAO.

15. GAO Legislation, op. cit., pp. 6-9 and 28-39.

16. 1976 Annual Report, op. cit., p. 2.

17. See Public Law 94-505 establishing Office of Inspector General for the Department of Health, Education, and Welfare and H.R. 8588, 95th Congress, 1st Session, establishing Offices of Inspector General in "certain executive departments and agencies."

ABOUT THE AUTHOR

Joseph Pois is Professor Emeritus of Public Administration in the Graduate School of Public and International Affairs of the University of Pittsburgh, where he had served as Chairman of the Public Administration Department and subsequently Associate Dean. His more than thirty years experience as a practitioner was focused on the financial, legal, and management aspects of the public and private sectors. He served as: Company Counsel and then Vice President, Treasurer, and Director of the Signode Corporation; Director of Finance of the State of Illinois under Governor Adlai E. Stevenson; Chief of the Administrative and Fiscal Reorganization Section of the U.S. Bureau of the Budget; and General Field Supervisor of Public Administration Service. He has been a consultant to the Commission on the Operation of the Senate, U.S. General Accounting Office, Indian Institute of Public Administration, U.S. Agency for International Development, Government of the Virgin Islands, U.S. Departments of Defense and State, and Brookings Institution. Pois was a member of the Chicago Board of Education and, more recently, the Pittsburgh Board of Public Education. He is a member of the Illinois and Pennsylvania Bars.